Face in the Mirror
A teachers' guide

*A teachers' guide for using poetry to support
good mental health in the classroom and beyond*

Judy Morris

This book accompanies
Face in the Mirror
Poems for mental & emotional wellbeing

First published in 2022

All living poets have given permission for their poetry to be used as part of this anthology.

Every effort has been made to trace and contact the copyright holders prior to publication.

If notified, the publisher undertakes to rectify any errors or omissions in the next edition of this volume.

The right of Judy Morris to be identified as the editor of this work has been asserted in accordance with the
Copyright, Designs and Patents Act 1988

British Library Cataloguing-in-Publication data
A catalogue record for this book is available from the British Library

ISBN: 978-1-919627-69-4

Every effort has been made to trace the copyright holders and obtain permission to reproduce this material.

Designed and typeset by
Carnegie Scotforth Book Production

Cover design by Julia Noble

This guide is dedicated to all young people out there.

Please be aware that this book contains references to trauma, clinical depression and loss.

There is a safety plan in this book to which you can refer if you feel affected by any of its content.

About the author

Judy Morris trained as a teacher and taught for over twenty-five years before becoming a headteacher and then an author. She has always been driven by a dynamic enthusiasm for writing, working with young people and helping them to find their own inner voice using poetry, stories and plays written specially for them.

Judy's classroom experience includes sspecialisms in Literacy, Special Educational Needs and Disability (SEND), and Personal, Social, Health and Economic Education (PSHE). The hallmark of her teaching has always been a deep concern for the wellbeing and happiness of her pupils, a core passion which is now reflected in this book.

The countryside surrounding her home in the beautiful Peak District of Derbyshire, a wild landscape that she has explored on foot and horseback, has served as a constant source of inspiration for her writing, imagination and creative energy.

Contents

Face in the Mirror

Lessons plans: Key Stage suitability   xi

Introduction

Poetry as therapy   1

A note on the use of poetry in COVID-19 recovery   1

What do the poetry themes represent and why were they chosen?   3

How poetry affects the brain   4

Slavery and racism   5

Gender and identity   5

The teaching guide set against the National Curriculum and statutory guidance   6

PSHE in the context of school inspections   6

How to use the poetry anthology and teaching guide   6

    Commentaries   7

    How to use the teaching plans   7

    Creative methods of delivery   8

    Differentiation   8

    Comparing two or more poems within a theme or across themes   9

    Key questions when comparing poems from the anthology   9

Establishing a worry box to accompany working with this anthology and as part of PSHE in the
classroom   9

Safety   10

    A safety plan for young people   10

Establishing ground rules before commencing the lessons   13

    Some suggested ground rules   13

Mindfulness: preparing students for learning   13

    Mindful starters   13

    Scalp and face massage   14

    Relaxing to music   14

    Be in a happy place   15

    The art of breathing   15

    Deep breathing in a seated posture   15

    Counting breaths in a seated posture   16

    Inhaling and exhaling whilst walking around the hall, playground or school field   16

    Attentiveness to the breath in a seated posture   16

    Breathing into the abdomen in a seated posture   16

    Standing posture   16

The role of assessment in learning   17

    Teacher assessment   17

    Peer assessment   18

    Evaluation sheets   18

      Upper KS2 formative (ongoing) self-assessment sheet   19

      KS3/4 Formative self-assessment comment stems   20

      Generic summative self-assessment sheet   21

Commentaries and lesson plans[1]

1. Who Am I?   24

New Kid	Paul Morris	25
I'm Nobody!	Emily Dickinson	31
Mongrel Moon	Peter Kalu	37
Kitchen Table	Paul Morris	43
Hands In Pockets	Peter Kalu	50

2. My Love, My Friendships   55

Be A Friend	Edgar Albert Guest	56
Friends	Abbie Farwell Brown	62
Isti Mirant Stella	Hannah Kate	67
A Poison Tree	William Blake	76
Sonnet 116	William Shakespeare	81
My other grandmother	Rosie Garland	88

3. It's Okay to be Different   94

Pretty/Different	Paul Morris	95
The Man In The Glass	Anonymous (after Peter Dale Wimbrow Sr.)	101
table	Hannah Kate	107
It's Okay	Judy Morris	115
Stargazer	Judy Morris	119

4. When Good Times Turn to Dark Times   124

day	Paul Morris	125
It Was Not Death, For I Stood Up	Emily Dickinson	131
Unsocial Media	Paul Morris	138
These Are Passing Clouds	Tesni Penney	144

5. I'm Alone   150

Hidden Tears	Mojisola Oladiti	151
Waving at Trains	Rosie Garland	158
Solitude	Ella Wheeler Wilcox	164

---

1   Wherever possible, poem titles in this book follow the poet's preferred or original form and orthography.

CONTENTS

1L	Paul Morris	171
Count That Day Lost	George Eliot	176

6. Losing and Remembering — 183

Do Not Stand at my Grave and Weep	Mary Frye	184
The mistake upon me	Aya Ahmad	190
The Wind on the Downs	Marian Allen	196
The Glove	Peter Kalu	202
the view from here	Paul Morris	207

7. Facing My Trauma — 215

Beyond the Morning Sun	Paul Morris	216
Dulce et Decorum est	Wilfred Owen	229
Your Poem Here	Hannah Kate	237
On Pudding Lane	Elaine Bousfield	243

8. I'm Standing Strong — 249

Recovery will come	Emily Jane	250
The Rainy Day	Henry Wadsworth Longfellow	256
Promise Yourself	Christian D. Larson	263
Old Tree	Judy Morris	270
Past, Present, Future	Emily Brontë	275
See It Through	Edgar Albert Guest	281

9. Looking for Happiness — 287

Delaunay's Dye	Hannah Kate	288
How Still, How Happy	Emily Brontë	293
When You Grow Up	Rosie Garland	300
Happy Thought	Robert Louis Stevenson	306

10. Trying to Find Answers — 310

Heartbeat Number 2	Paul Morris	311
On the Stork Tower	Wang Zhihuan tr. Kelvin Pak	318
If	Rudyard Kipling	323
you will heal	Emily Jane	331

11. Facing the Future Without Fear — 338

The Hourglass	Paul Morris	339
Life	Charlotte Brontë	345
The Road Not Taken	Robert Frost	352
Barter	Sara Teasdale	359
Invictus	William Ernest Henley	365
Face in the Mirror	Judy Morris	372

Poet biographies   381

Glossary of terms used in this book   387

Useful contact organisations for young people   394

With thanks...   396

Face in the Mirror

Lesson plans: Key Stage suitability

The lesson plans in this teaching guide are designed using activities, PSHE Association PSHE Education Programme of Study objectives and National Curriculum in England English Programme of Study objectives, which make them particularly suitable for use with the key stages set out below.

Teachers and other session providers may wish to adapt lesson plans to suit the needs of other age ranges, as required.

Poem	Poet	Key Stage*
1. Who Am I?		
New Kid	Paul Morris	U2, 3, 4
I'm Nobody!	Emily Dickinson	U2, 3, 4
Mongrel Moon	Peter Kalu	U2, 3, 4
Kitchen Table	Paul Morris	U2, 3, 4
Hands In Pockets	Peter Kalu	U2, 3, 4
2. My Love, My Friendships		
Be A Friend	Edgar Albert Guest	U2, 3, 4
Friends	Abbie Farwell Brown	U2, 3, 4
Isti Mirant Stella	Hannah Kate	U2, 3, 4
A Poison Tree	William Blake	U2, 3, 4
Sonnet 116	William Shakespeare	U2 (Y6), 3, 4
My other grandmother	Rosie Garland	U2, 3, 4

3. It's Okay to be Different

Pretty Different	Paul Morris	U2, 3, 4
The Man In The Glass	Peter Dale Wimbrow Sr.	U2, 3, 4
table	Hannah Kate	U2, 3, 4
It's Okay	Judy Morris	U2, 3, 4
Stargazer	Judy Morris	U2, 3, 4

4. When Good Times Turn to Dark Times

day	Paul Morris	3, 4
It Was Not Death, For I Stood Up	Emily Dickinson	3, 4
Unsocial Media	Paul Morris	U2, 3, 4
These Are Passing Clouds	Tesni Penney	4

5. I'm Alone

Hidden Tears	Mojisola Oladiti	3, 4
Waving at Trains	Rosie Garland	U2, 3, 4
Solitude	Ella Wheeler Wilcox	U2, 3, 4
1L	Paul Morris	U2, 3, 4
Count That Day Lost	George Eliot	U2, 3, 4

6. Losing and Remembering

Do Not Stand at my Grave and Weep	Mary Frye	U2, 3, 4
The mistake upon me	Aya Ahmad	U2, 3, 4
The Wind on the Downs	Marian Allen	U2, 3, 4
The Glove	Peter Kalu	U2, 3, 4
the view from here	Paul Morris	U2, 3, 4

7. Facing My Trauma

Beyond the Morning Sun	Paul Morris	U2, 3, 4
Dulce et Decorum est	Wilfred Owen	U2, 3, 4
Your Poem Here	Hannah Kate	3, 4
On Pudding Lane	Elaine Bousfield	U2, 3, 4

8. I'm Standing Strong

Recovery will come	Emily Jane	U2, 3, 4
The Rainy Day	Henry Wadsworth Longfellow	U2, 3, 4
Promise Yourself	Christian D. Larson	U2, 3, 4
Old Tree	Judy Morris	U2, 3, 4
Past Present Future	Emily Brontë	U2, 3, 4
See It Through	Edgar Albert Guest	U2, 3, 4

9. Looking for Happiness

Delaunay's Dye	Hannah Kate	U2, 3, 4
How Still, How Happy	Emily Brontë	U2, 3, 4
When You Grow Up	Rosie Garland	U2, 3, 4
Happy Thought	Robert Louis Stevenson	U2, 3, 4

10. Trying to Find Answers

Heartbeat Number 2	Paul Morris	U2, 3, 4
On the Stork Tower	Wang Zhihuan (tr. Kelvin Pak)	U2, 3, 4
If	Rudyard Kipling	U2, 3, 4
you will heal	Emily Jane	U2 (Y6), 3, 4

11. Facing the Future Without Fear

The Hourglass	Paul Morris	U2, 3
Life	Charlotte Brontë	U2, 3, 4
The Road Not Taken	Robert Frost	U2, 3, 4
Barter	Sara Teasdale	U2, 3, 4
Invictus	William Ernest Henley	U2, 3, 4
Face in the Mirror	Judy Morris	U2, 3, 4

*	**Upper Key Stage 2**	Years 5 and 6 — pupils aged 9 to 10/11 years
	Key Stage 3	Years 7 to 9 — pupils aged 11/12 to 14 years
	Key Stage 4	Years 10 and 11 — pupils aged 14/15 and 15/16 years

Introduction

Note on terminology:

Throughout this book we refer to 'young people' as a term to denote both younger and older children between Upper KS2 and the end of KS4. This corresponds approximately to the ages of nine to sixteen.

Poetry as therapy

Poetry is a distillation of language. It has concentrated meaning.

An ideal form for developing speaking and listening skills, poetry is essentially an oral medium with roots that are similar to song. The written poem is a stem of that root. Providing opportunities for young people to hear, to respond to, and to talk about poems introduces them to an enormous range of discussion opportunities: meaning, word choices, word sounds, rhyme, association and suggestion, description, humour, emotion — the list goes on.

In schools, poetry can be taught as part of the key reading, writing and speaking and listening areas of language development. But its effect and educative value are not limited to language development. Poetry can have a positive impact on the social and emotional learning of young people, and can provide them with a healthy outlet for their emotions as well as a means of accessing and understanding those feelings.

When young people are listening to poems being read or performed, they are building their listening skills. They learn to build the connection between word and meaning, between meaning and experience, to engage their emotions as well as their conscious minds in responding to what they have heard, and to exercise higher order skills such as empathy.

Whilst reading poetry enables young people to connect with the experiences of others and to find meaning in their own, writing poetry allows them to access a channel through which to release their innermost feelings and thoughts on a subject, theme or issue.

This teaching guide is intended to help young people to explore issues associated with mental health, wellbeing and relationships. The lesson plans provide opportunities for young people to talk about worries and concerns, to see their connections with others and with the world around them, and to empathise with others. The aim is to move away from stigmatising mental health problems, a state of affairs that still persists in society, and to be able to talk about mental health and wellbeing issues in a normalised, accepting and supportive forum.

A note on the use of poetry in COVID-19 recovery

We now know that 2020 saw the onset of the greatest public health crisis to have struck the United Kingdom in over a century. Almost every other country in the world has been affected to a greater or lesser degree by this global pandemic.

Young people have had to accommodate significant changes in their lives. They may have been unable to go to school or to keep up with their studies. They may have been unable to maintain contact with friends and family. They may have been ill themselves, or even lost people who were close to them. Many young people are likely to have experienced anxiety, depression, trauma, loss of sense of identity, loss of confidence or ambition for the future, any of a broad spectrum of psychological issues, some of which may persist long after the virus has gone away or ceased to be an active threat.

The thematic section headings in this teaching guide (which are mirrored in the headings in the accompanying poetry anthology *Face in the Mirror*) are also directly relevant to COVID-19 recovery in young people, addressing issues that are likely to be common consequences of the pandemic, of protracted lockdown and social isolation. These are summarised below by reference to section headings, with a few examples of direct applicability:

- ***Who Am I?***

  Loss of personal identity; loss of self-esteem; loss of ambition; the sense of hopelessness for the future.

- ***My Love, My Friendships***

  Separation issues; the absence or loss of family or friends; the end of relationships.

- ***It's Okay to be Different***

  Loss of the sense of personal choice; pressure from family to conform to expectations in the lockdown and afterwards; the feeling that personal decisions have been overridden by events in the wider world; loss of confidence; feeling under pressure from the constant stress caused by 24-hour news media.

- ***When Good Times Turn to Dark Times***

  The world feels dangerous because of community infection; doubts about the ability to cope; fear about the 'new normal'; general negativity.

- ***I'm Alone***

  Social isolation caused by lockdown; handling new concepts of self and self-discovery; managing personal space; making new relationships with people and with the natural world.

- ***Losing and Remembering***

  Loss of contact; loss of friends and loved ones; loss of familiar patterns of life; loss of hope or ambition for the future; remembering better times; remembering people and places we care for.

- ***Facing My Trauma***

  Dealing with personal trauma and post-traumatic stress; dealing with anxiety; the results of prolonged stress.

- ***I'm Standing Strong***

  Re-establishing firm foundations; building resilience; becoming and remaining positive.

- ***Looking for Happiness***

  Finding sources of happiness; happiness in small, everyday things; reflecting on happy times and looking forward to new ones.

- ***Trying to Find Answers***

  Not giving up; having confidence that things will get better, and that we will get better too; developing inner resilience; developing determination; being positive in the face of challenge.

- ***Facing the Future Without Fear***

  Encouraging optimism; looking forward to the future positively; fostering personal happiness; building a way forward.

What do the poetry themes represent and why were they chosen?

Young people are facing a rapidly changing world. To some extent it has always been so, but the pace of change in modern society seems to accelerate ever more quickly. Many of the issues that face young people are as old as the human race, whilst others are new and were unknown to their forebears.

Detailed insight into the lives of children and young people today is supplied by major surveys of their behaviours and attitudes. There is growing concern, and good cause for it, that young people are suffering from increasingly poor emotional health. Research bears this out.

In 2015 a survey was prepared by The Children's Society.[2] Over 53,000 children aged 8, 10 and 12 were surveyed across four continents and fifteen countries including Algeria, Colombia, Estonia, Ethiopia, Germany, Israel, Nepal, Norway, Poland, Romania, South Africa, South Korea, Spain, Turkey and England. The findings concluded that children in England were the least happy when compared to the other countries, particularly in relation to their appearance, self-confidence and their time at school.

In 2015 the HBSC England National Report[3] published the results of its survey on the physical and emotional wellbeing of 5,335 young people aged 11, 13 and 15 across England. Researchers noted that among these 'emotional wellbeing may be decreasing'.

According to the NHS report *The Mental Health of Children and Young People in England, 2020,*[4] the proportion of children experiencing a probable mental disorder increased over the three years prior to the report, from one in nine in 2017 to one in six in July 2020. In boys aged 5 to 16 the rate rose from 11.4% in 2017 to 16.7% in July 2020, and in similarly aged girls from 10.3% to 15.2% over the same time frame. The findings drew on a study sample of 3,570 children and young people aged between 5 and 22 years, surveyed in both 2017 and July 2020. The consensus appears to be that these rates continue to rise, driven by factors such as social and personal stresses and anxieties, and more recently by the COVID-19 pandemic, lockdown, isolation, educational distancing and associated issues and concerns.

The evidence suggests that young people are ever more concerned with issues to do with mental health, linked to relationships online and offline, body image, self-esteem, isolation and anxiety. The poems included in the anthology *Face in the Mirror* have been organised into themes which reflect many of these concerns.

The anthology includes classical and ancient poetry, as well as new writing by established poets and young writers. One would expect new writing, especially by young writers, to reflect the concerns and interests of young people today, and much of the new writing in the anthology was commissioned especially with that purpose in mind. However, the oldest poem in the anthology was written over 1,000 years ago. So how can such ancient writing be relevant to today's society? Poetry, like all art forms, expresses human experience, much of which is influenced by cultural and historical norms that change over time, such as concepts of gender and race and society. Yet in many ways so much else of deep human experience, such as joy and sadness and loneliness, love and hope and fear, are similar for us to how they were for our forebears hundreds or even thousands of years ago. As a classroom teacher for many years, the author of this guide used a wide range of material with

---

2   https://www.childrenssociety.org.uk/sites/default/files/TheGoodChildhoodReport2015.pdf

3   https://www.researchgate.net/publication/282857118_HBSC_England_National_report

4   https://digital.nhs.uk/data-and-information/publications/statistical/
     mental-health-of-children-and-young-people-in-england/2020-wave-1-follow-up

young people exploring this cross-cultural, cross-generational phenomenon, including the classics — Shakespeare, Tennyson, Ted Hughes and many others. Many were accessed by Upper Key Stage 2 pupils. The author found in her own teaching that the important thing is to introduce, contextualise and present the classic work in a way that is stimulating, interesting and relevant to the reader.

There are fifty-four poems in the anthology *Face in the Mirror*. Each poem can be seen as a mirror reflecting what a young person may be feeling, and can be used to help the student to examine their feelings more closely and to think about how they fit into an ever-changing world. Every poem chosen for inclusion in the collection can provide hope, comfort, confidence, and perhaps some guidance too.

The poems can also help young people to see and celebrate their own uniqueness, to accept themselves as different and to celebrate and cherish that difference. So much today is made of conformity with the expectations of society and peers, of the demand that they be like everyone else. But young people should not be afraid to cherish and express their individuality.

The poems in the anthology are intended to help young people understand that life can sometimes present us with dark and difficult times, but that however alone we might feel we are not on our own in our experiences. We can come through the bad times, survive our losses and our trauma, and know that recovery can come. One day we will feel stronger; we will look for happiness and find it. We will look for the answers to the problems that cloud our lives, and we will find them. And when we do, we can face our future without fear, stronger and more confident in ourselves. Each section of the anthology is a step on that journey of hope and redemption. The last, eponymously titled poem in the anthology seeks to draw all the themes together and summarises the journey the young person has been on in reading the collection.

How poetry affects the brain

Professor Adam Zeman, Professor of Cognitive and Behavioural Neurology at the University of Exeter Medical School and former chairman of the British Neuropsychiatry Association, worked with colleagues from the fields of psychology and English to carry out a study on thirteen volunteers, all faculty members and senior graduate students in English, in what he called 'a first foray into a rich and relatively unexplored neurological territory'.

In his 2013 paper *By Heart: An fMRI Study of Brain Activation by Poetry and Prose*,[5] Professor Zeman describes how state-of-the-art functional magnetic resonance imaging (fMRI) technology allowed researchers to visualise which parts of the brain are activated in processing various neurological activity associated with reading poetry and prose.

Subjects' brain activity was scanned and compared when reading literal prose (such as an extract from a heating installation manual), evocative passages from novels, easy and difficult sonnets, and their favourite self-selected poetry.

Remarkably, researchers found that poetry observably triggers our emotion centres in a way that is similar to the effect of music. In addition, the brain engages centres associated with 'literariness' — the faculty of linguistic processing — and with introspection, producing a more inwardly-directed pattern of brain activity.

---

5 Zeman, A., Milton, F., Smith, A., & Rylance, R. (2013). *By heart: An fMRI study of brain activation by poetry and prose.* Journal of Consciousness Studies, 20(9-10), 132–158.

Findings have also indicated that poetry stimulates a network of regions which is particularly active in the resting brain, and which has been linked functionally to forms of internally directed reasoning and thinking, including autobiographical memory, envisioning the future, thinking involving theory of mind, and moral decision making.

Unusual as it may seem to explore artistic and literary responses through scientific investigation — in some ways art and science can seem very dissimilar — it is clear that our brains do in fact respond to poetry in a complex way involving emotion, memory, language and introspection. These are precisely the faculties we need to access in order to allow young people to make connections with the world and with themselves, and most importantly with their own mental and emotional internal landscape.

Slavery and racism

Some of the poems in the poetry anthology and in this guide were written before or just after the abolition of slavery and at a time when racism was acceptable. Whilst none of the poets had a direct link to slavery, they may have had family connections or friends who were associated with the trade and profits of slavery.

A failing at that time was not to speak out about the deplorable practice or to be actively involved in the abolitionist movement. Some poets may not have spoken out when they had the opportunity to do so, and many were shaped by the norms and values of the times they lived in.

As educators and as readers, we still need to ask ourselves whether each of us individually has raised our voice sufficiently against the enduring effects of slavery and racism in our society today. Where we have seen an opportunity to support teachers by raising these questions in the material, we have done so. We are delighted to include poems in the anthology written by young poets and older poets from diverse cultural and ethnic backgrounds.

Gender and identity

There are also discussions around gender which may arise due to some of the poems we have selected for inclusion.

A notable example of this is Kipling's poem 'If' which has often been identified as a work that includes elements of toxic masculinity, for example in its encouragement to suppress emotion and to 'force your heart and nerve and sinew / To serve your turn long after they are gone' — that is, to keep going when it might be healthier to stop. The poem is also particularly male-centred, as is clear from the final lines 'you'll be a Man, my son!'. Does this poem speak to girls, and what does it have to say? Knowing what we know about toxic masculinity and the impact it can have on shaping boys' mental health, should we have selected such a poem? We feel that it was right to do so. This and all the other poems we have chosen should allow for debate and discussion of these issues and more, and to not include them would remove opportunity for such discussion.

We have explored such questions, including the applicability of the poem to all sexes and genders, in the Commentary and Lesson Plans to be found in this guide.

We hope that as educators you will work with the poems we have selected in a way which engages young people to question and challenge what they read, and to use poetry to explore their mental health and emotional wellbeing.

The teaching guide set against the National Curriculum and statutory guidance

The *National Curriculum in England: framework for key stages 1 to 4*[6] statutory guidance (last updated December 2014) states that all schools:

- must offer a curriculum which is balanced and broadly based
- must offer a curriculum that promotes the spiritual, moral, cultural, mental and physical development of pupils at the school and of society, and prepares pupils at the school for the opportunities, responsibilities and experiences of later life
- should make provision for personal, social, health and economic education (PSHE), drawing on good practice.

New Department for Education guidance[7] has been published for schools in England (June 2019) which states that from September 2020 three compulsory subjects in England will have to be delivered:

- Relationship Education in primary schools
- Relationship and Sex Education in secondary schools
- Health Education in state funded primary and secondary schools

Health Education will not be a new requirement in independent schools where PSHE education is compulsory. It is expected that independent schools will draw on the new statutory health guidance when planning their curriculum.

The new *Relationships Education, Relationships and Sex Education (RSE) and Health Education* statutory guidance[8] will serve to strengthen provision for the delivery of good quality PSHE education in schools. Schools are free to determine how to deliver the content in the new guidance. The poetry anthology and teaching guide seek to support the delivery of relationship and health education in schools as well as supporting others who work one-to-one with young people.

PSHE in the context of school inspections

There is a greater scope for PSHE education to be a focus of inspections under the latest Ofsted framework, with schools being required to say how their curriculum supports personal development. The anthology and teaching guide are valuable resources in helping teachers and leaders to support young people's wellbeing, as well as giving breadth and depth to the school's curriculum. In addition, the resources in the guide address issues around keeping young people safe, which also forms part of the scope of Ofsted inspection.

How to use the poetry anthology and teaching guide

The poetry anthology and teaching guide can be used by teachers and support staff in school to help address issues around mental health, wellbeing and relationship education. The lesson plans in the guide have been cross-referenced to the English National Curriculum and mapped to the PSHE Association programme of study 2020[9] that addresses content in the statutory guidance by reference

---

6   https://www.gov.uk/government/publications/national-curriculum-in-england-framework-for-key-stages-1-to-4/ the-national-curriculum-in-england-framework-for-key-stages-1-to-4#the-school-curriculum-in-england

7   https://assets.publishing.service.gov.uk/government/uploads/system/uploads/attachment_data/file/1019542/Relationships_ Education__Relationships_and_Sex_Education__RSE__and_Health_Education.pdf

8   https://assets.publishing.service.gov.uk/government/uploads/system/uploads/attachment_data/file/805781/Relationships_ Education__Relationships_and_Sex_Education__RSE__and_Health_Education.pdf

9   https://www.pshe-association.org.uk/

to 'learning opportunities', which are enumerated in each plan in this guide. The PSHE Association has developed a very comprehensive programme of study that is not limited to the statutory content. This to ensure that the learning opportunities offered in its programme are part of a broader and more comprehensive PSHE education than the statutory content alone would provide.

This teaching guide does not provide a prescriptive method of delivering the lesson plans it contains. They may be taught through links with the English curriculum, or as a series of dedicated PSHE lessons, or a combination of both. There are also opportunities for cross-curricular links with other subjects.

For countries that do not follow England's National Curriculum, the programme in this guide can be delivered without reference to the English national objectives in that programme of study, but may be linked by the teacher to their own national or local curriculums and standards. It can be delivered purely to support issues linked to the mental health, wellbeing and relationships of young people.

Commentaries

Each poem in the anthology is supported by a written Commentary in this guide. The Commentary provides information about the context, content and composition of each poem, as well as its message to young people. It is important to read the Commentary before planning and delivering the activities in a lesson plan as it will aid understanding of the poem, its themes and their relevance to the issues to be addressed in the lesson. It will help the person delivering the session to explore themes more deeply, to personalise the applicability of the text, and to be better prepared to address questions raised by young people. The Commentary has been incorporated to provide key personnel with the necessary background information and to facilitate young people's understanding of key issues.

There are literary devices that may be found in any given poem, such as rhyme, rhythm, metre, alliteration, repetition, symbolism, figurative language, imagery and so on. An explanation of their use in each poem will be found in the Commentary. A glossary of terms can be found at the back of this teaching guide to help teachers to guide young people towards a better understanding of how poetic conventions and literary forms are employed in the poems, and how they can help young people to build their own skills of communication, knowledge and understanding.

How to use the lesson plans

The lesson plans have been divided into sections with headings that mirror the layout of the accompanying poetry anthology *Face in the Mirror*. This enables teachers to locate poems on a given theme quickly and easily.

Each lesson plan lists the resources necessary for the session, including equipment for young people with special educational needs and disabilities (SEND). Post-it notes are often used in the sessions so that thoughts and feelings can be recorded, shared and displayed easily and flexibly.

The poems are suitable for young people to access from Upper Key Stage 2 (Years 5 and 6, aged between 9 and 11); Key Stage 3 (Years 7, 8 and 9, aged between 11 and 14); and Key Stage 4 (Years 10 and 11, aged between 14 and 16). However, they can also be used with young people over the age of 16 if the content suits their needs. The poems and lesson plans can be read and delivered in the order they are set out and in their entirety. However, schools, counsellors and others may choose to deliver all of the programme or parts of it, and this will be a decision for key adults working with young people.

There is no need to follow every activity within each lesson plan. Teachers and session leaders are best placed to know how much content to include in a lesson or programme to meet the needs of the young people with whom they are working. For that reason we have not included time allocations in lesson plans. The duration of the lesson will depend upon the teacher/leader's choice of activities from the plans provided, the length of the lesson and the needs of the individual group. Lesson plans are a menu of activities from which to select, and the teacher or session leader will wish to cherry-pick activities to suit the needs of the young people with whom they are working, or to supplement set activities with ideas and variations of their own. They may prefer to address a topic in a single lesson or to develop the ideas in the lesson plan over a series of lessons, allowing for more in-depth discussion.

Within each lesson plan there are creative cross-curricular links to other subject areas to help young people develop knowledge, skills and understanding through interconnected topics. The extension activities can help to engage young people further in their learning by providing a rich context for developing learning in other subject areas. This adds richness, breadth and depth to the school curriculum.

Key questions and open questions have been included in the lesson plans to help young people reflect and think more deeply about the poems they have read. Open questions are questions which, unlike closed questions, cannot be answered with just 'yes' or 'no'. Many open questions begin with 'what', 'how', 'why', 'when', 'where' or 'who', and answering them requires a more full and reasoned response than closed questioning. Open questioning may involve thinking about *why* one has a particular opinion or viewpoint, a deeper form of personal reflection, a valuable practice when considering mental and emotional wellbeing. The questions in the lesson plans have been written to help young people to reflect on their feelings, attitudes and understanding of the poems. This can help teachers to better access the young person's true thoughts and feelings about an issue and about themselves.

In each lesson plan there are main teaching activities that allow young people the opportunity to take part in focused discussions with a partner, small group or whole class. The activities are drawn from issues raised in the poems and the effects those issues can have on young people today. Collaboration with peers on learning tasks is actively encouraged, but there are opportunities for individual work too. A great deal of emphasis has been placed on developing speaking and listening skills, as well as reading for meaning within the lessons. There are lots of openings for pupils to write but these often flow from the lessons as pupils need time to plan and draft their writing.

Creative methods of delivery

There are also opportunities to develop working walls and classroom displays with classes, small groups or with a young person working on a one-to-one basis with a key adult. Working walls with key messages displayed are an important reminder to young people about what they have read, covered and discussed in the lessons. Teachers and support staff may choose to chart young people's involvement and progress as they move through the lessons using the information on the working walls as they progress through the plans.

Differentiation

There are a number of suggested teaching and extension activities for each of the lessons in the teaching guide. The activities are not prescriptive, and teachers should choose the activities they feel are most appropriate for their age group. The plans contain guidance information about the suitability of some of the poems with younger age groups and where applicable how to approach them so that they can access the content more readily.

For pupils who have problems writing in response to an activity, alternative tasks have been included to help pupils to structure their thoughts and ideas in a way that best suits their learning style and needs.

Formative assessment sheets have been differentiated for different key stages and can help teachers to track progress against PSHE objectives.

Comparing two or more poems within a theme or across themes

When working on a theme, young people can be given the opportunity to reflect on the poetry they have read by selecting two or more poems, then identifying how they are different and how they are similar in order to deepen appreciation and understanding of them. This can be done either whilst the work on the theme is in progress or once it has been completed. The poems can be chosen from within the same theme or across different themes. This can also help young people to revisit a theme they have covered already, to reinforce familiarity and to help build mental connections and associations.

How does one do this? Key questions to guide comparison are a way of helping young people to reflect on their understanding by talking with a partner, in a small group or with a key adult. Young people will then be in a better position to write about the poems in their books or journals once they have worked on some ideas because they will have more to think about and talk about, and a richer understanding of what they have seen.

When working on comparing poetry, it can be easier and more enjoyable for a young person to work with one or more other people rather than on their own. It is quite alright to work alone, but working with someone else allows the exchange of ideas, opinions, impressions, thoughts — and of course feeling and emotions.

Putting forward opinions, thoughts and feelings in a pair or group situation encourages critical thinking, self-awareness and the ability to express oneself clearly, and helps to build self-confidence. Considering what others have to say, and what they feel, builds the skills of communication and encourages the development and practice of empathy.

Key questions when comparing poems from the anthology

- What are the titles of the two poems and the names of their two poets?
- What are the similarities between the poems? What are the differences? You might like to think about the subject, the form, the language, the mood and emotion.
- What do you like about each of the poems? What do you dislike about them? Why? Give reasons for your opinions.
- How did the poems make you feel? Why? Give reasons for your opinions.

Establishing a worry box to accompany working with this anthology and as part of PSHE in the classroom

It is a good idea to set up a worry box in the class for any worries, issues or concerns the pupils may have at home or at school. It is a slotted cardboard box that resembles a ballot box, in which pupils may post a note to the teacher as a way of enabling them to have a say when they feel uncomfortable about speaking in a classroom setting. Alternatively the teacher can make a worry wallet, a pouch or envelope fixed to the wall, for the same purpose.

It is important that a pupil's anonymity is preserved at all times, and the teacher, classroom assistant or support worker should be sensitive about how it is used. It is important to consider carefully whether the pupil could be identified from their written note before reading it out. For the same reason, the worry box or worry wallet should be opaque. Teachers, classroom assistants and support workers may want to discuss the issues with the child or the whole class (with appropriate respect for the pupil's anonymity), depending on the worry. It may sometimes be necessary to pass on sensitive information to a PSHE lead or teacher with responsibility for safeguarding. The worry box should be checked daily, so that pupils' worries are addressed promptly.

Safety

Each lesson in this guide starts with young people referring to their safety plan.

A safety plan is a way of looking after yourself when you feel scared or worried or low.

When people are writing about their own thoughts and feelings, or reading about others' experiences, it can be unsettling and can sometimes be upsetting. Sometimes reading about others reminds us of our own situation. These reminders are called 'triggers'. A safety plan can be used with young people to explore ways in which they can keep themselves safe in case this happens and in case they are having a bad day mentally or emotionally. It is a good idea for *every* young person working on lessons in this guide to have their own safety plan.

A safety plan for young people

Everybody's safety plan is different because we are all unique. However, experience has shown us that it is important to ask certain questions to help the young person to build their own unique safety plan. There are suggestions below of the questions young people can ask themselves. However, if there are other questions and ideas that the young person thinks of they can be shared in class with the teacher or teaching support.

Please feel free to photocopy the plan below for use in lessons and sessions.

My Safety Plan

Feel free to decorate this. It is yours after all!

Keep your safety plan with you and use it when you need to.

Who can I talk to or get in touch with when I feel sad, scared or on my own with something? Who is on my caring friends and family list?

When I feel upset, what helps me to stay calm?

What are the warning signs I get that tell me I am feeling out of control? (Out of control here means overwhelmed by my feelings. Perhaps I become very angry or upset and start throwing things or maybe I run away and hide. Out of control will mean different things to different people).

What are some of the things I can do to help me from getting out of control?

What have I done in the past that has helped?

Are there things I can do to calm and soothe myself?

What would I say to someone else who is feeling like I am?

What nice things can I tell myself about me?

What would I say to someone else who is feeling like I am?

What could others do to help me feel safe?

Where is a safe place I can go?

What would be a good message or quote for me to remember every time I get worried, low or upset?

Establishing ground rules before commencing the lessons

Establishing ground rules before delivering the lesson plans can help to inculcate a positive, respectful shared learning ethos in the classroom or session setting. Ground rules are often referred to as a class contract or agreement. In the educational setting, it is one way to ensure that there is a safe teaching and learning environment. It is important for young people to be able to listen to each other's contributions and to value what has been said in the sessions. There is a lot of emphasis in the lesson plans on speaking and listening to encourage participation. The ground rules can be discussed with young people and then shared before the start of each session. These rules are by no means exhaustive, and young people may want to add their own suggestions. The ground rules should be displayed clearly and prominently in the classroom. Young people can also be given a copy to stick in their student books or files.

Some suggested ground rules

- Listen to what each person has to say.
- Be kind to each other and give support.
- Everybody's contribution is valuable, so respect what they have to say.
- Join in and ask questions if you want to.
- If a person does not want to say anything, they do not have to.
- Respect privacy by keeping the conversation in the room.
- Ask for further help and advice if you need it.

The ground rules should be kept to consistently and revisited at intervals before each session.

Mindfulness: preparing students for learning

When young people enter a classroom at the start of the school day, it can be useful to gauge how they are feeling. There may be individuals in a group whose mood is significant for their ability to take part or to learn effectively. Carrying out a simple activity during registration or when they are greeted by their session leader can be a way of assessing how receptive and open to learning they might be.

Here are three simple hand signals which young people can give to key adults as they arrive:
- Thumbs up to indicate that things are fine with the young person.
- Shake of the hand from side-to-side to indicate they are feeling a bit vulnerable or so-so.
- Thumbs down to indicate that they are not feeling okay.

Mindful starters

'Mindfulness means paying attention in a particular way; on purpose, in the present moment, and nonjudgmentally.'

Jon Kabat-Zinn[10]

---

10   Kabat-Zinn, J. (1994). *Wherever you go, there you are: Mindfulness meditation in everyday life* (p.4). New York: Hyperion

Incorporating mindfulness into classroom settings can help young people to reduce their stress and anxiety levels. It can also increase concentration and engagement as well as improving social skills, sleep, problem-solving and decision-making skills.

According to research carried out by Bupa,[11] scientists have used MRI scans to see how the brain changes when people practise mindfulness. The research has produced some very interesting results. Evidence suggests that particular areas of the brain may either shrink or grow in response to regular mindfulness practice. Here are a few examples:

- Mindfulness and stress. Research demonstrates that after practising mindfulness, the grey matter in the brain's amygdala, a region known for its role in stress, can become smaller.
- Mindfulness and creativity. The pre-frontal cortex, the area of grey matter in the brain which is responsible for things like planning, problem solving, and controlling emotions, can become thicker after practising mindfulness, demonstrating increased activity.
- Mindfulness and memory. An area of the brain known as the hippocampus, which helps memory and learning, can also become thicker after practising mindfulness.

Mindful starters are calming practices that help relax young people before they engage with the lesson plans. These can be introduced before the start of each session and should only take between five and ten minutes. The mindful starters do not require any resources — only chairs and space to move as required by the activity.

Research carried out in the US shows that stressed teachers impact students' learning outcomes. Students learn better in a climate that is emotionally positive. Studies have also shown that there is a link between positive emotional classroom climates and academic achievement. It is vital that classrooms should be positive learning environments, where young people feel valued and there is a culture of mutual respect.

Some effective mindful starters are described below.

Scalp and face massage

Close your eyes and rub, stroke and tap your scalp with your fingers for two minutes before gently massaging the forehead, temples and cheeks for a further couple of minutes. This exercise will help calm the muscles and relax the nerves. It also helps to improve the lymphatic system, an important part of the body's circulatory and immune system.

Relaxing to music

Begin the session with peaceful, melodic instrumental music, avoiding songs with lyrics upon which young people may be tempted to focus. Scientists have found that there are many benefits associated with listening to music. These include making people feel happier, lowering stress levels, reducing depression, elevating mood, strengthening learning and memory, improving health, aiding concentration and many more.

Making time to listen to music can have a calming and therapeutic effect in the classroom and can help to set the scene for a peaceful, thoughtful, productive session.

---

11   https://www.bupa.co.uk/newsroom/ourviews/mindfulness-my-brain

Be in a happy place

Visualisation is another powerful technique that can help young people to unwind, relieve stress and manage worries. Visualisation involves using mental imagery to achieve a more relaxed state of mind.[12] It works to expand a young person's ability to rest and relax by focusing the mind on a calming and serene image.

The young person should be asked to close their eyes and to think of a peaceful, relaxing scene. This can be a forest, a beach or a happy place where the young person feels relaxed. When visualising the calm and tranquil scene, ask the young person to think about what they are experiencing through all of their senses — to notice what they hear, smell and taste, and how their body feels. Towards the end of the activity take the time to return the young person gradually to the present. The practice of using visualisation also works well when tranquil music is played and helps to calm and relax the mind.

The art of breathing

The ancient art form of Qigong, which has its roots in China, focuses on breathing well for health and wellbeing. The techniques of Qigong were handed down through the generations to promote vitality and longevity. Relaxed breathing can help to calm tension in the nerves, so enabling physical relaxation throughout the whole body. A relaxed nervous system also helps decrease damaging mental and emotional stress. The following breathing activities are based on Qigong techniques and will help improve young people's mindfulness. Good posture, achieved easily by standing and sitting up straight, allows people to open up their lungs and breathe more freely and deeply. This can help to relieve stress. Good posture that supports the head and neck can help people to feel lighter, more confident and relaxed.

Some helpful Qigong practices are outlined below.

Deep breathing in a seated posture

Sit with feet apart and with hands resting on knees. There should be a gap under the arms to avoid a feeling of constriction and leave room for the breath. Sit comfortably on the chair, closer to the front than the back to allow space beneath the upper legs. The back, neck and head should be upright, with the chin pulled in as though the person is being pulled upwards by a thread running through the spine and out of the top of the head. Feet should be placed flat on the floor directly beneath the knees and about a hand span apart so that the thighs, knees and lower legs are separated but parallel. It is important to maintain good posture throughout the exercise — relax, but do not collapse. It is important to maintain this good postural alignment throughout the exercise.

Take in a deep breath through the nose, pause and release slowly, again through the nose. Repeat up to ten times. The eyes should be closed for this activity.

It is important to breathe only through the nose. Breathing through the mouth may be recognised by the brain as a stress response and encourage the release of stress hormones. Breathing through the nose avoids this. It is also important to include the pause between in-breath and out-breath, as this gives the body good opportunity to oxygenate the blood. Slowing the breathing is important because it allows the body to relax, dissipate stress hormones, and signals our parasympathetic nervous system to calm the body and mind.

---

12   https://www.verywellmind.com/visualization-for-relaxation-2584112

Deep breathing helps to reduce tension and relieve stress in the body. When you breathe deeply, it sends a message to the brain to calm down and relax, and the brain sends this message to your body. It also calms the parasympathetic nervous system, which controls the body's fight-flight-freeze responses, and has a measurable effect on reducing physical stress. When under stress, the body releases hormones that are intended to help deal with immediate threats; but when the stress trigger that causes this goes on for longer, then the continued presence of those hormones can have harmful effects on health. Qigong practice and similar slow breathing techniques help to reduce or eliminate this.

Counting breaths in a seated posture

Sit in the good postural alignment described above.

Breathe slowly and steadily through the nose.

Move on to counting the number of inhaled and exhaled breaths on each of your fingers over two minutes (inhaled and exhaled breath counts as one on your finger). As you practise this technique, breaths become longer and more relaxed. Maintain good postural alignments throughout the activity; make sure you do not slump — remember, relax but do not collapse. Young people can keep a log of their breaths to see how their performance in this exercise improves over time.

Inhaling and exhaling whilst walking around the hall, playground or school field

Apply the technique of counting each inhaled and exhaled breath (see above) while walking slowly. As you walk, place each foot down carefully from the heel to the ball of the foot. Move slowly, ensuring that each foot is placed firmly, the weight transferred to the stepping foot, and that you are balanced before taking the next step. Allow five minutes for this activity. Young people may want to keep a log of their breath counts over a period of time.

Attentiveness to the breath in a seated posture

Sit in the good postural alignment described above.

Take in slow, deep breaths and exhale slowly. Both in-breaths and out-breaths should be through the nose. Ask young people to think about how the breath feels. Ask: can you feel the air moving through your nose? Can you feel the air moving out through your nose? Does the air feel a little colder on the way in and warmer on the way out? Can you feel the air moving across the hairs in your nose or the back of your throat?

Breathing into the abdomen in a seated posture

Sit in the good postural alignment described above.

Take in a deep breath for a count of four. As you breathe in through the nose, breathe deep into the abdomen. Hold for a count of four and breathe out through the nose for a count of eight. Repeat this four times.

Standing posture

This activity requires young people to stand and relax in an upright position.

There should be enough space for each young person to stand without touching another person. Chairs should be available in case anybody wants to sit down at all during the activity.

Feet should be slightly apart and knees 'soft' and springy, not straight or stiff. It is important that there is a gap under the arms and that the arms and hands hang loose at the sides. The head should be upright with the chin slightly tucked in. This posture should be maintained during the activity.

Eyes should be closed. However, they can be opened if you feel unsteady on your feet.

Practise deep breathing into the body, breathing through the nose. Start with the airways and see if you can feel the air in the nostrils. Point out where the diaphragm is in the body (just under the base of the rib cage) and feel the effect of deep breathing in that part of the body. Can you feel your rib cage rise and fall? Move down to the abdomen. Take deep belly breaths. Can you feel the abdomen going in and out? After five minutes of steady breathing, ring a bell or give a quiet verbal signal for young people to open their eyes and to acclimatise to the light. Shift weight on the legs and feet, and fidget to restore the circulation after standing still.

The role of assessment in learning

There are many reasons why it is important that learning in PSHE education is assessed.

Assessment plays a major role in how young people learn, their motivation to learn, and how teachers teach. It is only by having the opportunity to reflect on their learning that young people's motivation increases, and this in turn improves their learning. Teachers need to feel confident that learning has taken place, to be able to demonstrate progress, and to identify and plan for future learning needs. Assessment also allows the leadership team to see the impact that PSHE education is having on pupils and on whole school outcomes. By not assessing PSHE education, one can describe the provision one is making but lack detail about its effectiveness on pupils.

Assessing learning in PSHE education can be achieved by using a combination of teacher assessment, pupil self-assessment and peer assessment.

There are three main types of pupil assessment:

- *Formative Assessment — generally known as 'assessment for learning' (AfL):*
  This is used to evaluate pupils' knowledge and understanding on a day-to-day basis and to tailor teaching accordingly.
- *Summative Assessment:*
  This is used to evaluate how much a pupil has learned at the end of a teaching period (end of a unit, topic, term or academic year).
- *Nationally Standardised Summative Assessment:*
  This is used by the UK Government to hold schools in England to account and to provide information on how pupils are performing in comparison to pupils nationally.

Teacher assessment

This is where a teacher reflects and makes judgments about a learner's starting point, needs, progress, participation and achievement. It also involves giving constructive feedback about performance and next steps.

The lesson plans support teacher assessment in the following ways:

- Through lesson observation, watching and listening to young people as they engage with the tasks they have been given to do.
- Through questioning — key questions have been produced for teachers and support staff in the teaching guide.
- Through reflection on the learner's contribution to discussion and participation in activities, and their writing (if any).
- Through young people's own written evaluations at the end of a lesson or after completion of a poetry theme.
- Through working walls and classroom displays of young people's ideas and contributions.
- Through the use of simple hand signals — thumbs up, shake of the hand and thumbs down — to assess how each young person has felt about the lesson.

Before each poetry theme is introduced, teachers may want to establish a baseline by asking the young person to draw or write what they know about the theme/subject. For example, what they understand by the terms 'bullying' or 'loneliness', and what this means to them. Mind maps are also a good way of linking ideas and can be introduced if a young person has not seen one before. At the end of a theme the same exercises can be repeated to see how the young person's knowledge and understanding has developed.

Peer assessment

Peer assessment opportunities have been built into many of the lesson plans so that peers can reflect and make helpful contributions about each others' knowledge, confidence, understanding, skills, participation and role in a group setting. This involves giving constructive feedback, moderated by the teacher or session leader.

Evaluation sheets

Below are some simple self-assessment sheets for young people to complete at the end of each session, upon finishing a theme, or when the programme has been completed. These can be used to assess understanding and learning in English as well as PSHE, and they allow young people the opportunity to reflect on what they have learned and how it made them feel.

Please feel free to photocopy the sheets for use in sessions.

Upper KS2 formative (ongoing) self-assessment sheet

How did the session go today?

Theme ....   Name ....

Date ....   Year group ....

How do you feel about your learning today?

Please put a tick next to the picture and comment which best describes how you feel.

I feel confident	I feel okay	I'm not sure / I need help

What would you like to say about your learning?

....

....

....

....

....

What questions would you like to ask?

....

....

....

....

....

Who do I ask or speak to if I need help?

....

....

....

....

....

Teacher's comments

....

....

....

....

....

KS3/4 Formative self-assessment comment stems

Using Post-it notes, ask young people to reflect on learning that has taken place in a session.

They are given a comment stem to complete on each Post-it note. These are then kept in the young person's book/file for the session leader to read. The comment stems could also be used to produce a self-assessment sheet if the session leader prefers.

I know .... (What I know now that I didn't know before)

I can .... (Skills I have learned)

I understand .... (What opinions or attitudes I have discussed or found out about)

Help available .... (What help is available if I need to talk)

Generic summative self-assessment sheet

This can be used with young people after they have completed part or all of a poetry theme or the whole programme of work. It can help to identify any gaps in the young person's learning, to find out what information has been retained, what the strengths and weaknesses are in the teaching and learning plans, and whether more work needs to be done to enrich the young person's understanding.

Please feel free to photocopy the sheet for use in sessions.

Pupil Self-assessment Sheet

End of theme / End of programme of work

Theme ....   Name ....

Date ....   Year Group ....

I have learned ....

....

....

....

....

I enjoyed ....

....

....

....

....

....

I found ....

....

....

....

....

I know how ....

....

....

....

....

....

Now I will ....

....

....

....

....

....

I would like to know ....

....

....

....

....

....

Teacher's/session leader's comments ....

....

....

....

....

Commentaries and lesson plans

Who am I?

24

Thinking about identity and belonging,
feelings of isolation,
and how one sees oneself...

New Kid

by Paul Morris

Commentary

I'm new to the school
With the same old rage;
It's a brand-new book
With a blotted page.
See I've got no worries,
I'm an 'ard man, me
'Cos me mam's Chuck Norris
And me dad's Bruce Lee,

And when I cry into my pillow
I don't let anybody see.

Got a face like a boulder
But me head's a state,
I'm me mam's little soldier
And me dad's best mate.
I'm a big-time shark
In a small-time pond,
'Cos me mam's a Terminator
And me dad's James Bond.
I'm a rich kid's nightmare,
I'm a poor kid's dream:

Stuff my mouth with the pillow
So they can't hear me scream.

Got an eye like a bullet,
Got a tongue like a dagger
And a fire in me gullet
And the moves like Jagger
And I'll see you right
But I'll rob you blind;
I've found
        A pound
And I've lost my mind,
'Cos I'm trapped in the mills of the daily grind...
Unpack my head
And there's nothing there:
Under the duvet of my confidence
Just the bed-bugs of despair —

What was that, Miss?
What am I writing?
Nothing Miss, really —
Nothing exciting.

What's that, Miss? Show you?
Let you see?
See, Miss: it's about nothing —
Just me…
　　　　Only me.

Context

'New Kid' was written during a school poetry-writing workshop in 2018, when the poet was visiting a school in Cheshire.

When he was walking through the school grounds on the way to the session, the poet passed a pupil in a brand-new uniform who was obviously new to the school. The pupil was boasting loudly to a small audience of others about their family, friends and special abilities, and about how important they had been in their previous school.

Content

The poem introduces us to a child — we are not quite sure whether a boy or a girl, but the "ard man' of line 6 would suggest the former — who is trying very hard to appear nonchalant and matter-of-fact about how little they care for school and how special and important they think they are. The child is new to their school, but brings with them the anger they felt at their previous school, and which perhaps they feel in other areas of their life too. For this child, the new school is not a new start, a clean slate, a chance to begin again and to do better. The child sees him- or herself as tough, and makes impossible claims for how tough his or her parents are as well. It seems that the child has a magnified sense of their own importance and is determined to deliver the message.

But there are intrusions into the grandiose narrative: references to crying into their pillow when nobody is looking, and stuffing their mouth with that pillow to prevent their cries from being heard (though we are left to speculate why, and what aspects of home life might lead to such distress). Among the overblown claims and self-aggrandisement there is humour and a hint of fragile desperation for acceptance, for respect, and perhaps for love.

Soon another picture emerges from the swagger and bluster: an intimation of an awareness of feeling trapped; an admission of lack of confidence and even of despair; a reluctance to share this with adults; and an admission that at the bottom of it all the hyperbole is driven by an underlying sense of personal worthlessness.

What we are seeing among the bravado and braggadocio is, we realise, the over-compensation of a vulnerable child who uses the outward show of magnified self-esteem as a mask — or perhaps as the armour of emotional self-defence.

Composition

The overall feel of the poem is fresh, young and energetic, with a sense of street poetry or spoken word performance. The language is informal and direct. The text is full of colloquialisms and a hint of linguistic 'looseness', or perhaps of dialect or an accent (*me head's a state, / … me dad's best mate*): does the speaker see him- or herself as 'street'? This builds to a high point as the far-fetched claims of the speaker increase, as though the speaker is using such language to reinforce their irreverence. As the poem progresses the almost self-conscious use of slang decreases as the child's vulnerability emerges.

The poem follows a conventional rhyme scheme which adds a sense of ease and dexterity, complementing the initial self-confidence of the speaker.

Despite its apparent informality there is clear and consistent rhythmic structure throughout the poem which lends the piece a driving, forward-moving impetus. The rhythmic pattern changes as the poem enters its final stanza, those nine lines having a less insistent and gentler, even tentative, pattern.

The child's revelations of vulnerability at lines 9 and 10, and at lines 21 and 22, are separated from the body of text as literal asides, emphasising their 'otherness'. However, the later revelations in lines 31 and following are the more shocking for appearing as part of the main flow of the poem, and as being more obviously central to the child's expression. There is not just intimation, but hard clarity.

The poem's narrative arc runs in phases, with a first phase building to a revelation of vulnerability (lines 1 to 10), then reprising a similar pattern (lines 11 to 22), before entering a longer phase which declines into the final and more prolonged admission of diminished self-confidence and vulnerability.

The overall cumulative effect is that of a mounting wave, rising and falling as it gathers strength, only to break and subside.

Message

The message of the poem is that outward shows of self-confidence sometimes hide a deeper and more concerning truth. A show of apparently exaggerated self-confidence and self-esteem may be a mask that hides just the opposite. It can be all too easy to respond to the superficial appearance of a young person (of anyone, in fact), taking them at face value and assuming that a confident and robust persona is all there is to be known if it is all that can be seen. A boastful, self-assured, self-important demeanour may be off-putting, or lead us to believe that someone is strong. But closer examination may reveal underlying vulnerability and need. Is the outward appearance all there is, or does it hide something more profound and more concerning?

We all, to a greater or lesser extent, adopt a façade to encounter and deal with the world. The truth may run much deeper.

Lesson plan: 'New Kid' by Paul Morris

Resources

Copies of the poem — ideally one per pupil, rulers for SEND pupils to follow a line when reading, flip chart paper for group activities, pens and pencils or marker pens. Extra paper should be made available for use if required.

Copies of pupils' safety plans to which they can refer throughout the session/lesson.

The lesson will cover oracy, reading and writing skills.

The session can be done in the round. or as a circle time activity, or at tables, or in an unstructured group. The lesson plan is suitable to use with pupils at Upper Key Stage 2, 3 and 4.

Links with the PSHE Association PSHE Education Programme of Study

Links have been made to the PSHE Association PSHE Education Programme of Study at Key Stage 2, 3 and 4 as follows:

KS2

- *H20. strategies to respond to feelings, including intense or conflicting feelings; how to manage and respond to feelings appropriately and proportionately in different situations*
- *H24. problem-solving strategies for dealing with emotions, challenges and change, including the transition to new schools*
- *H36. strategies to manage transitions between classes and key stages*

KS3

- *H6. how to identify and articulate a range of emotions accurately and sensitively, using appropriate vocabulary*
- *R22. the effects of change, including loss, separation, divorce and bereavement; strategies for managing these and accessing support*

KS4

- *H6. about change and its impact on mental health and wellbeing and to recognise the need for emotional support during life changes and/or difficult experiences*

Links with the National Curriculum

Links have been made to the National Curriculum for English at Key Stage 2, 3 and 4 as follows:

KS2 (Years 5 and 6) English programme of study

- *maintain attention and participate actively in collaborative conversations, staying on topic and initiating and responding to comments*
- *drawing inferences such as inferring characters' feelings, thoughts and motives from their actions, and justifying inferences with evidence*
- *discuss and evaluate how authors use language, including figurative language, considering the impact on the reader*
- *provide reasoned justifications for their views*

KS3 English programme of study

- *participating in formal debates and structured discussions, summarising and/or building on what has been said*
- *making inferences and referring to evidence in the text*
- *knowing how language, including figurative language, vocabulary choice, grammar, text structure and organisational features, presents meaning*

KS4 English programme of study

- *working effectively in groups of different sizes and taking on required roles, including leading and managing discussions, involving others productively, reviewing and summarising, and contributing to meeting goals/deadlines*
- *seeking evidence in the text to support a point of view, including justifying inferences with evidence*

- *analysing a writer's choice of vocabulary, form, grammatical and structural features, and evaluating their effectiveness and impact*

Teaching and learning activities

This poem can be used to introduce work on the theme of transition, for example to a new school, which can be an incredibly stressful time for pupils. A series of lessons can flow from the use of this poem. Please see the **Extension activities** below.

- Introduction — share aims of lesson.
- Refer pupils to their safety plans. Remind them of what a safety plan is for. Ask them to read through their own safety plan before they go further and answer any questions they may have.
- Read the poem (or teacher/leader to read it aloud) and discuss its content. Use of questions 'what-who-where-when-how-why':
  - What is this poem about?
  - Who is speaking in the poem?
  - Where is the poem set?
  - When you read the poem what picture do you form of the person who is speaking? How is this conveyed? Is the person tough, or is there something else in there too? What? Why do you think this?
  - How does the poem make you feel? Why and how does it do this?
  - Why do you think the poet uses language that is informal and direct? What is the poet trying to achieve?
- Divide pupils into small groups of four or five. Discuss the following with group members. What are the benefits of moving school/year group/college? In what way can this be a new start? What opportunities can a new start give you? What are you looking forward to? If it is something that will need work, how do you think you can achieve it? Why would you revert to your old behaviour if it was negative, if you have the chance to start over again? What are the benefits of 'turning over a new page'? Ask for a member of the group to act as a scribe to record suggestions and ideas.
- Take feedback and comments from pupils.
- Ask pupils to list worries/concerns about starting secondary school (Y6 pupils), entering a new year group (secondary pupils), or moving to a new secondary school. Can some of the worries be collated into groups? For example homework, bullying, punctuality, organisational skills, making new friends, etc.
- Ask pupils to think of ways to diminish worries/concerns. Discuss within the group. Ask for a scribe to record suggestions and ideas.
- Take feedback and comments from pupils.
- Explore together common experience and responses. Where can you go for help and support when you start your new school? Who can you talk to?
- Review what has been achieved in the lesson.
- Refer pupils to their safety plans as a place to look if they need help after leaving the lesson.

Extension activities

- Pupils to write their answers to the 'what-who-where-when-how-why' questions.
- Explore worries/concerns identified in the first lesson in more depth, dealing with each worry in a circle time activity. The number and length of lessons will depend on the number of issues identified in the first lesson. It will be important to come up with positive coping strategies so that pupils feel more confident when they are confronted with new situations.
- Cover work on self-confidence in drama or PSHE lessons. Divide the class into two groups. Pupils take it in turns to initiate a quick conversation with another pupil about themselves — a bit like speed dating. Pupils move around the group before swopping over. It is important to reinforce good eye contact, keeping shoulders straight, practising feeling self-confident by smiling and making conversation.
- Negative behaviour can often be a mask — something to hide behind. Make simple masks out of a sheet of card with two holes for the eyes. Do you feel different when you are wearing it? Try having a conversation with someone while you are wearing your mask. How does it make you feel different? Is it easier to speak out? Does it make you feel more or less confident or inhibited? Think about why this is so. Can you think about any other circumstances in which people use a mask, or perhaps a costume, to help them in their work? (e.g. police, armed forces, actors, performers, teachers, barristers, doctors, nurses — all people who are perceived differently because of their appearance when they are at work). Can you choose to 'wear a mask' for good in your daily life (e.g. to adopt a new, 'clean' persona)?
- In circle time activities, boost self-confidence by asking pupils to offer positive attributes of others within the group and to celebrate their uniqueness.
- Each pupil to make a list of their personal qualities and what they are good at. In art lessons, pupils to produce self-portraits using a variety of media. Display personal qualities next to portraits.
- Pupils to write their own creative poems around the theme of transition.

Cross-curricular/topic links

Cross-curricular and topic links may be explored for use in follow-up and for extension work in

- English
- Drama
- PSHE
- Art and Design

Differentiation

Opportunities for discussion in mixed ability pairs.

Differentiation by outcome e.g. quantity or complexity of issues identified, sophistication of response, level of inclusion/contribution, empathy.

Writing quantity outcomes will be differentiated/assessed/moderated according to teacher's expectations of quantity and depth; otherwise by outcome.

Differentiation through artwork as a means of expression.

I'm Nobody!

by Emily Dickinson

Commentary

I'm Nobody! Who are you?
Are you — Nobody — too?
Then there's a pair of us!
Don't tell! they'd advertise — you know!

How dreary — to be — Somebody!
How public — like a Frog —
To tell one's name — the livelong June
To an admiring Bog!

Context

'I'm Nobody!', sometimes known by its longer title of 'I'm Nobody! Who are you?', was first published in 1891 in a posthumous collection of the poet's work entitled *Poems, Series 2*. Fewer than a dozen of Emily Dickinson's poems were published during her lifetime, often anonymously, and they were edited heavily to conventionalise her idiosyncratic punctuation. Following Dickinson's death in 1886 at the age of fifty-five, her younger sister Lavinia discovered nearly 1,800 poems written but shared with nobody during the poet's increasingly solitary and reclusive life in Amherst, Massachusetts — the town in which she lived her whole life. These included eight hundred works that the poet had reviewed, revised, copied and assembled carefully into some forty manuscript books between 1858 and 1865. The first volume of her work was published four years after her death. However, until as late as the 1950s Dickinson's work was still often published in a manner that was significantly edited and altered from its original manuscript form.

From around the age of thirty-seven, Dickinson's behaviour began to change. She did not leave her home, spoke to visitors from the other side of a door rather than face to face, and although she was rarely seen by townsfolk (who appear to have considered her to be somewhat eccentric) especially during the last fifteen years of her life, when she was seen she was usually dressed in white. There is evidence from her letters to her brother that she had a growing sense of 'difference' between herself and others, and it is likely that health problems and the deaths of numerous friends and relatives weighed heavily upon her mind. These experiences informed the preoccupation of her lyric poetry with pain, grief, and love, as well as the nature and art from which she drew pleasure.

Content

'I'm Nobody!' expresses approval of outsiders, of people who are different, and is critical of dependency upon others' attention or approval for personal validation, going so far as to highlight the positive aspects of anonymity and even seclusion.

Opening with an emphatic and enthusiastic assertion of identity, the poet questions the reader and challenges them to consider how they identify themselves. If the reader considers themselves to be 'Nobody' too, then the poet seems excited that the two of them have found each other: being a 'Nobody' is a unifying trait and something of a badge of honour.

The poet addresses the reader in a confidential tone, exhorting them not to 'tell' others about their identity, because others would 'advertise' — that is, they would spread the fact of that identity which the poet seems to wish to keep secret.

The poet makes it clear that she would find it 'dreary' to be a 'Somebody', presumably an identity that is different from, if not in opposition to, the 'Nobody' she considers herself to be. She seems happy to be different from that alternative and perhaps more usual identity.

We are left in no doubt that the poet considers it negatively 'public' to makes one's voice heard repeatedly like a frog mired in the 'Bog' of society — a conventional and monotonous background noise which does nothing more than to have the individual step out of comfortable anonymity to assert their presence and, perhaps, to seek an attention that the poet does not value.

Composition

The poem is short, consisting of only eight lines divided into two quatrains. The first serves chiefly as a treatment of the speaker's meeting with the unidentified 'you', her advocating being a 'Nobody'; whilst the second is a more direct criticism of being a 'Somebody', with the negative connotations that the poet ascribes to that condition.

The overall tone of the work is ebullient, emphatic and direct, suggesting the speaker's confidence in her stance and opinions.

The verse composition uses rhyme, but sparingly and irregularly. The first and second lines rhyme, as do the sixth and eighth. The rhyme therefore appears decorative, rather than being structurally or linguistically integral to the composition, because it seems to be gratuitous or throwaway.

The work does not have a regular metre. However, it is interesting that of the poem's forty-two words, thirty-four are monosyllabic; and that the remainder, of which five words are trisyllabic and two disyllabic, all consist of words with even syllabic emphasis. The overall effect of this is that the lines feel as though they have a strong syllabic beat, though that beat is not a regular one, which lends the work a breezy pace and impetus.

The poem's punctuation is idiosyncratic in a way which marks it out unmistakeably as a work of Dickinson. The inclusion of dashes is capricious, their seemingly random appearance fulfilling no obvious purpose: it is not a matter of the poet using dashes instead of some other punctuation marks, as they are used where no other mark would appear to be necessary nor do they seem to inform the reading of the poem in any other way.

The use of capital letters is unconventional, with the poet applying them to what she considers to be significant nouns at variance with the usual practice in English. It may be conjectured that the capitalisation of 'Nobody' makes it read like a proper noun, and so lends it in some way the status of a particular title — with some irony, given the anonymity the word connotes. Indeed, the opening of the poem is a kind of parody. The speaker introduces herself with an oxymoron, stating an identity — 'Nobody' — which is simultaneously no identity at all, but is stated with an insistent and quite distinctively assertive sense of confidence.

The poem makes comprehensive use of anaphora as a compositional staple, with the self-pairings of 'Nobody' (lines 1 and 2), 'are you' (lines 1 and 2), 'how' (lines 5 and 6) and 'to' (lines 7 and 8). This helps to drive the emphatic tone of the work.

Figurative language is threaded through the entire piece. It is clear that 'Nobody' is metaphorical and not to be taken literally, the speaker being obviously a person rather than the 'not-a-person' that 'Nobody' literally implies. The name is rather intended to stand as a personal metaphor for the quiet, retired individual who, content with their own sense of self, does not seek validation through the acclamation or recognition of people at large, or those who claim some special ability or status — the 'Somebody' of line 5 (a noun also personalised, distinguished and elevated by its capitalisation). That 'Somebody' is again metaphorical, standing in opposition to 'Nobody', indicative of a person who either thinks him- or herself to be important or is considered so by others. The poem's only simile, the 'Frog', goes together with its final metaphor of the 'Bog' to which it calls: a composite image evoking the unthinking noise of the individual who constantly proclaims their presence to the 'Bog', the swamp or wasteland of society.

Message

It is clear from the tone of the work that people who prefer a quieter life do not have to lack a voice! We can prefer not to stick out in the crowd, but still have firm personal views and the voice to communicate them with good humour and enormous enthusiasm. It is not necessary to spend time asserting our identity to the world, and sufficient to know quietly just who we are.

The poem suggests the sense of solidarity or fellow feeling between two people whose connection occurs without the need for the approval of others. It is a kind of sympathy or affinity based upon their sharing a similar outlook. This is the focal paradox of the poem: that there is a community of people who, because of their shyness or quietness or personal preference for anonymity, are unlikely ever to meet. Yet it is a fellowship shared across humanity.

We may infer that people who do not seek attention may, like the poet herself, still make an important contribution to the sum of human experience and quietly live happy lives. Importantly, too, we see that even people who prefer not to push themselves forward may find a refreshing and joyful depth of empathy and connection with someone else who shares their own outlook on life.

Lesson plan: 'I'm Nobody!' by Emily Dickinson

Resources

Copies of the poem — ideally one per pupil, rulers for SEND pupils to follow a line when reading flip chart paper for group activities, pens and pencils or marker pens. Extra paper should be made available for use if required.

Copies of pupils' safety plans to which they can refer throughout the session/lesson.

The lesson will cover oracy and reading skills.

The session can be done in the round, or as a circle time activity, or at tables, or in an unstructured group. The lesson plan is suitable to use with pupils at Upper Key Stage 2, 3 and 4.

Links with the PSHE Association PSHE Education Programme of Study

Links have been made to the PSHE Association PSHE Education Programme of Study at Key Stage 2, 3 and 4 as follows:

KS2

- *H27. to recognise their individuality and personal qualities*
- *H28. to identify personal strengths, skills, achievements and interests and how these contribute to a sense of self-worth*

KS3

- *H1. how we are all unique; that recognising and demonstrating personal strengths build self-confidence, self-esteem and good health and wellbeing*
- *H3. the impact that media and social media can have on how people think about themselves and express themselves, including regarding body image, physical and mental health*
- *L24. to understand how the way people present themselves online can have positive and negative impacts on them*
- *R42. to recognise peer influence and to develop strategies for managing it, including online*

KS4

- *H2. how self-confidence self-esteem, and mental health are affected positively and negatively by internal and external influences and ways of managing this*
- *R35. to evaluate ways in which their behaviours may influence their peers, positively and negatively, including online, and in situations involving weapons or gangs*

Links with the National Curriculum

Links have been made to the National Curriculum for English at Key Stage 2, 3 and 4 as follows:

KS2 (Years 5 and 6) English programme of study

- *maintain attention and participate actively in collaborative conversations, staying on topic and initiating and responding to comments*
- *drawing inferences such as inferring characters' feelings, thoughts and motives from their actions, and justifying inferences with evidence*
- *discuss and evaluate how authors use language, including figurative language, considering the impact on the reader*
- *provide reasoned justifications for their views*

KS3 English programme of study

- *participating in formal debates and structured discussions, summarising and/or building on what has been said*
- *making inferences and referring to evidence in the text*
- *knowing how language, including figurative language, vocabulary choice, grammar, text structure and organisational features, presents meaning*

KS4 English programme of study

- *working effectively in groups of different sizes and taking on required roles, including leading and managing discussions, involving others productively, reviewing and summarising, and contributing to meeting goals/deadlines*
- *seeking evidence in the text to support a point of view, including justifying inferences with evidence*
- *analysing a writer's choice of vocabulary, form, grammatical and structural features, and evaluating their effectiveness and impact*

Teaching and learning activities

This poem can be used to introduce pupils to the themes of self-identity and self-worth which can help pupils to feel comfortable with who they are. The extension activities are designed to deepen awareness and understanding of this theme.

- Introduction — share aims of lesson.
- Refer pupils to their safety plans. Remind them of what a safety plan is for. Ask them to read through their own safety plan before they go further and answer any questions they may have.
- Read the poem (or teacher/leader to read it aloud) and discuss its content. Ask the following key questions:
    - What is this poem about?
    - What picture do you form of the person who is speaking in the poem? What evidence is there in the poem for this?
    - How does the poem make you feel? Why? How does it make you feel this way?
    - In the first line the speaker claims that she is 'a Nobody'. How is this a paradox? How can she be somebody and nobody at the same time? What does she mean? What does the poet mean by a 'Nobody'? She clearly thinks it is a positive thing: why? What do you think the poet means by 'a Somebody'? Why does she think it is negative to be a 'Somebody'? How does a 'Somebody' differ from a 'Nobody' in the poet's view?
    - How does the second stanza resonate with the culture of being a celebrity? How does it fit in with the culture of social media?
- Ask pupils to work with a partner or in small groups. Give each pair/group a piece of flip chart paper and ask them to divide the page into thirds. Write the following questions on the whiteboard for pupils to copy:
    - What pressures are there to look or to behave in a certain way?
    - Where do the pressures coming from? Pupils to brainstorm different forms of media which are used to convey information. It may be necessary to give a few prompts to get pupils started.
    - How can this impact on a person's mental health? Ask one of the pupils to act as a scribe.
- Take feedback and comments from pupils.
- Discuss with the whole class (or group) ways in which they can resist some of these pressures to conform to others' expectations. Compile a list on the whiteboard.
- Refer pupils back to the poem and reiterate the key message that finding self-worth can help you to be comfortable with who you are. You do not have to validate your worth through other people's opinions. Embrace yourself for who you are. Discuss this.
- Explore with pupils where they can go for help and support if they need to talk to someone.
- Review what has been achieved in the lesson.
- Refer pupils to their safety plans as a place to look if they need help after leaving the lesson.

Extension activities

- Pupils to write their answers to the key questions.
- Do you need to be a 'Somebody' to feel happy about being yourself? What does being a 'Somebody' mean in the context of social media? What are the positive and negatives of trying to be a 'Somebody' on social media?
- How important do you think it is to look for approval, praise and admiration from other people? Is it necessary for you to feel good about yourself? Why do you think these things?

- Discuss the use of punctuation in the poem. Pupils to comment on the use of punctuation and language in the poem. How does the poet's use of language contribute to the effect and impact of the poem? How could you make it even more powerful?
- Cover work on self-confidence in drama or PSHE lessons. Divide the class into two groups. Pupils take it in turns to initiate a quick conversation with another pupil about themselves — a bit like speed dating — aiming to find something they have in common each time. Pupils move around the group before swopping over. It is important to reinforce good eye contact, keeping shoulders straight, practising feeling self-confident by smiling and making conversation.
- In circle time activities, boost self-confidence by asking pupils to offer positive attributes of others within the group and to celebrate their uniqueness.
- Each pupil to make a list of their personal qualities and what they are good at.
- What are the positive and negative effects of social media on young people? Does it affect all young people the same way? Why? Discuss with a partner or in a small group.
- Pupils to write a balanced argument for and against the use of social media. Pupils can be encouraged to carry out research on the internet to look for the arguments before they draft their work.
- Discuss in PSHE lessons ways of managing the stress that may result from excessive use of social media or interacting with online content.
- Discuss what makes a good online friend. What are the qualities of a good online friend? What are the differences between an online friend and a 'real', present friend?
- What advice might you give to others who feel pressure from what they have encountered online? Pupils to discuss first and then write a reply as though they were an agony aunt (or agony uncle).

Cross-curricular/topic links

Cross-curricular and topic links may be explored for use in follow-up and for extension work in

- English
- Drama
- PSHE

Differentiation

Opportunities for discussion in mixed ability pairs.

Differentiation by outcome e.g. quantity or complexity of issues identified, sophistication of response, level of inclusion/contribution, empathy.

Writing quantity outcomes will be differentiated/assessed/moderated according to teacher's expectations of quantity and depth; otherwise by outcome.

Differentiation may also be through the use of key words rather than written sentences, or through artwork as a means of expression.

Mongrel Moon

by Peter Kalu

Commentary

You call me mulatto, mestizo, mixed
You see me through a gauze, a filter, a veil

You travel back along my double helix
See my past not my future

Listen up
I am the new dog
Barking at the bold new moon

I am the strange plant
Pushing through the cracks
In your backyard

I am the beauty that turns your understanding
uʍop ǝpᴉsdn

Look up. Look up.

There's a mongrel moon
In the sky tonight.

Context

Peter Kalu is a British writer of Danish and Nigerian parentage, whose fiction and poetry draw on his rich personal heritage.

His poem 'Mongrel Moon' is a compelling examination of what it means to be seen as different from the people among whom one lives, particularly in terms of race or heritage. It takes account of such factors as the use of divisive language and the language of difference; preoccupation with outmoded notions or judgments; the inevitability of change, particularly in a social context; and the value, positivity and beauty of difference.

Content

'Mongrel Moon' opens by establishing the difference of the speaker, who may be identified as the poet. He considers himself to be identified by others using words that allude to his having a diverse racial heritage.

The speaker is aware that he is seen by others as different, seen through 'a gauze, a filter, a veil' that may be seen as a metaphor for the preconceptions, or indeed prejudices, of the observer.

The speaker suggests that others consider him by reference to the 'double helix' of his DNA, a reference to his genetic — presumably racial — inheritance. In doing so, these observers are preoccupied by his origins, which are fixed in the past, rather than considering what direction the speaker's life might take in the present and future.

In emphatic terms, the speaker demands to be heard and declares his identity: 'the new dog', 'the strange plant', 'the beauty that turns your understanding upside down'. The newcomer into our society is unafraid, resolute, confident to be heard 'barking at the bold new moon'. He subverts the old order, challenging its understanding of things, 'pushing through the cracks' to make a place for himself close to the observer's established life and home. He brooks no refusal.

The reader is invited to raise his gaze above everyday life, and to notice that the world is being illuminated figuratively by a 'mongrel moon', a term that suggests the light cast on society by the combinative character of its new diversely-heritaged members.

Composition

The poem is written in free verse, with no rhyme scheme or regular metrical structure.

The poem's seven stanzas are delineated thematically. The first stanza establishes how the speaker (and, by extension, others like him) is seen by others; the second deals with the observer's preoccupations; the third stanza commands attention for this newcomer, the 'new dog', and declares the identity of the speaker; the fourth emphasises the speaker's identity and places him in the midst of the observer's territory; the fifth stanza lays claim to a 'beauty' that overturns the observer's world view; the sixth is an exhortation to the observer to look beyond him- or herself; the final stanza reiterates the undeniable and manifest presence of the speaker.

The poem's language is rich and nuanced. In the first line the poet uses terms — 'mulatto, mestizo, mixed' — that we might not be comfortable hearing in daily use. Yet his identity as part of a community of people to whom those words were applied historically by others gives him the liberty to use them freely, and in doing so to challenge the delicate sensibilities of the reader. This is particularly true of the poem's penultimate line and title, in which the word 'mongrel' is used, a word usually applied to describe a dog of mixed or indeterminate breed and hence carrying obviously derogatory overtones. Yet with a quiet insistence the poet implicitly asserts his right to the use of language that, when used by others, would seem especially offensive, and in so doing reclaims ownership of the term. It is an act of personal and social empowerment.

The poem is largely unpunctuated, which lends it a sense of free-flowing openness. The only punctuation occurs at the full stops in the penultimate line, which adds emphasis and imperative to the assertive, repeated 'Look up'; and at the end of the terminal line, which contributes a feeling of closure and finality.

Overall, the poem is laid out in an open form that supports the flow of phrasing and expression, exposing the lines to view and adding emphasis and cadence to them.

The twelfth line is set in inverted text: the speaker literally turns our perceptions upside down. Yet we realise quickly that although the text appears to be at odds with our conventions, it is nevertheless set in familiar type. This reinforces the poet's subtext that the new and unfamiliar has a universality at its heart: in just this way, though people such as the speaker may be thought of as new and perhaps unsettling, at the most profound level they are just fresh presentations of the familiar — people like us, like anyone else.

Message

The poem is an emphatic declaration of self: however different we may be from others, we are still ourselves, and we should be accepted as such.

Whatever the language people use to describe us, whatever their preconceptions and expectations of us might be, we are just who we are. We do not need to be like anyone else in order to be entitled to a sense of personhood, to assert our place among others in society. We should never be made to feel less that we are, less valid or valuable, entitled to less than our full dignity and respect, just because we are different.

Sometimes we need to assert our right to take our place in life, and to be accepted.

Lesson plan: 'Mongrel Moon' by Peter Kalu

Resources

Copies of the poem — ideally one per pupil, pencils or pens, rulers for SEND pupils to follow a line when reading, large sheets of flip chart paper.

Copies of pupils' safety plans to which they can refer throughout the session/lesson.

The lesson will cover oracy and reading skills.

The session can be done at tables or in an unstructured group. The lesson plan is suitable to use with pupils at Upper Key Stage 2, 3 and 4.

Links with the PSHE Association PSHE Education Programme of Study

Links have been made to the PSHE Association PSHE Education Programme of Study at Key Stage 2, 3 and 4 as follows:

KS2

- *H25. about personal identity; what contributes to who we are (e.g. ethnicity, family, gender, faith, culture, hobbies, likes/dislikes)*
- *H27. to recognise their individuality and personal qualities*

KS3

- *H1. how we are all unique; that recognising and demonstrating personal strengths build self-confidence, self-esteem and good health and wellbeing*
- *R3. about the similarities, differences and diversity among people of different race, culture, ability, sex, gender identity, age and sexual orientation*
- *R14. the qualities and behaviours they should expect and exhibit in a wide variety of positive relationships (including in school and wider society, family and friendships, including online)*

KS4

- *R1. the characteristics and benefits of strong, positive relationships, including mutual support, trust, respect and equality*

- *R5. the legal rights, responsibilities and protections provided by the Equality Act 2010*

Links with the National Curriculum

Links have been made to the National Curriculum for English at Key Stage 2, 3 and 4 as follows:

KS2 (Years 5 and 6) English programme of study

- *maintain attention and participate actively in collaborative conversations, staying on topic and initiating and responding to comments*
- *drawing inferences such as inferring characters' feelings, thoughts and motives from their actions, and justifying inferences with evidence*
- *discuss and evaluate how authors use language, including figurative language, considering the impact on the reader*

KS3 English programme of study

- *participating in formal debates and structured discussions, summarising and/or building on what has been said*
- *making inferences and referring to evidence in the text*
- *knowing how language, including figurative language, vocabulary choice, grammar, text structure and organisational features, presents meaning*

KS4 English programme of study

- *listening to and building on the contributions of others, asking questions to clarify and inform, and challenging courteously when necessary*
- *seeking evidence in the text to support a point of view, including justifying inferences with evidence*
- *analysing a writer's choice of vocabulary, form, grammatical and structural features, and evaluating their effectiveness and impact*

Teaching and learning activities

It will be necessary to explain the meaning of some of the words and phrases in the poem to aid understanding. For example, 'mulatto', 'mestizo', 'mongrel'.

- Introduction — share aims of lesson.
- Refer pupils to their safety plans. Remind them of what a safety plan is for. Ask them to read through their own safety plan before they go further and answer any questions they may have.
- Read the poem (or teacher/leader to read it aloud) and discuss its content.

  Ask key questions: What is the poem about? Why do you think the poet called it 'Mongrel Moon'? Pupils should be encouraged to annotate their poems and to write the meaning of some of the words in the margin. Pupils to take part in class/group discussion.
- Discuss in pairs or in small groups how the person in the poem says he is seen by others. How does this make you feel? How does he see himself and others like him? Why does he think that people like him are seen in this way? Record thoughts and feelings on flip chart paper.
- Each group to feed back to the rest of the class.
- How does the poet challenge racism and preconceptions regarding mixed-race heritage? Discuss and record observations on flip chart paper.
- Ask for feedback.

- Are there certain words that people are allowed to use about themselves and others like them, but that everyone else might not be allowed to use? This is sometimes called 'ownership' of a word. Why does this happen? Is it always a good thing? In what ways might it be good or bad? Find some of the words in the poem that the poet uses like this. Why do you think he has used these words? What message does it give to the reader?

- Review what has been achieved in the lesson. Draw pupils' attention to support that is readily available to help deal with issues that have been identified.

- Refer pupils to their safety plans as a place to look if they need help after leaving the lesson.

Extension activities

- Pupils to write answers to the key questions.

- Have you ever met someone about whom you were suspicious or negative, and then found that your concerns were unfounded? Perhaps it was someone you were afraid of, or who you thought would be difficult, but you then found they were a nice person. How did you feel about this? What did you think about the concerns you had had? If you are meeting someone who is unfamiliar or different from what you are used to, what is the best way to approach this? What should you do or not do, and why?

- How would you introduce yourself to someone who you knew was suspicious of you or thought negatively of you? How would you convince them that you are a good person? List your strategies and discuss them.

- Why do you think that people are suspicious or negative about other people who are not like them?

- Have you ever met someone you assumed would be nice or trustworthy, and then found that they were not? Perhaps it was someone you wanted to get on with or to trust, but you then found they were not a nice person or behaved badly towards you. How did you feel about this? What did you think about the experience you had had? Did it make you think differently about people? How might you stop yourself from having a similar experience in the future?

- Think about words that describe you. List them. Try to concentrate on positive things. Look through pictures online or in magazines that illustrate the adjectives that you have used to describe yourself then put them into a 'me cloud', a collage with a picture of you (or your name) in the middle surrounded by those positive words/images.

- Think of some of the negative words that describe you. How can you turn those negatives into positives?

- How do decide which group (or groups) of people you fit into? Discuss this. What does it mean to feel that you 'belong' to a particular group of people? Have you ever wanted to belong to a particular group of people but found that you could not? What happened and why? How did it make you feel or respond?

Cross-curricular/topic links

Cross-curricular and topic links may be explored for use in follow-up and for extension work in

- English
- PSHE
- Art and Design

Differentiation

Opportunities for discussion in class, groups, pairs.

Differentiation by outcome e.g. quantity or complexity of issues identified, sophistication of response, level of inclusion/contribution, empathy.

Writing quantity outcomes will be differentiated/assessed/moderated according to teacher's expectations of quantity and depth; otherwise by outcome.

Differentiation may also be through key words rather than written sentences, or through artwork as a means of expression.

Kitchen Table

by Paul Morris

Commentary

It was, I remember,
In the kitchen
In uneasy domesticity: she
And me, eleven.
The day was June,
Or something like;
Acid-drop sun
Bleaching the yard-wall copings
Bright and brittle.

She sat
Pinnied and sud-handed
Drying her fingers one by one;
Folded the towel and laid it down
Like an offering.
And so we were —
Separated by a kitchen table.

'You,' she said, 'will never be like them,
Never play their games or run with them,
Never be flares and platforms, mop-headed fashion-boy,
Knuckle-toe monkey boots, knit-collar car-coat,
Never "one-of-us".'
Her still-damp palm flatted her forehead,
Measuring her words' temperature,
Holding in memory.
'I know this,' she said, 'for it was so for me.
And we are one alike, you and I.'

Silence then,

Spreading to fill the space between us.

The clock I saw had stopped.

'No. You,' she said,
'You will never be "one-of-us".'
Words that to me, eleven,
Sounded an acid-drop curse.
'No no don't say don't say,' I said: no — *thought*, not said.
'No, you will never be never "one-of-us".'
Words' sound dropped — salt and acid —
On a June day,
Or something like.

43

And now, with her and me
Separated by a kitchen table and forty years
We're silent
          still.

Context

'Kitchen Table' was written in 2014.

The speaker looks back upon a seemingly simple encounter, but it is an exchange that has become fixed in his memory because of the effect he believes it has had upon him and the way he sees, and perhaps has experienced, life. We are left to speculate whether the event was as he describes, or whether it is the effect of memory, distance and experience that has made it so significant.

The poet has never identified the woman of the poem.

Content

The poem opens with the speaker establishing the scene over the first stanza: we are in a domestic kitchen; the speaker is eleven years old; it is June, probably (note 'Or something like', line 6); the vivid sun is shining harshly on the yard wall outside, scorching the stone. The boy (that is, the speaker) finds the situation 'uneasy' (line 3) and is clearly uncomfortable with the conversation that is to follow.

The speaker is sitting at a kitchen table with a woman who is not identified. We may speculate that she is his grandmother, mother, aunt or some other relative, as the scene is one of 'domesticity'. She is wearing an apron and drying her hands on a towel, which she fold and puts down (lines 10 to 16) as though it was a religious sacrifice or as if offering something to him — as indeed she is about to offer her thoughts. He seems aware that this is to be the setting in which something significant will occur — his 'And so we were —' (line 15) seems portentous.

The second stanza begins with the woman addressing the boy directly: 'You'. She tells him that he 'will never be like them' (line 17), a group of people who are unidentified. She says that he will never play or run with them, never dress like them (the fashions she describes place the scene in the early 1970s, and were worn by boys and young men). She says he will never be someone they accept; we may assume by now that by 'they' she is talking about boys of his age.

The woman touches her forehead, seeming to remember something (lines 22 to 24). She then says that she knows that life will be this way for him because that is the way it was for her, and she sees the two of them as being alike (lines 25 and 26).

There is then a long silence. Expressed by the fourth stanza and demarcated from the rest of the text by spacing above and below, the silence marks a moment of extreme focus, a moment of profound, significant change.

The very short fifth stanza is a single line. In the silence the speaker looks at the clock, which has stopped (line 29). We may wonder whether in the tension of that suspended moment it has actually stopped at all, or whether this moment of suspension of time merely seems that way to him. Is it real, or is it an effect of memory? However, the fact that it merits a stanza of its own identifies it as a pivotal moment, a moment of change.

The woman speaks again to begin the sixth stanza, emphasising her opinion that the boy will never be accepted by others of his age (lines 30 and 31). The speaker seems aghast and suggests that even at that young age, her words sound to him like a bitter curse; he wishes vehemently that she would stop, perhaps hoping that the effect of her negativity will be averted if it is left unspoken, but it is he who does not speak aloud (lines 32 to 34). He, a child, seems to understand the effect her words will have upon him whilst she, an adult, is oblivious of this. She repeats once again her conviction that the boy will never be 'one-of-us', one of a broader social group (line 35). In speaking her judgment, it is as if she has conferred a sentence upon him — that of being forever isolated and separate from his peers.

The speaker feels the sting of the words, which fall upon him like 'salt and acid' — both substances that are bitter and corrosive (line 36) — despite the brightness of the 'June day, / Or something like' (37 and 38). Though he is uncertain about precisely when the event took place, he has no doubt about how it felt.

The speaker's viewpoint returns to the present day in the seventh stanza, the last four lines of the poem (lines 39 to 42). He says that he and the woman are separated by a kitchen table, which may mean either that he is seated at a table again with her, or that it is the memory of the earlier encounter — or perhaps its effects upon him — that still stands between them. We may infer that the woman's words became fact, that the boy did not fit in with his peers, or perhaps that social integration has always been something with which he has struggled. Whether or not her words made any real difference to things, he identifies the kitchen table conversation as being somehow 'real', somehow instrumental in shaping either the events of his life or his view of relationships. He focuses on the silence that lay between them after she had passed her judgment upon him forty years before: one may speculate that he also felt such a silence, such a lack of true communication, between them at the time too, and feels that even after all this time the same lack of communication and understanding still separates them.

Composition

'Kitchen Table' is composed in free verse, without regular rhyme or metre.

The poem is divided into seven stanzas, arranged thematically. The first sets the scene and introduces the characters of the boy and the woman. The second sets the scene for their exchange. The third addresses what the woman says to the boy. The fourth describes the silence that follows. The fifth describes the sense of suspension of time that the speaker experienced at what he now recalls as a crucial moment in his life. The sixth stanza contains the woman's emphasis and, despite the boy's silent fear and antipathy towards what seems almost a prediction, her re-emphasis of her judgment. The seventh stanza finds the speaker looking back from the present and seeing how the personal separation between them, a chasm of mutual misunderstanding, has endured.

The layout of the poem contains two curious textual displacements. These occur at lines 28 and 42. The first of these is shift of the line to the right of the page to leave a large white space, a visual representation of the absence of words between the two characters at that moment. The second is again a shift of line to the right, but this time of a line fragment, the single word 'still' that ends the poem: this again creates a visual blank or 'silence' in the text, now symbolically reduced in its significance.

The poem's language and vocabulary is accessible and conversational. However, there are some unusual usages: 'copings' (= 'stones forming the top of a wall', line 8); 'pinnied' (= 'wearing a pinafore/ apron', line 11); 'sud-handed' (= 'with soapy hands', line 11); 'flatted' (= 'pressed flat', line 22).

The use of a string of hyphenated words in lines 19 and 20 gives the language a skipping, jog-trot quality that is evocative of the frivolousness of the cheap fashion the woman describes.

Punctuation is conventional.

Figurative language, apart from the simile 'like an offering' (line 14), is weighted strongly towards the use of metaphors. These are numerous, the poet — typically for his work — preferring short, taut metaphors which depend for their effect upon the implications and associations of one or two words: hence the awkwardness of the two (possibly related) characters is 'uneasy domesticity'; the too-vivid yellow sun is 'acid-drop'; the woman's words have the burning quality of 'salt and acid' (a recurrence of the scorching 'acid' motif); and the detachment between the boy and the woman is a 'silence'. A longer metaphorical device is the presentation of the seemingly stopped clock as an image of the apparent suspension of time, a moment of lacuna or immobility that forms in the boy's mind as he realises intuitively that the woman's words may affect his life ever afterwards — or as he remembers, with the distance of memory, how they did so.

Message

The message of the poem is that what we say to others may affect them profoundly, and in ways that we cannot necessarily predict.

Sometimes all that is needed to make someone feel different or separate from the group is to suggest that they do not fit in — if someone else sees one as an outsider it may be enough to make it so. Self-confidence and self-esteem may be fragile things.

Just because something bad has happened to us, there is no reason why we should wish to insist that others must be made to have a similarly negative experience, however much we may feel they should be part of it.

We should be careful how we speak to others, however well-intentioned we may think we are. Our words alone can have a life-changing impact.

We are invited to consider how even a domestic setting as innocent as a kitchen may be the scene of life-changing events. It is not the place that matters, but what happens there. As we spend so much of our lives at home, we should be careful that home remains a place of calm, safety and support.

The poem shows us that long after an event, whether or not we remember exactly what was said or the other details of the occurrence, it is often the emotion it triggered in us that we recall most vividly.

Lesson plan: 'Kitchen Table' by Paul Morris

Resources

Copies of the poem — ideally one per pupil, rulers for SEND pupils to follow a line when reading, pens and pencils or marker pens. Extra paper should be made available for use if required.

Copies of pupils' safety plans to which they can refer throughout the session/lesson.

The lesson will cover oracy, reading and writing skills.

The session can be done in the round (or as a circle time activity), or at tables, or in an unstructured group. The lesson plan is suitable to use with pupils at Upper Key Stage 2, 3 and 4.

Links with the PSHE Association PSHE Education Programme of Study

Links have been made to the PSHE Association PSHE Education Programme of Study at Key Stage 2, 3 and 4 as follows:

KS2

- *H25. about personal identity; what contributes to who we are (e.g. ethnicity, family, gender, faith, culture, hobbies, likes/dislikes)*
- *H27. to recognise their individuality and personal qualities*
- *H28. to identify personal strengths, skills, achievements and interests and how these contribute to a sense of self-worth*

KS3

- *H1. how we are all unique; that recognising and demonstrating personal strengths build self-confidence, self-esteem and good health and wellbeing*
- *H2. to understand what can affect wellbeing and resilience (e.g. life changes, relationships, achievements and employment)*

KS4

- *H1. to accurately assess their areas of strength and development, and where appropriate, act upon feedback*
- *H2. how self-confidence self-esteem, and mental health are affected positively and negatively by internal and external influences and ways of managing this*

Links with the National Curriculum

Links have been made to the National Curriculum for English at Key Stage 2, 3 and 4 as follows:

KS2 (Years 5 and 6) English programme of study
- *maintain attention and participate actively in collaborative conversations, staying on topic and initiating and responding to comments*
- *drawing inferences such as inferring characters' feelings, thoughts and motives from their actions, and justifying inferences with evidence*
- *discuss and evaluate how authors use language, including figurative language, considering the impact on the reader*
- *provide reasoned justifications for their views*

KS3 English programme of study
- *participating in formal debates and structured discussions, summarising and/or building on what has been said*
- *making inferences and referring to evidence in the text*
- *knowing how language, including figurative language, vocabulary choice, grammar, text structure and organisational features, presents meaning*

KS4 English programme of study

- *working effectively in groups of different sizes and taking on required roles, including leading and managing discussions, involving others productively, reviewing and summarising, and contributing to meeting goals/deadlines*
- *seeking evidence in the text to support a point of view, including justifying inferences with evidence*
- *analysing a writer's choice of vocabulary, form, grammatical and structural features, and evaluating their effectiveness and impact*

Teaching and learning activities

This poem can be used to introduce work on the theme of identity and relationships. It explores how someone else's concept of your identity can be unsettling and may have long echoes, either in the moment or in memory.

- Introduction — share aims of lesson.
- Refer pupils to their safety plans. Remind them of what a safety plan is for. Ask them to read through their own safety plan before they go further and answer any questions they may have.
- Read the poem (or teacher/leader to read it aloud) and discuss its content. Ask the following key questions:
  - What is this poem about?
  - What might be the relationship between the two people in the poem? Why do you think this?
  - How does the poem make you feel? Why? How does it do this?
  - What do you think the woman in the poem is trying to do? Why do you think this? What is the effect on the child? Why do you think this?
  - What advice would you give to the child about how to deal with what is being said by the woman?
  - What advice would you give the woman about what she is saying to the child?
- Arrange pupils into pairs. Discuss what makes you who you are. Think of things like name, age, family, heritage, what you like or dislike, your skills and interests, those unusual things that people might not know about you. Swop over and repeat the same questions. How do these things make you uniquely yourself?
- Think about how other people see you. How does this differ from how you see yourself? Why is this? Does it matter to you and why/why not? Pupils can help each other but should be sensitive to feelings.
- Swop over and repeat the same questions.
- Think of ways in which you would like to change or add to your identity. Try to think of small things as well as big ones. Why do you think these changes would/would not be good for you? How do you think you could achieve some of these smaller changes?
- Review what has been achieved in the lesson.
- Refer pupils to their safety plans as a place to look if they need help after leaving the lesson.

Extension activities

- Pupils to write their answers to the key questions.
- What is the message of the poem?
- Do you like the poem? Give reasons for your opinions.

- Younger pupils to write in more depth about their own identity under the title 'Who am I?' What is my family/heritage? What do I like/dislike? What am I good/not so good at? Where do I live? Where would I like to live or visit in the world? How would I like my life to be and how can I achieve it? When will I do things I consider important like going to college, getting a job, travelling, etc.? Why might I not be able to achieve the things I would like to (think of the barriers)? How can I try to overcome these barriers?

- Ask pupils to write their own identity poems using the title 'Who Am I?'.

- If you had a personal crest or symbol, what would it be? What would your motto be? Design the crest and put it on a personal flag. How would you use colour to convey personality?

- In drama lessons ask pupils to work in pairs on a conversation on the theme of 'I have never told you that I admire this about you, but...'. Each person takes turns to tell the other something admirable or positive that they see in them. Introduce other themes such as 'I wish I was like you because...' and 'You would make a great friend because...'. Each turn should try to build on what the other person has just said.

Cross-curricular/topic links

Cross-curricular and topic links may be explored for use in follow-up and for extension work in

- English
- Drama
- PSHE
- Art and Design

Differentiation

Opportunities for discussion in mixed ability pairs.

Differentiation by outcome e.g. quantity or complexity of issues identified, sophistication of response, level of inclusion/contribution, empathy.

Writing quantity outcomes will be differentiated/assessed/moderated according to teacher's expectations of quantity and depth; otherwise by outcome.

Differentiation may also be through key words rather than written sentences, or through artwork as a means of expression.

Hands In Pockets

by Peter Kalu

Commentary

> She walks, hands in pockets, hood up, slightly stooped.
> Instinctively, from my parked car, her little sister calls her name
> Brightly, twice.
> Little sister is unheard. Big sister rakes on towards the house.
> I guess I should add big sis's age group:
> Always plugged into iPods, headphones.
> And the weather the standard windy Northern grey
> And the dark, and she short sighted
> And the car headlights on, so we're actually invisible to her.
> And yet.

Context

Peter Kalu is of Danish-Nigerian parentage. He is an award-winning poet, playwright, short fiction writer and author of three young adult novels. Peter lives in Manchester, and much of his writing is based in a modern urban British setting.

The poet has said that he set the poem 'Hands In Pockets' against the landscape of a parental split, in which the older sister is not merely a stock surly teen afflicted by 'teenage rage', but is actually carrying with her the raw pain and anger of her parents' separation. She is confronted by the presence of her younger sister and father as she walks home in the dark.

Content

The poem captures a few moments of time in which the speaker describes the approach of a teenage girl, who we may assume to be his daughter and the sister of the younger girl he has with him in his parked car.

The older girl walks, hands in pockets (hence the poem's title), hunched against the bad weather.

Her younger sister, seeing her, calls out to her. The older girl does not seem to hear her, but carries on walking purposefully towards home, though she is dragging her feet from the weight of her situation (a parental split which, though not explicit from the poem, is its conceptual setting: see **Composition** below). We are not simply presented with a grumpy teen, unwilling to acknowledge her father and sister in the street: she is carrying an emotional burden of hurt, and whether it is directed at her father or at the whole situation, it is the emotion that comes out on top.

The speaker describes how the older girl is of the age to be 'always plugged into iPods, headphones'. Perhaps, therefore, she has an excuse for not hearing her sister calling to her. He builds upon this, offering the bad 'standard windy Northern grey' weather, the dark, the girl's short-sightedness and the glare of the car headlights as reasons why 'we're actually invisible to her'. He seems to have almost succeeded in convincing himself that this is why the girl will not acknowledge his presence. Like a card player, she literally and figuratively conceals her hand. But the fragility of the comfort the speaker can find in his own carefully constructed justification, the fact that he has not really convinced himself at all but that there remains something in the girl's manner that tells him that her actions are deliberate, is clear in his final, brittle 'And yet'.

Composition

'Hands In Pockets' is written as a single stanza in free verse, having no regular metre or rhyme scheme.

The language and vocabulary are conversational, and the few concessions to informality tend to sharpen focus on their subjects — for example in identifying the girls as 'little sister', 'big sister' and 'big sis' (lines 4 and 5). There is a tautness and sparseness of expression in the poet's very effective descriptions of the girl's appearance (line 1) and the weather (line 7) that contribute a convincing sense of verisimilitude to the piece.

The poet uses an effective and compelling neologism at line 4, the word 'rakes' ('Big sister rakes on towards the house'), a fascinatingly ambivalent coinage that seems to be evocative of a sense of purposeful movement. However, the poet himself has said that the word goes further than this, describing the girl dragging her feet in the way that, in his words, 'a rake is dragged across soil', and imagining how 'the weight of her situation metaphorically has her dragging herself through the pain of this parental split'. This is an intriguing insight into the way that a poet's mindscape informs the content and style of his writing.

The poem's punctuation is conventional and natural.

The use of enjambment enhances the poem's conversational tone. It is used particularly effectively in lines 7 to 10 where, combined with the use of anaphora (the repeated line openings of 'And the'/'And'), it adds impetus the speaker's attempt to build a framework of explanations (or, indeed, excuses) for the older girl's lack of acknowledgement — a framework that is given a destabilising blow by his final 'And yet.'

Figurative language is used sparingly. This is a poem of the literal and descriptive, rather than of woven imagery. The poet declines the use of simile. His inclusion of metaphor takes in the image implicit in 'sister rakes on towards the house' (see above), and that used to define 'big sis's age group' — she is 'Always plugged into iPods, headphones' (line 6).

Message

The message of the poem is subtle.

What we see may appear deceptively simple. Someone who appears to be just walking home, or perhaps someone who seems to be unhappy or even unaccountably angry, may have worries or other matters weighing on their mind that we do not know about.

We may find that, like the father and mother who occupy the silent hinterland of the poem, our actions have a greater effect on others that we might have wanted, hoped or expected. Our wishes, hopes and expectations make their effects no less real.

There are times when we might try to tell ourselves that someone's behaviour towards us is other than it appears — that they are not angry or hurt or worried, but something else. We might try to explain away the way we see them behaving, or to make excuses for them. But we may not be able to escape or avoid the fact that it is our actions that have made them that way.

We are to some extent shaped not just by factors such as our age, or by the expectations and hopes and wishes of others, but by our inner, often unrealised, landscape of experience: often difficult, sometimes painful, always intensely personal.

Lesson plan: 'Hands In Pockets' by Peter Kalu

Resources

Copies of the poem — ideally one per pupil, pencils or pens, flip chart paper, rulers for SEND pupils to follow a line when reading.

Copies of pupils' safety plans to which they can refer throughout the session/lesson.

The lesson will cover oracy and reading skills.

The session can be done at tables or in an unstructured group. The lesson plan is suitable to use with pupils at Upper Key Stage 2, 3 and 4.

Links with the PSHE Association PSHE Education Programme of Study

Links have been made to the PSHE Association PSHE Education Programme of Study at Key Stage 2, 3 and 4 as follows:

KS2

- *H23. about change and loss, including death, and how these can affect feelings; ways of expressing and managing grief and bereavement*
- *H31. about the physical and emotional changes that happen when approaching and during puberty (including menstruation, key facts about the menstrual cycle and menstrual wellbeing, erections and wet dreams)*
- *R9. how to recognise if family relationships are making them feel unhappy or unsafe, and how to seek help or advice*

KS3

- *R1. about different types of relationships, including those within families, friendships, romantic or intimate relationships and the factors that can affect them*
- *R22. the effects of change, including loss, separation, divorce and bereavement; strategies for managing these and accessing support*

KS4

- *H6. about change and its impact on mental health and wellbeing and to recognise the need for emotional support during life changes and/or difficult experiences*
- *R13. ways to manage grief about changing relationships including the impact of separation, divorce and bereavement; sources of support and how to access them*

Links with the National Curriculum

Links have been made to the National Curriculum for English at Key Stage 2, 3 and 4 as follows:

KS2 (Years 5 and 6) English programme of study

- *maintain attention and participate actively in collaborative conversations, staying on topic and initiating and responding to comments*
- *discuss and evaluate how authors use language, including figurative language, considering the impact on the reader*

KS3 English programme of study

- *participating in debates and structured discussions, summarising and/or building on what has been said*
- *knowing how language, including figurative language, vocabulary choice, grammar, text structure and organisational features, presents meaning*

KS4 English programme of study

- *working effectively in groups of different sizes and taking on required roles, including leading and managing discussions, involving others productively, reviewing and summarising, and contributing to meeting goals/deadlines*
- *analysing a writer's choice of vocabulary, form, grammatical and structural features, and evaluating their effectiveness and impact*

Teaching and learning activities

This poem is about what happens when a teenager encounters her father and little sister in a parked car as she is walking home in the dark. Mum and dad have recently split up and she is angry and hurt. It is important that pupils should know this context, which was established by the poet.

- Introduction — share aims of lesson.
- Refer pupils to their safety plans. Remind them of what a safety plan is for. Ask them to read through their own safety plan before they go further and answer any questions they may have.
- Read the poem (or teacher/leader to read it aloud) and discuss its content.

   Ask key questions:
   - What is the poem about?
   - How does the poem make you feel? How does it do this?
   - What is the theme of the poem?
   - What do you think the word 'rakes' means? Can you infer the meaning from the text? (See **Commentary**. The poet has said that the word describes how the teenager drags her feet like a rake across soil, because she is carrying a burden of pain and anger.)

- What image does the title of the poem conjure up? Pupils to take part in class/group discussions.
- How are little sister and the speaker invisible to big sister? Consider this in literal terms and emotional terms. Discuss in pairs or small groups.
- Each group to feed back to the rest of the class.
- What do we learn about big sister and the way she is feeling? Think about her actions and her behaviour. What is her coping strategy? Is this a healthy strategy? Why do you think this?

What is positive/healthy or negative/unhealthy about it? Discuss in pairs or small groups. Record observations on flip chart paper.

- Groups to feed back.
- What do you think big sister needs to do to address her hurt? How will this help her and those around her? Discuss in pairs and small groups. Record ideas on a flip chart.
- Ask for feedback.
- What do you think the needs are of adolescents and younger siblings? How are they similar and how do they differ? How can their needs be met and reconciled? What needs to happen? Do you think this actually happens, or do one's needs take precedence over the other? Discuss in pairs or small groups.
- Ask for feedback.
- Refer pupils to their safety plans as a place to look if they need help after leaving the lesson.

Extension activities

- Pupils to write answers to the key questions.
- Do you like/dislike the poem? Why? Give reasons for your opinions.
- Pupils to write about the form and structure of the poem.
- Circle time activities that focus on the changes that take place during puberty and teenage years.
- Pupils to explore the benefits of iPhones, the drawbacks of spending too much time on them, and the effect it can have on others.
- Circle time activities that centre around the importance of exercise and having time to relax.
- Pupils to reflect further on their own behaviours/needs and their interactions with family members and friends. How do you express your anger or dissatisfaction with family members, friends and others? Does this ever make you feel bad or get you into trouble? How does it do this? Can you strike a balance between your feelings and how you express them? How can you become more self-aware?

Cross-curricular/topic links

Cross-curricular and topic links may be explored for use in follow-up and for extension work in

- English
- PSHE

Differentiation

Opportunities for discussion in class, groups, pairs.

Differentiation by outcome e.g. quantity or complexity of issues identified, sophistication of response, level of inclusion/contribution, empathy.

Writing quantity outcomes will be differentiated/assessed/moderated according to teacher's expectations of quantity and depth; otherwise by outcome.

My Love, My Friendships

This section is about love and relationships —
friends, family and attraction...

Be A Friend

by Edgar Albert Guest

Commentary

Be a friend. You don't need money:
Just a disposition sunny;
Just the wish to help another
Get along some way or other;
Just a kindly hand extended
Out to one who's unbefriended;
Just the will to give or lend,
This will make you someone's friend.
Be a friend. You don't need glory.
Friendship is a simple story.
Pass by trifling errors blindly,
Gaze on honest effort kindly,
Cheer the youth who's bravely trying,
Pity him who's sadly sighing;
Just a little labor spend
On the duties of a friend.
Be a friend. The pay is bigger
(Though not written by a figure)
Than is earned by people clever
In what's merely self-endeavor.
You'll have friends instead of neighbors
For the profits of your labors;
You'll be richer in the end
Than a prince, if you're a friend.

Context

Edgar Albert Guest was born in Warwickshire, England in 1881. His family emigrated to the United States when Edgar was ten years old, settling in Detroit, Michigan. Two years later Edgar's father lost his job, and the boy began to find casual work after school. At the age of fourteen Edgar found employment as copy boy with *The Detroit Free Press*, an established local newspaper for which he would go on to work for almost sixty-five years. Edgar's father died just three years later, when the poet was seventeen.

Guest was soon promoted to police writer, then to exchange editor. In 1904, at the age of twenty-three, he began writing verse for the newspaper. His columns became extremely popular, and his daily topical verses eventually became the 'Breakfast Table Chat' feature that was syndicated to more than three hundred US newspapers.

Guest has been called 'the poet of the people'. His verse was hugely successful, largely because it was inspirational, optimistic and unashamedly sentimental. His style fitted in precisely with the contemporary American fashion for homespun, comfortable art with the nostalgic, rose-tinted flavour of everyday life in an idealised America. In the visual arts, this was the era of Norman Rockwell, and in many ways Guest was his literary equivalent.

In 1909 Guest's brother Harry published the poet's collection of poems, *Home Rhymes*, which consisted of verses taken from 'Breakfast Table Chat'. This was followed by a further collection in 1916, a book that sold over a million copies, and further collections of poetry followed almost annually — over twenty volumes taken from some 11,000 poems that Guest is believed to have written over his lifetime.

Though he was also a successful radio and television broadcaster for over twenty years, Guest described himself principally as 'a newspaper man who wrote verses'.

'Be A Friend' is a well-known and popular example of Guest's writing, extolling what were considered to be the simple and old-fashioned virtues and reflecting life in an empathetic, moral mirror.

Content

'Be A Friend' opens with an exhortation to do just that — to be a friend — and the poet returns repeatedly to this advice as the poem progresses.

We are told that money is unnecessary, but that we should have a 'sunny' outlook and the desire to help others to get on in their lives by offering a 'kindly hand' to someone who is friendless. We can be a friend to someone by being willing to give them, or indeed lend them, what they need.

The speaker assures us that we do not need 'glory' — that is, the satisfaction of personal fame. It is better to pursue the simplicity of friendship. We can show ourselves to be friends in many ways: by overlooking people's minor faults; by looking sympathetically upon someone's genuine effort; by encouraging young people; by showing compassion for those who are unhappy.

We are encouraged to exert 'just a little' work on what the poet considers to be the responsibilities and obligations of friendship.

The rewards of being a friend to others are commended to us, and we are told that we will get out of it no less than what we will bring to those others. We will receive a reward that is greater than the mere value of money that is earned by 'clever' people who work only for themselves. Rather, we will find that instead of just having neighbours — the people who surround us daily — those neighbours will become friends to us. This, we are told, is the real and greater wealth that we will earn if we are a friend to others.

Composition

'Be A Friend' is written as a single verse of twenty-four lines in rhyming couplets. The metrical structure is regular, consisting of six lines of eight syllables followed by two lines of seven, a total of eight lines, occurring three times in succession to make up the poem's twenty-four lines. This pattern of internal periodicity gives the poem, in effect, three internal stanzas or phases, though they are not differentiated as stanzas by layout in the usual way.

Each of these three 'internal stanzas' begins with the advice to 'Be a friend' (lines 1, 9 and 17), an anaphoric recurrence that adds emphasis to the poem's message. Similarly there is emphasis in the recurrence of 'Just' as a line opening (lines 2, 3, 5, 7 and 15).

The poem's language is a mixture of relatively informal, conversational, somewhat old-fashioned American English peppered with 'aesthetic' word-forms that one would be unlikely to find in everyday speech (e.g. 'unbefriended' , line 6; 'trifling errors', line 11; 'self-endeavor', line 20), and syntactic inversions (e.g. 'a disposition sunny', line 2; 'a little labour spend', line 15; 'people clever', line 19). These occurrences may seem a little self-conscious, but the original purpose of the poem as truly popular verse should not be overlooked: they work together with the straightforward rhyme scheme to give the piece a 'poetic' feel, perhaps intended for the casual reader who is not necessarily a regular consumer of poetry.

The use of punctuation is conventional, with both it and the occurrence of enjambment assisting the poem's conversational flow. This is a poem of worthy advice, and neither punctuation nor form are allowed complications that would tend to impede or dilute the gentle moral message.

Spelling follows American conventions, notable in the words 'labor' (line 15), 'self-endeavor' (line 20), 'neighbors' (line 21), and 'labors' (line 22). Whilst this does not in itself alter the overall effect of the poem, it serves as a reminder of its American origins.

The poet's use of figurative language is restrained. The sole simile assures us that the personal benefits of our friendship and the friends it brings us will leave us 'richer in the end / Than a prince' (lines 23 and 24). Otherwise the poet keeps to metaphor which is briefly descriptive: one's disposition should be 'sunny' (line 2); friendship is characterised as 'a simple story' (line 10); we are assured that compared with the pecuniary earnings of self-interested people, where friendship is concerned 'the pay is bigger' (line 17).

Message

The message of 'Be A Friend' is no less serious for the poem's apparent lightness of tone.

We are able to define ourselves as 'friends', not just to those with whom we are already close but to the wider world. We can put that definition into action in many ways: by being cheerful and positive; reaching out to those who might need it; by being kind, forgiving and generous with our time and attention; and by showing empathy.

Being a friend to others, especially those in need of friendship, help or support, need not cost us anything but the will and determination to do it.

Just showing the willingness to help someone else may be enough to create a connection of friendship with them.

When we set out to be a friend to other people, we benefit not only them but also ourselves, through the richness and deeper satisfaction of knowing that we are doing something good.

Lesson plan: 'Be A Friend' by Edgar Albert Guest

Resources:

Copies of the poem — ideally one per pupil, pencils or pens, flip chart paper or class whiteboard, plain A4 paper, rulers for SEND pupils to follow a line when reading.

Copies of pupils' safety plans to which they can refer throughout the session/lesson.

The lesson will cover oracy and reading skills.

The session can be done at tables or in an unstructured group. The lesson plan is suitable to use with pupils at Upper Key Stage 2, 3 and 4.

Links with the PSHE Association PSHE Education Programme of Study

Links have been made to the PSHE Association PSHE Education Programme of Study at Key Stage 2, 3 and 4 as follows:

KS2

- *R10. about the importance of friendships; strategies for building positive friendships; how positive friendships support wellbeing*
- *R11. what constitutes a positive healthy friendship (e.g. mutual respect, trust, truthfulness, loyalty, kindness, generosity, sharing interests and experiences, support with problems and difficulties); that the same principles apply to online friendships as to face-to-face relationship*

KS3

- *R1. about different types of relationships, including those within families, friendships, romantic or intimate relationships and the factors that can affect them*

KS4

- *R1. the characteristics and benefits of strong, positive relationships, including mutual support, trust, respect and equality*

Links with the National Curriculum

Links have been made to the National Curriculum for English at Key Stage 2, 3 and 4 as follows:

KS2 (Years 5 and 6) English programme of study
- *maintain attention and participate actively in collaborative conversations, staying on topic and initiating and responding to comments*
- *identifying how language, structure and presentation contribute to meaning*
- *discuss and evaluate how authors use language, including figurative language, considering the impact on the reader*

KS3 English programme of study
- *participating in formal debates and structured discussions, summarising and/or building on what has been said*
- *knowing how language, including figurative language, vocabulary choice, grammar, text structure and organisational features, presents meaning*

KS4 English programme of study
- *working effectively in groups of different sizes and taking on required roles, including leading and managing discussions, involving others productively, reviewing and summarising, and contributing to meeting goals/deadlines*

- *analysing a writer's choice of vocabulary, form, grammatical and structural features, and evaluating their effectiveness and impact*

Teaching and learning activities

This poem is about the importance of friendship. Being a friend to others, especially those in need of friendship, help or support, need not cost us anything but the will and determination to do it.

- Introduction — share aims of lesson.
- Refer pupils to their safety plans. Remind them of what a safety plan is for. Ask them to read through their own safety plan before we go further and answer any questions they may have.
- Read the poem (or teacher/leader to read it aloud) and discuss its content. Ask the following key questions:
  - What is the poem about?
  - Why has the poet chosen that particular title?
  - How does the poem make you feel? How does it do this?
  - Did you like or dislike the poem? Why? Give reasons for your opinion.
- With reference to the poem, ask pupils to list the characteristics of a friend. Pupils to work with a partner or in a small group. Record ideas on a flipchart.
- Ask for feedback.
- Do you agree or disagree with these characteristics? Pupils to discuss with a partner or in a small group. Ask for feedback.
- Conduct a class discussion about what qualities make a good friend and how can you check that you are behaving like a good friend. Think of things such as treating others as you would wish to be treated, or being there for them when you are needed. Ask pupils to suggest ideas. Record pupils' ideas on the whiteboard or on flip chart paper.
- Review what has been achieved in the lesson.
- Refer pupils to their safety plans as a place to look if they need help after leaving the lesson.

Extension activities

- Pupils to write answers to the key questions.
- Write about the importance of having friends and how they can help you.
- Write about the kinds of things you like doing with your friends.
- Write an advertisement looking for someone to be your friend. What qualities are you looking for in a friend?
- Ask pupils to talk about friendship problems in small groups. Think about having pupils roleplay their way through friendship problems. Peers to reflect on the problems and suggest alternative ways of dealing with them.
- Pupils to produce information pamphlets about the dangers of making online friendships and the risks associated with people they have never met.
- Write about the mood of the poem 'Be A Friend'.
- What is the poem's message?
- Write an advertisement or job application putting yourself forward as a possible friend to someone else. Be sure to tell them about your good qualities and what would make you a good friend. Mention what you want out of the friendship too.

Cross-curricular/topic links

Cross-curricular and topic links may be explored for use in follow-up and for extension work in

- English
- Drama
- PSHE

Differentiation

Opportunities for discussion in class, groups, pairs.

Differentiation by outcome e.g. quantity or complexity of issues identified, sophistication of response, level of inclusion/contribution, empathy.

Writing quantity outcomes will be differentiated/assessed/moderated according to teacher's expectations of quantity and depth; otherwise by outcome.

Friends

by Abbie Farwell Brown

Commentary

How good to lie a little while
And look up through the tree!
The Sky is like a kind big smile
Bent sweetly over me.

The Sunshine flickers through the lace
Of leaves above my head,
And kisses me upon the face
Like Mother, before bed.

The Wind comes stealing o'er the grass
To whisper pretty things;
And though I cannot see him pass,
I feel his careful wings.

So many gentle Friends are near
Whom one can scarcely see,
A child should never feel a fear,
Wherever he may be.

Context

Abbie Farwell Brown was born in Boston, Massachusetts in 1871. She was a descendant of Isaac Allerton who, together with his wife Mary and his three children, sailed to America in 1620 as one of the original Pilgrim Fathers on the historic voyage of the ship *Mayflower*.

Abbie began writing whilst still at school. Her poem 'Friends' appeared in her first book of children's poetry, *A Pocketful of Posies*, which was published in 1902, and early literary success led to a lifelong career as a writer of fiction, poetry, plays and song.

Despite her comparative success, details of the poet's life are scant and hard to find, nor is anything known about her specific inspiration to write 'Friends'.

Content

The poem is an apparently simple and accessible description of how nature, specifically the sky, sun and wind, can be sources of comfort, and how they can be reminders of other sources of friendship.

In the first stanza, the sky seen through a tree is likened to 'a kind big smile' — a friendly and joyful presence one can enjoy merely by looking up.

The second stanza speaks of sunshine flickering through leaves in the gently comforting terms of being like a mother's kiss.

Similarly the wind in the grass referred to in the third stanza is an unseen but benevolent force, gentle and careful, whispering quietly to the young listener.

The fourth and final stanza emphasises the identity of these natural forces and features as 'gentle Friends', almost as though they exist specifically to be sources of comfort. We are assured that there are so many such friends around, albeit practically invisible, that a child need never feel afraid.

Composition

The poem is written in four stanzas, each of them quatrains.

There is a regular rhyme scheme of ABAB. This common, easily followed pattern lends the poem a sing-song quality, as if the words were those of a nursery rhyme or song, which is particularly effective when the piece is read aloud.

The simple vocabulary and straightforward syntax mark the poem as a work that may be read and understood easily by younger children.

Punctuation is conventional, straightforward and minimal.

The poem makes strong use of imagery, and particularly of personification, in the likening of natural forces to friendly individuals. In so doing the poet gives those forces a greater agency, suggesting a larger power at work that interacts with children as a benevolent, protective presence.

The poet uses simile effectively, in instances such as 'The Sky is like a kind big smile' or describing the sunlight that 'kisses me upon the face / Like Mother, before bed'. She uses metaphor when speaking of the tree's 'lace / Of leaves above my head'; of how the wind comes 'To whisper pretty things', moving on 'careful wings'; and when describing how 'So many gentle Friends are near'.

Message

Abbie Farwell Brown was a writer of Christian texts. Indeed her first published children's book, *The Book of Saints and Friendly Beasts*, published in 1900, is a collection of Christian stories. In this poem we can see the features of a parable, a tale directed towards the purpose of teaching a moral lesson. The forces of Nature are essentially benevolent, an assemblage of elements that are naturally 'friends' to the young.

The poet suggests that simple personal interaction with the natural world can be a source of peace, relaxation and pleasure. Even in the busiest city, we can still see the natural wonder of the sky.

Lesson plan: 'Friends' by Abbie Farwell Brown

Resources:

Copies of the poem — ideally one per pupil, marker pens or coloured pens, pencils, erasers, plain A4 paper, rulers for SEND pupils to follow a line when reading.

Copies of pupils' safety plans to which they can refer throughout the session/lesson.

The lesson will cover oracy and reading skills.

The session can be done at tables or in an unstructured group. The lesson plan is suitable to use with pupils at Upper Key Stage 2, 3 and 4.

Links with the PSHE Association PSHE Education Programme of Study

Links have been made to the PSHE Association PSHE Education Programme of Study at Key Stage 2, 3 and 4 as follows:

KS2

- *H15: that mental health, just like physical health, is part of daily life; the importance of taking care of mental health*
- *H16. about strategies and behaviours that support mental health — including how good quality sleep, physical exercise/time outdoors, being involved in community groups, doing things for others, clubs, and activities, hobbies and spending time with family and friends can support mental health and wellbeing*

KS3

- *H10. a range of healthy coping strategies and ways to promote wellbeing and boost mood, including physical activity, participation and the value of positive relationships in providing support*

KS4

- *H7. a broad range of strategies — cognitive and practical — for promoting their own emotional wellbeing, for avoiding negative thinking and for ways of managing mental health concerns*

Links with the National Curriculum

Links have been made to the National Curriculum for English at Key Stage 2, 3 and 4 as follows:

KS2 (Years 5 and 6) English programme of study
- *maintain attention and participate actively in collaborative conversations, staying on topic and initiating and responding to comments*
- *identifying how language, structure and presentation contribute to meaning*
- *discuss and evaluate how authors use language, including figurative language, considering the impact on the reader*

KS3 English programme of study
- *participating in formal debates and structured discussions, summarising and/or building on what has been said*
- *knowing how language, including figurative language, vocabulary choice, grammar, text structure and organisational features, presents meaning*

KS4 English programme of study
- *listening to and building on the contributions of others, asking questions to clarify and inform, and challenging courteously when necessary*
- *analysing a writer's choice of vocabulary, form, grammatical and structural features, and evaluating their effectiveness and impact*

Teaching and learning activities

The poem is about the appreciation of nature and how natural forces and features such as the sun, sky and wind can provide comfort and solidarity if one is prepared to interact with them. The speaker finds peace and joy in nature and suggests that we may too.

- Introduction — share aims of lesson.
- Refer pupils to their safety plans. Remind them of what a safety plan is for. Ask them to read through their own safety plan before they go further and answer any questions they may have.
- Read the poem (or teacher/leader to read it aloud) and discuss its content. Ask the following key questions:
  - What is the poem is about?
  - Why do you think the poem's title is 'Friends'? Who are the 'gentle friends' in the poem?
  - How does the poem make you feel? Why do you think this? Give reasons for your opinions.
- What poetic devices are used in the poem? Pupils should be encouraged to think about the use of personification, similes, metaphors and alliteration and to highlight them in the poem using different coloured pens. Pupils may work on their own or with a partner.
- Did you like or dislike the poem? Give reasons.
- What rhyme scheme has the poet used?
- Discuss ways in which pupils relax in their spare time and invite them to sketch their own pictures of where they feel most relaxed. The pictures can be annotated with key words or phrases that indicate their thoughts and feelings about the place. This can help to identify locations where pupils think they are relaxing but are actually not.
- Share sketches/drawings with a partner and talk about them giving each other constructive feedback and suggestions.
- What are the barriers to finding somewhere to relax? How can these be overcome? Discuss with a partner or a key adult and suggest ways of overcoming them. If there are no barriers, use the examples below for pupils to reflect on:
  - I can't relax at the park — there's always trouble.
  - I can't relax at home. Mum and her new boyfriend are always arguing.
- Review what has been achieved in the lesson.
- Refer pupils to their safety plans as a place to look if they need help after leaving the lesson.

Extension activities

- Pupils to write answers to the key questions.
- Pupils to paint their own relaxing pictures. The paintings can be abstract, focusing on colours associated with calmness. The artwork can be displayed around school with positive, relaxing messages.
- Think about ways of relaxing in lessons to avoid feeling stressed or anxious. Discuss and share ideas.
- Think about ways of relaxing outside school. Pupils to write about the health benefits of relaxation and how they can manage their study programme to avoid feeling stressed and anxious particularly on the lead up to examinations. Wherever possible signpost pupils to activities that they might access in their locality. Share with pupils online services that are available (e.g. Mind, the mental health charity). Look at tips and exercises to help pupils relax.

Cross-curricular/topic links

Cross-curricular and topic links may be explored for use in follow-up and for extension work in

- English
- PSHE
- Art and Design

Differentiation

Opportunities for discussion in class, groups, pairs.

Differentiation by outcome e.g. quantity or complexity of issues identified, sophistication of response, level of inclusion/contribution, empathy.

Writing quantity outcomes will be differentiated/assessed/moderated according to the teacher's/session leader's expectations of quantity and depth; otherwise by outcome.

Differentiation may also be through key words rather than written sentences, or through artwork as a means of expression.

Isti Mirant Stella

by Hannah Kate

Commentary

March 1986: The European Space Agency launched Giotto, a robotic spacecraft designed to study Halley's Comet.

I dazzled you from day one,
though you didn't really understand
what it meant. But the regularity,
the uniqueness of our connection
seemed to tell you there was something
more than coincidental orbits.

Then, last time, you thought
(with analysis that denied romance)
it was time to get to know me better,
to find out what was in my heart.
After millennia, you decided our paths
should do more than simply cross.

But we were on opposite sides of the sun
and conditions just weren't right.
You saw what you wanted to see,
you knew what you wanted to know.
It didn't matter what else I could tell you,
because it was over as soon as it began.

Your interest in me began to fade,
but you were right to say I had to go.
Speeding away in the opposite direction.
Eccentricity, velocity, parabolic trajectory
would never fit with your heliocentric plodding.
And I have other orbits to cross.

I'll be back. An elliptical ellipsis,
and then I'll shooting star across your skies
like a thick tapestried omen,
a star that makes the captains of ships err.
You'll be moving in the same old circles
And me? I'll be dazzling again.

Context

'Isti Mirant Stella' was written by Manchester-based poet, author, publisher, broadcaster and academic Hannah Kate.

The poem's title is Latin and means 'they marvel at the star'. This phrase is a quote taken from the Bayeux Tapestry, the wool-embroidered linen pictorial record of the Norman preparations for their invasion of England, and the Battle of Hastings that then led to their conquest of the country. It is believed to have been commissioned by Bishop Odo, half-brother to William the Conqueror, and made in England in the 1070s. One of the scenes in the artwork depicts six men pointing up towards a strange star which trails a tail: this is now generally assumed to be Halley's Comet, which passed through the skies six months before King Harold's defeat and death. The appearance of such comets was taken at the time to be an omen of disaster (the word 'disaster' itself literally means 'bad/evil star'), as Halley's Comet has been associated for centuries with the defeat or death of kings, and the occurrence of natural catastrophes.

The poet uses the metaphor and imagery of the transient, powerful comet, together with the device of personifying the comet and the Earth, to speak about the dynamics and power of human relationships.

Content

The poem opens with a poet's note about the launching in 1986 of a space probe designed to study Halley's Comet. The reality of the historically infamous comet being studied scientifically, and the prospect of its true nature being revealed, is set up in counterpoint to the net of mysterious human influence that the poet is about to weave.

The speaker addresses an individual directly. This person seems to be someone other than the reader, so we are eavesdropping on a conversation. From clues that we may discern as the poem progresses, however, we may take the speaker and the person she is addressing to be Halley's Comet and the Earth respectively. But they are personifications, and so speak as 'usual' people would. Throughout the poem there is this duality between the two aspects of the conversation, between comet and Earth, person and person.

'Isti Mirant Stella' is an allegorical poem, conveying both literal and symbolic meaning. The duality of the poem's content makes it complex to analyse — there are two strands of meaning that are closely intertwined, or indeed superimposed upon one another. The first strand of meaning is the more literal treatment of Halley's Comet travelling through space, encountering and re-encountering the Earth. The second is the allegorical treatment of a relationship between two people, the 'comet', who is energetic and brilliant, and the 'other person', who is more steady and staid. Their conversation uses the astronomical imagery of comet and planet. We may think of these two strands as the 'comet/Earth context' and the 'person/person context' respectively.

The following analysis considers each stanza in turn, comparing the 'comet/Earth context' and the 'person/person context'. The beginning of each is printed in **bold typeface** to help the reader to navigate through each stanza. It is followed by a briefer summary of the 'person/person context' within the poem, the one which is most relevant to the dynamics of human relationships.

In the first stanza the speaker opens by stating how she has always dazzled the other person, who did not 'understand / what it meant' (lines 2 and 3), by which she means the significance of her dazzling him. The regularity with which the two encountered each other suggested there 'was something / more than coincidental orbits' (lines 5 and 6), that is that there was more to their meetings than their paths simply crossing. **In the comet/Earth context**, this could refer to the comet dazzling the people of Earth with its light, but those people not knowing whether the passing of the comet had some greater significance. It has seemed that there is more significance to the meetings than just the preset paths of two objects moving through space — some sense of deeper meaning.

In the person/person context, the stanza refers to how the speaker has always metaphorically 'dazzled' the other person, who could not understand why they were so smitten. The fact that the two of them crossed paths in what seemed a special way gave the impression that there was something special or significant in their encounters.

In the second stanza, the speaker says that the last time they met, the other person thought it was time to learn more about her and what was at her heart. That person's wish to find out more was considered unromantic (line 8), which suggests that they had a more scientific or intellectual curiosity rather than taking the speaker for what she is or merely allowing the 'romance' of her mystery to continue unexamined. After a long time of these encounters (line 11), the other person had decided that they should do more than just allow these meetings to happen, and decided to try to learn more. **In the comet/Earth context**, this suggests that the last time the comet visited (the last visit of Halley's Comet was in 1986, the one before that in 1910 — it visits every 75–76 years) the people of Earth now wanted to study the comet as something more than just a 'romantic' or mysterious object, but one that could be studied scientifically and its true nature discovered. **In the person/person context**, the speaker suggests that the other person has decided 'to get to know me better' (line 9), with a sort of unromantically analytical sense. They have decided that they should not just continue to encounter each other in that same old way (line 12).

The third stanza sees the speaker describing how she and the other person were, in figurative terms, worlds apart: 'conditions just weren't right' (line 14) for them to be together. She tells the other person that he 'saw what [he] wanted to see' (line 15) and 'knew what you wanted to know' (line 16), that it did not matter what she could say because their involvement ended very quickly ('over as soon as it began', line 18). **In the comet/Earth context**, the speaker (who is the comet, we should remind ourselves) refers to how she and the Earth cannot know each other when they are far apart in their orbits through space, 'on opposite sides of the sun' (line 13). The Earth's interest is limited: it sees what it wants to see, knows what it wants to know. There is little communication, so to speak, between them because they are in close proximity for such a short time. **In the 'person/person' context**, the speaker refers to how conditions between herself and the other person were not right to get to know each other better. The other person read into her character what they wanted to see there, and took only what they wanted to know without seeing or knowing the whole person. Communication did not matter between them, because the relationship was 'over as soon as it began' (line 18).

The fourth stanza opens with the speaker observing the transient nature of the person's interest in her, though she feels it is right that they should part (lines 19 and 20). She is 'speeding away in the opposite direction' (line 21) from the other person. Her irregular nature, her speed and path (line 22) are incompatible with the regular 'plodding' of the other person (line 23). She has other 'orbits' — other paths — to cross (line 24), other people to encounter. **In the comet/Earth context**, this suggests the comet fading to sight as the two planetary objects move apart. The path of the comet is quick, curving away through space, at odds with the Earth 'plodding' regularly around the sun (line 23). The comet expects that she will cross the paths of other objects in space (line 24). **In the person/person context**, the speaker describes how the other person loses interest in her quickly; but she acknowledges that it is right for them to be apart. She moves too quickly for this other person. They are incompatible because the speaker's path through life is quick, unusual, curving away elsewhere whilst the other person carries on tediously around the same point in life — their life revolves around something else, something that seems of little concern to the speaker, who anyway has other people to interact with.

The fifth stanza opens with a defiant, almost arrogant 'I'll be back' (line 25): the speaker continues on her way, unfazed by what she has left behind her and intending to return nevertheless. She will travel

69

on a path that brings her back, having unfinished business, before returning again dynamically (lines 25 and 26). She is 'a thick tapestried omen' (line 27), richly textured and deep, her return heralding something significant. She is, she asserts, something that leads people astray ('makes the captains of ships err', line 28). **In the comet/Earth context**, the comet expects to return to encounter Earth again. Her orbital path (an ellipse, as orbital paths usually are) always carries the promise of unfinished business, a metaphorical 'ellipsis', referring to the punctuation mark that may be used to create suspense before a thought, or at the end of a sentence, or may indicate that there is more to be said. On her return to Earth, the comet will appear again in the skies (line 26): this is a heavily nuanced and meaning-laden portent of things to come ('thick tapestried omen', line 27). However, 'thick tapestried' is also a reference to the depiction of Halley's Comet in the Bayeux Tapestry (see **Context** section above): the comet's reappearance is significant enough to merit commemoration. The 'star' (i.e. the comet) can lead people astray, such as the 'captains of ships' (line 28) who may mistake her for a navigational marker, for something predictable and reliable. The comet will find the Earth following its usual path ('moving in the same old circles', line 29). When she reappears, she will again be so bright as to dazzle onlookers (line 30). **In the person/person context**, the speaker confidently predicts her return. Though she takes her own path, it leads her back and implies unfinished business, things yet to be done or said (the 'elliptical ellipsis' of line 25). She will then be back, dramatically, in the life of the other person, as someone whose return means that exciting things will start to happen (lines 26 and 27). She is someone who can lead even steady, responsible people astray (line 28). She will find the other person following their usual, regular way of life ('moving in the same old circles', line 29). But the speaker will be surprising, brilliant, 'dazzling' (line 30) again.

Summary of person/person context

The poem is an account of the relationship between two people. The first, the speaker, is energetic and bright. She has dazzled the other person from the time they first met. The other person did not really understand the effect she had, but the relationship seemed unique and therefore special.

The other person then decided to try to engage more closely in the relationship, to take more interest in it.

However, the two people were too different, and conditions were not right for the relationship to develop further. The other person saw what they wanted to see in the relationship, and it ended quickly.

The other person's interest in the speaker faded. But the speaker thought it was right that it should do so. She could continue with her swift, energetic, eccentric life. She knew she would never fit in with the other person's staid ways. Anyway, she had other things to do.

The speaker will return to the other person's life. There is unfinished business between them, things yet to be done or said or experienced. The speaker's return always means that things will start happening — she is known for it. She knows she may lead people astray. She will find the other person living the same old steady life. But she will be dazzling again.

Composition

'Isti Mirant Stella' is a narrative allegorical poem, composed in five stanzas of free verse, unrhymed and without regular metre.

The language is conversational, the punctuation such as might be used had the piece been presented as prose.

The organisation of stanzas serves the progression of the narrative: the establishment of identity, character and relationship; the burgeoning of the relationship; problems with the relationship; dissolution and parting; return, renewal and a re-emphasis of character.

There are a few words the meaning of which might be clarified for younger readers: 'eccentricity' (= 'irregularity, unconventionality', or in the astronomical sense 'deviation from being circular', line 22), 'parabolic' (= 'a curved, symmetrical path', but also 'expressed in parables, i.e. stories, images or allegory', line 22), 'heliocentric' (= 'having the sun at its centre, moving around the sun'), 'elliptical' (= 'shaped like an ellipse, a regular oval shape' in the astronomical sense, but in the linguistic sense 'using or involving ellipsis, especially so as to be difficult to understand', line 25), 'ellipsis' (= 'an indication that something has been left out of speech or writing, or that something is left unsaid', line 25).

The work may be read as containing an extended use of personification, with the comet and the Earth standing for two people engaged in the dynamics of a tentative and apparently problematic relationship.

The poem is an extended metaphor, in which human relationships are discussed in terms of the interaction between astronomical objects. The instances of individual metaphor and the interplay between them can be derived from the comparison between the 'comet/Earth context' and 'person/ person context' in the **Content** section above.

Message

Sometimes people who are very different from each other may be attracted, either romantically or as friends. That attraction may not be equal, and might be greater for one person than the other. But there has to be something of shared value between people, or at least something that each person individually gets out of the relationship, in order for it to survive and thrive. It is up to us to decide when we see something in another person that attracts us to them, and how attracted we feel, and what we get out of that.

It may seem that there is something special or unique in a relationship that appears to give it a particular importance or significance. But it is up to everyone to decide how much a relationship really means to them. One-sided relationships, whether they are romantic or friendship, often turn out to be unsatisfying and are unlikely to last.

When we get to know somebody better we may find out that they are not what we thought when we first got to know them. It is acceptable to change our opinions of the person and the relationship we have tried to share with them if this happens.

Sometimes, however much one person might want a relationship to work out, whether romantically or as friends, it is not to be. People can seem to be too far apart, perhaps in their personalities or interests, for the relationship to succeed. Our preferences or personal characteristics may simply be incompatible. We must decide whether the other person is right for us — and we cannot insist that they should think we are right for them if they think we are not, however much we might want the relationship.

Even though we may not be able to stay in a relationship with someone else, we may still encounter them from time to time. When we do, it should not come as a surprise that we find the same feelings of attraction that we felt before, and it may be that a romance or friendship that did not work the first time may succeed the second time around. But we should remember that people tend to stay more or less the same, seldom changing greatly, with the same sort of personal characteristics they always had. If it was not to be before, then perhaps it never will.

Sometimes, however dazzled we are by someone — or however dazzled they think we should find them — we know in our hearts that we are not right for each other. However much we might like someone else, some relationships are not meant to last.

Lesson plan: 'Isti Mirant Stella' by Hannah Kate

Resources

Copies of the poem — ideally one per pupil, pens and pencils, flip chart paper, dictionaries, rulers for SEND pupils to follow a line when reading.

Copies of pupils' safety plans to which they can refer throughout the session/lesson.

The lesson will cover oracy and reading skills.

The session can be done at tables or in an unstructured group. The lesson plan is suitable to use with pupils at Upper Key Stage 2, 3 and 4.

Links with the PSHE Association PSHE Education Programme of Study

Links have been made to the PSHE Association PSHE Education Programme of Study at Key Stage 2, 3 and 4 as follows:

KS2

- *H17. to recognise that feelings can change over time and range in intensity*
- *H23. about change and loss, including death, and how these can affect feelings; ways of expressing and managing grief and bereavement*

KS3

- *R21. how to manage the breakdown of a relationship (including its digital legacy), loss and change in relationship*
- *R22. the effects of change, including loss, separation, divorce and bereavement; strategies for managing these and accessing support*

KS4

- *R11. strategies to manage the strong emotions associated with the different stages of relationship*
- *R13. ways to manage grief about changing relationships including the impact of separation, divorce and bereavement; sources of support and how to access them*

Links with the National Curriculum

Links have been made to the National Curriculum for English at Key Stage 2, 3 and 4 as follows:

KS2 (Years 5 and 6) English programme of study

- *maintain attention and participate actively in collaborative conversations, staying on topic and initiating and responding to comments*
- *identifying how language, structure and presentation contribute to meaning*
- *discuss and evaluate how authors use language, including figurative language, considering the impact on the reader*

KS3 English programme of study

- *participating in formal debates and structured discussions, summarising and/or building on what has been said*
- *knowing how language, including figurative language, vocabulary choice, grammar, text structure and organisational features, presents meaning*

KS4 English programme of study

- *listening to and building on the contributions of others, asking questions to clarify and inform, and challenging courteously when necessary*
- *analysing a writer's choice of vocabulary, form, grammatical and structural features, and evaluating their effectiveness and impact*

Teaching and learning activities

The poet uses metaphorical language in this poem to explore the incompatibility of two people and the breakdown of a relationship. The effects are heartfelt as the relationship deteriorates, but the poem's narrative ends with the speaker coming back stronger and brighter after the breakup. The poem can be explored with different age groups and could cover family breakups or the breakdown of friendships and relationships. The title of the poem is taken from a panel of the Bayeux Tapestry in which a group of men are watching Halley's Comet. The title means 'they marvel at the star'.

When working with Upper KS2 pupils, the session leader may wish to read the **Commentary** section for this poem for a full overview, but to focus particularly on the *Summary of person/person* contextual comments which examine the interpersonal aspects of the work in particular. It is not necessary to go into great depth about the astronomical metaphor with this age group: closer analysis of the relationship between astronomical and interpersonal metaphor may be better undertaken with older pupils.

- Introduction — share aims of lesson.
- Refer pupils to their safety plans. Remind them of what a safety plan is for. Ask them to read through their own safety plan before they go further and answer any questions they may have.
- Read the poem (or teacher/leader to read it aloud) and discuss its content. Ask the following key questions:
  - What does the title of the poem mean?
  - What is the poem about?
  - How does the poet use personification and or metaphorical language in the poem?
  - Did the relationship between the two people in the poem ever really get off the ground? Why do you think this? Why are things this way between the two people in the poem?
- With a partner or in a small group, look up the meaning of the following words and phrases from the poem in a dictionary: eccentricity, velocity, parabolic trajectory, heliocentric plodding, elliptical, ellipsis. What effect do you think the poet was trying to create by choosing these words? How does the poet achieve this effect?

- In pairs or small groups discuss the reasons for the breakdown of the relationship in the poem from the viewpoint of each of the people in the poem. Record on a flip chart. Why is it important to look at the reasons from both parties in the poem? Relationships do break down and people can fall out of love with each other. It is important to explore the reasons from both sides.

- Take feedback from the groups.

- Have you ever experienced a breakup or the deterioration of a valued relationship? What happened? How did you come to terms with the breakup? Was there any help available? Do you think things might have been different if you had been able to get help? How and why?

- Take feedback from the groups.

- Have you ever wanted to be friends with someone, but they did not want it? How did you come to terms with it? How did it leave you feeling? How could you have handled this better?

- Take feedback from the groups.

- In pairs or small groups discuss ways of getting over a breakup or a rejection. Refer initially to the poem and then discuss more widely in terms of breakdown in a family, friendship or relationship.

- Take feedback from the groups.

- Review what has been achieved in the lesson.

- Refer pupils to their safety plans as a place to look if they need help after leaving the lesson.

Extension activities

- Pupils to write answers to the key questions.

- Did you like or dislike the poem? Give reasons for your opinions.

- What poetic devices are used in the poem? Encourage pupils to think about the use of personification, metaphor and allegory and to highlight them in the poem using different coloured pens.

- Imagine you are a star or comet. Give yourself a name. What makes you unique and special? Use descriptive words and phrases to describe your uniqueness and how you stand out from other stars or comets. Create a comet picture with the comet's tail consisting of the words and phrases that describe you.

- Research Halley's Comet. Produce a fact file about it.

- Find images of stars on the internet. Create your own cosmic picture with you as the main star.

- Describe the changes of mood in the poem. How does the mood change towards the end of the poem?

- What is the poem's message?

Cross-curricular/topic links

Cross-curricular and topic links may be explored for use in follow-up and for extension work in

- English
- PSHE
- Art and Design
- Science

Differentiation

Opportunities for discussion in class, groups, pairs.

Differentiation by outcome e.g. quantity or complexity of issues identified, sophistication of response, level of inclusion/contribution, empathy.

Writing quantity outcomes will be differentiated/assessed/moderated according to teacher's expectations of quantity and depth; otherwise by outcome.

Differentiation may also be through key words rather than written sentences, or through artwork as a means of expression.

A Poison Tree

by William Blake

Commentary

I was angry with my friend:
I told my wrath, my wrath did end.
I was angry with my foe:
I told it not, my wrath did grow.

And I watered it in fears
Night and morning with my tears,
And I sunned it with smiles
And with soft deceitful wiles.

And it grew both day and night,
Till it bore an apple bright,
And my foe beheld it shine,
And he knew that it was mine.

And into my garden stole
When the night had veil'd the pole;
In the morning, glad, I see
My foe outstretch'd beneath the tree.

Context

'A Poison Tree' was written by William Blake in 1794 and was first published in the poet's collection *Songs of Experience*. The poet was talented in visual as well as literary arts. He was a visionary whose poems, paintings and prints displayed considerable skill from an early age. He was a committed Christian, but was hostile to almost all forms of organised religion. An artist known for his expressiveness and creativity as well as for the philosophical and mystical traits of his work, Blake is seen as a free-thinking Pre-Romantic, his work an important part of the Romantic movement.

'A Poison Tree' was originally entitled 'Christian Forbearance'. At the time of its composition, 'polite' middle- and upper-class society largely required the suppression of strong emotion. However, Blake considered this emotional repression to be unhealthy and was in favour of a more expressive mode of interaction.

In line with much of Blake's thinking, his attitudes towards the opening up of negative emotion with a view to dispersing and neutralising it may be seen as visionary. His stance, with his emphasis on examination of the psyche, seems strikingly modern.

Content

The poem focuses on the emotion of anger, and what may occur when it is suppressed and allowed the opportunity to grow unseen. An examination of the darker side of the human mind, the poem considers the more extreme consequences that may occur if anger is allowed to flourish internally.

The poem's speaker opens by recounting how, when angry with a friend, he told the friend of his feeling of 'wrath'; in doing so his anger was brought to closure. The implication is that exposing such emotion to its subject, to whom the speaker presumably feels he can confide his feelings, has a cleansing effect. In essence, the exposure of dark emotion to the light of day disperses that darkness.

Antithetically, the speaker is not able to discuss his anger with his enemy, with whom he cannot — or will not — be so emotionally open. The result of this is that the speaker's anger remains internalised to his own mind, with disastrous results.

The speaker's suppressed, internalised anger grows, in the manner of a seed. He nourishes that anger with his feelings of fear and unhappiness, by pretending to be cheerful when he is not and by other apparently gentle deceptions. The seed of the speaker's anger becomes not a mere shoot but a metaphorical tree — the Poison Tree of the poem's title.

Soon the Poison Tree bears a fruit which, though seemingly attractive, is deadly.

The speaker's enemy approaches the toxic fruit under cover of night, and the next morning is found lying beneath the tree, presumably dead. Having finally encountered the full might of the speaker's anger he has been overwhelmed, and presumably destroyed, by it. Far from being concerned at his foe's death, the speaker is chillingly glad at seeing the lethal outcome of his anger. The poem ends quite abruptly, with no reflection upon the quality of the speaker's shocking pleasure at his enemy's dire fate.

Composition

The poem consists of a four stanzas of four lines. Each stanza is made up of two rhyming couplets with the rhyme scheme AABB.

The first two couplets alternate lines with metre of seven stressed syllables with lines of eight. The rest of the poem, some twelve lines (six couplets), maintains a consistent metre of seven stressed syllables. The structure appears to falter in the third line of the second stanza, where the monosyllabic 'sunned' results in a line of six stressed syllables rather than seven; this might be avoided if one reads the word disyllabically as 'sunnèd'; this is in line with the poem's antiquated language, though it should be noted that the diacritic is not indicated in Blake's original manuscript.

The vocabulary of the poem is archaic, with the poet utilising words such as 'wrath' (= 'anger'), 'wiles' (= 'tricks' or 'deceits'), 'beheld' (= 'saw') and 'stole' (= 'crept'). This archaic language supports the poem's sense of dignity and gravity, which suits the seriousness of its topic. It also adds to the poem something of a biblical quality which is in line with its allusion to the metaphorical, mystical fruit or apple.

In the Bible story, at the heart of the Garden of Eden is the Tree of Knowledge of Good and Evil, the fruit of which God tells Adam and Eve they must not eat. They eat the attractive fruit, and its consumption leads to calamity. Similarly, the poem's speaker's anger creates a fruit that, when approached by his enemy, produces catastrophic results. Both metaphorical fruits are forbidden and dangerous.

The poet repeatedly places the emphasis of his language on himself, using 'I', 'my' or 'mine' no fewer than seventeen times in a poem of just over one hundred words. In doing so, he refers his actions and their consequences back to himself: it is his actions and omissions that have made the difference to the person against whom he has directed his anger, and the responsibility for the dire consequences is his too.

Message

'A Poison Tree' highlights the damage to both self and others that can result from suppressing anger.

The poem encourages us to bring our dark feelings into the light so as to defuse and neutralise them, releasing negative emotions and moving on with life before anger harms our own health and wellbeing and that of others.

Lesson plan: 'A Poison Tree' by William Blake

Resources:

Copies of the poem — ideally one per pupil, pencils or pens, flip chart paper or class whiteboard, plain A4 paper, rulers for SEND pupils to follow a line when reading.

Copies of pupils' safety plans to which they can refer throughout the session/lesson.

The lesson will cover oracy and reading skills.

The session can be done at tables or in an unstructured group. The lesson plan is suitable to use with pupils at Upper Key Stage 2, 3 and 4.

Links with the PSHE Association PSHE Education Programme of Study

Links have been made to the PSHE Association PSHE Education Programme of Study at Key Stage 2, 3 and 4 as follows:

KS2

- *H17: to recognise that feelings can change over time and range in intensity*
- *H18: about everyday things that affect feelings and the importance of expressing*
- *H20: strategies to respond to feelings, including intense or conflicting feelings; how to manage and respond to feelings appropriately and proportionately in different situations*

KS3

- *H7: the characteristics of mental and emotional health and strategies for managing these*

KS4

- *H7: a broad range of strategies — cognitive and practical — for promoting their own emotional wellbeing, for avoiding negative thinking and for ways of managing mental health concerns*
- *H8: to recognise warning signs of common mental and emotional health concerns (including stress, anxiety and depression), what might trigger them and what help or treatment is available*

Links with the National Curriculum

Links have been made to the National Curriculum for English at Key Stage 2, 3 and 4 as follows:

KS2 (Years 5 and 6) English programme of study

- *maintain attention and participate actively in collaborative conversations, staying on topic and initiating and responding to comments*
- *identifying how language, structure and presentation contribute to meaning*
- *discuss and evaluate how authors use language, including figurative language, considering the impact on the reader*

KS3 English programme of study

- *participating in structured discussions, summarising and/or building on what has been said*
- *knowing how language, including figurative language, vocabulary choice, grammar, text structure and organisational features, presents meaning*

KS4 English programme of study

- *working effectively in groups of different sizes and taking on required roles, including leading and managing discussions, involving others productively, reviewing and summarising, and contributing to meeting goals/deadlines*
- *analysing a writer's choice of vocabulary, form, grammatical and structural features, and evaluating their effectiveness and impact*

Teaching and learning activities

The poem was written in 1794, a time when people were encouraged to bottle up their emotions. 'A Poison Tree' uses antithesis, metaphor and biblical associations to highlight the self-damage that can occur if anger is suppressed. It is useful to use the commentary to explain these terms with pupils when you are introducing and talking about the poem, and to talk about the historical context in which this poem was written. It will be necessary to lead pupils step-by-step through the poem to ensure they understand its message.

- Introduction — share aims of lesson.
- Refer pupils to their safety plans. Remind them of what a safety plan is for. Ask them to read through their own safety plan before they go further and answer any questions they may have.
- Read the poem (or teacher/leader to read it aloud) and discuss its content. Ask the following key questions:
  - What do you think the poem is about?
  - Why do you think the poem is called 'A Poison Tree'?
  - What poetic features are used in the poem? Refer to the use of metaphors, antithesis and biblical associations.
  - Which words are archaic in the poem? Explain the meaning of the words or ask pupils to look them up.
  - Did you like or dislike the poem? Why? Give reasons for your opinions.
- With reference to the poem, ask pupils to discuss what happens when the speaker in the poem discusses his/her anger with a friend. Compare and contrast with what happens when it is suppressed. What could the speaker have done to communicate his/her feelings? What could the speaker have done to control or defuse those harmful feelings? Pupils to work with a partner or in a small group. Ask for feedback.

- Discuss with a partner an occasion when you held back your anger and were glad that you did. How did you manage it? Was this a positive or a negative experience and why? What do you think would have happened if you had not been able to contain your anger on that occasion?
- Discuss with a partner an occasion when you lost your temper. What happened? How did it make you feel? What were the consequences? What could you have done to prevent the anger from spilling out? Pairs to draw up a list of coping strategies on flip chart paper. Ask pairs to share their lists.
- How can anger impact on the health and wellbeing of others? Discuss in pairs or small groups.
- Review what has been achieved in the lesson.
- Refer pupils to their safety plans as a place to look if they need help after leaving the lesson.

Extension activities

- Pupils to write answers to the key questions.
- Write about the importance of friends and how they can help if you have a problem.
- Write an advertisement for a friend. What qualities are you looking for in a friend? What qualities do you have to offer as a friend to someone else?
- Pupils to produce self-help guides about anger management. These could be displayed around school for other pupils to read.
- What are the physical effects of anger on the body? How can you tell when you are starting to get angry? How can you then calm yourself? Think of some strategies and examine them in detail. Pupils to produce their own fact sheets.
- Make a list of anger behaviours e.g. slamming the door, throwing things, shouting. Make a list of strategies to alleviate those particular behaviours.
- Pupils to write their own empathetic, descriptive pieces of writing. Pupils may be given pictures showing angry expressions as a writing stimulus. If there is more than one person in a picture, what is the relationship or dynamic between them? Why do you think this? What has been done or said to make the person angry? What has just happened? What is going to happen? How could the situation have been avoided? How can it be fixed? What could you do to help if you were with the person in the picture?

Cross-curricular/topic links

Cross-curricular and topic links may be explored for use in follow-up and for extension work in

- English
- PSHE

Differentiation

Opportunities for discussion in class, groups, pairs.

Differentiation by outcome e.g. quantity or complexity of issues identified, sophistication of response, level of inclusion/contribution, empathy.

Writing quantity outcomes will be differentiated/assessed/moderated according to teacher's expectations of quantity and depth; otherwise by outcome.

Sonnet 116

by William Shakespeare

Commentary

Let me not to the marriage of true minds
Admit impediments. Love is not love
Which alters when it alteration finds,
Or bends with the remover to remove:
O no! it is an ever-fixed mark
That looks on tempests and is never shaken;
It is the star to every wand'ring bark,
Whose worth's unknown, although his height be taken.
Love's not Time's fool, though rosy lips and cheeks
Within his bending sickle's compass come:
Love alters not with his brief hours and weeks,
But bears it out even to the edge of doom.
If this be error and upon me proved,
I never writ, nor no man ever loved.

Context

Sonnet 116 is the oldest English poem in this guide. At some four centuries old, it is almost twice as old as the next oldest, Blake's 'A Poison Tree'. Naturally its language differs from our modern idiom. To the reader who is unfamiliar with the English of Shakespeare's time, the language may seem strange and it is easy to become caught up in its use of what is often described popularly as 'Old English'. But Sonnet 116 is not written in Old English, nor Middle English either. Shakespeare writes in Early Modern English (otherwise known as Early New English), and with the exception of a few unfamiliar words and images it is surprisingly close to the English we speak today. We should be no more afraid of reading it than we are of any new or unfamiliar accent or dialect.

To help the reader who is getting used to Shakespeare, a full textual 'translation' of Sonnet 116 into modern idiom is included below. It is not intended to be literal, nor are the rhyme or metre retained, but the text preserves the meaning and pacing of the original.

Do not let me acknowledge reasons why minds that are true
Should not be joined together. Love is not truly love
If it changes when the other person changes,
Or if it stops when the other person takes away their love:
O no! it is an unmoveable guiding point
That faces storms and is never shaken;
It is the star that guides every lost ship,
Whose value is unknown, although its height can be measured.
Love is not put down by Time, though pink lips and cheeks
Will be destroyed by the sweep of its curved sickle:
Love does not change with the passage of Time's brief hours and weeks,
But carries on even till Doomsday.
If this is wrong and it can be proved that I am wrong,
Then I never wrote, and nobody has ever truly loved.

Content

The speaker opens by stating the wish that he should not introduce any barriers to prevent 'true minds' from being joined together (lines 1–2). Though we may speculate that he is talking about romantic love, this is not necessarily the case and much of what he says can also be applied to, for example, the love we find in a close friendship or within family relationships.

Love is not truly love — it is in fact less than true love — if it changes when it finds 'alteration', meaning a change in circumstances or in the behaviour of the person who is loved (lines 2–3). Similarly, love is not truly love if it 'bends' — or distorts itself — so much that it goes away when the person whom one loves stops loving (lines 3-4). In short, true love does not change when the other person changes, and does not stop because the other person does not love any longer. The speaker exclaims his emphatic belief that love is not like this: 'O no!' (line 5).

The imagery in lines 5 to 8 is nautical. We are told that far from being a shifting or impermanent thing, love is constant — an 'ever-fixed mark' (line 5) that can withstand a storm without being damaged or harmed (line 6). True love can be like a sea-mark — something like a rock or a beacon or a lighthouse that never moves — and can help the individual 'wand'ring bark' (= 'lost ship') to navigate through life and its storms, as love can help the person who seems lost in life. Love is like a star by which we can find our way, something secure that can provide a reliable reference point to navigation through life for those who are lost or aimless — the 'every wand'ring bark' (where 'bark' = 'ship') of line 7. This 'star' of love is something the true value of which is not known, although its height can be measured; but the word 'worth' (line 8) may also signify the star's figurative astrological value, and so the importance of love to the individual's life and future.

The speaker tells us that love is not to be put down by time, is 'not Time's fool' (line 9). Physical beauty and appearance, which may have something to do with attraction and so with the onset of love, are admittedly subject to time's destructive powers and come within its 'bending sickle's compass' (line 10) — the sweep or 'compass' of the figurative blade, the scythe with which personified Time reaps his harvest and cuts down physical beauty. But though beauty is diminished by time, true love is not. Love, we are told, does not change with time's 'brief hours and weeks' (line 11), but endures all things even to the very end ('bears it out even to the edge of doom', line 12).

The poem's final two lines are an emphatic endorsement of love. If someone can prove to the speaker that he is wrong about love (line 13), then he never wrote the words of the poem (line 14). However, he clearly *did* write it, suggesting how vehemently he believes that no such proof could ever be offered and that he is absolutely right about love. If anyone were to prove that he is wrong about love, then in the speaker's opinion nobody has ever really loved anyone (line 14), because love can only be true love if, as he has so described so vividly, it is unwavering, unshakeable and everlasting. The speaker is adamant about this, and the emphatic toughness of his words add real strength, force and conviction to the end of the sonnet.

Composition

The sonnet originated as a verse form in 13th century Italy, most commonly for love poems. It was popularised by the work of Renaissance poets such as Petrarch. The Italian sonnet form (known as the Petrarchan sonnet) consists of fourteen lines of iambic pentameter with the rhyme scheme ABBAABBACDECDE. The sonnet is in two parts, the first of eight lines outlining a question or problem, then six lines proposing a resolution; the transition between the two, the 'volta' or 'turn' occurs in the ninth line. However, the work we are considering is not an Italian sonnet.

The sonnet was introduced to England in the early 16th century by Sir Thomas Wyatt and was particularly fashionable in the 1590s — though intriguingly William Shakespeare is usually disparaging of the verse form when he mentions it in his plays.

Sonnet 116 is a Shakespearean sonnet, the poet's own form. It is written in iambic pentameter and follows a structure of three quatrains finished by a couplet, with a rhyme scheme of ABABCDCDEFEFGG. The volta occurs in the thirteenth line.

The language is Early Modern English. Grammar, syntax and some elements of vocabulary may be unfamiliar to the young reader, but these are addressed in the **Content** section above.

The poet makes use of caesura — metrical pause — for emphasis and reflection. This can be seen at line 2 after 'impediments', line 5 after 'no', line 8 after 'unknown', line 9 after 'fool'. The most significant, however, may be that in the final line after 'writ', where the poet adds a brief moment of pause and gravitas before concluding with the dire consequences that would follow if he were to be proven wrong about love.

The poem incudes some personification, chiefly in relation to time which is given the capitalisation of a proper noun, Time (line 9), and the male persona of a divine force, charged with his 'hours and weeks' (line 11) and his figurative 'bending sickle' (line 10) with which he takes his harvest of human beauty.

The use of repetition again adds emphasis to the work. Anaphora is deployed in the repeated 'Love' that opens lines 9 and 11. The same word is used in the diacope of line 2, 'Love is not love', and further diacope is used in line 3 ('alters when it alteration finds') and line 4 ('remover to remove').

The poem uses three distinct sets or themes of imagery. In the first quatrain it is the imagery of the Christian marriage service: the 'admit impediments' of line 2 is redolent of that part of the service, a part with which Shakespeare as a married man and a churchgoer would have been familiar, that asks those who are marrying whether they know of 'any impediment, why ye may not be lawfully joined together in Matrimony'. The second quatrain, lines 5 to 8, is replete with nautical imagery as discussed in the **Content** section above. The third quatrain, lines 9 to 12, uses the imagery of personified time (see **Content** section above). It may be added that there is also some evidence of legal imagery in the final couplet: the poet considers whether 'error' could be 'upon me proved' (line 13), the courtroom terminology of the legal trial, and the fourth word of line 14, 'writ', not only means 'wrote' but is also the technical legal term for a formal written order issued by a court. This is, in figurative terms, the poet standing trial willingly for his belief in love.

Message

Love that is genuine, whether it is romantic love or the love of friends or family or any other kind, is constant and does not change easily. It is not easily taken away.

Love is something to which we can look for guidance and comfort when we feel lost or aimless. It can help to show us the right way to go in life and the right things to do.

Even in difficult times, love is something we can rely on. At such times it is perhaps even more important to us than ever.

We may know we have love, that we love someone else or that they love us, but we may not realise just how important that love can be to our lives.

Many things in life will change and some of them, such as physical attractiveness, will change with time. But real love is not subject to the changes of time. It can still remain with us, whatever those other changes might be, all our lives.

Sometimes we will encounter something in life that seems like love but is not genuine. It may be something that is easily taken away, or that seems to come and go, or that seems to depend on some other factor such as how we look or what we do for the person who is supposed to love us. When this happens, we are wise to question whether or not what we are seeing is real love. We should not settle for less.

Love, whether it is someone else's love for us or our love for them, should be something that is steady, dependable and trustworthy.

Lesson plan: Sonnet 116 by William Shakespeare

Resources

Copies of the poem — ideally one per pupil, pens and pencils, flip chart paper, rulers for SEND pupils to follow a line when reading.

Copies of pupils' safety plans to which they can refer throughout the session/lesson.

The lesson will cover oracy and reading skills.

The session can be done at tables or in an unstructured group. The lesson plan is suitable to use with pupils at Upper Key Stage 2 (Y6), 3 and 4.

Links with the PSHE Association PSHE Education Programme of Study

Links have been made to the PSHE Association PSHE Education Programme of Study at Key Stage 2, 3 and 4 as follows:

KS2

- *R1. to recognise that there are different types of relationships (e.g. friendships, family relationships, romantic relationships, online relationships)*
- *R2. that people may be attracted to someone emotionally, romantically and sexually; that people may be attracted to someone of the same sex or different sex to them; that gender identity and sexual orientation are different*

KS3

- *R1. about different types of relationships, including those within families, friendships, romantic or intimate relationships and the factors that can affect them*
- *R2. indicators of positive, healthy relationships and unhealthy relationships, including online*

KS4

- *R1. the characteristics and benefits of strong, positive relationships, including mutual support, trust, respect and equality*

- *R3. to respond appropriately to indicators of unhealthy relationships, including seeking help where necessary*

Links with the National Curriculum

Links have been made to the National Curriculum for English at Key Stage 2, 3 and 4 as follows:

KS2 (Years 5 and 6) English programme of study
- *maintain attention and participate actively in collaborative conversations, staying on topic and initiating and responding to comments*
- *identifying how language, structure and presentation contribute to meaning*
- *discuss and evaluate how authors use language, including figurative language, considering the impact on the reader*

KS3 English programme of study
- *participating in formal debates and structured discussions, summarising and/or building on what has been said*
- *knowing how language, including figurative language, vocabulary choice, grammar, text structure and organisational features, presents meaning*

KS4 English programme of study
- *listening to and building on the contributions of others, asking questions to clarify and inform, and challenging courteously when necessary*
- *analysing a writer's choice of vocabulary, form, grammatical and structural features, and evaluating their effectiveness and impact*

Teaching and learning activities

Sonnet 116 is about the constancy and permanency of love and how it does not change. It is likely that it is romantic love that Shakespeare is talking about, although the poem can also be applied to other sorts of love such as deep friendship or parental love. To help pupils to understand the sonnet it will be necessary to go through the poem to explain its meaning. Please see the **Commentary** which provides a lot of contextual information about the poem: the **Comments** section includes a complete rendition of the poem into modern English which session leaders should feel free to use if the original Shakespearean English is distracting.

Work around this sonnet could be split into two lessons or delivered as a longer teaching session. It is suggested that the lesson should be covered in two sessions, as described below, to allow discussion around the theme of love which is broad-ranging and deep. If two lessons are being taught a natural break comes before introducing Sonnet 116. Teachers may choose some or all of the discussion points in the main activity depending on the age and maturity of their pupils.

Session 1
- Introduction — share aims of lesson.
- Refer pupils to their safety plans. Remind them of what a safety plan is for. Ask them to read through their own safety plan before they go further and answer any questions they may have.
- Ask the pupils to write their own definition of love beginning with the line 'Love is...'
- Ask for feedback.

- Are there different types of love? Discuss in pairs or in small groups.
- Ask for feedback.
- Do you think love is permanent or temporary? If it changes, how might it change and why? Discuss in pairs or small groups.
- Ask for feedback.
- Ask the pupils to reflect on the phrase 'Love is not love if…'. Think about clues that tell you that someone is not being sincere when they tell you they love you e.g. love is not love if he hits me, love is not love if she asks me to do something that makes me feel uncomfortable.
- When might someone tell you that they love you or pretend to love you when they really do not? This might be a helpful vehicle for broader discussion on cyber safety and exploitation and should be continued in the extension activities. Discuss in small groups.

Session 2

- Read the poem (or teacher/leader to read it aloud) and discuss its content. Ask the following key questions:
  - Who was Shakespeare? Provide some background information about him and the time he lived.
  - When was Sonnet 116 written?
  - What is a sonnet?
- What is the poem about? Go through the poem line by line. Look at some of the words that Shakespeare uses and compare them with their meanings (see **Content** in the **Commentary** section for a complete translation into modern idiom). Pupils can annotate their copies of the poem to aid understanding of words, phrases and their meaning.
- Ask pupils to reflect on the poem and to discuss the following question. How important do you think love is in life? Why is it important — or not, if you think it is not? Pupils to work with partners or in small groups and to record their thoughts on flip chart paper.
- Ask for feedback.
- Ask pupils to revisit their definitions of 'Love is…' having read Sonnet 116 and taken part in group discussions. Are there any alterations you would like to make? Are you happy with your definition, and why? Is there any way to refine your definition? As a result of what you have learned, what further thoughts do you have about the different types of love?
- Review what has been achieved in the lesson.
- Refer pupils to their safety plans as a place to look if they need help after leaving the lesson.

Extension activities

- Did you like the poem? Give reasons for your opinion.
- Find out more about Shakespeare's life and times and read more of his sonnets and plays.
- In PSHE lessons continue discussions around cyber safety and how to avoid exploitation on chat sites.
- What is the theme of the poem?
- Write about the form, structure, language and rhyme scheme of the poem.
- What is the message of Sonnet 116?
- What does Sonnet 116 say about love?
- Look at the imagery in the poem and explain why the poet uses these images.

- What is the difference between love and friendship? Using the poems in this section of the guide, discuss the question and try to reach a consensus.
- Produce the poem as a storyboard with images that can be painted or drawn to reflect what love is.
- Practise reading the poem with intonation and expression. Each pupil to act it out front of an audience.
- Produce a glossary for the poem.
- In what ways do you think that love was the same in Shakespeare's time as it is now? In what ways was it different? Why do you think these things?
- In the middle of the sonnet Shakespeare uses a lot of nautical imagery to describe love. Decide on a type of imagery and write a passage describing your experience of love, which might be love for family, a friend, a pet or something else. You might, for example, think of the imagery of travel, fashion, nature, music or another theme. Produce artwork to depict images of love using your theme.

Cross-curricular/topic links

Cross-curricular and topic links may be explored for use in follow-up and for extension work in

- English
- PSHE
- Art and Design
- Drama

Differentiation

Opportunities for discussion in class, groups, pairs.

Differentiation by outcome e.g. quantity or complexity of issues identified, sophistication of response, level of inclusion/contribution, empathy.

Writing quantity outcomes will be differentiated/assessed/moderated according to teacher's expectations of quantity and depth; otherwise by outcome.

Differentiation may also be through key words rather than written sentences, or through artwork as a means of expression.

My other grandmother
by Rosie Garland

Commentary

My other grandmother

came out when her daughter wasn't looking.
Grabbed my knitted mitten as we escaped

from the house, door shushing its lips
over the stiff coir mat. She could stretch

my mother's five-minute scuttle to the post office
into an hour. She sang songs with words that did-

n't fit, took an interest in beetles
and what happened when you trod on one,

the way a spider plucked its legs
across the webstrings, the incredible reek of gutters.

She let me run ahead, drag myself
through hedges backwards, fall

into puddles, skin my elbows, sky dive
out of trees. Taught me how to bounce,

how to race snails up my arms,
the perfect moment to prise off a scab.

Knew the time to untwig my hair, spit-rub me clean.
When to smooth her skirt, her face, into sensible pleats.

We climbed the steps holding our breath
for the grown-up voice telling us to wipe our feet.

Context

Rosie Garland has often said that one of her earliest and happiest memories is being read to by her grandmother, an experience that gave her a lifelong love of reading.

'My other grandmother' is, we may reasonably suppose, an example of autobiographical poetry. It is an affectionate examination of the poet's memory of her relationship with her maternal grandmother, who is depicted as a liberating and somewhat anarchical presence. At least this is the case when they are away from the poet's mother.

When they are in mother's presence, grandmother is neat, restrained and orderly. But when mother is not around, grandmother introduces the child to an absorbing alternative world of freedom and fascination. Grandmother seems to understand the things that fascinate the child, her curiosity and the need to run around and get dirty, and encourages her to explore these things — indeed, she joins in with her granddaughter in enjoying them! It is this subversive alter ego, the 'other grandmother' of the title, that the poem celebrates.

Content

'My other grandmother' opens with the poet identifying the 'otherliness' of her grandmother when her daughter (the poet's mother) is not looking.

Together, the poet and her grandmother escape from the house to find things that interest and stimulate them. They share a fascination for small, unnoticed phenomena in nature. The child/poet is allowed to run free, to get dirty and risk herself whilst her grandmother teaches her how to avoid getting hurt.

The relationship between the grandmother and child resembles that of one child with another — only the grandmother is the far more experienced 'child', passing on her wisdom to the child/poet.

The grandmother knows the right time to go home, to clean and tidy themselves up ready to re-enter the more strait-laced atmosphere of mother's home.

The pair, now on their best behaviour and the grandmother having become 'sensible' again, enter the house waiting for the voice of an acknowledged 'responsible' adult figure, the child/poet's mother, to tell them to wipe their feet.

Composition

The poem is written in free verse, without a rhyme scheme or regular metrical structure.

It is organised in eleven stanzas. These do not appear to be organised thematically, nor is there any other apparent structural reason for this layout. However, they gather the poem's text into double-lined groupings (one hesitates to call them 'couplets' due to the absence of rhyme and regular metrical length which that term typically implies). These pairs give the poem a long and subtle sense of pulse, of emphasis and release, that helps to drive it along.

Punctuation is conventional. The language is conversational and the vocabulary conservative, the only exceptions being the probably unfamiliar 'coir' (line 5), the name of a type of coconut fibre often used to make doormats, and the neologism 'untwig' (line 18), which is applied in the sense of 'to remove twigs from'.

The poet uses enjambment freely throughout the piece, in line with its discursive flow. In the third stanza she goes further, splitting the word 'didn't' so that its first three letters end line 7 whilst its last two letters carry over to the following stanza and begin line 8. This adds an amusing visual, literal pun to the reference to grandmother singing 'songs with words that didn't fit', as the words themselves do not fit the line length.

Figurative language includes the extended metaphor of the 'other' grandmother. We are not seeing two grandmothers, but rather two aspects of the same person. There is an attractive metaphor at line 4, with the door 'shushing its lips / over the stiff coir mat', where the 'shushing' is an onomatopoeic representation of the sound of the door brushing the mat. At lines 12–13 we learn that grandmother allows the child/poet to 'drag myself through hedges backwards', which may be literal given the boisterous activities being described, but which of course also has a familiar metaphorical, idiomatic application with the meaning of 'to look dishevelled'. At lines 18–19 the poet refers to how her grandmother 'Knew the time... / ...to smooth her skirt, her face, into sensible pleats', and this carries a delightful zeugma in which the 'sensible pleats' are both those of her clothing and, figuratively, the staid arrangement of her features (and perhaps the wrinkles of old age too) that grandmother reassumes before she enters the house.

Message

'My other grandmother' is a touching account of the close relationship between a child and the childlike energy of an older person.

We see that people are not necessarily as we first perceive them, and that sometimes the better or most exciting part of their character can be hidden from immediate view.

We should be cautious about judging others superficially, based upon our expectations or their appearance. Under the surface, things can be very different indeed.

In the energetic and dynamic relationship between the poet and her grandmother we gain insight into how deeply the experience of a close connection with another person — even someone who appears to be very different from us — can affect and influence us. Among the most valuable gifts that life has to offer is the sense of growth and fulfilment that we can derive from a close personal rapport with a family member, a friend, or some other significant person in our life.

Lesson plan: 'My other grandmother' by Rosie Garland

Resources

Copies of the poem — ideally one per pupil, pens and pencils, Post-it notes, rulers for SEND pupils to follow a line when reading.

Copies of pupils' safety plans to which they can refer throughout the session/lesson.

The lesson will cover oracy and reading skills.

The session can be done at tables or in an unstructured group. The lesson plan is suitable to use with pupils at Upper Key Stage 2, 3 and 4.

Links with the PSHE Association PSHE Education Programme of Study

Links have been made to the PSHE Association PSHE Education Programme of Study at Key Stage 2, 3 and 4 as follows:

KS2

- *R1. to recognise that there are different types of relationships (e.g. friendships, family relationships, romantic relationships, online relationships)*

KS3

- *R1. about different types of relationships, including those within families, friendships, romantic or intimate relationships and the factors that can affect them*

KS4

- *R1. the characteristics and benefits of strong, positive relationships, including mutual support, trust, respect and equality*

Links with the National Curriculum

Links have been made to the National Curriculum for English at Key Stage 2, 3 and 4 as follows:

KS2 (Years 5 and 6) English programme of study

- *maintain attention and participate actively in collaborative conversations, staying on topic and initiating and responding to comments*
- *drawing inferences such as inferring characters' feelings, thoughts and motives from their actions, and justifying inferences with evidence*
- *identifying how language, structure and presentation contribute to meaning*
- *discuss and evaluate how authors use language, including figurative language, considering the impact on the reader*

KS3 English programme of study

- *participating in debates and structured discussions, summarising and/or building on what has been said*
- *making inferences and referring to evidence in the text*
- *knowing how language, including figurative language, vocabulary choice, grammar, text structure and organisational features, presents meaning*

KS4 English programme of study

- *listening to and building on the contributions of others, asking questions to clarify and inform, and challenging courteously when necessary*
- *seeking evidence in the text to support a point of view, including justifying inferences with evidence*
- *analysing a writer's choice of vocabulary, form, grammatical and structural features, and evaluating their effectiveness and impact*

Teaching and learning activities

This is a poem which encapsulates beautifully the relationship between a grandmother and her granddaughter. It is told by the child in the poem who recounts some of the happy childhood experiences and memories she had with her grandmother.

- Introduction — share aims of lesson.
- Refer pupils to their safety plans. Remind them of what a safety plan is for. Ask them to read through their own safety plan before they go further and answer any questions they may have.
- Read the poem (or teacher/leader to read it aloud) and discuss its content. Ask the following key questions:
  - What is the poem is about?
  - Did you like the poem? Give reasons for your opinions.

- How would you describe the child's relationship with her grandmother?
- What do you think the phrase 'spit-rub me clean' means? Is this a phrase we use today? Think of some other words or phrases that you have heard older people use, but which are not used commonly today.

- What activities do grandmother and granddaughter take part in? Ask pupils to discuss in pairs or small groups and to highlight key words and phrases in the poem.
- Take feedback from the groups.
- What is the mood of the poem? How do you know? Talk to a partner.
- Ask for feedback.
- What does the poem tell you about the grandmother's outlook on life? How do you infer this from the poem?
- Which of the grandmother and granddaughter's activities would you have enjoyed doing and why? Invite contributions from pupils.
- In pairs or in small groups talk about an event/activity that you have taken part in with a family member or friend. Where were you? Who were you with? What made it special? How did it make you feel and why?
- Ask for feedback.
- Review what has been achieved in the lesson.
- Refer pupils to their safety plans as a place to look if they need help after leaving the lesson.

Extension activities

- Pupils to write answers to the key questions.
- Write about the form and structure of the poem.
- Describe what you know about the grandmother in the poem.
- Describe what you know about the child in the poem.
- Write a story about a special friendship. It might involve a pet, a friend or a family member.
- What is the poem's message?
- Illustrate the poem with drawings of the activities that the grandmother and granddaughter take part in.
- Distribute sample comic strips to groups of children or display them on the interactive whiteboard. There are lots of examples to be found on the internet. Working with one comic strip at a time, discuss how the comic-strip creator combines text, quotes, and images to tell a story or to convey a message. 'My other grandmother' creates a series of images that resemble a comic strip. Invite pupils to create their own comic strips to tell about a personal experience or to tell about specific activities that take place in the poem, including lots of thoughts and feelings. Ask pupils to draft their comic strips and edit them with the help of a partner. Pupils to share their finished pieces of work in small groups.
- For KS4 pupils, see whether you can turn this free verse into a regularly metrical, rhymed poem. You might have to think about changing some of the words, but try to retain the sense and story of the original poem.
- When the grandmother is with her granddaughter she is relaxed, adventurous and childlike. But when she is with the child's mother (who is her own daughter), her behaviour is more reserved. Think of times and circumstances in your life when you behave a certain way with one group of people, but quite differently with another. Why do you do this? How do you know how to behave with each group? Which is the real 'you'? Think about a time you

felt that you had to behave differently with a certain group of people, and it made you feel uncomfortable: how else could you have dealt with the situation?

Cross-curricular/topic links

Cross-curricular and topic links may be explored for use in follow-up and for extension work in

- English
- PSHE
- Art and Design

Differentiation

Opportunities for discussion in class, groups, pairs.

Differentiation by outcome e.g. quantity or complexity of issues identified, sophistication of response, level of inclusion/contribution, empathy.

Writing quantity outcomes will be differentiated/assessed/moderated according to teacher's expectations of quantity and depth; otherwise by outcome.

Differentiation may also be through key words rather than written sentences, or through artwork as a means of expression.

It's Okay to be Different

94

*This section is about making choices/decisions
and feeling confident about being oneself,
in a world where celebrity and media images
of physical perfection rule...*

Pretty/Different
by Paul Morris

Commentary

1.

All we want from you's perfection
Cos you know perfection sells;
We just want you to be different —
Just like everybody else.

We just want you to be pretty
And we want you to feel great:
Just buy the hundred-quid ripped jeans
And lose a little weight…

Well we say a little weight, my love —
We mean a stone or two,
Cos if you don't have that thigh gap
No-one's going to fancy you.

We won't say you're unattractive,
No we'd never be so mean,
But you're nothing like the models
In our online magazine.

How will you ever get on?
How'll you ever reach your peak,
If your hair is not immaculate
And your eyebrows aren't on fleek?

Cos you'll never show your face,
Your chance for happiness is gone,
If all your shoes aren't Jimmy Choos
And your bag's not a Vuitton.

We don't demand conformity,
But we know you'd like to be
Just like a million fakers, makers
Of a self-serving celebrity.

Get your selfie onto Instagram —
Come on, get that picture took
So all the trolls and haters
Can drop in and take a look —

95

2.

NO
NOT IN MY NAME! No takers
For your haters
Your fakers
'Ideal image' makers —
I'm not a fool yet
For your Russian roulette
When your dreams of looking dreamier
Twist to anorexia
Bend to bulimia —
Flashing lashings of passion
But just fascists of fashion —

You don't pause for the pain
You cause when you spit hate again —
Insane
That you paint us all with the same stain —

You see
I care for my caring
More than the clothes that I'm wearing —
Less for my hair
Than for the brain under there —

In my mirror I see
Me —
My security
Is knowing I'm free to be
What I choose to be
In my heart
My caring
In every part I'm sharing
In my will to be
Me —

Life's too precious to waste my youth.
You keep your pressures:
This is my life, my treasures —
MY truth.

Context

'Pretty/Different' was written in response to an ongoing media discussion about peer and commercial pressures for young people to look and dress according to certain expectations, and how those young people react to those pressures. This cycle of pressure and reaction is linked to issues such as body image, and associated high-profile problems such as body dysmorphia, eating disorders and depression. Fashion companies deploy large advertising budgets specifically to target young people, creating a desire among many to conform to perceived expectations and in turn generating peer pressure upon others, often in their social group, to follow those trends. The poem imagines and personifies these blandishments and pressures, and the direct reaction to them of a young person who declares their individuality.

Content

The poem is written in two distinct parts. The first weaves together the subtle, seductive but emphatic pressures of the fashion business, the media and peers to conform to their norms; whilst the second part imagines a powerful, almost violent, personal reaction to those pressures in an explosion of emotion that interrupts and drowns out the first voice. Whilst the first part, under the guise of caring about 'you', refers to social and media-driven standards of beauty such as body shape, weight, clothing, makeup, hairstyles and expensive personal accessories, the more raw voice of the second part concentrates on the inner and true beauties of freedom of choice, individuality, compassion, and faithfulness to oneself.

Composition

The poem's first part opens with a suggestion that the speaker — the voice of fashion, the media and peer pressure — is advising for the reader's own good. The eight stanzas that follow are rhymed, metrical and quite regular: in other words, they conform to 'rules' of poetry writing. The stanzas are of four lines, with a conventional rhyme scheme of ABCB. The lines of each stanza alternate seven or eight syllables with six or seven, with some freedom of hand in the metre. Punctuation is regular and conventional. The regularity and conventionality of composition bolster the overall impression of predictability and conformity.

By contrast the second part of the poem, the reply, is free-form, unmetrical and does not follow a regular rhyme scheme, though there are some internal rhymes and assonances suggestive of street or performance poetry styles. It opens with a capitalised, shouted 'NO / NOT IN MY NAME!' and a clear statement that the speaker is aware of the pressure under which they are being placed — a declaration of awareness and resistance. Rhymes and assonances occur apparently haphazardly, sometimes with machine-gun rapidity, suggesting an emotionally-driven, off-the-cuff reaction, and defying regular rules of rhyme placement just as the voice defies the imposition of expectations. The section finishes with a four-line verse in which the speaker applies a more settled form of rhyme, whilst still defying regularity of metre. The overall effect of the composition of this section is one of angry yet articulate rebuttal, defiance, and emphatic declaration of personal identity.

Message

The poem invites us to question the origin and wholesomeness of demands for conformity of appearance that are commonly made of young people. These are often made by people who stand to gain from young people's concern to be included, to be seen as 'one of the group'.

We are shown the importance of recognising the origin and motivation of demands for our conformity, particularly from commercial quarters, and of questioning them.

Our response need not be violent but may be emphatic; need not be regular but may be divergent without being chaotic; and may be intelligent without being conventional or complacent. We are invited to recognise the pressures we are under, and to declare our independence and our own unique personal identity.

Lesson plan: 'Pretty/Different' by Paul Morris

Resources

Copies of the poem — ideally one per pupil, rulers for SEND pupils to follow a line when reading.

Copies of pupils' safety plans to which they can refer throughout the session/lesson.

The lesson will cover oracy, reading and writing skills.

The session can be done at tables or in an unstructured group. The lesson plan is suitable to use with pupils at Upper Key Stage 2, 3 and 4.

Links with the PSHE Association PSHE Education Programme of Study

Links have been made to the PSHE Association PSHE Education Programme of Study at Key Stage 2, 3 and 4 as follows:

KS2
- *R15. strategies for recognising and managing peer influence and a desire for peer approval in friendships; to recognise the effect of online actions on others*
- *L16. about how text and images in the media and on social media can be manipulated or invented; strategies to evaluate the reliability of sources and identify misinformation*
- *L9. about stereotypes; how they can negatively influence behaviours and attitudes towards others; strategies for challenging stereotypes*

KS3
- *H3. the impact that media and social media can have on how people think about themselves and express themselves, including regarding body image, physical and mental health*
- *R42. to recognise peer influence and to develop strategies for managing it, including online*

KS4
- *H2. how self-confidence self-esteem, and mental health are affected positively and negatively by internal and external influences and ways of managing this*
- *H3. how different media portray idealised and artificial body shapes; how this influences body satisfaction and body image and how to critically appraise what they see and manage feelings about this*
- *H18. the ways in which industries and advertising can influence health and harmful behaviours*

Links with the National Curriculum

Links have been made to the National Curriculum for English at Key Stage 2, 3 and 4 as follows:

KS2 (Years 5 and 6) English programme of study
- *maintain attention and participate actively in collaborative conversations, staying on topic and initiating and responding to comments*

- *discuss and evaluate how authors use language, including figurative language, considering the impact on the reader*
- *learning a wider range of poetry by heart*
- *preparing poems and plays to read aloud and to perform, showing understanding through intonation, tone and volume so that the meaning is clear to an audience*

KS3 English programme of study

- *participating in debates and structured discussions, summarising and/or building on what has been said*
- *improvising, rehearsing and performing play scripts and poetry in order to generate language and discuss language use and meaning, using role, intonation, tone, volume, mood, silence, stillness and action to add impact.*
- *analysing a writer's choice of vocabulary, form, grammatical and structural features, and evaluating their effectiveness and impact*

KS4 English programme of study

- *analysing a writer's choice of vocabulary, form, grammatical and structural features, and evaluating their effectiveness and impact*
- *improvising, rehearsing and performing play scripts and poetry in order to generate language and discuss language use and meaning, using role, intonation, tone, volume, mood, silence, stillness and action to add impact.*

Teaching and learning activities

- Introduction — share aims of lesson.
- Refer pupils to their safety plans. Remind them of what a safety plan is for. Ask them to read through their own safety plan before they go further and answer any questions they may have.
- Read the poem (or teacher/leader to read it aloud) and discuss its content.
- Ask the following key questions:'
  - What is the poem about?
  - Why do you think it was written in two parts?
  - What is the difference in the rhyme scheme between the first part of the poem and the second part?
  - Why do you think it has been written in this way?
- Discuss any words or expressions that pupils may not be familiar with e.g. 'on fleek'. Can you infer the meaning of the word or expression from the text?
- What pressures are there on pupils today? Discuss use of negative images/messages on social media, peer pressure, etc.
- Ask for pupil feedback around pressures to conform. What pressures have you experienced? How did it affect how you saw yourself, and your self-esteem? How did you deal with it?
- Divide the class into groups of two or three. Each group to perform a verse of the poem. Explain that they are going to perform the poem and that it will be necessary to learn a verse off by heart. Talk about how the poem will be delivered. The first part, for example, may need to show insincerity and sarcasm, whilst the second part may need to show defiance and resistance.
- Review what has been achieved in the lesson.
- Refer pupils to their safety plans as a place to look if they need help after leaving the lesson.

Extension activities

- Pupils to write answers to the key questions.
- Continue to work with pupils on performing the poem in English or drama lessons. Pupils to learn the poem off by heart. Discuss ways of fitting gesture and action to convey, for example, refusal, defiance, resistance, strength. It could be performed in assembly for the whole school or for different year groups.
- Make a display of adverts or photographs that depict unrealistic expectations or show airbrushed images of celebrities. Why are they unrealistic? What do advertisers hope to gain by this? Discuss with pupils.
- Consider what a realistic version of one of the pressurising adverts would look like.
- Why do advertisers choose not to use realistic images?
- Pupils to write their own poems on the theme of identity. These could be displayed around school.
- Make a display of leaflets and posters to signpost help available from different services or within school.
- Establish a worry box in the classroom or setting. Pupils post their worries and these are addressed or referred by the teacher for further assistance and support.

Cross-curricular/topic links

Cross-curricular and topic links may be explored for use in follow-up and for extension work in

- English
- PSHE
- Drama

Differentiation

Opportunities for discussion in class, groups, pairs.

Differentiation by outcome e.g. quantity or complexity of issues identified, sophistication of response, level of inclusion/contribution, empathy.

The Man In The Glass

Anonymous (after Peter Dale Wimbrow Sr.)

Commentary

When you get what you want in your struggle for self
And the world makes you king for a day
Just go to the mirror and look at yourself
And see what that man has to say.

For it isn't your father, or mother, or wife
Whose judgment upon you must pass
The fellow whose verdict counts most in your life
Is the one staring back from the glass.

He's the fellow to please — never mind all the rest
For he's with you, clear to the end
And you've passed your most difficult, dangerous test
If the man in the glass is your friend.

You may fool the whole world down the pathway of years
And get pats on the back as you pass
But your final reward will be heartache and tears
If you've cheated the man in the glass.

Context

'The Man In The Glass' is a poem with a surprisingly complicated history. It exists in many variations and with a number of different titles. All of these are thought to be based upon a poem entitled 'The Guy In The Glass' which was written by Peter Dale Wimbrow Sr. Born in 1895, Wimbrow was a musician, singer, radio performer and songwriter, and founded *The Indian River News* newspaper in June 1948.

Wimbrow wrote 'The Guy In The Glass' in 1934 for publication in *The American Magazine*. The piece rapidly grew in popularity, becoming a popular verse often passed between people with no credit for authorship. As a result, as early as 1938 there were published inquiries as to the poem's original author. The situation was complicated further when in 1983 the American advice columnist Ann Landers (actually a series of writers publishing under a pseudonym) included the poem in her column, attributing its authorship incorrectly to an unnamed man who died as a result of drug abuse. Numerous correspondents to the column then either claimed or attributed authorship, only one of whom named the original author correctly, and Wimbrow (who had died in 1954) was duly credited as the poem's true originator.

The work has achieved something of a life of its own, having been redrafted and amended many times by various hands, some of whom claimed authorship but many of whom remained anonymous. Often this rewriting was because Wimbrow's original had made heavy use of American 1930s American vernacular, at the expense of general comprehensibility.

In recent years the Wimbrow family has taken steps to assert their forebear's authorship of the original poem, which is not generally disputed.

The version which is reproduced here is a reworking of Wimbrow's original, in language that, without much of the unfamiliar Thirties US idiom, is likely to be more accessible to the modern young reader.

Content

The poem is a consideration of the importance of being true to ourselves whatever others may think.

What is important, we are told, even when we are getting what we want in life ('struggle for self', line 1) and feeling as though we are getting ahead ('king for a day', line 2), is to ask whether we can judge ourselves and our own conduct positively — going 'to the mirror' (line 3) to 'see what that man has to say' (i.e. to consult the judgment of the person we see in our own reflection, line 4).

We are told that satisfying the standards of our parents or partner (line 5) is less important than the 'verdict [that] counts most in your life' (line 7), which is 'staring back from the glass' (i.e. the mirror of our own self-judgment, line 8). Irrespective of the judgment of others, we must be able to pass our own judgment of ourselves.

We should disregard the opinions of others (line 9) and stand apart, relying on our own self-judgment as we must always be able to live with ourselves (lines 9 and 10). It may be difficult (and, in the poet's view, precarious) for us to judge ourselves against our own standards, but it is a test that we should try to pass to be on the best of terms with ourselves (lines 11 and 12).

It does not matter how we have made the world — that is, everybody around us — think of us or how much approval or praise we may have received (lines 13 and 14). Ultimately, we are told, we will only be unhappy if we have cheated ourselves out of being able to hold a good opinion of our own conduct (lines 15 and 16).

We must stand apart from the opinions of the world around us and do what we know is right for us, being true and honest to ourselves.

Composition

'The Man In The Glass' is written in four stanzas each of four lines, with the rhyme scheme ABAB.

The verse is composed in anapests, a metrical foot consisting of two unstressed syllables followed by a stressed syllable (in effect, 'da-da-DUM', though the initial unstressed beat of a line may be omitted). Lines consist of alternating anapestic tetrameter (four anapestic metrical feet per line) and anapestic trimeter (three anapestic feet per line), which give the poem a lively and rapid pace.

The vocabulary and language of the poem are conversational and informal, with some minor vestiges of the original American vernacular, notably 'king for a day' (line 2). The resulting poem has a breezy, rather hearty feel, as though one were receiving avuncular good advice.

Punctuation is minimal, demarcating each stanza as a single sentence. The use of the dash in the first line of the third stanza provides an effective caesura that adds emphasis to the advice that follows — 'never mind all the rest'.

The poet makes consistent use of personification throughout the poem in the form of 'the man in the glass', the reflected image of oneself in the mirror and also conceptually the self facing the self.

In giving that character the ability to make either positive or negative judgments about the person who is looking into it, the faculty of evaluation and judgment is externalised. It is not simply a person judging him- or herself but an external, trustworthy 'friend' (line 12) whose good opinion is of paramount importance; yet that friend is, of course, oneself.

The poem contains no simile, but uses metaphor to support and embellish its theme. As well as the 'man in the glass' metaphor, there is the second extended metaphor of judgment. Repeated reference is made to 'judgment', 'verdict' and passing a 'test' (lines 6, 7 and 11 respectively), all externalised legal images for the critical faculty of evaluating the quality of one's character and actions. We are encouraged to see our conduct as something that should be weighed in the balance, a serious undertaking but one that is suggestive of applying the highest standards of conduct to ourselves and then maintaining them.

We are encouraged not to rely upon the appraisal of ourselves by others, not even those to whom we are close, nor to submit to the often unreliable 'court of public opinion' as others might do. We should stand apart from this, evaluating ourselves against the values and conduct of the person we would like to be, scrupulously and honestly, striving to improve and, it might be suggested, to impress ourselves.

Message

Whilst the opinions of other people matter, it can be a powerful tool for growth and self-development to have a personal code of standards to which we hold ourselves. This does not need to be a formal thing, but simply a set of values to which we decide to adhere.

Whatever others may think is right for themselves or others or even for us, it is essential that we should be true and honest to ourselves. Sometimes people will advise us in their own best interests, not ours. We are each unique, not quite like anybody else who has ever lived or ever will live, and so we must decide for ourselves what is right for us. We may take guidance from others, but ultimately we must be our own unique selves.

It can often feel as though we must gauge ourselves by comparison with others — parents, siblings, friends, peers, or those whom we aspire to emulate. We should remember, though, that our differences are what make each of us uniquely ourselves, and that uniqueness is something to be cherished.

Lesson plan: 'The Man in the Glass', Anonymous
(after Peter Dale Wimbrow Sr.)

Resources:

Copies of the poem — ideally one per pupil, pencils or pens, Post-it notes, class whiteboard, plain or lined A4 paper, rulers for SEND pupils to follow a line when reading.

Copies of pupils' safety plans to which they can refer throughout the session/lesson.

The lesson will cover oracy and reading skills.

The session can be done at tables or in an unstructured group. The lesson plan is suitable to use with pupils at Upper Key Stage 2, 3 and 4.

Links with the PSHE Association PSHE Education Programme of Study

Links have been made to the PSHE Association PSHE Education Programme of Study at Key Stage 2, 3 and 4 as follows:

KS2

- *H27. To recognise their individuality and personal qualities*
- *R11. what constitutes a positive healthy friendship (e.g. mutual respect, trust, truthfulness, loyalty, kindness, generosity, sharing interests and experiences, support with problems and difficulties); that the same principles apply to online friendships as to face-to-face relationships*

KS3

- *H1. how we are all unique; that recognising and demonstrating personal strengths build self-confidence, self-esteem and good health and wellbeing*
- *R2. indicators of positive, healthy relationships and unhealthy relationships, including online*
- *R42. to recognise peer influence and to develop strategies for managing it, including online*

KS4

- *H1. to accurately assess their areas of strength and development, and where appropriate, act upon feedback*
- *R1. the characteristics and benefits of strong, positive relationships, including mutual support, trust, respect and equality*
- *R28. to recognise when others are using manipulation, persuasion or coercion and how to respond*

Links with the National Curriculum

Links have been made to the National Curriculum for English at Key Stage 2, 3 and 4 as follows:

KS2 (Years 5 and 6) English programme of study
- *maintain attention and participate actively in collaborative conversations, staying on topic and initiating and responding to comments*
- *identifying how language, structure and presentation contribute to meaning*
- *discuss and evaluate how authors use language, including figurative language, considering the impact on the reader*

KS3 English programme of study
- *participating in formal debates and structured discussions, summarising and/or building on what has been said*
- *knowing how language, including figurative language, vocabulary choice, grammar, text structure and organisational features, presents meaning*

KS4 English programme of study

- *working effectively in groups of different sizes and taking on required roles, including leading and managing discussions, involving others productively, reviewing and summarising, and contributing to meeting goals/deadlines*
- *analysing a writer's choice of vocabulary, form, grammatical and structural features, and evaluating their effectiveness and impact*

Teaching and learning activities

Many young people believe that when they do things to please their peers, they will be popular and accepted. They may go against the advice of their parents, carers and teachers or their own common sense, only to find themselves in trouble and still not popular with the peers whose approval they had valued. This poem and the accompanying teaching activities enable pupils to explore what it means to have integrity and honesty with oneself. Sometimes this integrity and honesty means challenging the status quo or at least acknowledging to themselves that there is nothing wrong with them thinking or behaving differently from others.

- Introduction — share aims of lesson.
- Refer pupils to their safety plans. Remind them of what a safety plan is for. Ask them to read through their own safety plan before they go further and answer any questions they may have.
- Read the poem (or teacher/leader to read it aloud) and discuss its content. Ask the following key questions:
  - What do you think the poem is about?
  - Who do you think the man in the glass is? Why is it important to please that person?
  - How did the poem make you feel? Why? How did it do this? Give reasons for your opinions.
  - Did you like or dislike the poem? Give reasons for your opinions.
  - Can you find an example of a metaphor in the poem? Can you explain the meaning of it?
  - What rhyme scheme has the poet used? Why do you think he has used this scheme?
- What do you understand by the term 'be true to yourself'? Ask pupils to spend time in pairs or small groups thinking about this and what it means.
- Ask for feedback.
- Why is it important to stay true to yourself in life rather than letting peers take you down a path that you know you should not tread? How might this impact negatively on you and others? How can you stay strong? Ask pupils to discuss and feed back.
- What might be the reasons for not wanting to listen to yourself and your own better judgment? In pairs ask pupils to write their thoughts on Post-it notes. These can be stuck on a whiteboard for the teacher to read out.
- Ask pupils to reflect on an occasion when a peer asked them to do something that they did not want to do but they went along with it. What happened? Were there any consequences? Pupils to discuss this in pairs and in small groups.
- Take feedback.
- Working with a partner or in a small group, come up with a list of suggestions on how to stay true to yourself.
- Partners or small groups to feed back.
- Review what has been achieved in the lesson.
- Refer pupils to their safety plans as a place to look if they need help after leaving the lesson.

Extension activities

- Pupils to write answers to the key questions.
- Write a story which involves a dilemma between friends and involves the central character having to make a firm decision to do the right thing.
- Ask pupils to talk about friendship problems in small groups. Think about having pupils roleplay their way through a peer pressure situation. Pupils to reflect on the pressure and suggest ways of dealing with it.
- Pupils to produce information pamphlets, leaflets or guidance about how to resist peer pressure on social media.
- What pressures are there in society for young people to conform to other people's expectations and goals? Ask pupils to brainstorm ideas and then to think of ways of dealing with them.
- Pupils to reflect on their own uniqueness. What do they think their talents and skills are? What skills do they feel they lack? How confident do they feel about themselves and their learning? How can we address issues of skills and confidence?
- Younger pupils to draw two pictures of themselves. In the first picture they are invited to think of words to describe themselves and their qualities. Pupils can do this on their own or with a trusted friend or partner. The partner may suggest qualities that they see in their friend which can help to boost their self-confidence and self-esteem. On another sheet of paper pupils are invited to write about skills or qualities they feel they lack. Working with a trusted friend or adult they are asked to explore ways of improving these skills.
- Write about the message of the poem.
- Discuss the use of personification in the poem.

Cross-curricular/topic links

Cross-curricular and topic links may be explored for use in follow-up and for extension work in

- English
- Drama
- PSHE
- Art and Design

Differentiation

Opportunities for discussion in class, groups, pairs.

Differentiation by outcome e.g. quantity or complexity of issues identified, sophistication of response, level of inclusion/contribution, empathy.

Writing quantity outcomes will be differentiated/assessed/moderated according to teacher's expectations of quantity and depth; otherwise by outcome.

Differentiation may also be through key words rather than written sentences, or through artwork as a means of expression.

table

by Hannah Kate

Commentary

this tree wants to be a table
but then
a tree that isn't a table is no tree at all
being a table is natural for a tree
to be planed and smoothed and
varnished and oiled and
french polished all with loving care
this is what a tree is grown for
this is what a tree desires
there is nothing sadder than a tree
hardened and twisted through years
of neglect and lack of attention
diseased limbs and wasted wood
for a tree that isn't a table is no tree at all

this tree demands to be a table
but then
a tree that isn't a table is no tree at all
this tree has chosen its carpenter
the tools that will work on its surface
which axe which saw which chisel blade
which hands which oils which sandpaper
this tree knows what shape
of table it wants to be and how
and when and why it will be used
and if the carpenter does a shoddy job
this tree will send him away and
find another then another then another
cos a tree that isn't a table is no tree at all

all trees should become tables
but then
a tree that isn't a table is no tree at all
everyone knows that trees
are crying out to be tables and crying
out for tools to turn them into tables
and there are books and films to show
a carpenter how to use tools and make
trees into tables and make
trees happy to be tables because really
ask any table
they say they like the varnish
and tables tell saplings all the time
that a tree that isn't a table is no tree at all

this tree will be a table
but then
a tree that isn't a table is no tree at all
a tree cannot really refuse
to be a table though some of them will try
a tree that wants to be with other trees
a tree that wants to seal up its knots
from tools that should file its bark
but what use is a tree that isn't a table
what's the point in letting it grow
what's the point in giving it space
and if a carpenter makes it into a table
he's only behaving as a carpenter should
cos tools that don't make tables are no tools at all

Context

'table' was written by Manchester-based poet, author, publisher, broadcaster and academic Hannah Kate.

The poet is reserved regarding the original intention of the poem, preferring to allow the reader their own interpretation of the poem and taking the view that much of a poem's significance is made in the mind of the reader. However, it would be interesting to speculate whether the piece arises from Hannah's extensive experience as an educationist and academic. It is therefore upon this, the interpretation of this guide's author, among the many that could no doubt be applied to the work, that the interpretive elements of this commentary will be based.

Content

The poem is a discussion of the merits and suitability of a tree for fulfilling a particular purpose: that of becoming (or rather, of being made into) a table.

The speaker discusses how suitable the tree is for the purpose of being made into a table, and how natural and desirable it is for a tree to be made into a table. We are told of all the care and effort that goes into the transformation of the tree into a table, how it is the tree's purpose in life to become a table, and how sad it is for a tree to be neglected and go to waste by being left in its natural state.

The speaker describes the care and skill that the carpenter applies to turning the tree into a table, and how the tree cooperates with — perhaps even demands — the process of its own transformation as it knows what shape of table it wishes to become and how it will be used. The tree will even reject the carpenter and choose another if it feels that he is not doing a good job of the manufacturing process.

We are told that the process is one to which everyone, even the tree itself, subscribes enthusiastically, and there is a strong sense of disapproval for those who dissent or depart from it: as the speaker repeats throughout the poem, 'a tree that isn't a table is no tree at all'. The carpenters who do this work have access to many resources to show them how to do their work well, but also to show them how to make trees happy to go through the process of being made into tables.

The speaker admits that trees cannot really refuse the process of being made into tables, though some of them do try to do so. These trees may try to remain as they are, with other similar trees, but the speaker questions the point of allowing these trees to grow and giving them space, and again challenges the value of a tree that is not a table.

We are told that the carpenters who carry out this process are only doing what they should do, because if they did not do so then their tools, the means by which the work is done, would not be fulfilling their purpose and would be 'no tools at all'.

The content of this poem is clearly highly metaphorical. We understand as readers that the situation the poet describes does not pertain literally to the real world, but the poem acquires a quite different significance if we read it as a tour-de-force of anthropomorphism in which the poet is using the imagery of trees and their transformation into tables to denote people who are subject to the forces of change. In this reading the poet is not talking about trees but people: the turning of trees into tables by carpenters using tools in a process of manufacture actually stands for the turning of people into a socially sanctioned 'end product' through a process effected by those tasked with doing so and given the means to do it.

This might for example include the process of formal education where the 'tree' is the young person or student, the 'table' is the schooled or trained individual, the 'carpenter' is the teacher, and the 'tools' the teaching techniques. Just as 'there is nothing sadder than a tree / hardened and twisted through years / of neglect and lack of attention / diseased limbs and wasted wood' (lines 10–13), so there is nothing sadder that human potential that has gone to waste through lack of education. Just as 'this tree demands to be a table' (line 15), so young people may demand the transformation of formal education in order to pursue their life goals. Just as 'if the carpenter does a shoddy job / this tree will send him away and / find another then another then another' (lines 25–27), so the young person who wants to be educated will go from teacher to teacher until the process of their education is, as they see it, complete. Just as one may 'ask any table / they say they like the varnish / and tables tells saplings all the time / that a tree that isn't a table is no tree at all' (lines 39–42), so those who have passed through education's transformation will insist that they enjoyed the process and the 'finish' it has conferred upon them, and tell other younger people that in order to be 'somebody' they must follow the process themselves.

In this reading the repeated 'a tree that isn't a table is no tree at all' then becomes the equivalent of 'a person who is not educated is no person at all'. This reflects a certain conventional and quite narrow societal view, particularly among educators, that in order to be 'real people' or 'somebody' (so to speak), young people must have passed through conventionally transformative formal education. They must not be permitted, however much they may wish it, to refuse the process, to be with others like themselves, be allowed to grow in another less conventional direction, or be given space of their own (as may be seen in the poem's final stanza).

As stated in the **Context** section above, the poet is an educationist and academic, so it is interesting to speculate whether the piece arises from her experience of formal education and how it may not necessarily be right or a 'best fit' for all. This is not to be understood as an indictment of formal education in any way, but merely an observation of how it sometimes works. Society is rarely asked to explain why it is necessary to make young people into something it finds useful, nor why it should be that particular useful thing, nor why it is considered useful. Likewise the very people who deliver the process rarely have to offer a reason for their doing so except for its being just what they do, and that the means by which they do it somehow *have* to be used to serve the process. Yet nobody asks: why 'tables' — why not something else, and why do we need so many of that same thing? And why can a tree (that is, a young person) sometimes not just be left as they are, or allowed to follow an unconventional way of living and learning that may fit them better? These are legitimate questions to raise regarding education and the transformation of the individual by society, and it is a function of poetry to ask such important questions.

It must be emphasised, though, that this is only one possible interpretation of the poem and one of a number of no less plausible constructions that can be placed upon the work. It might equally refer to the effects of consumer culture, where the 'tree' is the young person (or indeed another 'to-be-shaped' individual), the 'table' is the fully-shaped material consumer, the 'carpenter' is the businessman, and the 'tools' the advertising or other means of persuasion to consume. It might refer to drug culture, in which the 'tree' is the still-clean young person, the 'table' is the habitual drug-taker, the 'carpenter' is the pusher or other committed drug-user who shapes innocence into corruption, and the 'tools' the drugs themselves or the pressure to take them. Or one might think of a scenario relating to peer pressure, where the 'tree' is the young person, the 'table' is the person who complies and conforms to 'how we do things', the 'carpenter' is the pressurising peer group member, and the 'tools' the means of applying peer pressure. There are no doubt many others, and it is thought-provoking to explore them and their implications.

Composition

'table' is written ostensibly as a form of encomium, a poem in which a person, thing, or abstract idea is glorified or praised. However, one may consider this to be a cover for the poem's true purpose, which is to question or satirise those processes in society that seek to turn people into a standardised 'product'.

The poem is written as free verse, in four stanzas each of fourteen lines without rhyme scheme or regular metre. However, the poem makes effective use of repetition in the form of anaphora in the first three lines of each stanza, which adds a sense of rhythm and emphasis to the opening of the verse.

The text of the poem is entirely unpunctuated and does not use capital letters, though the line construction and content adds a certain element of demarcation to the flow of the language. The effect of this is to cause the reader to concentrate particularly closely on flow and expression.

The poem's vocabulary is straightforward and accessible, with use of some informal forms such as 'cos' (lines 28 and 56) and simple abbreviations such as 'isn't', 'what's' and 'he's' throughout. There are few words that young people are unlikely to have met.

The language is somewhat formalised, conveying the feeling that the reader is being addressed in an attempt to persuade him or her of the merits of the speaker's argument — something that is in line with the apparent purpose of the poem being an encomium. This is supported by the use of repetition throughout the poem, notably the frequent refrain that 'a tree that isn't a table is no tree at all', which reinforces its message.

The poet makes no use of simile, but the entire poem may be read as an extended metaphor (see **Content** section above) in which the transformation of tree into table by carpenters stands for the educational transformation of young people into a socially desirable end product by those charged with effecting that change. Some of the metaphorical equivalencies used in one reading of the poem — that of its referring to formal education — are explored in the **Content** section above; others will become readily apparent as one reads, and it is fascinating to explore how the metaphorical imagery of the poem can fit with other scenarios of change imposed upon young people, or indeed people in general. The extended metaphor of the poem also relies upon the extensive personification of the image of the tree throughout the poem, again as discussed in the **Content** section.

Message

There is pressure all around us to be something that others want us to be. Sometimes they will succeed in persuading us that this is what we ourselves want, even if at heart we know it is not. This may apply to many things in life, whether it is education that seeks to send us along a conventional route to which we are unsuited, or pressure to become a money-driven consumer, or pressure from peers to behave just like them even when it against our better judgment. It is important to remember to be true to ourselves and our nature, and to be willing to be different from what others expect us to be.

Sometimes we may be faced with a weight of opinion, perhaps even commonly-held opinion, which tells us that unless we conform to others' expectations then we are in some way unworthy or less than complete. This can place a considerable pressure upon us to comply with others' wishes. However, we should try not to depend on others too much for our sense of validation and we should try to do what we believe is right for us.

It may take a great amount of personal determination to resist the temptations or pressures of others, even pressures that may make us want to be like others, to fit in, and that we may find very convincing. It may be helpful for us to realise that sometimes there is little or no good reason why others may try to compel us to behave in a certain way, except that they want us to do it with no other real justification. We may have to choose between doing what others want and being true to our own selves.

Sometimes it may seem that the whole of society is placing pressure upon us. Whilst keeping our calm and harming nobody, we should be willing to assert our own identity and our right to be ourselves, our right to be different.

Lesson plan: 'table' by Hannah Kate

Resources

Copies of the poem — ideally one per pupil, marker pens, flip chart paper, rulers for SEND pupils to follow a line when reading.

Copies of pupils' safety plans to which they can refer throughout the session/lesson.

The lesson will cover oracy, reading and writing skills.

The session can be done at tables or in an unstructured group. The lesson plan is suitable to use with pupils at Upper Key Stage 2, 3 and 4.

Links with the PSHE Association PSHE Education Programme of Study

Links have been made to the PSHE Association PSHE Education Programme of Study at Key Stage 2, 3 and 4 as follows:

KS2

- *H25. about personal identity; what contributes to who we are (e.g. ethnicity, family, gender, faith, culture, hobbies, likes/dislikes*

KS3

- *H1. how we are all unique; that recognising and demonstrating personal strengths build self-confidence, self-esteem and good health and wellbeing*
- *H3. the impact that media and social media can have on how people think about themselves and express themselves, including regarding body image, physical and mental health*

KS4

- *H2. how self-confidence self-esteem, and mental health are affected positively and negatively by internal and external influences and ways of managing this*
- *H3. how different media portray idealised and artificial body shapes; how this influences body satisfaction and body image and how to critically appraise what they see and manage feelings about this*

Links with the National Curriculum

Links have been made to the National Curriculum for English at Key Stage 2, 3 and 4 as follows:

KS2 (Years 5 and 6) English programme of study

- *maintain attention and participate actively in collaborative conversations, staying on topic and initiating and responding to comments*
- *identifying how language, structure and presentation contribute to meaning*
- *discuss and evaluate how authors use language, including figurative language, considering the impact on the reader*

KS3 English programme of study

- *participating in formal debates and structured discussions, summarising and/or building on what has been said*
- *knowing how language, including figurative language, vocabulary choice, grammar, text structure and organisational features, presents meaning*

KS4 English programme of study

- *working effectively in groups of different sizes and taking on required roles, including leading and managing discussions, involving others productively, reviewing and summarising, and contributing to meeting goals/deadlines*
- *analysing a writer's choice of vocabulary, form, grammatical and structural features, and evaluating their effectiveness and impact*

Teaching and learning activities

This is a very deep and thoughtful poem that challenges social norms and expectations. A tree is not a tree unless it has been turned and fashioned into a beautiful, planed table. This process is never challenged and is self-perpetuating. Is this similar to the way that young people are being channelled to conform to what society expects from them, and changed into something that society finds desirable? The meaning of this poem can be read on many levels and discussed in as great a depth as you wish.

- Introduction — share aims of lesson.

- Refer pupils to their safety plans. Remind them of what a safety plan is for. Ask them to read through their own safety plan before they go further and answer any questions they may have.
- Read the poem (or teacher/leader to read it aloud) and discuss its content.

  Ask key questions:
  - What is the poem about?
  - What is the theme of the poem?
  - The words 'wants', 'demands', 'should' and 'will' are used in sentences in each stanza. These are examples of imperatives. What effect does the poet create by using these words?
  - What is the message of the poem?
- 'A tree that isn't a table is no tree at all'. Do you agree or disagree with this statement? Why do you think this? What do you think this phrase means in the context of the poem? Ask pupils to discuss with a partner or in small groups. Record thoughts on a flip chart.
- Ask for feedback.
- The tree only has validation and approval when it has been turned into a table that is beautifully planed and useful. What social expectations and pressures do you think are brought to bear on young people today to make them acceptable and useful to society? Where do these expectations come from? How can you let your own unique individuality shine through in the face of these expectations? How can you do this without other people finding it confrontational? Does it matter if they do? Is it necessary to be useful to society, and what does that even mean? Ask pupils to work in small groups and to record their thoughts on a flip chart.
- Ask for feedback.
- One of the reasons we strive to meet expectations is because of what we see on social media — people comparing themselves to others. Discuss ways of resisting pressures from others. Ask pupils to record their thoughts on a flip chart.
- Ask for feedback.
- Review what has been achieved in the lesson. Draw pupils' attention to support that is readily available to help deal with issues that have been identified.
- Refer pupils to their safety plans as a place to look if they need help after leaving the lesson.

Extension activities

- Pupils to write answers to the key questions.
- Do you like the poem? Give reasons for your opinions.
- 'A tree cannot really refuse to be a table though some of them will try'. How can young people resist pressures in society that are being brought to bear on them? Pupils to write about the pressures and possible ways to escape them.
- Write about the form and structure of the poem, commenting on the use of language and the repetition of words and phrases to persuade the reader.
- Ask pupils to photograph trees in their natural surroundings. Pupils to draw, paint or produce collages of them using bark rubbings or pieces of twig/leaves.
- Pupils to describe one of the trees that they have photographed. What is special and unique about it? If the tree was a person, what sort of person would it be? Why do you think this?
- Ask pupils to bring in photographs of themselves and objects that have special meaning to them. This might include certificates, trophies, a piece of jewellery, a soft toy, etc. Ask pupils to talk about their uniqueness and why the objects they have brought in are special to them. What do these objects say about them as people? Why do you think this? A class display of

photographs and writing can be created around the theme of 'Who am I?'. This display can be produced for the start of a new academic year in primary or secondary school.

- Pupils to write their own poems about being unique.
- Describe the processes involved in transforming trees into tables. Who or what is involved? What do the tools do? What is the purpose of the process? Discuss how this might apply figuratively to other processes that people are put through.
- Think of some processes that young people might be invited, tempted or pressurised to go through, such as becoming a member of a gang, taking drugs, training for a job, or forced marriage. In each case consider: who or what is the tree, the thing that is being changed; what is the table, the end product; who or what is the carpenter, who carries out the process; what are the tools, by which the change is carried out? Can you think of other transformations we go through in life? Do we always need someone to change us, or can we change ourselves? Why do you think this?
- Are tables more beautiful than trees? Discuss why or why not. Are there different standards of beauty at work here? What are they?
- How did the poem make you feel? How did it do this? Why did you feel this way?
- What is the mood of the poem?
- Compare and contrast the poems 'table' and 'Old Tree' (see Section 8 of this guide, **I'm Standing Strong**). The two poems look at trees in their different states, both natural and as a raw material to be turned into something else.

Cross-curricular/topic links

Cross-curricular and topic links may be explored for use in follow-up and for extension work in

- English
- PSHE
- Art and Design

Differentiation

Opportunities for discussion in class, groups, pairs.

Differentiation by outcome e.g. quantity or complexity of issues identified, sophistication of response, level of inclusion/contribution, empathy.

Writing quantity outcomes will be differentiated/assessed/moderated according to teacher's expectations of quantity and depth; otherwise by outcome.

Differentiation may also be through key words rather than written sentences, or through artwork as a means of expression.

It's Okay

by Judy Morris

Commentary

It's okay to be different,
It's okay to be me:
My difference is who I am —
My own personality.

I don't have to look a certain way,
I don't have to think the same:
I can be whatever I want to be,
My life, my look, my name!

I don't have to fit your pattern,
I don't have to play your game —
I can shine the light I want to shine
And burn with my own flame!

I can be the self I truly am,
The voice I want to speak:
I'm me, and I am beautiful.
I'm me: I am unique.

Context

'It's Okay' was written with the purpose of celebrating the uniqueness and freedom of young people, and to recognise the talents and beauty we all have as individuals. The poet suggests that we do not have to conform to stereotypes or to the expectations of others, but should be free to be ourselves. The poem was written in Halkidiki, Greece, in 2018.

Content

The poem opens by a simple declaration that it is 'okay' to be oneself. The theme is developed with increasing emphasis, by reference to the individual's personality, looks and behaviour. We are told that we may disregard the expectations and pressures of peers and of society at large to conform to external expectations, in favour of asserting our unique individuality and freedom.

Composition

The poem consists of four stanzas, each of four lines, with a relaxed rhyme scheme of ABCB.

The metre is similarly relaxed, with first lines of eight or nine syllables, second lines of six or seven, third lines of eight or nine, then last lines of six or seven again.

Punctuation is conventional.

The overall effect of the poem in performance is one of gathering and rising emphasis, and is anthemic in tone.

Message

The message of the poem is directed to young people: be yourself. Do not allow others to change you, to dictate who you are or how you behave, or to put you under pressure to conform to norms that they and others try to impose.

You are yourself, the only you there has ever been or ever will be. You are unique, and this should be recognised, respected and celebrated.

Lesson plan: 'It's Okay' by Judy Morris

Resources

Copies of the poem — ideally one per pupil, marker pens, rulers for SEND pupils to follow a line when reading, large sheets of flip chart paper.

Copies of pupils' safety plans to which they can refer throughout the session/lesson.

The lesson will cover oracy, reading and writing skills.

The session can be done at tables or in an unstructured group. The lesson plan is suitable to use with pupils at Upper Key Stage 2, 3 and 4.

Links with the PSHE Association PSHE Education Programme of Study

Links have been made to the PSHE Association PSHE Education Programme of Study at Key Stage 2, 3 and 4 as follows:

KS2

- *H21. to recognise warning signs about mental health and wellbeing and how to seek support for themselves and others*
- *H27. to recognise their individuality and personal qualities*
- *R15. strategies for recognising and managing peer influence and a desire for peer approval in friendships; to recognise the effect of online actions on others*
- *L9. about stereotypes; how they can negatively influence behaviours and attitudes towards others; strategies for challenging stereotypes*

KS3

- *H1. how we are all unique; that recognising and demonstrating personal strengths build self-confidence, self-esteem and good health and wellbeing*
- *H3. the impact that media and social media can have on how people think about themselves and express themselves, including regarding body image, physical and mental health*
- *H12. how to recognise when they or others need help with their mental health and wellbeing; sources of help and support and strategies for accessing what they need*
- *R42. to recognise peer influence and to develop strategies for managing it, including online*

KS4

- *H2. how self-confidence self-esteem, and mental health are affected positively and negatively by internal and external influences and ways of managing this*

- *H3. how different media portray idealised and artificial body shapes; how this influences body satisfaction and body image and how to critically appraise what they see and manage feelings about this*
- *H10. how to recognise when they or others need help with their mental health and wellbeing; to explore and analyse ethical issues when peers need help; strategies and skills to provide basic support and identify and access the most appropriate sources of help*
- *R37. to recognise situations where they are being adversely influenced, or are at risk, due to being part of a particular group or gang; strategies to access appropriate help*

Links with the National Curriculum

Links have been made to the National Curriculum for English at Key Stage 2, 3 and 4 as follows:

KS2 (Years 5 and 6) English programme of study

- *maintain attention and participate actively in collaborative conversations, staying on topic and initiating and responding to comments*
- *discuss and evaluate how authors use language, including figurative language, considering the impact on the reader*

KS3 English programme of study

- *participating in formal debates and structured discussions, summarising and/or building on what has been said*
- *knowing how language, including figurative language, vocabulary choice, grammar, text structure and organisational features, presents meaning*

KS4 English programme of study

- *working effectively in groups of different sizes and taking on required roles, including leading and managing discussions, involving others productively, reviewing and summarising, and contributing to meeting goals/deadlines*
- *analysing a writer's choice of vocabulary, form, grammatical and structural features, and evaluating their effectiveness and impact*

Teaching and learning activities

The poem is directed to young people as an encouragement to be themselves, to celebrate their uniqueness, and not to conform unthinkingly to stereotypes or to the expectations of others.

- Introduction — share aims of lesson.
- Refer pupils to their safety plans. Remind them of what a safety plan is for. Ask them to read through their own safety plan before they go further and answer any questions they may have.
- Read the poem (or teacher/leader to read it aloud) and discuss its content.

  Ask key questions:
  - What is the poem about?
  - How do we celebrate difference and uniqueness?
  - How does the poem make you feel? Pupils to take part in class/group discussion.
- What pressures are there on young people today? Discuss use of negative images/messages on social media, peer pressure, etc. How have you or someone you know been affected by any of these? Have you ever put pressure on someone else? How could you have dealt with the situation differently? Pupils to record their thoughts on flip chart paper based on personal experience.

- Each group to feed back to the rest of the class.
- Groups to discuss ways of dealing with negative images/messages on social media, peer pressure. Where can people go for help if they feel low or have a worry/concern? Record ideas on flip chart paper.
- Each group to feed back.
- Write down three unique qualities about yourself or a friend. Make sure that these are positive. Share thoughts.
- Review what has been achieved in the lesson. Draw attention to support that is readily available to help deal with issues that have been identified.
- Refer pupils to their safety plans as a place to look if they need help after leaving the lesson.

Extension activities

- Pupils to write answers to the key questions.
- Pupils to write their own identity poems with positive messages.
- Display portraits of pupil faces with positive messages that have been written about them by other pupils.
- Circle time activities that focus on a person's individual strengths.
- Write and produce information booklets, leaflets, posters to signpost help available from services.
- Establish school ambassadors so that pupils have a point of reference if they need to talk to someone about a worry or an issue.
- Write a letter to an agony aunt (or agony uncle) about a worry or concern. The agony aunt should think about the concern and write a reply.
- Establish a worry box in the classroom or setting. Pupils post their worries and these are addressed by the teacher.

Cross-curricular/topic links

Cross-curricular and topic links may be explored for use in follow-up and for extension work in

- English
- PSHE
- Art and Design

Differentiation

Opportunities for discussion in class, groups, pairs.

Differentiation by outcome e.g. quantity or complexity of issues identified, sophistication of response, level of inclusion/contribution, empathy.

Writing quantity outcomes will be differentiated/assessed/moderated according to teacher's expectations of quantity and depth; otherwise by outcome.

Differentiation may also be through key words rather than written sentences, or through artwork as a means of expression.

Stargazer

by Judy Morris

Commentary

Diamond-bright,
You radiate brilliance and inner beauty.

In a tumultuous Universe
Where planets collide
And worlds end — or seem to —
And comets crash,
The deafening din
Drowns out all tranquillity
And the Darkness blankets everything.

But you,
Stargazer,
You let your inner light break through.
One Light to pierce the Darkness you are.

Stargazer: shine.

Context

'Stargazer' was written in 2019. The poet describes having the concept of the poem come to her in the middle of a dark autumn night, after looking out of the window to see whether there was a moon visible in the sky. The comparative brightness of the stars against the black sky, and of a single tiny point of light against the darkness, inspired the thematic metaphor of inner light.

Content

The poem opens with the speaker addressing an unknown person, assuring them that they radiate inner light and beauty which is 'diamond-bright'. The speaker refers to the seemingly chaotic nature of our Universe, and how both the apparent turmoil of existence and a pervasive sense of darkness can obscure our experience.

The poet asserts the importance of the person whom she addresses as 'Stargazer', suggesting that they go beyond the usual in being a metaphorical source of illumination, and praising his or her ability to allow their 'inner light' to 'pierce the Darkness' of life.

The poem ends with an exhortation to the Stargazer to 'shine'.

Composition

The poem is written in free verse, without a rhyme scheme or regular metrical structure.

No two adjacent lines have the same syllabic value. However, it is noticeable that where the speaker is addressing her subject, the Stargazer, most directly, she does so with her shortest lines: this occurs in lines 1, 10, 11 and 14. This conveys a sense of the speaker's openness and frankness, and of a simplicity and honesty that does not require verbosity.

The text of the poem is organised in four themed stanzas. The first introduces the poem's silent protagonist, the Stargazer. The second addresses philosophically the perceived chaos and obscurity of an apparently disordered reality. The third stanza focuses closely upon the Stargazer, presenting him or her as possessing a precious and extraordinary quality. The final stanza is a single line, an unequivocal encouragement to the Stargazer to continue to manifest their metaphorical inner light.

Punctuation is conventional.

The poem's vocabulary is straightforward and uncomplicated, which supports its directness. The language renders more accessible the philosophical musings of lines 3 to 9, as well as grounding the extended use of metaphor throughout the poem — noting that the poem is in effect a single extended metaphor.

It is notable that the poet capitalises the word 'Darkness' as a proper noun. This is not a mere absence of light but a greater, personified force that can be repelled or held at bay by one's figurative inner light.

That the poet makes use of epithet in identifying the poem's subject as 'Stargazer' (lines 11 and 14) is clear. But her initial mode of address — 'Diamond-bright' — can also be read as epithetical. The two epithets are similar in their references to light; but whereas 'Diamond-bright' has an intensity and literal hardness, 'Stargazer' implies a gentler, more contemplative and softer quality of illumination. The poem's subject has his or her gaze fixed on higher things, looking beyond the darkness and difficulty of life.

Message

The message of 'Stargazer' is a gentle, direct and intimate recognition of how an individual's metaphorical inner light can be a vital factor that repels the negativity of a seemingly chaotic, dark and uncaring life. This benevolent force extends beyond the individual, as light extends beyond its source. We are left to speculate as to what the precise nature of that light might be: perhaps it is positivity, love, intuition, or something else. We must all find our inner light and do our best to shine.

Lesson plan: 'Stargazer' by Judy Morris

Resources

Copies of the poem — ideally one per pupil, pencils or pens, dictionaries, paper, rulers for SEND pupils to follow a line when reading.

Copies of pupils' safety plans to which they can refer throughout the session/lesson.

The lesson will cover oracy, reading and writing skills.

The session can be done at tables or in an unstructured group. The lesson plan is suitable to use with pupils at Upper Key Stage 2, 3 and 4.

Links with the PSHE Association PSHE Education Programme of Study

Links have been made to the PSHE Association PSHE Education Programme of Study at Key Stage 2, 3 and 4 as follows:

KS2

- *H16. about strategies and behaviours that support mental health — including how good quality sleep, physical exercise/time outdoors, being involved in community groups, doing things for others, clubs, and activities, hobbies and spending time with family and friends can support mental health and wellbeing*
- *H27. to recognise their individuality and personal qualities*
- *H28. to identify personal strengths, skills, achievements and interests and how these contribute to a sense of self-worth*

KS3

- *H1. how we are all unique; that recognising and demonstrating personal strengths build self-confidence, self-esteem and good health and wellbeing*
- *H10. a range of healthy coping strategies and ways to promote wellbeing and boost mood, including physical activity, participation and the value of positive relationships in providing support*

KS4

- *H2. how self-confidence self-esteem, and mental health are affected positively and negatively by internal and external influences and ways of managing this*
- *H7. a broad range of strategies — cognitive and practical — for promoting their own emotional wellbeing, for avoiding negative thinking and for ways of managing mental health concerns*

Links with the National Curriculum

Links have been made to the National Curriculum for English at Key Stage 2, 3 and 4 as follows:

KS2 (Years 5 and 6) English programme of study

- *maintain attention and participate actively in collaborative conversations, staying on topic and initiating and responding to comments*
- *discuss and evaluate how authors use language, including figurative language, considering the impact on the reader*
- *use dictionaries to check the spelling and meaning of words*

KS3 English programme of study

- *participating in formal debates and structured discussions, summarising and/or building on what has been said*
- *knowing how language, including figurative language, vocabulary choice, grammar, text structure and organisational features, presents meaning*
- *consolidate and build on their knowledge of grammar and vocabulary through:*

- *extending and applying the grammatical knowledge set out in English Appendix 2 to the key stage 1 and 2 programmes of study to analyse more challenging texts*

KS4 English programme of study

- *listening to and building on the contributions of others, asking questions to clarify and inform, and challenging courteously when necessary*
- *analysing a writer's choice of vocabulary, form, grammatical and structural features, and evaluating their effectiveness and impact*
- *consolidate and build on their knowledge of grammar and vocabulary through... studying their effectiveness and impact in the texts they read*

Teaching and learning activities

- Introduction — share aims of lesson.
- Refer pupils to their safety plans. Remind them of what a safety plan is for. Ask them to read through their own safety plan before they go further and answer any questions they may have.
- Read the poem (or teacher/leader to read it aloud) and discuss its content.

  Ask key questions:

  - What is the poem about? Are there any clues in the title? Pupils to take part in class/group or paired discussion.
  - What is the poem's message?
  - How does the poem make you feel? Why?

- Can you find examples of verbs in the poem? Circle or underline them. How do they help build interest and intensity?
- Discuss the form and structure of the poem including use of dashes.
- What do you understand by the phrase 'tumultuous Universe'? Pupils should be encouraged to use dictionaries to look up words they do not know.
- Ask pupils to reflect on whether they have experienced dark or chaotic moments in their lives. Working with a partner or in a small group ask pupils to share. Was there anything that helped you to get through it? What was it, and how did it help you? What (or what else) might have helped?
- Ask each pupil to list positive attributes about themselves. This activity could be done with the help of a friend or a key adult. The positive attributes should be referred to whenever the young person is feeling low or bad about themselves to help lift their mood and to help them feel better about themselves.
- Ask pupils to reflect on ways of remaining positive in school and at home. What things might help? Ask for suggestions and record ideas.
- Review what has been achieved in the lesson. Draw pupils' attention to support that is readily available to help deal with issues that have been identified.
- Refer pupils to their safety plans as a place to look if they need help after leaving the lesson.

Extension activities

- Pupils to write answers to the key questions.
- Pupils to write their own Stargazer poems substituting some of the nouns, adjectives and verbs with new ones. Pupils can use a thesaurus to find alternative words.
- Pupils to write their own acrostic poem using the word 'shine' or a synonym for it.

- Pupils to write their own poems on a different theme e.g. their street or home, a river, the sea, the beach, a woodland or forest using a range of nouns, verbs and adjectives.
- Pupils to decorate their list of positive attributes for inclusion in their workbooks or journals.
- Circle time activities that focus on pupils being positive about themselves.
- Pupils to draw or paint pictures of positive images that help to reinforce positivity and personal happiness.

Cross-curricular/topic links

Cross-curricular and topic links may be explored for use in follow-up and for extension work in

- English
- PSHE
- Art and Design

Differentiation

Opportunities for discussion in class, groups, pairs.

Differentiation by outcome e.g. quantity or complexity of issues identified, sophistication of response, level of inclusion/contribution, empathy.

Writing quantity outcomes will be differentiated/assessed/moderated according to teacher's expectations of quantity and depth; otherwise by outcome.

Differentiation may also be through artwork as a means of expression.

When Good Times Turn to Dark Times

This section is about self-doubt, low self-esteem, depression and bullying...

day

by Paul Morris

Commentary

she stares down the day like the barrel of a gun
and closes her eyes
to the glare of the dark

no echo for her
no fragment of light

no day
today

just
the push to compartmentalise
and classify
                categorise

she sits in the dark in the midsummer sun
and listens to the silence
of a roaring world

Context

'day' is a poem about depression, and explores the sense of isolation and numbness that can be such a distressing part of that illness. It is important to note that it is not literally about someone who is being threatened with a gun, but whose sense of depression makes her feel threatened by the ordinary world. Many people, particularly those who have not experienced it, think that depression is about sadness, having something to be actively unhappy about and manifesting this. Addressing this preconception, the poet speaks to the sense of detachment, emotional flatness and absence that people with depression may experience whilst unwell.

Content

The poem is an intimate description of a girl or woman who is overwhelmed by her depression to the point of being passive, separated from the everyday goings-on of the world around her. She is sitting outside 'in the midsummer sun', yet the darkness she experiences is internal to her.

The poem opens by describing how its subject receives passively her realisation that the day will be one of active depression, staring into the coming day as though it is the barrel of a gun with which she is being threatened. It is essential to note that this is not intended to be a literal reference to being threatened with a weapon, nor to suicide.

This idea of being threatened with a weapon may be unsettling to some children and young people. However, analogy and metaphor are key devices used in poetry to illustrate complex thoughts and emotions, and although the 'gun' is not real the immediacy of the sense of threat of looking down the barrel of a weapon conveys the sense of vulnerability that the poet seeks to convey.

The question may be asked, too, whether the subject of the poem is actually looking down the gun barrel from the position of its being trained on her, or whether it is she who is 'aiming' at the day with a sense of trying to keep it under control.

The subject's only reaction is to close her eyes to exclude her surroundings — or perhaps to exclude herself from them. This is characteristic of some people's depressive illness, where they will tend to dive more deeply into themselves in the face of a depressive episode rather than necessarily rising to meet the world. The subject's sense of isolation is such that none of the sounds or sights of the everyday world seem to be for her — 'no echo for her / no fragment of light'. She seems to perceive the day frankly and simply as having been lost, consumed by her illness, rendered void as shown in the lines 'no day / today'. That she realises the cause of her detachment and the attitudes of others towards her, and feels the pressure and futility of those things, is suggested by 'the push to compart-mentalise / and classify / categorise': the day has become about her illness, not about her living the day for itself. Her sense of isolation is emphasised.

Composition

The piece is written in what appears to be free verse, approximating the cadence of natural speech. However upon careful inspection the situation is found to be more complex, just as someone's psychological state may appear usual, unremarkable, but reveal itself only upon closer consideration.

There is an involved and fluid structure apparent within the poem. The rhythms and metre of the first and final stanzas mirror each other, though imperfectly so as to hide the relationship. The stanzas also establish the subject's sensory status within her day: she tries to block out and hide its sights but cannot avoid its intrusions completely, though they still appear to exclude her and to evade having real relevance to her.

The two lines of the second stanza are of equal syllabic value; and this is also the case for the stark declaration of the third stanza. These pairings add a sense of measure, a sort of ticking monotony and flatness that adds to the sense of oppression of language.

The intrusion of the busy fourth stanza is heralded by the single, dropped 'just', followed by two lines (the second of which is broken as 'classify / categorise') which again are syllabically equal, despite their comparative busyness. Whilst the words in those lines are uncharacteristically fussy for the poem's bare simplicity, this still places the language within the subject's strictly metred descriptive style.

The main text of the poem consists of only fifty-eight words, of which forty-six, by far the majority, are monosyllabic. This lends the work a stripped-back, 'scrubbed' feel. All but three of the remaining words in the poem are disyllabic, the bareness of language suggesting the flatness of the subject's emotional state. This simplicity of language is interrupted only in the penultimate stanza with 'compartmentalise /and classify / categorise', the intrusive judgment implicit in the words being mirrored up by their invasive, polysyllabic length.

It is notable that the text of the poem is entirely in lower case letters, as is the title, and that it is unpunctuated. The poet uses language which renders these compositional conventions unnecessary. The words themselves, the starkness of their expression, allow no room for ambiguity of reading, just as the emotional state of its subject seems plain and unambiguous to her, needing no pointing-up or elaboration. Even the most straightforward conventions of writing are stripped away in the face of the subject's crushing condition.

Message

The poem encourages us to consider how someone with depressive illness may feel left out of the world around them. They may feel that the world does not notice them, and that otherwise ordinary, daily experiences cease to be relevant to them.

Having to contend with the weight of their emotional condition, people with depressive illness may become introspective, requiring all their strength to deal with the tumult within their own emotions. Their resulting quietness may be deceptive, and hide a deeper problem which only reveals itself more fully under closer scrutiny.

Depression can be lonely, isolating, numbing, leaving those who experience it to withdraw into themselves or to perceive the world as unfriendly and excluding.

Lesson plan: 'day' by Paul Morris

Resources

Copies of the poem — ideally one per pupil, rulers for SEND pupils to follow a line when reading.

Copies of pupils' safety plans to which they can refer throughout the session/lesson. The lesson will cover oracy, reading and writing skills.

The session can be done in the round, or as a circle time activity, or at tables, or in an unstructured group. It is suitable to use with pupils at Key Stage 3 and 4.

Links with the PSHE Association PSHE Education Programme of Study

Links have been made to the PSHE Association PSHE Education Programme of Study at Key Stage 3 and 4 as follows:

KS3

- *H11. the causes and triggers for unhealthy coping strategies, such as self-harm and eating disorders, and the need to seek help for themselves or others as soon as possible [NB It is important to avoid teaching methods and resources that provide instruction on ways of self-harming, restricting food/inducing vomiting, hiding behaviour from others etc., or that might provide inspiration for pupils who are more vulnerable (e.g. personal accounts of weight change).]*
- *H12. how to recognise when they or others need help with their mental health and wellbeing; sources of help and support and strategies for accessing what they need*

KS4

- *H8. to recognise warning signs of common mental and emotional health concerns (including stress, anxiety and depression), what might trigger them and what help or treatment is available*

- *H9. the importance of and ways to pre-empt common triggers and respond to warning signs of unhealthy coping strategies, such as self-harm and eating disorders in themselves and others [NB It is important to avoid teaching methods and resources that provide instruction on ways of self-harming, restricting food/ inducing vomiting, hiding behaviour from others etc., or that might provide inspiration for pupils who are more vulnerable (e.g. personal accounts of weight change).]*

Links with the National Curriculum

Links have been made to the National Curriculum for English at Key Stage 3 and 4 as follows:

KS3 English programme of study

- *participating in formal debates and structured discussions, summarising and/or building on what has been said*
- *knowing how language, including figurative language, vocabulary choice, grammar, text structure and organisational features, presents meaning*
- *recognising a range of poetic conventions and understanding how these have been used*

KS4 English programme of study

- *working effectively in groups of different sizes and taking on required roles, including leading and managing discussions, involving others productively, reviewing and summarising, and contributing to meeting goals/deadlines*
- *analysing a writer's choice of vocabulary, form, grammatical and structural features, and evaluating their effectiveness and impact*

Teaching and learning activities

This poem lends itself to a lot of discussion — individual, paired, group and class — about the difficult topic of depression.

Please read the **Commentary** that accompanies the poem as it contains figurative language and references to weapons which may be unsettling to some children and young people. It will be important to check for any potential emotional triggers before using the poem.

- Introduction — share aims of lesson.
- Refer pupils to their safety plans. Remind them of what a safety plan is for. Ask them to read through their own safety plan before they go further and answer any questions they may have.
- Read the poem (or teacher/leader to read it aloud) and ask the following questions:
  - What is this poem about?
  - Is the gun real or figurative? Why is the image of a gun used by the poet?
  - How does the poem make you feel? How does it do this? Why?
  - How does the language that the poet uses contribute to the way the poem makes you feel?
- Examine the compositional structure of the poem. Please see **Commentary** for this poem.
- Have you ever been faced with something you felt was too big to cope with? How did you deal with it? e.g. anger, introspection, seeking help, self-doubt. Did it work? Did it make things better or worse? Why/why not? How might you have dealt with it better? Paired activity or group activity.
- Faced with a similar challenge to the one discussed above, would you do things differently? Why do you think this? What did you learn from that situation?

- Do you have a safe place when you feel low or worried? How does your safe place work for you? Have you ever told anyone about this? Why? Paired activity/group activity.
- Do you ever feel excluded from the world around you? How? How do you cope with it? Paired activity/group activity.
- Read this quote from William Shakespeare's play *Hamlet*: 'There's nothing good or bad but thinking makes it so'. Do you think this is true? Why, or why not? Can you give an example from your own experience of when the way you thought about something made it better or worse? Class discussion.
- You are going into a new year/class/school e.g. high school. How is this positive? How is this negative? Can the same things be both according to how they are viewed? Work through this example with the pupils (negatives are in the left column, positives the right) and discuss as a class.

At high school...	
I'll lose friends	I'll have opportunities to make new friends
Nobody knows me	I'll have a fresh start
I'll be anxious	I'll be excited
I'll meet new people	I'll meet new people

Ask pupils for more ideas about things that have either positive and negative aspects or both, depending on how you view them.

- Review what has been achieved in the lesson.
- Refer pupils to their safety plans as a place to look if they need help after leaving the lesson.

Extension activities

- Pupils to write answers to the key questions.
- Pupils to write about a personal experience of a time in their life when they felt low, how they reacted to that feeling, what they did to try to remedy it, and how this worked.
- Pupils to reflect on issues that worry them, for example relationships etc. Pupils to write about one of these issues and come up with ways of dealing with it.
- Artwork in black and white or shades of grey that reflect flatness of mood, detachment from the world, a bad day. What images might show this?
- Prepare the poem to read aloud and to perform, showing understanding through intonation, tone and volume so that the meaning is clear to an audience.
- Invite speakers to come into school to raise awareness around mental health e.g. Mind, Childline, Samaritans, Mental Health Foundation, a GP, an educational psychologist.
- Display posters around the school/setting so pupils know where to go to access help and support.

Cross-curricular/topic links

Cross-curricular and topic links may be explored for use in follow-up and for extension work in

- English
- Drama
- PSHE
- Art and Design

Differentiation

Opportunities for discussion in mixed ability pairs/groups.

Differentiation by outcome e.g. quantity or complexity of issues identified, sophistication of response, level of inclusion/contribution, empathy.

Writing quantity outcomes will be differentiated/assessed/moderated according to teacher's expectations of quantity and depth; otherwise by outcome.

Differentiation may also be through artwork as a means of expression.

It Was Not Death, For I Stood Up

by Emily Dickinson

Commentary

It was not Death, for I stood up,
And all the Dead, lie down —
It was not Night, for all the Bells
Put out their Tongues, for Noon.

It was not Frost, for on my Flesh
I felt Siroccos — crawl —
Nor Fire — for just my Marble feet
Could keep a Chancel, cool —

And yet, it tasted, like them all,
The Figures I have seen
Set orderly, for Burial,
Reminded me, of mine —

As if my life were shaven,
And fitted to a frame,
And could not breathe without a key,
And 'twas like Midnight, some —

When everything that ticked — has stopped —
And Space stares — all around —
Or Grisly frosts — first Autumn morns,
Repeal the Beating Ground —

But, most, like Chaos — Stopless — cool —
Without a Chance, or Spar —
Or even a Report of Land —
To justify — Despair.

Context

The only surviving draft of 'It Was Not Death, For I Stood Up' in the poet's own hand can be dated to 1862, although it appears that she returned to the work later to revise it and to add some alternative word choices.

The poem was first published in 1891 in a posthumous collection of Dickinson's work entitled *Poems, Series 2*. Fewer than a dozen of her poems were published during her lifetime, often anonymously, and they were edited heavily to conventionalise her idiosyncratic punctuation.

The poem's proposed dating places it a few years into the period when Dickinson had taken on the task of caring for her bed-ridden mother, which coincided with a period of immense productivity in her poetry writing. It was around this time in her life that Dickinson's behaviour had begun to change and she had become more reclusive: it may be the relative seclusion of her life was conducive to her flow of poetical composition. This was also the time at which Dickinson seems to have been contemplating the publication of her work, and wrote to the literary critic Thomas Wentworth Higginson seeking guidance and advice. Higginson praised her work, but suggested that Dickinson should delay publication until she had written for longer, apparently unaware that she had already had some work published. Dickinson valued his advice, referring to him as her 'Dear friend', and it seems that his advice and interest in her work was a source of comfort and support for the poet: indeed she later told him that he had saved her life in 1862.

For further information regarding the poet's life, see the **Context** section to the commentary on her poem 'I'm Nobody!' in Section 1 of this guide, **Who Am I?**

Content

When reading the poem for meaning it should be remembered that Emily Dickinson's punctuation is usually idiosyncratic and capricious. It may be easier for the reader not to take too much account of it, as it can be misleading; for example, most of the dashes are essentially meaningless and some other marks, such as the comma in line 8, have no discernible function.

The poem opens with the speaker, who may be the poet herself, seeming to be confused and disoriented, unsure about her condition. She is not dead, because she is standing whereas the dead lie down (lines 1 and 2). It is not night-time, because the noon bells are ringing (lines 3 and 4). It is not cold, because she can feel warm winds on her skin (lines 5 and 6) — although what should be a pleasant sensation is vitiated as she feels the warmth 'crawl'. It is not burning hot, because her feet are as cold as marble, cold enough to keep a church chancel — a large open area at the front, around the altar — cool (lines 7 and 8).

What the speaker is sensing nevertheless feels like all of those things, like death and night and cold and fire; to her it has the taste of all of them (line 9). We are told that the people who the speaker has seen prepared for burial, those who have died, remind her of her own condition (lines 10 to 12).

The speaker feels as though her life had been cut down, pared down and put into a frame, a constricting shape — perhaps even a coffin, like the dead she has seen (lines 13 and 14). She is not able to breathe without a key, something external to herself that opens the restricted place in which she feels locked and allows her to take the air she needs (line 15).

It is like midnight (line 16), the very opposite of the noon referred to in the first stanza when the pealing of the bells reminded her that she was alive. Now it is a time when everything that has been in motion during the day has stopped, when time itself seems to have stopped and it feels as though the very space around her is watching (lines 17 and 18). It is as though she is surrounded by horrid white frost (see **Composition** section below for the dual meaning of 'grisly'), as appears on autumn mornings — though 'morns' also sounds like 'mourns', reminding us of the death to which she has been referring (line 19). 'Repeal the beating ground' (line 20) is a highly enigmatic and problematic phrase which may refer to the way that the autumnal frosts have covered the fertile earth that teems and beats with life, bringing to the ground a temporary releasing ('repeal') from supporting its living burden.

Most of all, though, the speaker's life is 'like Chaos' (line 21). This may be read in the modern sense of its being a state of utter disorder and confusion; or in the classical Greek sense in which chaos (χάος) means 'emptiness, void, abyss, chasm' — so not merely disorder, but an aching emptiness. It is endless and cold, without any prospect of fortune ('Chance', line 22), a state like being adrift at sea without the sight of a distant ship or of land to help her find her way back to shore. If such a thing were to be seen then at least the knowledge that she is distant from something that is better than her current lost condition would help to justify the sense of hopeless unhappiness she feels (lines 22 to 24).

Composition

'It Was Not Death, For I Stood Up' is written in six stanzas of quatrains. Its rhyme scheme is ABCB, though the rhymes are in all but one instance (stanza 5) imperfect or slant rhymes, formed by words that have similar but not identical sounds.

The metrical structure consists of alternating lines of iambic tetrameter (four metrical feet of da-DUM), and iambic trimeter (three metrical feet of da-DUM), though line 13 is catalectic (i.e. missing its final syllable to leave the final foot incomplete).

The poem's language and vocabulary have a certain archaic, formal feel. Whilst this is to be expected to some extent, given the poem's date, it also conveys a certain slightly stiff carefulness, as of someone feeling their way and expressing themselves with a clipped, cautious tone. There are a few words for which the young reader will appreciate guidance: 'Tongues' (= 'voices' or 'sound', line 4), 'Siroccos' (= 'warm winds' from the Mediterranean winds of that name that bring hot and humid air, line 6), 'Chancel' '(= 'part of a church near the altar reserved for the clergy and choir', line 8), 'Repeal' (= 'cancel, quash', line 20), 'Stopless' (= 'unceasing, never-ending', line 21), 'Spar' (= 'wooden pole used in the rigging of a sailing ship', line 22).

One might suggest that the fragmented punctuation in the present poem is intended to be suggestive of the speaker's disjointed state of mind. However, erratic punctuation is a characteristic feature of Dickinson's writing that has been much discussed by critics and scholars since her work was first published. It is therefore probably best for the reader not to take too much account of it, as it is difficult to say with any certainty that a particular instance of punctuation was intended by the poet to enhance or convey a subtlety of meaning (even if it actually does so) when so much of the other punctuation in her work rather does the opposite or appears essentially random.

Whilst Dickinson's unconventional punctuation is one of the most discussed idiosyncrasies of her writing, another less prominent though still present eccentricity is her occasionally erratic spelling. In the present poem this gives rise to an intriguing question of meaning. In the fifth stanza, at line 19, Dickinson describes 'Grisly frosts'. The word 'grisly' means 'horrid' or 'causing horror or disgust', whilst the homophonic 'grizzly' is an archaic word meaning 'grey or white'. It is unclear whether the poet intends here to convey an emotional reaction to the numbing, enervating frost, or address its colour. It may be that the word Dickinson uses is a spelling error and that she meant 'grizzly'. The resulting ambiguity, however, adds depth and nuance to the brief description.

The poet's use of capitalisation is curious. She capitalises her nouns quite consistently, only seven out of thirty-one being left uncapitalised — though she also capitalises two adjectives and a verb. It would be tempting to speculate whether this capitalisation is intended to add a sense of gravitas and weight to each of the nouns, dignifying it and adding a sense of portent, perhaps even person-ifying them (although such a mass of personification loses the individual distinction that the device confers upon a word). Perhaps what the poet intends us to see is a confusion of seeming significance, a turmoil in which we have to decide whether the importance that things seem to bear is in fact legitimate, much like the state of mental confusion she depicts.

Dickinson makes use of anaphora in the openings to lines 1, 3 and 5, suggesting a state of persistent questioning — the speaker cannot define what the things she is experiencing really are, and so turns to deciding what they are not.

The poem can be read as an extended metaphor for the speaker's — perhaps the poet's — confused and troubled state of mind. The proliferation of metaphorical imagery about death (stanzas 1 and 3), burial (stanzas 3 and 4), heat and cold (stanzas 2 and 5) and being lost (stanza 6) all contribute their parts towards this sum of complex perplexity. Ultimately what we take from the work is not chiefly the formality of compositional conventions, the way the words appear on the page, but rather the way that Dickinson uses her idiosyncratic style to covey the unease and disorientation of mental dislocation.

Message

It can be frightening to experience emotional distress, especially for the first time or in a way that one has not experienced it before. There may be a feeling that the usually familiar world has become something confusing, somehow not quite itself, perhaps even nightmarish! We may feel that we too are not quite the people we thought we were, and we may not understand what is happening to us to make us feel this way. Things may feel quite different from what we are used to, and we may react to them unusually.

Sometimes one of the greatest problems associated with experiencing dark times in our lives is trying to understand just what is going on. We may lack a suitable frame of reference, and though we try to compare our problems with things we have experienced before we may find that nothing quite fits. We should not be afraid to seek help from people, especially professional people, who might be able to work alongside us to explore what is happening and give us guidance.

For some people, it is not necessary that they should feel bad in a particular way: a sense of detachment from the familiar features of our daily lives may be enough to leave us feeling scared, disorientated and confused. We may not know what we want or need. Once again, help from a professional may help to calm us and give us a perspective on what we are experiencing.

When we experience difficult times, it may feel as though only we have ever gone through something like this before. We may feel as though nobody else has ever shared these feelings. But if we seek help we will find that many people have experienced what we are experiencing, and that they have made sense of it and recovered their equilibrium. This understanding is unlikely to be the whole answer to our problems, but it may help us to know that others have passed this way before and it may give us hope.

It may be particularly hard when we feel, or are perhaps told by others, that there is no good reason to feel that life has become dark. For example, sometimes people might tell us that there is no reason for us to feel sad or depressed, and that we should be ashamed to feel bad when there are so many good things around us — we have a home and food and people who care for us. This can make us feel as though we are somehow not entitled to feel unwell or troubled, especially when we ourselves are having problems understanding why we are feeling the way we are. Professional people will not speak to us in this way, and we should not be reluctant to seek help from people like teachers, doctors or counsellors. We should not feel that we are always to blame for our own problems.

Life is sometimes difficult and confusing. With time, patience and help, we can look forward to experiencing good times again.

Lesson plan: 'It Was Not Death, For I Stood Up' by Emily Dickinson

Resources

Copies of the poem — ideally one per pupil, pens or pencils, marker pens, flip chart paper, rulers for SEND pupils to follow a line when reading.

Copies of pupils' safety plans to which they can refer throughout the session/lesson. The lesson will cover oracy and reading skills.

The session can be done in the round, or as a circle time activity, or at tables, or in an unstructured group. It is suitable to use with pupils at Key Stage 3 and 4.

Links with the PSHE Association PSHE Education Programme of Study

Links have been made to the PSHE Association PSHE Education Programme of Study at Key Stage 3 and 4 as follows:

KS3

- *H7. the characteristics of mental and emotional health and strategies for managing these*
- *H12. how to recognise when they or others need help with their mental health and wellbeing; sources of help and support and strategies for accessing what they need*

KS4

- *H8. to recognise warning signs of common mental and emotional health concerns (including stress, anxiety and depression), what might trigger them and what help or treatment is available*
- *H10. how to recognise when they or others need help with their mental health and wellbeing; to explore and analyse ethical issues when peers need help; strategies and skills to provide basic support and identify and access the most appropriate sources of help*

Links with the National Curriculum

Links have been made to the National Curriculum for English at Key Stage 3 and 4 as follows:

KS3 English programme of study
- *participating in formal debates and structured discussions, summarising and/or building on what has been said*
- *knowing how language, including figurative language, vocabulary choice, grammar, text structure and organisational features, presents meaning*

KS4 English programme of study
- *listening to and building on the contributions of others, asking questions to clarify and inform, and challenging courteously when necessary*
- *analysing a writer's choice of vocabulary, form, grammatical and structural features, and evaluating their effectiveness and impact*

Teaching and learning activities

Emily Dickinson wrote many poems about death. She also wrote often about depression. This poem describes what it can feel like to be gripped by despair and depression.

Pupils will need to be guided through this poem as the speaker (who may be Emily Dickinson speaking for herself about her own condition) attempts to understand what she is feeling and experiencing when she is deeply depressed. To aid understanding of some of the language, see the **Composition** section of the **Commentary** to this poem.

- Introduction — share aims of lesson.
- Refer pupils to their safety plans. Remind them of what a safety plan is for. Ask them to read through their own safety plan before they go further and answer any questions they may have.
- Read the poem (or teacher/leader to read it aloud) and ask the following key questions:
  - What do you think this poem is about?
  - What emotions does the speaker experience in this poem?
  - What is the poem's message?
- The poet describes a prevailing mood of hopelessness, which leads to depression. In groups ask pupils to reflect on what they think depression is. Ask pupils to record their thoughts on a flip chart.
- Take feedback. There are varying degrees of depression, ranging from times when students feel 'down' or 'sad' to full diagnosable clinical depression.
- Working in small groups ask pupils to brainstorm events or periods of time when they have felt sad, low, down or depressed. It can be their own experiences or those of others. Ask one of the group members to record the experiences on a flip chart.
- Ask for feedback from each group and share experiences. Display the flip charts in the classroom for pupils to read. Explain that when we are depressed, we do not feel, think or act the way we normally do. Go back to the poem and pick out some of the indicators of depression.
- Explain to pupils that if a person is clinically depressed, they often find it difficult to get out of their low mood. It affects the person's ability to carry on with daily life. When the feelings of sadness, hopelessness or despair last longer than a few weeks and interfere with school life and activities, professional help is needed. Professionals can give counselling and medication to help them get back to feeling normal again. Talk to pupils about what is likely to be involved in the process of seeking professional help. Ask for their own experiences of seeking help: what were the positives and negatives, what was easier or harder than they thought it would be, what recommendations or advice would they have for others? It is important to talk about the help available so that pupils know where to go for support, and to share our experiences where we can.
- Share and signpost sources of available help.
- Review what has been achieved in the lesson.
- Refer pupils to their safety plans as a place to look if they need help after leaving the lesson.

Extension activities

- Pupils to write their answers to the key questions.
- Discuss the differences between unhappiness and depression, in terms of their features and how they should be encountered and treated.

- In circle time activities or in a one-to-one situation ask pupils to reflect on issues that worry them. For example, exam stress, starting a new school, feeling confident in class, etc. Identify some more of these stress points. Discuss ways of identifying and dealing with the issues that arise from them.
- Invite speakers to come into school to raise awareness around mental health e.g. Mind, Kooth, Childline, Samaritans, Mental Health Foundation, a GP, an educational psychologist.
- Display posters around school/setting so pupils know where to go to access help and support.
- Pupils to produce posters (to be displayed around school) that alert peers to the signs of depression.
- Produce information leaflets about depression. Pupils can use the web to find out more about the subject.

Cross-curricular/topic links

Cross-curricular and topic links may be explored for use in follow-up and for extension work in

- English
- PSHE
- Art and Design

Differentiation

Opportunities for discussion in mixed ability pairs/groups.

Differentiation by outcome e.g. quantity or complexity of issues identified, sophistication of response, level of inclusion/contribution, empathy.

Writing quantity outcomes will be differentiated/assessed/moderated according to teacher's expectations of quantity and depth; otherwise by outcome.

Differentiation may also be through key words rather than written sentences, or through artwork as a means of expression.

Unsocial Media
by Paul Morris

Commentary

We are happy to believe that writing is about sharing meaning.
In the early 21st century this is not always so, and even textspeak has its dark, hidden side.

hru m8?
ib 4u
somy?
well ykwykd

icbw
we cud b f2f
still aap
a3

bcnu soon
wubu2?
nwo m8
i'll b w8ing 4u

rsn
b comin around
not jk not jp
not jja

tmwfi
i'm sete
toy
crbt

so it's bau
we're 'bff'
say 'lma'?
nfw m8 —
never

* * * * * * * * * * * * * * * *

How are *you*, mate?
I'm back for you.
Sick of me yet?
Well you know what *you* can do…

It could be worse:
We could be face-to-face.
Still, always a *pleasure* —

Anytime, anywhere, anyplace.

Be seeing *you* soon —
What you been up to?
No way out, mate —
I'll be waiting for *you*.

Real soon now
Be coming around:
Not just kidding, not just playing
Not just joking around…

Take my word for it,
I'm smiling ear-to-ear
Thinking of you
Crying real big tears…

So it's business as usual
We're 'best friends forever'.
Say 'leave me alone'?
No freakin' way, mate —

Never.

Context

'Unsocial Media' was written in 2018 as a response to the poet's discussions in writing and poetry workshops with young participants. There was a common perception among them that adults were relatively unaware of the importance of social media in young people's lives. It was felt that adults did not generally realise the extent to which social media could be used by peers for negative purposes, such as to apply emotional pressure or to oppress or bully, inverting the purpose for which social media (or, viewed broadly, electronic communications media) were developed. It was remarked that textspeak, the vernacular language in which texts are sometimes written, may look like fun to adults who are not familiar with it, and it may be assumed that messages are innocuous when in fact they are not.

The poem shows how the superficially fun, trivial appearance of textspeak can, like any means of communication, hide a more sinister purpose.

Content

The poem is reproduced here in two forms which are intended to be read together: the textspeak version and its full, 'translated' English text.

The textspeak format of the poem could appear almost impenetrable to someone who is unfamiliar with the idiom, but its meaning may be quite apparent to young people who use the language regularly (note that textspeak has a number of versions or dialects, the one in the poem being taken from the *Wiktionary Glossary of Textspeak*, July 2018).

The English translation of the textspeak poem may be more readily comprehensible for the general reader. The poem presents an imaginary series of six darkly suggestive texts from an unnamed sender — one for each stanza, the final one with its single-word rider, 'Never' — and can also be read as a single extended text message. Its tone is menacing, making its threats by implication rather than directly or overtly.

The effect of the poem is cumulative, with the imaginary sender's sinister intentions becoming clearer as the poem progresses.

Composition

The poem consists of six four-line stanzas, the final stanza having a single-word rider by which the last word is detached from the line end for emphasis. The rhyme scheme is ABCB.

The metre is rhythmical but quite irregular, with the first lines of the first three stanzas having an emphatic, thumping four beats, achieved by the syllables each being equally stressed. The overall effect of the body of each stanza is wheedling and almost sing-song, an effect heightened by the use of informal, insincerely courteous, mock-friendly vocabulary.

Punctuation is conventional.

The poem's title alludes to the world of popular electronic communications media and their distortion (in this case, in the form of a text) into something negative.

The ending is ominous, leaving the reader to fear for what might happen next.

Message

The message of the poem is intended to demonstrate how an apparently informal, everyday piece of text communication can hide a sinister meaning behind unfamiliar, obscure textspeak. We are invited to consider where else among the lives of young people threatening or negative messages might be hidden — perhaps even in plain view.

Threats do not have to be overt, and sometimes the most intimidating behaviour can be disguised within an everyday, familiar and deceptively friendly medium.

Lesson plan: 'Unsocial Media' by Paul Morris

Resources

Copies of the poem — ideally one per pupil, pens and pencils or marker pens, rulers for SEND pupils to follow a line when reading.

Copies of pupils' safety plans to which they can refer throughout the session/lesson.

The lesson will cover oracy, reading and writing skills.

The session can be done in the round, or as a circle time activity, or at tables, or in an unstructured group. It is suitable for Upper Key Stage 2, 3 and 4.

Links with the PSHE Association PSHE Education Programme of Study

Links have been made to the PSHE Association PSHE Education Programme of Study at Key Stage 2, 3 and 4 as follows:

KS2

- *R19. about the impact of bullying, including offline and online, and the consequences of hurtful behaviour*
- *R20. strategies to respond to hurtful behaviour experienced or witnessed, offline and online (including teasing, name-calling, bullying, trolling, harassment or the deliberate excluding of others); how to report concerns and get support*

KS3

- *R38. to recognise bullying, and its impact, in all its forms; the skills and strategies to manage being targeted or witnessing others being bullied*

KS4

- *R31. the skills and strategies to respond to exploitation, bullying, harassment and control in relationships*

Links with the National Curriculum

Links have been made to the National Curriculum for English at Key Stage 2, 3 and 4 as follows:

KS2 (Years 5 and 6) English programme of study

- *maintain attention and participate actively in collaborative conversations, staying on topic and initiating and responding to comments*
- *articulate and justify answers, arguments and opinions*
- *discuss and evaluate how authors use language, including figurative language, considering the impact on the reader*
- *provide reasoned justifications for their views.*

KS3 English programme of study

- *participating in formal debates and structured discussions, summarising and/or building on what has been said*
- *knowing how language, including figurative language, vocabulary choice, grammar, text structure and organisational features, presents meaning*
- *recognising a range of poetic conventions and understanding how these have been used*

KS4 English programme of study

- *listening to and building on the contributions of others, asking questions to clarify and inform, and challenging courteously when necessary*
- *seeking evidence in the text to support a point of view, including justifying inferences with evidence*
- *analysing a writer's choice of vocabulary, form, grammatical and structural features, and evaluating their effectiveness and impact*
- *make an informed personal response, recognising that other responses to a text are possible and evaluating these*

Teaching and learning activities

This is a really good poem for discussion about bullying on social media and ways of dealing with it. The poem is written in textspeak which pupils often use when they are communicating with each other.

- Introduction — share aims of lesson.
- Refer pupils to their safety plans. Remind them of what a safety plan is for. Ask them to read through their own safety plan before they go further and answer any questions they may have.
- Read the poem (or teacher/leader to read it aloud) and discuss its content without the use of the transcript initially. Ask the following key questions:
  - Are there any clues from the poem's title what it might be about?
  - Why do you think the poet decided to write a poem in text speak?
  - What is the poem about? Why do you think this?
  - Did you like the poem? Give reasons for your opinions.
- Discuss the translation with the pupils.
- Class discussion about who might write such a message and why, who they might send it to and why, and what might be the impact of the message.
- How can bystanders respond when they become aware of bullying, taking into account issues of safety and effectiveness?
- Discuss how the poet builds up feelings of intimidation disguised behind a friendly medium. The effect of the poem is cumulative, with the imaginary sender's sinister intentions becoming clearer as the poem progresses.
- Discuss the rhyme scheme and the use of insincere, mock-friendly vocabulary.
- Working in pairs or small groups, pupils to highlight examples of insincere vocabulary within the poem. How can language be used to deceive or to hide aggression?
- Discuss with pupils how the poem makes them feel and why.
- Have pupils ever received intimidating or bullying messages either on their phone or on social media? What happened? How was this dealt with? Pupils to work in small groups or pairs to discuss.
- Take feedback.
- Discuss reporting arrangements in school and who to go to for help and support. Include in this people they can speak to from agencies such as Childline and NSPCC. Reiterate the message that bullying should never be tolerated.
- Review what has been achieved in the lesson.
- Refer pupils to their safety plans as a place to look if they need help after leaving the lesson.

Extension activities

- Pupils to produce their own posters, leaflets and poems about anti-bullying. These can be displayed around school.
- Pupils to design an anti-bullying logo. This could be run as a competition with the winning entry/entries being displayed.
- Pupils to write responses to the key questions.
- Display information about where to get help and advice if a pupil is being bullied. Display information from external agencies, with contact details.
- Produce posters, leaflets and poems about mobile phone and online safety.

- Invite guest speakers into school or setting, for example, a representative from Childline or NSPCC.
- Further work around online safety — keeping passwords safe, not sharing indecent images on mobile phones or on social media.
- Look at what the law says about bullying on social media and the consequences of actions when people decide to bully or intimidate others.

Cross-curricular/topic links

Cross-curricular and topic links may be explored for use in follow-up and for extension work in

- English
- PSHE
- Art and Design
- ICT

Differentiation

Opportunities for discussion in mixed ability pairs.

Differentiation by outcome e.g. quantity or complexity of issues identified, sophistication of response, level of inclusion/contribution, empathy.

Writing quantity outcomes will be differentiated/assessed/moderated according to teacher's expectations of quantity and depth; otherwise by outcome.

Differentiation may also be through key words rather than written sentences, or through artwork as a means of expression.

These Are Passing Clouds
by Tesni Penney

Commentary

They always want me to describe my feelings.
The problem is I can't feel a thing.
My mind is steel wool,
my vision distorted in grey clouds.

If anything manages to infiltrate the numbness,
it's an abrasive thought
scratching the surface of my brain.
I don't even feel the pain, just more sadness.

Crouched in a dark, damp tunnel
slowly filling up;
with my own thoughts drowning me.
I struggle to keep you to myself —

I don't flinch anymore as you
gnaw away slowly
corroding my hope like an ulcer
eating my flesh.

Why can no one else see the damage?

My days are joyless,
my nights cold,
left alone with painful memories
ebbing and flowing with the clouds.

A voice interrupts my thoughts, softly
offers me a hand to hold, reaches
across the void to guide me
from the dark, from the damp.

Eyes wide open I see as for the first time.
My friends, family, strangers, all
willing to help dig me from my mind's trap —
willing to share their tested advice on me.

"Don't worry,"
"These clouds will pass, the light
finds a way to shine through, and
your grey skies won't last forever.

These are passing clouds."

Context

'These Are Passing Clouds' is one of many poems on the theme of mental health written by Tesni Penney, a young contemporary poet from the English Peak District who uses her poetry to explore her own feelings.

The poem uses the imagery of the grey and stormy weather of the poet's native county to reflect the stormy emotional landscape of the speaker.

Content

The poem opens with the speaker describing how some unspecified people — 'they' — want her to describe her feelings (line 1), and the problems she has in doing so. She speaks of how she is numbed, her mind and vision clouded (lines 2 to 4). We may speculate that these people are either those close to her, such as her family or friends, or perhaps professionals such as doctors, teachers, therapists or counsellors.

The only thing that gets through the speaker's numbness is her own thought, which seems to scratch at her brain (lines 5 to 7). She experiences the feeling as sadness rather than pain (line 8).

The speaker feels confined, claustrophobic and stifled by her own thoughts (lines 9 to 11). She addresses what may be her own depression or distress — the 'you' that she struggles to keep to herself (line 12), and tells this personified condition how she no longer reacts as it slowly devours her hope in life (lines 13 to 16).

There is a conflicting sense of both wonder and clarity in the speaker's question of why nobody else is able to see the damage she feels she is experiencing (line 17). She wonders at her inability to understand why others cannot see what is happening within her, yet also the clarity in her insight that there is something there to be seen.

Returning to description of her interior world, the speaker tells us how her days are without happiness and her nights are cold (lines 18 to 19). She feels alone with memories that cause her pain and that seem to come and go with the clouds she feels inside (see first stanza, lines 3 and 4).

At the volta of the poem, the speaker's thoughts are interrupted by a voice and she is offered someone's hand (lines 22 to 23). The voice and hand come to the speaker across what she sees as a void that separates her from the 'usual' world, and they come to guide her from the darkness and discomfort in which she has been swathed (lines 24 to 25).

The speaker now becomes aware as though seeing for the first time, her eyes now open (line 26) to all the people who are willing to help deliver her from the trap her mind has set for her (lines 27 to 28). They are willing to share advice that they have 'tested' (line 29). The speaker now hears what these people have to say to her. She is advised not to worry (line 30), that light will break through the gloominess that shadows her life (lines 31 to 32), that the dark skies will not be permanent (line 33), and that the clouds that cover her will pass (line 34). We are left to ask ourselves whether the speaker, though she has certainly heard this advice, finds it meaningful or helpful or comforting, or whether its terms of reassurance will really offer a key to the peace and light she seeks.

Composition

'These Are Passing Clouds' is written in free verse, without a rhyme scheme or regular metrical structure.

The poem is organised in ten stanzas, consisting of four unrhymed, irregular quatrains followed by a single-line stanza, with this pattern then repeated. Each stanza deals broadly thematically with an aspect of the speaker's condition: her inability to feel; the pain of her thoughts; the claustrophobia of her mental landscape; the devouring nature of her illness; her puzzlement at others' inability to see the damage her condition causes; the isolation and bleakness she feels; the establishment of contact; her renewed perception of others; the advice she receives; and the transitory nature of her unhappiness. The two isolated lines of stanzas 5 and 10 may be seen as key, the first of them being a moment of questioning both of self and the world, and the second a moment of realisation of the impermanence of the 'clouds' encountered in life.

The punctuation of the work is conventional. The language is conversational and the vocabulary conservative, the only exceptions being the probably unfamiliar 'infiltrate' (= 'penetrate' or 'filter through', line 5) and 'ulcer' (= 'a sore in which the skin will not heal', line 15). The tone of composition lends the piece a highly effective sense of emotional suppression, an introspective and self-questioning character that is evocative of the speaker's situation.

The poet uses enjambment freely throughout the piece, following the discursive flow of language, with each line giving emphasis to a distinct aspect or nuance of thought and expression.

Figurative language chiefly includes the extended metaphor (indeed the controlling metaphor) of the 'clouds' that pervade the speaker's mind, which occurs in stanzas 1, 6, 9 and 10. Other metaphor supports or refers to this image of greyness or cloudiness directly throughout the work, including 'steel wool' (line 3), 'ebbing and flowing' (line 21), the 'dark' and 'damp' of lines 9 and 25, and 'grey skies' (line 33). The imagery associated with the portrayal of her condition as a corrosive, consuming illness (stanza 4) stands out from this as particularly intense. The absence of simile throughout the poem serves to magnify the centrality of metaphor to the speaker's mode of expression: nothing in her life is like something else — it does not *seem so* but *is so*, vivid to her in its immediacy and subjective reality. We may speculate that at least some of the force of the advice the speaker receives in stanzas 9 and 10 derives from its being expressed to her in the sort of metaphorical terms that sit closest to her personal frame of reference.

The final phase of the poem — the 'tested advice' of the penultimate and final stanzas — presents the possibility of subtle ambiguity. The speaker may consider the advice to be 'tested' in the sense of 'tried and tested' (i.e. reliable and likely to be efficacious) and therefore welcome; or she may intend to imply that it is somehow intrusive, noting that it is to be shared 'on' her (with its sense of imposition and the speaker's passivity) rather than *with* her. We may also wonder whether the final single-line stanza, isolated textually for greater emphasis and referring to the passage of the clouds from her life, may to some small extent refer to the passing of this well-meaning intrusion into the speaker's inner world.

Message

The message of the poem speaks of the overshadowing that we may feel when we are mentally or emotionally unwell. It can be of help for us to realise that we are not the only people to experience such feelings, and that we are not alone in living through them. Yet that overshadowing — those clouds — can pass and the brightness return to our lives.

When we are unhappy we may feel fogged. It can be hard to think clearly, or to exercise the same clarity of mental vision that we may have when well. We may feel that there is no room in us for anything but sadness and pain. But we should remember that light, peace and happiness may be closer than we think.

We may feel isolated, or that nobody understands how we feel. Yet those around us — family, friends, professionals — may see more than we realise and understand more than we believe they do. Just as we are looking for someone to come to our aid, they may be looking for ways in which to help us when we need it most.

However long we may have been in pain, there is always the possibility of feeling the help of those who reach out to us, and learning to meet, accept and seek their help and advice. That advice may sometimes seem quite simple, but it may be intended to help us to realise that we share in the human experience, and that many people have felt — and still feel — what we feel now. We should never feel that there is any stigma attached to seeking or accepting help. The help we receive may not be perfect, but combined with our own strength it can be enough to help us to drive the clouds from our lives and let the light come through.

It is important to ask for help when it is needed, to accept it when it is offered, and to take every opportunity we can to achieve happiness.

Lesson plan: 'These Are Passing Clouds' by Tesni Penney

Resources

Copies of the poem — ideally one per pupil, pencils or pens, flip chart paper, rulers for SEND pupils to follow a line when reading.

Copies of pupils' safety plans to which they can refer throughout the session/lesson. The lesson will cover oracy and reading.

The session can be done in the round, or as a circle time activity, or at tables, or in an unstructured group. It is suitable to use with pupils at Key Stage 4.

Links with the PSHE Association PSHE Education Programme of Study

Links have been made to the PSHE Association PSHE Education Programme of Study at Key Stage 4 as follows:

KS4

- *H8. to recognise warning signs of common mental and emotional health concerns (including stress, anxiety and depression), what might trigger them and what help or treatment is available*

Links with the National Curriculum

Links have been made to the National Curriculum for English at Key Stage 4 as follows:

KS4 English programme of study

- *listening to and building on the contributions of others, asking questions to clarify and inform, and challenging courteously when necessary*
- *seeking evidence in the text to support a point of view, including justifying inferences with evidence*
- *analysing a writer's choice of vocabulary, form, grammatical and structural features, and evaluating their effectiveness and impact*

Teaching and learning activities

This poem lends itself to a lot of discussion — individual, paired, group and class conversations around the theme of depression.

- Introduction — share aims of lesson.
- Refer pupils to their safety plans. Remind them of what a safety plan is for. Ask them to read through their own safety plan before they go further and answer any questions they may have.
- Read the poem (or teacher/leader to read it aloud) and ask the following questions:
  - What can you infer from the title of the poem?
  - What is this poem about?
  - What is the poet's message?
  - What is the tone of the poem? Use evidence to support your views.
- In pairs or in small groups discuss the speaker's experience and understanding of depression. What advice is given? Do you think this is good advice and if so, what is good about it? Why do you think this? Are there any problems with the advice and if so, what are they and how could you improve on them? Is all advice good advice? Why do you think this? Record key points on a flip chart.
- Ask for feedback from the groups.
- The poet uses metaphorical language in the poem. Can you find an example of a metaphor in this poem? How does it work to convey the poet's meaning? Can you find an example of a simile? Again, how does it work to convey the poet's meaning? Pupils to work in pairs or small groups. Revise work on metaphors and similes if pupils need more help to understand what they are and how they are used in stories and poetry. Show them examples on the whiteboard. Ask pupils to reflect on what is being represented by the clouds.
- Ask for feedback from all the groups.
- Why is it important to talk about depression? Why do you think the young poet chose to write about this subject? Pupils to take part in a class discussion. It will also be important to talk about help available if pupils ever feel depressed or low.
- Review what has been achieved in the lesson.
- Refer pupils to their safety plans as a place to look if they need help after leaving the lesson.

Extension activities

- Pupils to write answers to the key questions.
- The speaker says 'My mind is steel wool', which creates the impression of her mind being a dense, grey cloud. To what extent do you think the poem is about the clouds clearing and the speaker seeing more clearly? How does this help the speaker?
- Write about the structure and layout of the poem (how it is constructed and how it is set out on the page). What is the significance of the two single-line stanzas 5 and 10?

- Produce a piece of artwork which reflects the mood of the poem or the use of metaphorical language. Can you find images that act as metaphors?
- Can you think of any metaphors that are personal to your own relationship with your moods or sense of wellbeing? An example might be 'I am the sea. When I am happy, I am calm, rippling and sunny. Sometimes I am stormy and unwelcoming.'
- Prepare the poem to read aloud and to perform, showing understanding through intonation, tone and volume so that the meaning is clear to an audience.
- Invite speakers to come into school to raise awareness around mental health e.g. Mind, Kooth, Childline, Samaritans, Mental Health Foundation, a GP, an educational psychologist.
- Display posters around school/setting so pupils know where to go to access help and support.
- How did the poem make you feel? Give reasons for your opinions.

Cross-curricular/topic links

Cross-curricular and topic links may be explored for use in follow-up and for extension work in

- English
- PSHE
- Art and Design

Differentiation

Opportunities for discussion in mixed ability pairs/groups.

Differentiation by outcome e.g. quantity or complexity of issues identified, sophistication of response, level of inclusion/contribution, empathy.

Writing quantity outcomes will be differentiated/assessed/moderated according to teacher's expectations of quantity and depth; otherwise by outcome.

Differentiation may also be through artwork as a means of expression.

I'm Alone

This section is about seeking personal space; about feelings of loneliness and isolation...

Hidden Tears

by Mojisola Oladiti

Commentary

When rejection hits you
And you've nowhere to turn
You try to lean on the ones who loved you.
But the darkness shoots and you
RUN.

Tried to find your bright light
'Cause all your dreams have fallen apart,
But you're stuck in the dark night
So you don't want to restart
AGAIN.

When depression sticks
And you feel left out
It's like your heart's fallen,
Like it's spinning about.
Others outside having fun,
Bug smiles on their faces —
Can't be with them so
                            you're
                                  done.
What sets us apart is
That they know the basics
ALWAYS.

There's more to me
Than they see.
I feel the need to talk but they never listen.
We all want to be in the centre of attention:
I got mine in the centre of misperception.
The things they say hurt more than ice —
Don't they know I can see through their eyes?
TRANSPARENT.

Thought you could go by your own rules in our world?
They said it was cute
'Cause you've got to obey their every word.
They'll always keep you on mute.
They say don't judge a book by its cover
Though they got everyone to hate me and say
I always lie.
Don't know why
I even ever bother
Waiting for someone to say goodbye
FOREVER.

Context

Mojisola Oladiti is a Nigerian-born writer who is based in Manchester. A keen and accomplished athlete who has represented her county as a middle-distance runner, Mojisola's dynamism and energy are reflected in her poem 'Hidden Tears', which she wrote when a student at Manchester's Cedar Mount Academy.

As a proud young woman writer, Mojisola is motivated by the potential of her work to reach and help others.

Content

The poem's powerful opening addresses the reader directly, and admits through her use of the so-called 'generic-you' (see **Composition** section below) for the possibility that both she and the reader may have shared similar experience.

We are confronted with the harsh reality that may accompany anxiety, depression or mental trauma: the impact of one's sense of rejection (line 1); the feeling that one is trapped (line 2); the attempt to find support in loved ones (line 3); the feeling of threat that can come from one's mind being in a dark place (line 4); and the compulsion to escape (line 5).

We are told that when presented with the destruction of our dreams for the future that anxiety or depression may cause (line 7), we may try to find something within ourselves to metaphorically light our way forward (the 'bright light' of line 6). However, we may find that we are unable to get out of the inner darkness in which we find ourselves (line 8), and that we may not be able to face trying to get our lives moving again (lines 9–10). The capitalised prominence of 'AGAIN' emphasises how the experience may be a repeated one, and we may infer that if we experience recurring depression or anxiety we may become reluctant to start again after the discouragement of previous setbacks.

Depression sometimes 'sticks' (line 11) to the person it affects, and may leave them feeling excluded or detached (line 12). The effects can be disorientating and disheartening (lines 13–14). While other people are able to enjoy themselves outside, annoying in their happiness (lines 15–16) to someone who cannot share it, the depressed person cannot be with them and so feels their separation (lines 17–19). We are told that what sets the depressed person apart is the sense that other people always seem to know how things are done (lines 20–22) when they themselves feel they do not, or are unable to cope.

The speaker, who now speaks more for herself and less generally, asserts that there is more to her than others see (lines 23–24). She wants to talk but feels that others will not listen to her (line 25). We all want to be noticed, but the speaker locates herself as misunderstanding or misunderstood — perhaps both — 'in the centre of misperception' (lines 26–27).

The things other people say are cold and sharp, they 'hurt more than ice' (line 28), and the speaker wonders whether those who say such things know that she is able to see their intentions and how they perceive things, even perhaps how they perceive her — seeing as though 'through their eyes' (line 29), a referred point of view that with insight she considers to be emphatically 'TRANSPARENT' (line 30).

The speaker adopts the persona of the 'others' to address the reader, seeming to claim ownership of the everyday world for themselves and asking whether 'you' (the speaker or the reader — whoever has experienced anxiety or depression) think they can go by their own rules in *their* world (line 31). She then switches back to her own point of view to tell the reader how 'they' (that is the 'others') were delighted that you — the speaker or the reader, sharing the same experience — had to do what they said, to follow their standards ('obey their every word', line 33).

The speaker feels that the 'others' try to keep her/us from speaking (line 34), a further reference to how they do not listen, which she established in line 25. She suggests that they have induced 'everyone to hate me and say / I always lie' (lines 36–37).

The speaker seems both angry and dejected, feeling that she does not know why she bothers with others, or perhaps with the affairs of daily life. She may feel a sense of impending and perhaps repeated loss, or perhaps one of abandonment, which may suggest the departure or abandonment of friends or others that may be associated with her mental health problems — she is 'waiting for someone to say goodbye / FOREVER' (lines 40–41). Perhaps she is simply tired of waiting for others to show her the same basic courtesies ('waiting for someone to say goodbye') that she shows them.

Composition

'Hidden Tears' is written in five stanzas without regular metre, but in which the poet uses an irregular pattern of rhyme.

In the first stanza lines 1, 3 and 4 rhyme (*you/you/you*). In the second stanza lines 1 and 3 rhyme (*light/night* — or by extension *bright light/dark night*), as do lines 2 and 4 (*apart/restart*). The second stanza rhymes lines 2 and 4 rhyme (*out/about*), lines 3, 5 and 9 with use of half rhyme (*fallen/fun/done*), and lines 6, 10 and 11 (*faces/[apart] is/basics*). The fourth stanza rhymes lines 1 and 2 (*me/see*), lines 3, 4 and 5 with the use of half rhyme and assonance (*listen/attention/misperception*), and lines 6 and 7 paired with the use of half rhyme (*ice/eyes*). The fifth and final stanza sees rhymes in lines 1 and 3 with the use of half rhyme (*world/word*), lines 2 and 4 (*cute/mute*), lines 5 and 9 again with half rhyme (*cover/bother*), and lines 6, 7, 8 and 10 with half rhyme (*say/lie/why/goodbye*).

The use of half rhyme (otherwise known as sprung rhyme, slant rhyme or oblique rhyme) is commonly found in rap music, allowing greater flexibility in connecting words, and for spoken word artists it helps the performer to avoid obvious or clichéd rhymes, thus offering greater versatility of language manipulation. In the case of 'Hidden Tears', the poet's use of the device adds a sense of gritty authenticity to the work, a 'street' feel that magnifies its impression of hard, lived understanding.

Lines are generally short and punchy, delivered with the force of a series of sharp blows. Longer lines serve not only expositionally but also to prevent any feeling of comfortable regularity, keeping the reader's attention fixed on the quick-moving language.

Vocabulary is generally conversational, with constructions tending towards youthful vernacular usages. She also uses common axiom — 'They say don't judge a book by its cover' — to further establish her vernacular tone. However, the poet is bold in her use of language that describes starkly the hard experience that is the poem's chief theme.

The poem's punctuation is sparse, restricted carefully to the minimum necessary to delineate and clarify meaning.

In the third stanza, the seventh, eighth and ninth lines could form a single line, but in breaking this up visually the poet has succeeded in lending a percussive emphasis to each syllable of the 'so / you're / done'.

A similar percussive effect is achieved by the final line of each stanza, in every case a single word that lends particular stress to an action or circumstance that the poet has developed in the verse.

A significant characteristic of the poem is the shifting points of view and reference. From line to line this may be that of the speaker, the 'others' with whom the speaker experiences such difficulty, or the world in general — a rapidly-changing whirl that may suggest the disorientation of the speaker's situation or the pressure of both internal and external views that the speaker feels. However, the poet also uses a further point of view or reference in the work — that of the reader who is invited, or indeed compelled, to identify with the speaker. This is achieved through the particular use the poet makes of the pronoun 'you'. In everyday English this is used simply as the second-person pronoun, but in this poem it is often used as a third-person singular pronoun, equating approximately to the indefinite pronoun 'one' meaning broadly 'a person' — though also having the same clearly-implied intention that it be construed as referring to the speaker, equating with 'me' or 'I'. This usage, where 'you' refers not just to an intended individual or group but to anyone, or by extension to the speaker him- or herself, is referred to as the 'generic-you'. It is common in some English vernacular usage, but the reasons that may underlie that usage are seldom considered. Researchers have conducted experiments focusing on why people adopt this usage, and results have shown that the generic-you often helps the user to cope with negative experiences, allowing them to 'normalise' the experience and reflect on it from a distance, explaining a personal situation whilst at the same time drawing the listener/reader into the experience and attempting to make it into something to which many people will relate. Studies suggest that people speaking or writing about a negative personal experience will tend to use the generic-you more than people who are describing a neutral personal experience. The generic-you can be a means of achieving psychological distance from negative experience, providing a way to move beyond individual perspective to include others in what is understood to be common experience. In 'Hidden Tears' the poet uses the generic-you to draw in the reader, to both suggest that the reader may have shared the speaker's experience and to make the vital point that it requires only an access of poor mental health for them to do so.

The poet makes sparing use of figurative language, with simile confined to 'It's like your heart's fallen, / Like it's spinning about' (stanza 3, lines 3–4), and 'hurt more than ice' (stanza 4, sixth line). Metaphor is used with a more lavish hand, including 'the darkness shoots' (stanza 1, line 4), 'your bright light' (stanza 2, line 1), 'you're stuck in the dark night' (stanza 2, line 3), 'I got mine in the centre of misperception' (stanza 4, line 5), 'Don't they know I can see through their eyes?' (stanza 4, line 7), 'keep you on mute' (stanza 5, line 4), and arguably 'Waiting for someone to say goodbye' (stanza 5, line 10).

Message

The poem reminds us of the shared experience of mental illness, and particularly depression. It is a surprisingly common occurrence.

Mental illness and depression can result in feelings of rejection, alarm, dislocation and disorientation. The world may appear to be a threatening place, and other people — perhaps even those to whom we would turn first for help — may seem distant from us. We may react to our feelings, particularly if they are unfamiliar, in fear or even panic. We can feel as though we are being driven further, distanced or even isolated from other people, even those who would actually want to help us, and that we are alone. But we may remember that those people are there to help, and we should try to accept or seek help whenever we need it.

When we are unwell it may feel as though we cannot find our way to the things that motivated us before, that helped to give us our identity or made us feel like who we really are. If this happens repeatedly it can be disheartening and make us reluctant to try to keep getting up when we are figuratively knocked down. Still, we should remember that people like parents and teachers may understand how we feel, and we should try to trust them.

It may seem that other people are enjoying the world when we are not, or that we are not having our voices heard when others are, which can make it feel as though others know some hidden secret of success that has not been shared with us. This can heighten our sense of exclusion from daily life, and perhaps lead us to feel that we do not really want to be part of the wider world. However, the feeling that other people understand the world better than we do is not necessarily true: everybody can find life difficult and confusing, and sometimes people have to work hard not to show just how puzzling life can be for them. They may be making a show of confidence that they do not really feel. Again, people like parents and teachers may be familiar with this.

We may think that other people do not perceive us as we wish to be perceived, or as we really are. We may feel a lack of attention or that what others say or do is hurtful, whether or not they actually mean it to be. This can simply be a result of how our mental health makes us see ourselves, and how we project this onto others around us. Still, at the heart of everything we remain ourselves and the help of others, if we accept it, can help us to get back to the self with whom we are comfortable.

Lesson plan: 'Hidden Tears' by Mojisola Oladiti

Resources

Copies of the poem — ideally one per pupil, pencils or pens, flip chart paper, rulers for SEND pupils to follow a line when reading.

Copies of pupils' safety plans to which they can refer throughout the session/lesson. The lesson will cover oracy and reading.

The session can be done in the round, or as a circle time activity, or at tables, or in an unstructured group. It is suitable to use with pupils at, Key Stage 3 and 4.

Links with the PSHE Association PSHE Education Programme of Study

Links have been made to the PSHE Association PSHE Education Programme of Study at Key Stage 3 and 4 as follows:

KS3

- *H7. the characteristics of mental and emotional health and strategies for managing these*
- *H12. how to recognise when they or others need help with their mental health and wellbeing; sources of help and support and strategies for accessing what they need*
- *R14. the qualities and behaviours they should expect and exhibit in a wide variety of positive relationships (including in school and wider society, family and friendships, including online)*

KS4

- *H5. the characteristics of mental and emotional health; to develop empathy and understanding about how daily actions can affect people's mental health*
- *H8. to recognise warning signs of common mental and emotional health concerns (including stress, anxiety and depression), what might trigger them and what help or treatment is available*

Links with the National Curriculum

Links have been made to the National Curriculum for English at Key Stage 2, 3 and 4 as follows:

KS3 English programme of study

- *participating in debates and structured discussions, summarising and/or building on what has been said*
- *knowing how language, including figurative language, vocabulary choice, grammar, text structure and organisational features, presents meaning*

KS4 English programme of study

- *listening to and building on the contributions of others, asking questions to clarify and inform, and challenging courteously when necessary*
- *analysing a writer's choice of vocabulary, form, grammatical and structural features, and evaluating their effectiveness and impact*

Teaching and learning activities

This poem lends itself to a lot of discussion — individual, paired, group and class conversation particularly around the theme of depression.

- Introduction — share aims of lesson.
- Refer pupils to their safety plans. Remind them of what a safety plan is for. Ask them to read through their own safety plan before they go further and answer any questions they may have.
- Read the poem (or teacher/leader to read it aloud) and ask the following questions:
  - What is this poem about?
  - How does the poem make you feel? How does it do this? Give reasons for your opinions.
  - How is the speaker in the poem seen and treated by her peers? What do you think about the way she is treated? If you were with her, what advice would you give her?
- What do you think the phrase 'bug smiles on their faces' means? Invite comments from the class.
- What is the significance of the words written in capital letters? Why do you think the poet chose to write them in capital letters? What effect does this create? Discuss in pairs or small groups.
- Ask for feedback.
- The poet uses the phrase 'when depression sticks'. In small groups discuss what you know about depression and how it affects the speaker in the poem. Brainstorm thoughts and record on flip chart paper. Pupils may want to look up the meaning of the word 'depression' in the dictionary. Younger pupils will need more explanation about what depression is.
- Ask for feedback.

- What support/help do you think the young person in the poem needs from her peers, her family and her teachers? What do you think she should do to let others know how she is feeling? Use evidence wherever possible from the poem to inform your answer. Pupils to work in pairs or small groups. Record answers on flip chart paper.
- Ask for feedback.
- Review what has been achieved in the lesson.
- Refer pupils to their safety plans as a place to look if they need help after leaving the lesson.

Extension activities

- Pupils to write answers to the key questions.
- Prepare the poem to read aloud and to perform, showing understanding through intonation, tone and volume so that the meaning is clear to an audience.
- Invite speakers to come into school to raise awareness around mental health e.g. Mind, Childline, Samaritans, Mental Health Foundation, a GP, an educational psychologist.
- Display posters around school/setting so pupils know where to go to access help and support.
- Did you like the poem? Give reasons for your opinions.
- If a person with depression is 'stuck in the dark night' (stanza 2), what does a brighter day look like? Ask pupils to write about happy experiences in their lives, how it made them feel and the effect it had on their mood.
- What is the poem's message?
- Write about the importance of strong, supportive friendships. Are friends really your friends if they are not kind towards you? What is a true friend?
- Write about the form, structure and rhyme scheme of the poem.

Cross-curricular/topic links

Cross-curricular and topic links may be explored for use in follow-up and for extension work in

- English
- PSHE

Differentiation

Opportunities for discussion in mixed ability pairs/groups.

Differentiation by outcome e.g. quantity or complexity of issues identified, sophistication of response, level of inclusion/contribution, empathy.

Writing quantity outcomes will be differentiated/assessed/moderated according to teacher's expectations of quantity and depth; otherwise by outcome.

Waving at Trains

by Rosie Garland

Commentary

On the bridge, I wave at every woman. Half the population
of Great Britain; thirty million according to Miss Grant.
A hundred women in each train, two trains on the way

to school, three on the walk home, makes five hundred;
times five days a week equals two thousand five hundred
which goes into thirty million too many times for me to work out.

I scratch the numbers in my notebook, string beads
of zeros across the bottom of each page to calculate
how long I've got to do this before I've waved to every single one.

Then I can be sure that one of them was her. The woman
who gave birth to me three thousand seven hundred
and twelve days ago, including leap years.

She will see something familiar in my hand,
read its semaphore, and know.

Context

Rosie Garland describes herself as having been 'born in London to a runaway teenager'.

In an interview with *The Telegraph* newspaper in 2014, Rosie described her experience of being
an adopted child, and how wanted and loved she had felt in the care of what she came to see as
her 'real' family. But she described too how when she reached her early 30s, about twenty years
previously, it had niggled that she still had not answered the question 'Where do I come from?' — a
simple curiosity about her origins. This poem reflects the pain, poignancy and longing of a child who
is lit by that curiosity.

Content

'Waving at Trains' is written in the voice of a child, who we may identity with the poet. She says that
she is 'three thousand seven hundred and twelve days' old — 'including leap years' — which makes
her ten years old, and also suggests the mathematically precise, intelligent mind she has applied to
her extraordinary project.

The speaker describes how she stands on a railway bridge and waves at passing trains. This is a
solitary occupation, but she is trying to make a connection. In particular the speaker is waving at the
women passengers. According to Miss Grant, presumably her teacher, women account for half the
population. The speaker has started to do the arithmetic to work out how long it would take to wave
to a number of women equal to all the women in the country, assuming one hundred women per
train, five trains per day, five days per week; she cannot complete the calculation because the number
of women is so large. She was hoping to work out how long it would take her to wave to them all.

We learn that it is only by doing this, and waving at every woman in the country, that the speaker can be sure that somewhere among them she will wave to her birth mother.

The speaker is confident that if her birth mother sees her wave she will recognise who the speaker is.

The young speaker's plan appears naïve: we can see that not every woman in the country will be a passenger on that train at some time, nor will every woman passenger see her waving. There is a sense of loneliness behind her actions, which are solitary. This is a hopeful plan, though ultimately an impractical one, which is lent a poignancy by the young speaker's attempts at a mathematical precision against which her innocent hopefulness is counterpointed. But the sincerity of the wish behind the plan is clear, confident and touching.

Composition

The poem is written in free verse, unrhymed and without regular metre.

The five stanzas consist of four three-line verses and a final verse of two lines.

The language is conversational, with straightforward vocabulary and punctuation. This suits the informal, intimate address of the child who is telling us of her plans. The vocabulary contains only one word that is likely to be unfamiliar to a younger reader: the word 'semaphore', a term which properly refers to a system of sending messages by holding the arms, two flags or poles in various positions according to an alphabetic code, but by extension in this case indicates a gesture or visual signal that will convey a message.

The poem is largely literal, which fits well with the child speaker's mathematically methodical approach to her quest and the simplicity of her desire. Figurative language and other literary devices are used little. Lines 7 to 8 include the metaphorical description of how the speaker will 'string beads / of zeros across the bottom of each page' when she tries to calculate the magnitude of her task. The final line uses 'semaphore' metaphorically to describe the communicated message of the 'something familiar in my hand' that she hopes her mother will see: the phrase 'in my hand' is probably meant in the sense of 'about my hand' rather than suggesting that the child is holding an object in it.

Message

'Waving at Trains' speaks of the lengths to which we will go to find out who we are, to understand our true identity and to get in touch with our origins. Even if the task will not bear critical examination, even when the task we set for ourselves is too great or too unrealistic ever to be practical, we will sometimes tell ourselves that our plans might just work, or are better than not knowing — at least we are doing *something*. This may be particularly true of us wanting to find our family connections, our roots. Without them we may have an enduring sense of being somehow disconnected, separated or alone.

We find it comforting to believe that somewhere in the teeming world there is somebody who will recognise us for who we really are. We want to be known, to be understood.

Our plans and aims may seem doomed to failure, but hope and persistence are powerful and can keep us going even when the odds seem to be stacked against us. We may find something else that helps us to fulfil our aims, or someone to whom we can reach out for guidance, support and understanding.

Lesson plan: 'Waving at Trains' by Rosie Garland

Resources

Copies of the poem — ideally one per pupil, pens or pencils, calculators, dictionaries, plain or lined paper, rulers for SEND pupils to follow a line when reading.

Copies of pupils' safety plans to which they can refer throughout the session/lesson.

The lesson will cover oracy, reading and writing skills.

The session can be done at tables or in an unstructured group. The lesson plan is suitable to use with pupils at Upper Key Stage 2, 3 and 4.

Links with the PSHE Association PSHE Education Programme of Study

The learning opportunities below are not covered by the draft DfE statutory guidance *Relationships Education, Relationships and Sex Education (RSE) and Health Education*, but they form part of a broader programme for schools when they are covering work on bereavement.

Links have been made to the PSHE Association PSHE Education Programme of Study at Key Stage 2, 3 and 4 as follows:

KS2

- *H23. about change and loss, including death, and how these can affect feelings; ways of expressing and managing grief and bereavement*
- *H25. about personal identity; what contributes to who we are (e.g. ethnicity, family, gender, faith, culture, hobbies, likes/dislikes)*

KS3

- *R22. the effects of change, including loss, separation, divorce and bereavement; strategies for managing these and accessing support*
- *H2. to understand what can affect wellbeing and resilience (e.g. life changes, relationships, achievements and employment)*

KS4

- *R13. ways to manage grief about changing relationships including the impact of separation, divorce and bereavement; sources of support and how to access them*
- *H2. how self-confidence self-esteem, and mental health are affected positively and negatively by internal and external influences and ways of managing this*

Links with the National Curriculum

Links have been made to the National Curriculum for English at Key Stage 2, 3 and 4 as follows:

KS2 (Years 5 and 6) English programme of study

- *maintain attention and participate actively in collaborative conversations, staying on topic and initiating and responding to comments*
- *discuss and evaluate how authors use language, including figurative language, considering the impact on the reader*
- *draft and write by:*

  selecting appropriate grammar and vocabulary, understanding how such choices can change and enhance meaning

KS3 English programme of study

- *participating in formal debates and structured discussions, summarising and/or building on what has been said*
- *knowing how language, including figurative language, vocabulary choice, grammar, text structure and organisational features, presents meaning*
- *plan, draft, edit and proof-read through:*

  considering how their writing reflects the audiences and purposes for which it was intended

KS4 English programme of study

- *working effectively in groups of different sizes and taking on required roles, including leading and managing discussions, involving others productively, reviewing and summarising, and contributing to meeting goals/deadlines*
- *analysing a writer's choice of vocabulary, form, grammatical and structural features, and evaluating their effectiveness and impact*
- *adapting their writing for a wide range of purposes and audiences: to describe, narrate, explain, instruct, give and respond to information, and argue*

Teaching and learning activities

This poem deals with the search for personal connection. The speaker is alone and we feel her sense of loss and isolation.

- Introduction — share aims of lesson.
- Refer pupils to their safety plans. Remind them of what a safety plan is for. Ask them to read through their own safety plan before they go further and answer any questions they may have.
- Read the poem (or teacher/leader to read it aloud) and discuss its content.

  Ask key questions:

  - What is the poem about?

  - How does the poem make you feel? How does it do this? Give reasons for your opinions.

  - What is the significance of the title?

  - What does the word 'semaphore' mean in the poem? Pupils to look up the meaning of the word in a dictionary. In what ways do we 'semaphore' or telegraph our meaning to others without communicating directly? How do we give away how we think or feel?

- In pairs or small groups work out the age of the child in the poem.
- Why are numbers so important to the child? Discuss in pairs or small groups.
- Ask for feedback.
- What help does the child need? Discuss with a partner or in small groups.

- Imagine you are the child in the poem. Describe what goes through your mind as you stand alone on the bridge and look at each passing train. Pupils may want to draft their writing using scaffolding prompts. Scaffolding prompts for the writing task may help pupils to record their ideas. These can be written on the whiteboard for pupils to write notes about before they complete the main writing task. Consider:
  - Where are you standing?
  - Describe what you can see around you.
  - How often do you go there?
  - What times of day do you visit?
  - Why do you choose that place to stand and wave at the trains?
  - Who are you hoping to see and why?
  - What thoughts and feelings go through your mind as you stand on your own and wave at the trains?
  - Describe one or more of the women's faces on the train as they look out of the window.
  - What are you hoping for?

- Review what has been achieved in the lesson. Draw pupils' attention to support that is readily available to help deal with issues that have been identified.

- Refer pupils to their safety plans as a place to look if they need help after leaving the lesson.

Extension activities

- Pupils to write answers to the key questions.

- Pupils to complete the writing task from the main activity. Pupils should be encouraged to share their work and to make changes where necessary.

- If there is so little chance of actually making contact with her birth mother, the woman that the girl imagines to be on the train, why bother waving? What does it achieve for the girl who is waving? Do you think that what the girl is doing is better than just doing nothing? Why do you think this?

- Imagine that one day you find that woman on the train. You wave, she waves back and there is instant recognition. She jumps off the train at the next station and you run towards each other. What happens next? What do you say to each other? What are the good and bad, easy and difficult things you will each have to deal with?

- In pairs act out and explore the first meeting between the child and the woman. Start with this dialogue prompt: 'Who are you? Have we met before?'

- Create a list of the questions that the child might want to ask the woman. Think carefully about the sort of language you would use to ask those questions. How might the woman reply?

- Pupils to write their own poems in the style of Rosie Garland's work. It might be about the loss of a family member or a pet, or trying to find someone that you have lost from your life such as a friend with whom you have lost contact.

- Think of alternative titles for Rosie Garland's poem.

- Did you like the poem? Give reasons for your opinions.

- Turn the poem into a letter from a child to her mother, father, grandparent or pet.

- Write a series of diary entries as though you were the child in the poem. Recount what you do each day and how you feel. What has the girl learned from her experiences?

- Circle time activities that concentrate on the release of feelings and emotions over the loss of a relative, a friend or beloved pet.

Cross-curricular/topic links

Cross-curricular and topic links may be explored for use in follow-up and for extension work in

- English
- Drama
- PSHE

Differentiation

Opportunities for discussion in class, groups, pairs.

Differentiation by outcome e.g. quantity or complexity of issues identified, sophistication of response, level of inclusion/contribution, empathy.

Writing quantity outcomes will be differentiated/assessed/moderated according to teacher's expectations of quantity and depth; otherwise by outcome.

If the main writing task presents too much of a challenge for some pupils then the focus might be on answering the scaffolding prompts or using the prompts to produce a comic strip with words and pictures, with help if necessary. The lines of prompted text might also be assembled to create a prose poem.

Pupils' responses to the main activity could be recorded by the session leader and transcribed if writing is problematic.

Solitude

by Ella Wheeler Wilcox

Commentary

Laugh, and the world laughs with you;
Weep, and you weep alone;
For the sad old earth must borrow its mirth,
But has trouble enough of its own.
Sing, and the hills will answer;
Sigh, it is lost on the air;
The echoes bound to a joyful sound,
But shrink from voicing care.

Rejoice, and men will seek you;
Grieve, and they turn and go;
They want full measure of all your pleasure,
But they do not need your woe.
Be glad, and your friends are many;
Be sad, and you lose them all, —
There are none to decline your nectared wine,
But alone you must drink life's gall.

Feast, and your halls are crowded;
Fast, and the world goes by.
Succeed and give, and it helps you live,
But no man can help you die.
There is room in the halls of pleasure
For a large and lordly train,
But one by one we must all file on
Through the narrow aisles of pain.

Context

'Solitude' is perhaps Ella Wheeler Wilcox's best-known and most popular poem. Indeed its first line — and arguably its second too — are now proverbial.

The poet herself described the circumstances of the poem's composition. On a February morning in 1883 she was a passenger on a train travelling to Madison, the capital city of the US state of Wisconsin, having been invited to attend the governor's inaugural ball. On taking her seat in the carriage she saw a young woman whom she knew and who was, as she expressed it 'the bride of a year, the widow of a week, a lovely girl I had last seen radiant with happiness'. The young widow was weeping, indeed sobbing, and Wilcox did her best to console her. Later that evening, radiant in a new white gown made especially for the ball, the poet was happily examining her appearance in the mirror when she recalled the figure of the young widow in black. The contrast between not only their appearances but also their emotional lots in life impressed itself upon her, and in her remorse the first quatrain of 'Solitude' came to her mind. The poet went on to finish the work and it was first published in *The New York Sun* newspaper later that month, earning Wilcox the sum of $5 in the process. It was included in her second book of collected poetry, *Poems of Passion*, before the end of that year.

Ella Wheeler Wilcox was born in Wisconsin in 1850. Her family considered themselves to be intellectuals, and grasp of the English language was a respected and much-valued ability among them. Wilcox read keenly, though it is believed that there were few books in her childhood home: the family lost most of its wealth due to the failure of her father's business.

As a child Wilcox was a precocious writer, and began to compose poetry from the age of eight. Her first poem was published when she was only thirteen years old: she reportedly believed that if the newspaper accepted a piece of her writing for publication then she would at least receive a copy of the paper in which her piece was printed, which would supply her craving for new reading material. Unfortunately the poem itself is lost, and Wilcox herself was later unable to remember even the poem's topic. However, it was enough to begin a writing career and she had become recognised as a poet in her own right by the time she left high school.

Wilcox married the year after her first book was published. She went on to develop interests in spiritualism, theosophy (a then-new spiritual philosophy that emphasised individual spiritual awareness of God) and New Thought (a spiritual movement — for further information about this see the **Context** section to the poem 'Promise Yourself' by Christian D, Larson in Section 8 of this guide, **I'm Standing Strong**). She wrote for New Thought publications, advocating animal rights and vegetarianism.

Wilcox produced a number of books of fiction and several collections of poetry in her lifetime. Some of her poetry was deemed to have crossed the line into indecency, and for some time her work was banned from the shelves of many American public libraries. Her work has remained controversial, with her poems often being cited in anthologies of 'bad verse'. Whatever Wilcox's view may have been of her own work we may see her as a popular poet rather than a literary one, writing plainly accessible verse that was generally concerned with cheerful, hopeful, optimistic matters.

Content

The speaker addresses the reader directly. She sets out a series of comparisons between a happy life and an unhappy one, and how the world around you may treat us differently if we have the latter rather than the former.

We are told that if we laugh, the world will laugh with us — that if we are happy, everyone around us will want to be included in that happiness (line 1). If we weep — that is, if we are unhappy — then those around us will not want any part of our sorrow (line 2). The world is, the speaker says, a sad place that must take its happiness wherever it can, even from others (line 3); it has enough unhappiness of its own so that it does not need or want to share in the sorrows of others (line 4).

If we sing, expressing joy, the world around us will respond to us and join in (line 5). If we sigh with sadness, it is lost as the world around us does not want to hear it (line 6). The world rejoices with our joy, but is reluctant to join in with sorrow (lines 7 and 8).

The speaker tells us that if we are joyful other people will want to be with us (line 9), but that if we show grief they will prefer to leave us alone (line 10). People want to take a full share of the good things we have (line 11) but they do not need, or perhaps want, any part of our unhappiness (line 12). If we appear to be happy, people will want to be our friends (line 13); if we are sad, those 'friends' will not stay around (line 14). Nobody turns down the good things we have to offer (line 15), but when things turn bitter for us they leave us to deal with them on our own (line 16).

If we have plenty and want to share it with others, people will want to enjoy the good times (line 17), but when we have little people will leave us to it (line 18) and pass us by. We may feel that it is good for the quality of our lives for us to do well and to give some of what we gain to others (line 19), but that does not mean that there will be anyone there for us when we need them most (line 20). Wherever there is pleasure, there seems to be room for a magnificent crowd of people willing to enjoy it (lines 21 and 22), but when we have to deal with pain we must do so alone (lines 23 and 24).

In many ways this may appear to be a rather pessimistic poem. This seems rather a hopeless picture: people only want us when it is good for them, the poet seems to say — cheer up or nobody will want anything to do with you! This need not be understood as the poet's personal philosophy, but rather a commentary on human nature. It seems that the poet is indeed telling us that we must look happy if we want to have friends, and that we must give to others if we want them to be around us. She seems to be telling us, too, that others will only want us when we have something pleasurable to share with them such as happiness or good times or even wealth, but that they will not want anything to do with us when we are unhappy or have less to offer them. Is the alternative to happiness, to faking it if we cannot be happy naturally, really that we must be alone? Not at all: we need not take things that far. It is certainly a natural human trait for people to want to be happy and to be around happiness, to gravitate towards happiness and to shy away from unhappiness, because it often seems that the world has relatively little of the former and too much of the latter. Yes, there will be some people who will be friendly only when they are getting what they want out of the relationship. But this should not lead us to believe that everyone will behave the same way towards us. That is not so. We may surely hope that there will be some people who will behave differently and will be loyal to us in our times of trouble. There will always be those we can rely on to be with us, to support us, and to be on our side whether we are happy or sad. These, whether they are family or friends or those who work to help us, are true friends.

Composition

'Solitude' is composed as a didactic poem in three stanzas of octets (otherwise known as octaves). The rhyme scheme is ABCBDEFE; the third line of each stanza contains an internal rhyme, the rhyme occurring between the word at the midway point of the line and its final word.

The oddly complex metre of the poem (couplets of trochaic trimeter followed by a line of iambic tetrameter, finished with an iambic trimester) is far less important in itself — this was never meant to be literary poetry — than the jauntily bouncy rhythmical effect this creates in reading. Whilst this seems to support the poem's theme if we see it as one of pursuing happiness, which might well have been the poet's original intention, it sits rather uncomfortably if we view that theme as being a kind of caution that unless we constantly present a cheerful face to the world we will find ourselves alone. This may be the poet's strategy, in line with the mores of her time, either for delivering an encouraging message or attempting to sugar a bitter pill of reflection on human nature.

The poem's punctuation is conventional. Its language bears some slightly grandiose touches of 'poetic' vocabulary to lend weight to the subject matter (e.g. 'Feast, and your halls are crowded', line 17). There are several words that, whilst not obscure, may need to be clarified for the younger reader: 'mirth' (= 'joy, happiness', line 3), 'bound' (= 'rebound, bounce back', line 7), 'shrink' (= 'be reluctant, hesitate, line 8), 'grieve' (= 'be unhappy, show grief', line 10), 'woe' (= 'unhappiness, misery', line 12), 'nectared' (= 'sweetened', line 15), 'gall' (= 'bitterness', line 16), 'fast' (= 'go without food', line 18), 'lordly' (= 'magnificent, impressive', line 22), 'train' (= 'followers, household, hangers-on', line 22), 'aisles' (= 'passageways, paths', line 24).

The work contains a breadth of figurative language and imagery. Much of it reworks a similar figure, that of people being attracted by happiness and plenty but keeping their distance from unhappiness and want. The laughter and weeping to which lines 1 and 2 refer is not necessarily literal, but indicative of happiness and sadness in life. Similarly, the singing and sighing of lines 5 and 6 are intended to signify the expression of joy or sadness, and not to be understood literally; nor do 'the echoes' of line 7 and 8 connote an intelligent agency capable of deliberate response, but rather the tendencies of the world to respond positively to signs of happiness and to shy away from the contrary. The 'nectared wine' of line 15 suggests metaphorically the good and sweet things that happiness has to offer, the 'gall' of line 16 (actually bile, the proverbially bitter fluid contained in the gallbladder) its unpalatable opposite. The food metaphor is continued into the lines that follow, lines 17 and 18, with the proverbial feast-and-famine imagery where people flock to the happy, rich table but shun the need of poverty and sorrow. The final metaphorical device of lines 21 to 24, that of the crowded assembly of wealth and happiness contrasted with the solitariness of pain, rounds off the piece.

The poet makes use of repetition as a recurring device. In lines 1 and 2 she deploys epanalepsis, a poetic device in which the same or closely related words are repeated at or close to the beginning and end of a sentence or clause (in line 1 'laugh'/'laughs', in line 2 'weep'/'weep') for emphasis and to enhance the rhetorical impact of these two key thematic words.

Message

It may feel as though when we are happy, everyone around us is keen to share part of our happiness and good fortune, but that when we are sad people keep their distance. Although there may be some truth in this, and it is human nature to go towards happiness and away from its opposite, still we should remember that being unhappy sometimes changes how we see things. We may feel that people are avoiding us even when they really are not. It can be easy to see our own unhappiness and feelings of isolation as a kind of reflection in others, a projection of the way we feel.

Some people may say that they have 'enough of their own troubles' as a reason not to listen to others' problems. Sometimes this is an excuse: they just do not want to hear someone else's troubles. But it might also be that issues in their own lives mean that they only have enough energy to concentrate on their own difficulties. We can never tell what burden someone might be carrying secretly. But even if one person cannot listen to our problems or help us with them, we should not feel alone and we should not be put off asking someone else. It should always be possible to find somebody who is willing to listen and to help.

Life contains good times and bad. We should try to remember that even if we feel that life is going badly and that we are alone in our unhappiness, things will change eventually. We are not truly alone, and things will get better. We can help things to change for the better more quickly if we speak to family, friends, teachers, counsellors, or other people who can offer us guidance and good advice.

It might be true that everyone experiences unhappiness and loneliness from time to time, but that does not mean that our own experiences do not matter. There is no hierarchy of unhappiness. Just because someone else may be having a worse time than us is no reason why our feelings are less real or less valid. We should never feel bad about feeling bad.

We may be tempted to try to look happy and to hide our sadness and pain when we feel it, especially if we believe that people will not want to be with us and we are afraid that people will keep away. It is understandable that we should try to look cheerful, but we should try not get into the habit of bottling up our negative feelings or hiding them. We run the risk of keeping bigger and ever bigger problems inside us, until they become so big and strong that they overwhelm us. There is a saying that 'sunlight is a great cleanser', meaning that it is usually better to get negative things out into the open and to deal with them. We are stronger with others' help and support.

Lesson plan: 'Solitude' by Ella Wheeler Wilcox

Resources

Copies of the poem — ideally one per pupil, rulers for SEND pupils to follow a line when reading.

Copies of pupils' safety plans to which they can refer throughout the session/lesson.

The lesson will cover oracy and reading skills.

The session can be done at tables or in an unstructured group. The lesson plan is suitable to use with pupils at Upper Key Stage 2, 3 and 4.

Links with the PSHE Association PSHE Education Programme of Study

Links have been made to the PSHE Association PSHE Education Programme of Study at Key Stage 2, 3 and 4 as follows:

KS2

- *H16. about strategies and behaviours that support mental health — including how good quality sleep, physical exercise/time outdoors, being involved in community groups, doing things for others, clubs, and activities, hobbies and spending time with family and friends can support mental health and wellbeing*

KS3

- *H13. the importance of, and strategies for, maintaining a balance between school, work, leisure, exercise, and online activities*

KS4

- *H8. to recognise warning signs of common mental and emotional health concerns (including stress, anxiety and depression), what might trigger them and what help or treatment is available*

Links with the National Curriculum

Links have been made to the National Curriculum for English at Key Stage 2, 3 and 4 as follows:

KS2 (Years 5 and 6) English programme of study
- *maintain attention and participate actively in collaborative conversations, staying on topic and initiating and responding to comments*
- *discuss and evaluate how authors use language, including figurative language, considering the impact on the reader*

KS3 English programme of study

- *participating in formal debates and structured discussions, summarising and/or building on what has been said*

- *knowing how language, including figurative language, vocabulary choice, grammar, text structure and organisational features, presents meaning*

KS4 English programme of study

- *working effectively in groups of different sizes and taking on required roles, including leading and managing discussions, involving others productively, reviewing and summarising, and contributing to meeting goals/deadlines*

- *analysing a writer's choice of vocabulary, form, grammatical and structural features, and evaluating their effectiveness and impact*

Teaching and learning activities

This poem is about the relationship between the individual and the outside world. The title 'Solitude' might make us think it is about loneliness, but it is more about having responsibility for ourselves. It may be necessary with younger pupils to lead them through the poem and to explain some of the more difficult vocabulary to aid understanding. Pupils should be encouraged to annotate the poem as the teacher/therapist goes through each stanza.

- Introduction — share aims of lesson.

- Refer pupils to their safety plans. Remind them of what a safety plan is for. Ask them to read through their own safety plan before they go further and answer any questions they may have.

- Read the poem (or teacher/leader to read it aloud) and talk about the poem, including:

    - The poem is called 'Solitude'. What does this word mean?

    - What is the poem about? Why do you think this?

    - What is the message of the poem?

    - The poem was written a long time ago. How do you know? What clues are there to indicate this?

- Ask pupils to reflect on the word 'solitude'. Where do you find solitude? When do you look for solitude or quiet? Ask for feedback from pupils and record ideas on the whiteboard.

- What is the difference between solitude and loneliness? Ask pupils to discuss this in small groups. The difference is volition — what you want. Solitude is being on your own and that can be enjoyable. Loneliness is what you feel when you are on your own but want to be with other people. It is possible to feel lonely when surrounded by other people if you are not interacting with anyone and you want to. So, solitude can turn into loneliness if you have been okay on your own but start to feel that you need to interact with others. Similarly, loneliness may become easier if you become more at ease away from the company of others. Imagine that Shaila says she is always happy with her own company and does not need others around her. Is this always a good thing? Why might Shaila be saying this? Joe says he feels lonely at home even though he has a big family. Why might this be? Do you have any good advice for Joe?

- Life is full of ups and downs. We all encounter moments of joy and sorrow. Ask pupils to work in pairs or small groups to reflect upon times in their life when this has been the case. What helped you to get through the difficult times? Sometimes you need space. Sometimes you need people.

- Spend a few minutes inviting pupils to share their personal memories of difficult times and happy times with the whole class.
- Review what has been achieved in the lesson.
- Refer pupils to their safety plans as a place to look if they need help after leaving the lesson.

Extension activities

- Pupils to write answers to the questions in the first part of the lesson.
- The poet uses pairs of words to contrast emotions. Ask the pupils to highlight pairs of words in the poem.
- The poet uses personification. Ask pupils to highlight examples and explain their meaning.
- Ask pupils to identify examples of alliteration and rhyming words in the poem.
- Life is a mixture of joy and sorrow. How can we positively use solitude?
- What is the tone of the poem?
- Did you like or dislike the poem? Give reasons for your opinions.
- Pupils to write their own acrostic poems using the word 'solitude' or to write their own poems on either loneliness or solitude.
- In PSHE lessons ask pupils to think about ways they can help others when they are in need.

Cross-curricular/topic links

Cross-curricular and topic links may be explored for use in follow-up and for extension work in

- English
- PSHE

Differentiation

Opportunities for discussion in class, groups, pairs.

Differentiation by outcome e.g. quantity or complexity of issues identified, sophistication of response, level of inclusion/contribution, empathy.

Writing quantity outcomes will be differentiated/assessed/moderated according to teacher's expectations of quantity and depth; otherwise by outcome.

1L

by Paul Morris

Commentary

Friend, there are times I know you feel alone:
But I'll be here for you. Hope's never gone.
Talk to me, friend. The smallest things can make
A change. You're not *alone*: we are *all one*.

Context

'1L' was written for this anthology at the first Christmas following the poet's father's death, a time that prompted him to consider the great difference that even a small amount of sympathetic interaction can make at certain times in our lives and the sense of welcome support that can come from someone inviting us simply to talk, reminding us that we are not alone.

Content

The poem opens with a short, direct address to an unidentified, unknown listener whom the speaker calls 'friend'. The speaker reassures this friend that he is aware that they sometimes feel alone, which we infer to be a source of unhappiness for them, and he immediately assures the friend of his wish to help them.

The speaker tries to offer comfort with the reflection that there is always hope, which is 'never gone'. He reassures the friend that they can talk to him, reflecting that even small things 'can make a change' in life.

The speaker ends with the observation that his friend should not feel isolated, and that we are not alone in life but connected to others.

Composition

The poem consists of a single stanza composed as a rubaʿi, a verse form of Persian origin that is conventionally written as a quatrain with the rhyme scheme AABA or AAAA. '1L' is set in iambic pentameter, following the rubaʿi rhyme scheme AABA, and therefore combines elements of both Eastern and Western poetic traditions.

Neither the narrator nor his (or her) addressee are identified, although the latter is addressed as 'friend', which seems to be intended to be taken either at face value (that is, that the person actually is a friend) or as an indication of the narrator's good intentions towards them.

The language of the poem is direct and unembellished, which accords with both its brevity and the directness of its mode of address. It is a straightforward offer of help, made in persuasive and accessible terms. It is imbued with a sense of urgency which renders it brisk rather than brusque.

Punctuation is conventional, and is applied as it would have been had the piece been expressed as prose.

The piece is remarkable for its inclusion of no less than three masculine caesuras in just four lines — that is, breaks in the verse that follow a stressed syllable, occurring where one phrase ends and the following one begins. They are demarcated by the first full stop in the second line; the full stop in the third line; and the first full stop in the fourth line, following the enjambment from the third line. The effect is to enhance the sense of directness and to lend a brisk, staccato feel to the language — again, one that agrees with the directness of the speaker.

The punning fourth line, in which the narrator states that his friend is 'not *alone*' but that 'we are *all one*', is intended rhetorically rather than humorously. It is this portion of the poem from which the work derives its name. Having said that 'The smallest things can make / A change' the narrator counterpoises *'alone'* with the contradictory, notionally opposite *'all one'* — these being italicised by the poet for emphasis. The conceptual difference between the former and the latter, diametrical opposites, seems immense — the difference between solitude and a sharing sense of inclusion with the rest of humanity. And yet when written down, the two differ by only a single letter: the one L that, when added to the first word 'alone', produces the latter phrase 'all one'. Hence the title '1L' emphasises how little can separate the sense of solitude from that of belonging, and reminds us how large is the difference that apparently small things can make.

Message

The message of the poem is to emphasise how even a brief recognition of our unhappiness, our sense of isolation or loneliness, can make a positive difference.

The feeling that someone understands us and is prepared to listen to us can be extremely comforting and encouraging, as can the assurance that we are part of something bigger than ourselves rather than having to feel remote or separated from others. This can take a lot of support, but sometimes it can require only something very small to make a positive and significant difference to us.

Lesson plan: '1L' by Paul Morris

Resources

Copies of the poem — ideally one per pupil, marker pens, large sheets of flip chart paper, writing paper, pens or pencils, rulers for SEND pupils to follow a line when reading.

Copies of pupils' safety plans to which they can refer throughout the session/lesson.

The lesson will cover oracy, reading and writing skills.

The session can be done at tables or in an unstructured group. The lesson plan is suitable to use with pupils at Upper Key Stage 2, 3 and 4.

Links with the PSHE Association PSHE Education Programme of Study

Links have been made to the PSHE Association PSHE Education Programme of Study at Key Stage 2, 3 and 4 as follows:

KS2

- *H15. that mental health, just like physical health, is part of daily life; the importance of taking care of mental health*
- *H19. a varied vocabulary to use when talking about feelings; about how to express feelings in different ways;*
- *H21. to recognise warning signs about mental health and wellbeing and how to seek support for themselves and others*

KS3

- *H1. how we are all unique; that recognising and demonstrating personal strengths build self-confidence, self-esteem and good health and wellbeing*
- *H2. to understand what can affect wellbeing and resilience (e.g. life changes, relationships, achievements and employment)*
- *H12. how to recognise when they or others need help with their mental health and wellbeing; sources of help and support and strategies for accessing what they need*

KS4

- *H2. how self-confidence self-esteem, and mental health are affected positively and negatively by internal and external influences and ways of managing this*
- *H8. to recognise warning signs of common mental and emotional health concerns (including stress, anxiety and depression), what might trigger them and what help or treatment is available*
- *H10. how to recognise when they or others need help with their mental health and wellbeing; to explore and analyse ethical issues when peers need help; strategies and skills to provide basic support and identify and access the most appropriate sources of help*

Links with the National Curriculum

Links have been made to the National Curriculum for English at Key Stage 2, 3 and 4 as follows:

KS2 (Years 5 and 6) English programme of study

- *maintain attention and participate actively in collaborative conversations, staying on topic and initiating and responding to comments*
- *discuss and evaluate how authors use language, including figurative language, considering the impact on the reader*
- *draft and write by:*

  selecting appropriate grammar and vocabulary, understanding how such choices can change and enhance meaning

KS3 English programme of study

- *participating in formal debates and structured discussions, summarising and/or building on what has been said*
- *knowing how language, including figurative language, vocabulary choice, grammar, text structure and organisational features, presents meaning*
- *applying their growing knowledge of vocabulary, grammar and text structure to their writing and selecting the appropriate form*

KS4 English programme of study

- *listening to and building on the contributions of others, asking questions to clarify and inform, and challenging courteously when necessary*

- *analysing a writer's choice of vocabulary, form, grammatical and structural features, and evaluating their effectiveness and impact*

- *adapting their writing for a wide range of purposes and audiences: to describe, narrate, explain, instruct, give and respond to information, and argue*

Teaching and learning activities

- Introduction — share aims of lesson.

- Refer pupils to their safety plans. Remind them of what a safety plan is for. Ask them to read through their own safety plan before they go further and answer any questions they may have.

- Read the poem (or teacher/leader to read it aloud) and discuss its content.

  Ask key questions:

  - What is the poem about?

  - How does the poem make you feel? How does it do this? Give reasons for your opinions.

  - What is the significance of the title and the words written in italics?

  - Why do you think the poem is so brief?

- Discuss the form and structure of the poem. Pupils to take part in class/group discussion.

- Have you ever felt alone or unhappy? What were the circumstances that led to you feeling like this? Provide prompts if students are struggling to think of an experience e.g. a sibling or family fallout, an issue in school involving another pupil or pupils, not feeling like you fit in, loss of a family member or pet, struggling with exams or schoolwork, being unwell. Pupils to share their experiences in pairs or small groups.

- Groups to discuss ways of dealing with unhappiness. Where can people go for help if they feel low or have a worry or concern? How can these places or people be helpful? Record ideas on flip chart paper.

- Each group to feed back.

- Pupils to draft a short piece about a time they needed help. Were they able to get it? How? If they could not, why was this?

- Review what has been achieved in the lesson. Draw pupils' attention to support that is readily available to help deal with issues that have been identified.

- Refer pupils to their safety plans as a place to look if they need help after leaving the lesson.

Extension activities

- Pupils to write answers to the key questions.

- Pupils to write a short piece about a time when they helped someone who needed it. How did it feel to be able to help someone? Why did it feel like this?

- Pupils to write a short piece on what might stop them from seeking help if they felt they needed it. Consider factors such as not knowing where to go for help, family or peer pressure, embarrassment, pride. Are these good reasons? How can we get over these barriers?

- Circle time activities that focus on a person's positive qualities e.g. kindness, being a good listener, patience.

- Write and produce information booklets, leaflets, posters to signpost help available from services.

- Establish school ambassadors so that pupils have a point of reference if they need to talk to someone about a worry or an issue. Together, draw up a list of guidelines for how those ambassadors will do their job.
- Write a letter to an agony aunt (or agony uncle) about a worry or concern. The agony aunt should think about the concern and write a reply. Write the reply from the agony aunt.
- Establish a worry box or worry wallet in the classroom or setting. Pupils post their worries and these are addressed by the teacher.

Cross-curricular/topic links

Cross-curricular and topic links may be explored for use in follow-up and for extension work in

- English
- PSHE
- Art and Design

Differentiation

Opportunities for discussion in class, groups, pairs.

Differentiation by outcome e.g. quantity or complexity of issues identified, sophistication of response, level of inclusion/contribution, empathy.

Writing quantity outcomes will be differentiated/assessed/moderated according to teacher's expectations of quantity and depth; otherwise by outcome.

Differentiation may also be through key words rather than written sentences, or through artwork as a means of expression.

Count That Day Lost

by George Eliot

Commentary

If you sit down at set of sun
And count the acts that you have done,
And, counting, find
One self-denying deed, one word
That eased the heart of him who heard,
One glance most kind
That fell like sunshine where it went —
Then you may count that day well spent.

But if, through all the livelong day,
You've cheered no heart, by yea or nay —
If, through it all
You've nothing done that you can trace
That brought the sunshine to one face —
No act most small
That helped some soul and nothing cost —
Then count that day as worse than lost.

Context

George Eliot is the pen-name assumed by Mary Anne Evans, an English poet, novelist, poet, journalist and translator whose work chiefly came to prominence in the third quarter of the nineteenth century. She is celebrated as one of the leading writers of the Victorian era, and her novel *Middlemarch*, first published in eight instalments between 1871 and 1872, has been described as the greatest novel in the English language.

Evans was provided with an education that was not often afforded to women at the time. She attended a boarding school between the ages of five and nine with her older sister Christiana, moving on to two other schools in the English Midlands from ages nine to thirteen and then thirteen to sixteen. After the age of sixteen she had little formal education. But thanks to her father's position as estate manager of Arbury Hall in Warwickshire she was allowed access to the library of a great country house, a privilege which helped her to extend her own learning and the breadth of her reading. Her visits to the wealthy estate also stimulated her awareness of the contrast between the wealth of landowning gentry and the lives of the often much poorer estate workers, and the theme of such parallel lives later recurred in much of her fiction.

Evans's early life was influenced by her family's Anglican religion, and she was exposed to other denominations of Christianity during her school days. However, in her twenties she began to question her religious faith, though she continued to attend church with her father for whom she kept house until his death in 1849. She would go on to reject religious belief completely.

It was during the nine years that Evans was keeping house for her father at Foleshill, near Coventry, that she began a close friendship with Charles and Cara Bray, free thinkers whose home, Rosehill, was a meeting-place for people with radical views. There she met luminaries such as Robert Owen, Herbert Spencer, Harriet Martineau and Ralph Waldo Emerson. Through this connection, Charles Bray agreed to publish some of Evans's earliest writing, including reviews, in his newspaper *The Coventry Herald and Observer*.

A mere five days after her father's funeral Evans, then 30 years old, travelled to Switzerland with the Brays. On her return to England in 1850, Evans (who was now calling herself Marian rather than Mary Ann) moved to London, determined to become a writer. She stayed at the house of John Chapman, a radical publisher who had published her first major literary work — an English translation of Strauss's *The Life of Jesus* — in 1846. He had recently acquired *The Westminster Review*, a left-wing journal. Evans joined its staff and was appointed as its assistant editor the following year. Though women writers were no longer uncommon, this role of editor of a literary magazine was an unusual achievement for a woman.

Evans's journalistic writing was filled with comments on her views of Victorian society and social thought, expressing sympathy for the 'lower classes' and criticising organised religion, at odds with the widely held beliefs of the time.

Although female authors were published under their own names during Evans's lifetime, her adoption of the masculine nom de plume George Eliot for her fiction and poetry appears to have resulted from her wish to break free of the stereotype of women's writing being limited to insubstantial romances, and also to encourage her fiction to be considered separately from her widely known work as editor and critic. She may also have wanted to put some distance between her increasingly controversial, if not scandalous, private life (she was having an affair with a married man at the time) and the court of public opinion.

Evans produced seven novels between 1859 and 1876. Though she is perhaps better known as a novelist than a poet, it is worthy of note that her first publication was in fact a poem, 'Knowing That Shortly I Must Put Off This Tabernacle', which appeared in *The Christian Observer* when Evans was 20 years old. 'Count That Day Lost' dates from the end of her writing career: it was first published posthumously in 1887, one of the last of Evans's works to see the new light of day.

Content

The speaker describes a situation in which we sit down in the evening (line 1) and take stock of the things we have done that day (line 2). She says that if we find that we have done one selfless thing that has helped somebody (lines 4 to 5), or even looked at someone in a way that brightened their day (lines 6 to 7), then we can think of the day as having been spent well (line 8). Even in these small acts we have done some good.

However, if throughout that day we have done nothing to cheer someone, even by the smallest 'yes' or 'no' (lines 9 to 10), and if we can find nothing we have done to make anyone smile (lines 11 to 13), even the tiniest thing that cost us nothing but still helped someone (lines 14 to 15), then the day is worse than lost (line 16).

The value of a day — whether it has been spent well or has had no value — is to be measured not by what we have done for ourselves but by what we have done to make things better for others. Our significance lies not only in what we are to ourselves, but in the difference our lives make to the lives of the people with whom we have even the smallest interaction.

Composition

'Count That Day Lost' is an epistolary poem, addressing the reader directly and giving advice or guidance. It is composed in two rhymed octets or octaves, stanzas of eight lines having the rhyme scheme AABCCBDD, with the rhymes changing between the two stanzas. Pairs of lines each of eight syllables are separated by single lines of four syllables, making each stanza syllabically 8, 8, 4, 8, 8, 4, 8, 8.

The first stanza is concerned with what one might do to behave positively towards others in order to have, in the poet's estimation, spent the day well; whilst the second stanza addresses how by failing to do even a little good for others one will have 'lost' the day.

Being intended to address the reader directly, the poem's language is generally relatively straight-forward. However, it is somewhat archaic (or perhaps archaising) and this presents some vocabulary that may be unfamiliar to the young reader: 'set of sun' (= 'sunset', line 1), 'self-denying' (= 'selfless' or 'self-sacrificing', line 4), 'livelong' (= 'entire' or 'whole', line 9), 'yea' (= 'yes', line 10), 'nay' (= 'no', line 10). The archaic feel of the language is particularly apparent in syntactical inversions in formulations such as 'One glance most kind' (line 6) instead of the more familiar 'one very kind glance'; 'You've nothing done' (line 12) instead of 'you've done nothing'; 'No act most small' (line 14) instead of 'no tiny act'; and 'nothing cost' (line 15) instead of 'cost nothing'.

The poet makes repeated use of the words 'count' or 'counting', which appear in lines 2, 3, 8 and 16. This is a poem that is concerned with keeping tally of one's actions, of accounting for oneself and being accountable for the quality of one's actions in relation to others. The repetition of certain words in both stanzas, such as 'heart' (lines 5 and 10) and 'sunshine' (lines 7 and 13) help to create the effect of reflection between the two stanzas, the well-spent day and the 'lost' day.

The use of figurative language is restrained. However, the chief example is quite ingenious. In the first stanza there is the simile of the glance that 'fell like sunshine' (line 8), and the poet redeploys the noun in a metaphorical setting in the second stanza, 'brought the sunshine to one face' (line 13).

Significantly, we should note that the poet's emphasis is very much on the reader and their actions. The word 'you' (appearing too in the abbreviation 'you've') appears no fewer than six times in sixteen lines. This emphasises the distinctly personal nature of the reader's responsibility: to be an individual who is responsible for their own actions and their relationship to the good they should (in the poet's estimation) do for others. Doing good may be a general responsibility, but we are each alone in our accountability for our deeds.

Message

We are encouraged to reflect on what we have done each day and what, if anything, we have done for others. It may not be enough merely to have done no harm: we are encouraged to do positive good.

We may feel that as individuals we can do little or nothing to make the world a better place. But sometimes the smallest and simplest things — a word, a gesture, even a look — can make a genuine difference for good and change somebody's day for the better. These actions may be tiny, costing nothing and requiring no real effort except the will to do good for others and be kind to them. If we do not do these little things then in fact we may find ourselves feeling that we have let ourselves down simply because we have missed the chance to do something positive in the world.

At times when we feel alone, or when we feel as though nobody does much to help us, the sense that we have tried to help others even in the smallest ways can make us feel positive about ourselves. It can give us a feeling that we are not alone but are immersed in a world filled with people who share the same sorts of thoughts and feelings that we have, and this can help us to feel less alone and more connected.

Lesson plan: 'Count That Day Lost' by George Eliot

Resources

Copies of the poem — ideally one per pupil, pens and pencils, plain or lined paper, rulers for SEND pupils to follow a line when reading.

Copies of pupils' safety plans to which they can refer throughout the session/lesson.

The lesson will cover oracy and reading skills.

The session can be done in the round, or as a circle time activity, or at tables, or in an unstructured group. The lesson plan is suitable to use with pupils at Upper Key Stage 2, 3 and 4.

Links with the PSHE Association PSHE Education Programme of Study

Links have been made to the PSHE Association PSHE Education Programme of Study at Key Stage 2, 3 and 4 as follows:

KS2

- *H18. about everyday things that affect feelings and the importance of expressing feelings*
- *R11. what constitutes a positive healthy friendship (e.g. mutual respect, trust, truthfulness, loyalty, kindness, generosity, sharing interests and experiences, support with problems and difficulties); that the same principles apply to online friendships as to face-to-face relationships*

KS3

- *H2. to understand what can affect wellbeing and resilience (e.g. life changes, relationships, achievements and employment)*
- *R14. the qualities and behaviours they should expect and exhibit in a wide variety of positive relationships (including in school and wider society, family and friendships, including online)*

KS4

- *H2. how self-confidence self-esteem, and mental health are affected positively and negatively by internal and external influences and ways of managing this*
- *H8. to recognise warning signs of common mental and emotional health concerns (including stress, anxiety and depression), what might trigger them and what help or treatment is available*

Links with the National Curriculum

Links have been made to the National Curriculum for English at Key Stage 2, 3 and 4 as follows:

KS2 (Years 5 and 6) English programme of study

- *maintain attention and participate actively in collaborative conversations, staying on topic and initiating and responding to comments*
- *discuss and evaluate how authors use language, including figurative language, considering the impact on the reader*
- *provide reasoned justifications for their views*

KS3 English programme of study

- *participating in formal debates and structured discussions, summarising and/or building on what has been said*
- *knowing how language, including figurative language, vocabulary choice, grammar, text structure and organisational features, presents meaning*

KS4 English programme of study

- *working effectively in groups of different sizes and taking on required roles, including leading and managing discussions, involving others productively, reviewing and summarising, and contributing to meeting goals/deadlines*
- *analysing a writer's choice of vocabulary, form, grammatical and structural features, and evaluating their effectiveness and impact*

Teaching and learning activities

This poem has an important message which will need to be unpicked through shared discussion: that life without helping others around you is worthless and isolating. Only if you do good deeds for the community do you 'gain' the day. If you do not do anything good or say anything kind to others around you, or help them in some way however small, then the day is wasted and you have missed the opportunity to make the world a little better for others and yourself.

- Introduction — share aims of lesson.
- Refer pupils to their safety plans. Remind them of what a safety plan is for. Ask them to read through their own safety plan before they go further and answer any questions they may have.
- Read the poem (or teacher/leader to read it aloud) and discuss its content. Ask the following key questions:
  - What is this poem about?
  - What is it about doing good for others that might make you feel less alone, more connected, and better about yourself?
  - What does the speaker consider a 'day well spent'?
  - What does the speaker consider a day 'worse than lost'?
  - What are the messages of the poem?
- With a talk partner discuss whether you agree with the messages of the poem. Give reasons for your opinions.
- Talk partners briefly feed back to the rest of the group.
- What, for you, is a good day? Each pupil to write a few lines about it.
- What, for you, is a bad day? Each pupil to write a few lines about it.
- What can you or others do to help make a day feel better? Consider this in terms of it being better for others and being better for yourself.
- Discuss how people's moods can be affected by what others say and do. A kind word or a smile can bring about a difference. Why do you think this is? An unkind word or a

thoughtless remark can equally have a big effect. Why is this? Present the following table to pupils and ask them to work with a friend to complete it with their own examples. First work through the examples in the table to ensure that they are clear about what they must do.

Action	Before	After
I offered a classmate some extra help with their maths.	She was unsure what to do and lacked confidence.	She knew what to do. She felt much better about her maths work. She didn't feel worried anymore. I felt good for helping.
I listened to my friend talking to me about something he was worried about in class.	He felt anxious and worried. He could not concentrate or learn properly.	He felt much happier. He had some advice and suggestions to think about. He felt like somebody cared. I was glad to have been able to make a difference.

- Take feedback and comments from pupils.
- Review what has been achieved in the lesson.
- Refer pupils to their safety plans as a place to look if they need help after leaving the lesson.

Extension activities

- Pupils to write their answers to the key questions.
- Write about the rhyme scheme, structure and language of the poem.
- Find out more about the historical context of the poet's time and why women writers often wrote under a male pseudonym.
- For older pupils, discuss the pressures people feel not to do something because of their sex, skin colour, religion, age or other personal characteristics.
- What did you like and dislike about the poem? Why did you think this? Give reasons for your opinions.
- Look up the meaning of some of the words and phrases in the poem e.g. 'One self-denying deed'.
- Write a short poem on the same theme as 'Count That Day Lost'.
- Somebody suggests that you should live by the principle 'commit random acts of kindness everyday'. Discuss or write about how this might be a good thing or a bad thing and how you could achieve it . What would be the barriers to the success of this principle? What might a society be like where everybody lived by this principle?

Cross-curricular/topic links

Cross-curricular and topic links may be explored for use in follow-up and for extension work in

- English
- PSHE
- History

Differentiation

Opportunities for discussion in mixed ability pairs.

Differentiation by outcome e.g. quantity or complexity of issues identified, sophistication of response, level of inclusion/contribution, empathy.

Losing and Remembering

This section is about losing, mourning
and remembering...

Do Not Stand at my Grave and Weep

by Mary Frye

Commentary

Do not stand at my grave and weep;
I am not there. I do not sleep.
I am a thousand winds that blow.
I am the diamond glints on snow.
I am the sunlight on ripened grain,
I am the gentle autumn rain.

When you awaken in the morning's hush,
I am the swift uplifting rush
Of quiet birds in circled flight.
I am the soft stars that shine at night.
Do not stand at my grave and cry;
I am not there. I did not die.

Context

'Do Not Stand at my Grave and Weep' was originally composed, it is said, on a brown paper shopping bag. This might seem an unusual choice of writing medium for a poet, but Mary Frye was a florist by profession.

Born in Dayton, Ohio, Mary was orphaned at the age of three. She grew to become a keen reader with an extraordinary memory.

'Do Not Stand at my Grave and Weep' was written in 1932. Mary reportedly composed the poem, the only one of her works to have received significant public notice, when a young Jewish girl from Germany, Margaret Schwarzkopf, was staying with the Frye family. Margaret's mother was ill in Germany, but as antisemitic unrest was increasing in that country it was feared that Margaret might be imprisoned or killed if she returned to visit her. Sadly Margaret's mother died and her daughter's devastation, heightened by the fact that she had been unable to see or talk to her mother before she passed away, touched Mary Frye (who, it should be remembered, had lost her own parents in early childhood) very deeply. One day Mary, finding that the words of the poem 'just came to her' (as she described it) seemingly unbidden, took a brown paper shopping bag and wrote down twelve lines of verse which, at first, were untitled.

Though the poet never published her poem, Mary made numerous copies for private circulation and many people found consolation in the piece. In time the poem became widely known, being written on thousands of bereavement cards and becoming a standard work to be read aloud at funerals. The work became known all over the English-speaking world and in 1996 won recognition as 'The Nation's Favourite Poem' in the United Kingdom.

For many years the poem's origins were forgotten. Then in the late 1990s Mary Frye, who was by then in her late nineties, came forward to claim authorship, and poem and poet were reunited in the public imagination.

Content

The poem's speaker is the voice of a person who has died, addressing someone they have left behind in life. It is not necessary to imagine this as a supernatural conversation, but rather as gentle words of comfort spoken to the imagination of the bereaved person.

The speaker asks the listener not to stand crying by their grave because that is not where they are (lines 1 and 2). The speaker is to be found in the wind (line 3), in the sparkle of light on snow (line 4), in the sunlight shining on a field of ripe grain (line 5), and in the gentle rain of autumn (line 6). In these quiet natural things the bereaved listener will find something of the life-force of the speaker.

The speaker says that when the listener awakes in the still of the morning (line 7), they are to be found in the quick rising flight of quiet birds circling (lines 8 and 9). The speaker is in the stars that shine in the night sky (line 10). The bereaved listener should not cry by the speaker's grave (line 11) because they are not really there, and they are not truly dead (line 12).

The living essence of the speaker can be found in all these beautiful elements of nature, and whilst this is so they are not really gone from the world.

Composition

'Do Not Stand at my Grave and Weep' is written in two stanzas, each of which is a sestet (that is, a verse of six lines) composed of three rhyming couplets in iambic tetrameter with the rhyme scheme AABBCC.

The language of the poem is formal but uncomplicated. The vocabulary is easily accessible, respectful and gentle. These are features of the writing which may have contributed considerably to the poem's extraordinary popular appeal.

The use of punctuation is unobtrusive and serves to divide the text into sentences or clauses that rarely exceed a single line's length, the only exception being the easy-flowing enjambment between lines 8 and 9.

The poet makes use of anaphora in the repeated 'I am' that opens lines 2, 3, 4, 5, 6, 8, 10 and 12. The effect of this is a quietly persistent reiteration of the speaker's continuing existence, of their presence not only throughout the poem but throughout the natural phenomena it describes — wind, light, reflection, rain, the movement of living things. It is the living who are able to say 'I am', and the speaker is softly, insistently reassuring us that those who appear to have gone from life are still very much part of it.

The extent to which figurative language can be observed in the poem depends very much upon the reader's viewpoint. If the reader takes the philosophical view that people who have passed away are literally still present in the natural world around us, then it might be said that there is no figurative language at all in the piece. If, however, the reader believes that it is more a case of our seeing things in nature that remind us of some characteristic of someone who has passed away, some sense or aspect of them that is shared with what we observe, then for that reader the poem is clearly interwoven throughout with an opulent tapestry of metaphor and personification, in the rich evocation of all the things 'I am'.

Message

The message of the poem is that people who have passed away are in some ways still with us. Whether we believe that the person literally remains with us in spirit, or that we can still see some aspects of their character reflected in the world around us, we are not entirely without them.

Our imaginations can help to evoke not only the memory of the person who has gone, but also some sense of what it felt like for us to have them with us.

A person's life is more than simply where they stand or how they look or what they say. It is about all the good things they leave with us, the lessons their life has taught us, the good example they have shown. Even when our relationship with the person has had its problems, we can still come to a kind of peace and acceptance through the power of understanding and imagination.

Whenever we see something that reminds us of the person we have lost, then they are not truly gone from our lives. They have stopped growing old or getting sick or having any of the problems that the rest of us experience, and we can think of them as having become a part of something greater. We carry them with us forever in our hearts and minds, and they remain as much a part of us as we are of the natural world around us.

Lesson plan: 'Do Not Stand at my Grave and Weep' by Mary Frye

Resources

Copies of the poem — ideally one per pupil, pens and pencils, Plain or lined paper, rulers for SEND pupils to follow a line when reading.

Copies of pupils' safety plans to which they can refer throughout the session/lesson.

The lesson will cover oracy, reading and writing skills.

The session can be done in the round, or as a circle time activity, or at tables, or in an unstructured group. It is suitable for Upper Key Stage 2, 3 and 4.

Links with the PSHE Association PSHE Education Programme of Study

The learning opportunities below are not covered by the DfE statutory guidance: Health Education and Relationships Education/RSE but they form part of a broader programme for schools when they are covering work on bereavement.

Links have been made to the PSHE Association Programme of Study for PSHE Education at Key Stage 2, 3 and 4 as follows:

KS2

- H23. *about change and loss, including death, and how these can affect feelings; ways of expressing and managing grief and bereavement*

KS3

- *R22. the effects of change, including loss, separation, divorce and bereavement; strategies for managing these and accessing support*

KS4

- *R13. ways to manage grief about changing relationships including the impact of separation, divorce and bereavement; sources of support and how to access them*

Links with the National Curriculum

Links have been made to the National Curriculum for English at Key Stage 2, 3 and 4 as follows:

KS2 (Years 5 and 6) English programme of study
- *maintain attention and participate actively in collaborative conversations, staying on topic and initiating and responding to comments*
- *discuss and evaluate how authors use language, including figurative language, considering the impact on the reader*
- *provide reasoned justifications for their views*

KS3 English programme of study
- *participating in formal debates and structured discussions, summarising and/or building on what has been said*
- *knowing how language, including figurative language, vocabulary choice, grammar, text structure and organisational features, presents meaning*

KS4 English programme of study
- *listening to and building on the contributions of others, asking questions to clarify and inform, and challenging courteously when necessary*
- *analysing a writer's choice of vocabulary, form, grammatical and structural features, and evaluating their effectiveness and impact*
- *make an informed personal response, recognising that other responses to a text are possible and evaluating these*

Teaching and learning activities

This is a strong poem for discussion about remembrance and loss because it is in the form of a monologue which is relatable and easy to follow. The emotions are deep but expressed in accessible terms.

- Introduction — share aims of lesson.
- Refer pupils to their safety plans. Remind them of what a safety plan is for. Ask them to read through their own safety plan before they go further and answer any questions they may have.
- Read the poem (or teacher/leader to read it aloud) and discuss its content. Ask the following key questions:
  - What is the poem about? How do you know? Working in pairs ask pupils to spend some time talking about it. Take feedback.
  - Who is the voice of the poem? Why do you think this? Invite answers from pupils.
  - What is the tone of the poem?
  - What is the theme of the poem?

- The words 'I am' are repeated throughout the poem. Why do you think the poet has done this?
- Discuss the use of alliteration, imagery and metaphor in the poem.
- Discuss the rhyme scheme — twelve lines of rhyming couplets.
- There are short statements in the first six lines. How does this affect the pace of the poem?
- Identify any words or phrases with which pupils are unfamiliar. Can pupils think of any more familiar words the poet might have used in place of the unfamiliar ones?
- How does the poem make you feel? How does the language make you feel this way? Working in pairs ask pupils to spend a few minutes reflecting on this.
- Divide the class into small groups and introduce the two case studies below. Ask each group to say how they could be a good friend to the people in each of the case studies, and what they could say or do to support their two friends who have lost someone they loved very much.
    - A boy in your class, Charlie, recently lost his younger sister in a tragic car accident.
    - Zainab came to school today feeling terribly upset because her dog had to be put down last evening.
- Take feedback from each group.
- Review what has been achieved in the lesson.
- Refer pupils to their safety plans as a place to look if they need help after leaving the lesson.

Extension activities

- Pupils to write responses to the questions in the teaching and learning section.
- Did you like the poem? Why do you think this? Give reasons for your opinions.
- Research Mary Frye. What can you find out about her life, and when and why she wrote the poem?
- Write a short biography of Mary Frye's life.
- Pupils to paint, draw or produce collages of a beautiful idyllic place to help the pupil remember someone or something (for example a pet) they have lost and to think of him/her in a beautiful surrounding.
- Pupils to write about their own personal experience of loss and how it made them feel.
- Create a memory tree for someone or something you have lost. At the centre of the branches is the picture or name of the person/object. Along each branch record a different way in which you remember him/her/it, the details you remember, and how it makes you feel to think about this person or thing. Pupils can design their own tree and put on as many or as few branches as they wish.
- Produce a collage memory board. Pupils can bring photographs and images along with 'I remember...' statements about their loved one. This can help to bring solace and comfort.
- Write a letter to someone and tell him/her about the person who died and the things you miss most.

Cross-curricular/topic links

Cross-curricular and topic links may be explored for use in follow-up and for extension work in

- English
- PSHE

- History
- Art and Design

Differentiation

Opportunities for discussion in mixed ability pairs.

Differentiation by outcome e.g. quantity or complexity of issues identified, sophistication of response, level of inclusion/contribution, empathy.

Writing quantity outcomes will be differentiated/assessed/moderated according to teacher's expectations of quantity and depth; otherwise by outcome.

Differentiation may also be through key words rather than written sentences, or through artwork as a means of expression.

The mistake upon me
by Aya Ahmad

Commentary

To those whose lives have been marked by
the political decisions of previous generations.

A.A.

The mistake upon me
The impact upon me
The unconscious act
The inalterable event

The unforgettable date

The good deal for them
The mistake for me
The new life for them
The murder of my generation

The belief
The desire:
That hope will progress as we progress.

Context

Aya Ahmad's earliest poetry was written in Syria, the country from which she and her Kurdish family escaped war and oppression in the mid-2010s. Her talent as an English language writer developed swiftly, being recognised in 2017 and 2018 with prizes in Manchester's Portico Sadie Massey Awards for Young Readers and Writers.

'The mistake upon me' was written in 2018 and is among Aya's earlier poetical works in the English language.

Like much of Aya's work, 'The mistake upon me' is rooted in the poet's experience of war and the effects it wreaks on those whose lives are changed profoundly by conflict.

Content

'The mistake upon me' is written in two distinct parts: a dedication, which the poet specified should form an essential element of the work, and the body of the poem itself.

The dedication suggests that the victims of wrong mentioned in the poem are what it terms 'those whose lives have been marked by the political decisions of previous generations'. It is signed with the poet's initials.

The poem refers to an unidentified 'mistake' and an unspecified 'impact' of which the speaker is, or has been, the object. This may be the 'act' or 'event' which are described in the following two lines as 'unconscious' and 'inalterable'. The speaker gives the reader no details about the nature of the act/event, nor its/their effects. We are left to speculate (informed by the dedication) that these are political acts, the consequences of which may not have been foreseen by those who did them but which nevertheless have changed the speaker's life. It is clear that whatever they are, she has found them significant, powerful, or even epochal.

The speaker mentions a date which is 'unforgettable', though the reasons for this, and its relationship (if any) to the act/event, remain unclear. Again, we may infer from the dedication that the date refers to a politically significant event.

We are told of a 'deal' which has been 'good' for an unidentified 'them', but which has been a 'mistake' for the speaker. Again, the precise nature of this transaction is not elucidated, though she goes on to state that there has been a 'new life' for these unspecified others, whilst her own generation has suffered 'murder'.

Overall, and informed by the dedication, we are left to infer that the poem refers to decisions, probably political or social in nature, that have been made at some notable point by people of generations previous to that of the speaker. Those decisions were good for them, but have been the cause of harm and unhappiness for the speaker and those of later generations, including the deaths of others of the speaker's generation.

As the dedication is signed with the poet's initials, we may identify her as the voice within the poem. It is therefore likely that the events to which she is referring are those political upheavals that occurred in her family's native Syria, as a result of which the poet first came to the United Kingdom after she and her family experienced the estrangement of leaving their homeland and the personal loss which such forced exile brings.

Though the speaker and her generation have clearly suffered as a result of various events and the actions of others, the tone of the final stanza is positive: a hope that as people 'progress', so there will be greater cause of hope for the world.

Composition

'The mistake upon me' is an unusual work with some complex poetic features.

The opening dedication is a prose couplet which appears to be intended to disambiguate the poem that follows, but only to the extent of rooting its references in a political context. The dedication is signed with the poet's initials, which indicates the personal nature of the message and probably identifies her as the poem's speaker.

The verse phase of the poem consists of four stanzas: the first a quatrain; the second a single line; the third another quatrain; and the fourth a tercet.

The poet does not employ rhyme or regular metre. Line lengths are short and punchy, emphasising the poet's directness of address. This effect of directness is further supported by the straightforward vocabulary she uses, and by the absence of figurative language.

A remarkable feature of the poem is the repeated use of the definite article to begin all but the final line. This lends a sense of weight to the events the speaker describes, locating them in her lived experience even if they are outside the reader's and reinforcing our impression of the personal nature of the writing.

Similarly, the poet uses simple language to high effect in deploying the repetition of personal pronouns to establish a sense of differing identity within the poem — a 'them and us/me' of those who have made the harmful decisions and those who have suffered the consequences.

Punctuation is almost absent from the text. There is a full stop to signify the end of the dedication, and another to mark the end of the poem, but otherwise there is only one mark — the colon at the conclusion of the penultimate line that sets up the poem's final note of hope. This gives the work an inexorable sense of movement, unhindered by stops or pauses.

There is an almost tidal shifting of sense within the stanzas. In the first stanza, the first two lines refer to the speaker, whilst the next to shift focus to depersonalised acts/events. This depersonalisation is carried forward in the single line of the second stanza. The third stanza alternates allusions to the culpable 'them' with references to the speaker and her generation. The final stanza seems redemptive, taking a possibly passive 'belief' to an active 'desire', and locating it in the ability of people (this time identified as a unified 'we' rather than the earlier 'them and us/me' duality) to achieve progress.

Message

'The mistake upon me' concerns itself with the effects on young people of the actions and decisions of older ones. Though the poet has couched this in terms of politics, the principle is applicable to all sorts of decisions that older people make which affect younger generations.

People very often make decisions that are good for them, without thinking through the consequences for others of their actions. Changes that are imposed upon others may be surprisingly negative for them, lending those changes a stark broader significance.

We should do our best to think through how our decisions might affect others, and to avoid doing things that might be good for us but harmful to others. Yet even if negative consequences do result from others' decisions, we should not lose sight of the belief and hope that things can, with the belief and desire to achieve it, be better.

Lesson plan: 'The mistake upon me' by Aya Ahmad

Resources

Copies of the poem — ideally one per pupil, pens and pencils or marker pens, rulers for SEND pupils to follow a line when reading.

Copies of pupils' safety plans to which they can refer throughout the session/lesson.

The lesson will cover oracy and reading skills.

The session can be done in the round, or as a circle time activity, or at tables, or in an unstructured group. It is suitable for Upper Key Stage 2, 3 and 4.

Links with the PSHE Association PSHE Education Programme of Study

The learning opportunities below are not covered by the draft DfE statutory guidance: Health Education and Relationships Education/RSE but they form part of a broader programme for schools when they are covering work on loss.

Links have been made to the PSHE Association PSHE Education Programme of Study at Key Stage 2, 3 and 4 as follows:

KS2

- *H23. about change and loss, including death, and how these can affect feelings; ways of expressing and managing grief and bereavement*
- *H36. strategies to manage transitions between classes and key stages*

KS3

- *R22. the effects of change, including loss, separation, divorce and bereavement; strategies for managing these and accessing support*

KS4

- *R13. ways to manage grief about changing relationships including the impact of separation, divorce and bereavement; sources of support and how to access them*

Links with the National Curriculum

Links have been made to the National Curriculum for English at Key Stage 2, 3 and 4 as follows:

KS2 (Years 5 and 6) English programme of study
- *discuss and evaluate how authors use language, including figurative language, considering the impact on the reader*
- *provide reasoned justifications for their views*

KS3 English programme of study
- *participating in structured discussions, summarising and/or building on what has been said*
- *knowing how language, including figurative language, vocabulary choice, grammar, text structure and organisational features, presents meaning*

KS4 English programme of study
- *analysing a writer's choice of vocabulary, form, grammatical and structural features, and evaluating their effectiveness and impact*
- *make an informed personal response, recognising that other responses to a text are possible and evaluating these*

Teaching and learning activities

This is a good poem for discussion about loss and the consequences of one's decisions. It is open to wide interpretation and personalisation, and is a strong backdrop onto which to project one's own experiences and feelings.

- Introduction — share aims of lesson.
- Refer pupils to their safety plans. Remind them of what a safety plan is for. Ask them to read through their own safety plan before they go further and answer any questions they may have.
- Read the poem (or teacher/leader to read it aloud) and discuss its content.
  Ask the following key question:
  - What do you think the poem is about? Working in pairs or small groups ask pupils to spend some time talking about it.
- Take feedback.
- Why do you think the poem is called 'The mistake upon me'? What mistake do you think has taken place? Why do you think this is important to the poet? Discuss in pairs or small groups.
- Take feedback.
- Personal pronouns 'me' and 'them' are used several times in the poem. How does this create a sense of difference?
- What is the tone of the poem? Does it change later in the poem?
- What do you understand by the line 'The unconscious act'?
- Why do you think the line 'The unforgettable date' stands alone in the poem? What is the effect of this unknown milestone upon the reader?
- Discuss how your decisions can have unforeseen consequences for others. Has an older person ever made a decision that affected you in ways that they did not foresee, or that seemed good for them but bad for you? How do you think those bad effects could have been avoided? Explore this in discussion.
- Ask for feedback.
- Review what has been achieved in the lesson.
- Refer pupils to their safety plans as a place to look if they need help after leaving the lesson.

Extension activities

- Did you like or dislike Aya's poem? Why do you think this? Give reasons for your opinion.
- What is the message of the poem?
- Discuss in pairs and small groups how this poem made you feel and why.
- Ask pupils to write their own poems in the style of Aya's poem. Ask pupils to replace the words in bold for alternative synonyms. Pupils may use a thesaurus to find alternative words.

The **mistake** upon me

The **mistake** upon me
The **impact** upon me
The unconscious **act**
The **inalterable** event

The **unforgettable** date

The **good deal** for them
The **mistake** for me
The **new** life for them
The **murder** of my **generation**

The **belief**
The **desire**:
That hope will **progress** as we **progress**.

- Ask pupils to read one another's poems. Have pupils used effective synonyms in their poems? Peers to review each other's poems.
- Pupils to read out their poems in class or in small groups.
- Ask pupils to illustrate their poems. Poems could be displayed in the classroom or in a class book.
- Pupils to produce artwork to accompany their poems. The pictures may be drawn or painted.
- Pupils to write their own poems about one of the following: upheaval, loss of identity, loss of personal freedom, personal loss, the effects of someone else's decision upon us.

Cross-curricular/topic links

Cross-curricular and topic links may be explored for use in follow-up and for extension work in

- English
- Drama
- PSHE
- Art and Design

Differentiation

Opportunities for discussion in mixed ability pairs.

Differentiation by outcome e.g. quantity or complexity of issues identified, sophistication of response, level of inclusion/contribution, empathy.

Writing quantity outcomes will be differentiated/assessed/moderated according to teacher's expectations of quantity and depth; otherwise by outcome.

Differentiation may also be through artwork as a means of expression.

The Wind on the Downs

by Marian Allen

Commentary

I like to think of you as brown and tall,
As strong and living as you used to be,
In khaki tunic, Sam Brown belt and all,
And standing there and laughing down at me.
Because they tell me, dear, that you are dead,
Because I can no longer see your face,
You have not died, it is not true, instead
You seek adventure in some other place.
That you are round about me, I believe;
I hear you laughing as you used to do,
Yet loving all the things I think of you;
And knowing you are happy, should I grieve?
You follow and are watchful where I go;
How should you leave me, having loved me so?
We walked along the towpath, you and I,
Beside the sluggish-moving, still canal;
It seemed impossible that you should die;
I think of you the same and always shall.
We thought of many things and spoke of few,
And life lay all uncertainly before,
And now I walk alone and think of you,
And wonder what new kingdoms you explore.
Over the railway line, across the grass,
While up above the golden wings are spread,
Flying, ever flying overhead,
Here still I see your khaki figure pass,
And when I leave the meadow, almost wait,
That you should open first the wooden gate.

Context

'The Wind on the Downs' was written in 1917 by Marian Allen (full name Eleanor Marian Dundas Allen), a British writer who was born in 1892 in Sydney, Australia. By 1908 she and her family had moved to England and were living in Oxford where, in 1913 or 1914, Marian met Arthur Tylston Greg, an Oxford University law student to whom she became engaged. At the outbreak of World War I in 1914, Arthur took a commission as a second lieutenant in the 3rd Cheshire Regiment. After seven months at the front, he was seriously wounded in May 1915. However, Arthur then joined the Royal Flying Corps and returned to the war. He was killed in action at the controls of his aircraft in April 1917, just two months after graduating as a pilot with the rank of captain. He was twenty-two years old.

Marian finished writing her poem 'The Wind on the Downs' on 10th May 1917, just a few days after receiving the news of her fiancé's death. Indeed she poured her grief into her poetry writing. The poem first appeared in the eponymous sixty-three-page collection of poetry that Marian published in 1918, which was dedicated 'To A.T.G.'.

Marian continued to write poetry in remembrance of her lost fiancé for many years after his death, and went on to become a successful children's author and illustrator. She never married.

Content

Though its rawness is mitigated by the gentleness of the poet's writing style, 'The Wind on the Downs' is a work that is filled with the agony and incredulity of new and devastating loss.

The poem is autobiographical, and there is no doubt that the speaker is intended to be the poet herself and the 'you' to whom she speaks her recently deceased fiancé, Arthur.

In the first half of the poem, the poet seems to be trying to come to terms with the unthinkable fact of her fiancé's death. She addresses him directly, describing him as she remembers him when he was alive, wearing the uniform and leather 'Sam Brown' cross-belt of a British officer (lines 1–4). She goes on to express her disbelief that he is dead, suggesting instead that he has gone to 'seek adventure in some other place' (lines 5–8), yet describing how she still hears him and believes he is with her (lines 9–10). She appears confused as to how to react to her loved one's death: remembering his happiness, she is uncertain about associating him with grief (lines 11–12); and she finds it impossible that, having loved her, he should leave her (lines 13–14).

The poem moves into its second half in similar vein, with the poet recalling walking with her fiancé and reflecting on how it had seemed then, seems now, and always will seem, impossible that he should die (lines 15–18). She describes having been easy in each other's company, and having looked forward to a future with him that has now been replaced by solitude and the memory of him: it is clear that she still thinks of him as alive, somewhere perhaps beyond death (lines 19–22). The familiar location through which the poet walks serves as a reminder of him to the extent that she can still envisage him passing by, whilst the 'wings' overhead — a reference perhaps to wild birds — call to mind his association, as a Royal Flying Corps pilot, with flight (lines 23–26). The poet's evocation of Arthur, her memory of his presence, is so vivid to her that as she leaves the meadow she almost waits for him to open the gate for her, a little courtesy that we may infer he used to do for her (lines 27–28).

The overall impression is of the poet's emotional pain and incredulity at the loss of the man she loved so much. In the constant reminders of the familiar things they shared and experienced together, she finds echoes of his continued presence and evokes him vividly in her imagination.

Composition

'The Wind on the Downs' consists of twenty-eight lines, conceived as two Shakespearean sonnets — a verse form often associated with romantic love — combined consecutively into one continuous verse.

Structurally, the Shakespearean sonnet consists of three quatrains and one couplet, written in iambic pentameter. Overall, the sonnet's rhyme scheme is ABABCDCDEFEFGG. The first fourteen lines of 'The Wind on the Downs' follow this structure, with the latter half doing like likewise.

One might discern a volta at the end of the fourteenth line, where the first sonnet gives way to the second. This coincides with the muted anguish — gentle, dignified, but no less agonised — of the poet's 'How should you leave me, having loved me so?'. This marks the point at which she moves from the desperate doubt of the poem's first half into the comparative resignation and the wistful seeking of comfort in memory that characterise the second.

The vocabulary of the poem is straightforward, the punctuation and syntax conventional, reflecting the language of everyday speech within the idioms of the time. This lends the work a poignancy and a touching directness, leaving us with the sense that the poem is not an artistic contrivance but is couched in the very words the poet would wish to say to her departed beloved in person.

The poem is epistolary, addressed to the poet's fiancé directly as one might when writing a letter. In fact many of the poems written by Marian Allen at this tragic time were epistolary and had Arthur as their subject, and these may be seen as a continuation of the correspondence she had carried on with him throughout the war, whilst he was on active service.

There is little use of specific figurative language in the poem. The poet's description of Arthur as being present and around her, or of his exploring 'new kingdoms', may be literal expressions of her feelings and some religious or spiritual conviction. The description 'golden wings' of line 24 seems otherwise to be as close to specific metaphor as the poet comes. Yet the entire poem is suffused with the non-literal, as a figurative address to someone who can no longer read it.

Message

'The Wind on the Downs' is a poetic demonstration of the power of loss and of memory.

Loss, caused by someone's death or their removal from us, may cause devastating grief. We will naturally find in the world around us reminders of the person we have lost, and this can either renew our pain or help to assuage it. We may find the pain of loss to be numbing, confusing, or perhaps even life-changing. But we may also find in it the power to create something new, to start again, and to learn about ourselves and our place in the world.

In the midst of life's most terrible times, we can still find both strength and beauty.

Lesson plan: 'The Wind on the Downs' by Marian Allen

Resources

Copies of the poem — ideally one per pupil, pens and pencils, plain or lined paper, rulers for SEND pupils to follow a line when reading. There is a wonderful short animated film of the poem on YouTube produced by The Poetry Society, which pupils might like to watch. The poem is read by Olivia Vinall and may be found at https://www.youtube.com/watch?v=5bfLMt3VoqM

Copies of pupils' safety plans to which they can refer throughout the session/lesson.

The lesson will cover oracy and reading skills.

The session can be done in the round, or as a circle time activity, or at tables, or in an unstructured group. It is suitable for Upper Key Stage 2, 3 and 4.

Links with the PSHE Association PSHE Education Programme of Study

The learning opportunities below are not covered by the DfE statutory guidance: Health Education and Relationships Education/RSE but they form part of a broader programme for schools when they are covering work on bereavement.

Links have been made to the PSHE Association PSHE Education Programme of Study at Key Stage 2, 3 and 4 as follows:

KS2

- *H23. about change and loss, including death, and how these can affect feelings; ways of expressing and managing grief and bereavement*

KS3

- *R22. the effects of change, including loss, separation, divorce and bereavement; strategies for managing these and accessing support*

KS4

- *R13. ways to manage grief about changing relationships including the impact of separation, divorce and bereavement; sources of support and how to access them*

Links with the National Curriculum

Links have been made to the National Curriculum for English at Key Stage 2, 3 and 4 as follows:

KS2 (Years 5 and 6) English programme of study
- *maintain attention and participate actively in collaborative conversations, staying on topic and initiating and responding to comments*
- *discuss and evaluate how authors use language, including figurative language, considering the impact on the reader*
- *provide reasoned justifications for their views*

KS3 English programme of study
- *participating in formal debates and structured discussions, summarising and/or building on what has been said*
- *knowing how language, including figurative language, vocabulary choice, grammar, text structure and organisational features, presents meaning*

KS4 English programme of study
- *listening to and building on the contributions of others, asking questions to clarify and inform, and challenging courteously when necessary*
- *analysing a writer's choice of vocabulary, form, grammatical and structural features, and evaluating their effectiveness and impact*
- *make an informed personal response, recognising that other responses to a text are possible and evaluating these*

Teaching and learning activities

This is a highly effective poem for discussion about remembrance and loss. Miriam's fiancé Arthur Greg was killed in action in 1917. The poet recalls with vivid clarity and emotion some of the special times she spent with Arthur, particularly the walks they used to take together along the canal towpath in Oxford.

- Introduction — share aims of lesson.
- Refer pupils to their safety plans. Remind them of what a safety plan is for. Ask them to read through their own safety plan before they go further and answer any questions they may have.
- Read the poem (teacher/leader to read it aloud) or watch The Poetry Society's animated film *The Wind on the Downs* (see above) and discuss its content. Ask the following key questions:
  - What is the poem about?
  - How does the poem make you feel? How does it do this? Give reasons for your opinions.
  - Do you like the poem? Give reasons by reference to the poem.
- Discuss the importance of word choice. How does the poet use different words to make the reader understand her feelings or mood? Discuss with a friend or in a small group.
- Take feedback from each group.
- What picture do we develop of Arthur Greg? Working with a partner or in a small group, pick out some of his qualities. Write a description of Arthur from what Marian says about him.
- Take feedback.
- Think about a memorable occasion in your life. What made it memorable? It may have been a happy time or a sad time. What positive/happy things can you draw from that memory? Give pupils the option to write about their memory or to use the technique of write and draw to using key words and phrases to encapsulate their memory.
- Review what has been achieved in the lesson.
- Refer pupils to their safety plans as a place to look if they need help after leaving the lesson.

Extension activities

- Pupils to write responses to the key questions in the teaching and learning section.
- Research Marian Allen's life. What can you find out about her life, and particularly the time when she wrote the poem?
- Why do you think the poet found it necessary to write this poem so soon after Arthur's death?
- Create a memory box for a deceased loved one. What words or pictures would you put in the box?
- Write a short biography of Marian Allen.
- Produce a story board of the poem with images that catch the essence of the work. Key words and phrases may be taken from the poem and included in the pictures.
- Imagine you are Marian writing a letter to your fiancé. In your letter reflect on all the happy times you had together. Include thoughts, feelings and emotions in your writing.
- Work on reading the poem with intonation and stress before recording it. Try to make it sound natural, as though you were just speaking to someone. Remember that this is an epistolary poem (i.e. it is like a letter) and so it is written just as though Marian was speaking to Arthur. Ask pupils to reflect on the recorded readings and to suggest ways in which they might be improved.

- What do you think the reference to 'golden wings' represents in the poem? For example, was it the plane Arthur was flying when he died? Is it wild birds? Or is it something else? Give reasons for your opinions.
- The poem provides scope for researching the role and experience of women in WW1 and the early 20th century.
- Produce a PowerPoint of the poem. Produce pictures and illustrations to accompany the words of the poem. A sound file of a pupil reading the poem can be included.

Cross-curricular/topic links

Cross-curricular and topic links may be explored for use in follow-up and for extension work in

- English
- PSHE
- History
- ICT
- Art and Design

Differentiation

Opportunities for discussion in mixed ability pairs.

Differentiation by outcome e.g. quantity or complexity of issues identified, sophistication of response, level of inclusion/contribution, empathy.

Writing quantity outcomes will be differentiated/assessed/moderated according to teacher's expectations of quantity and depth; otherwise by outcome.

Differentiation may also be through key words rather than written sentences, or through artwork as a means of expression.

The Glove

by Peter Kalu

Commentary

She had worn it once, now it was mine. I waited till night, till my phone stopped ringing, till the generators finally ceased their clatter, and there was no light nor any possibility of light. Then, as air warmed and thickened in the room, I eased open the evidence bag, took hold of it, and, finger by finger, slipped it on. She'd had large hands, mine were small (that joke we had when we walked hand in hand through the market — the impracticality of walking like that). I raised the glove to my face and breathed. She was still there.

Context

Peter Kalu is a British writer of Danish-Nigerian heritage, and is an award-winning poet, playwright, short fiction writer and author.

Much of the poet's work reflects the deeper experiences of life lived by the people of the places he has visited and come to know, and of the city of Manchester where he now lives.

Content

The speaker has possession of an object which, at first, he does not specify in the poem, but which from the title we might understand to be a glove. It once belonged to someone else — the 'she' of line 1 — but is now his.

He waits until night-time when it is dark and quiet. He does not say where he is, but the speaker is somewhere that seems to rely upon a noisy generator for domestic electricity, and this goes off at night. He has waited not only until it is dark but until there is no 'possibility of light' (line 2).

The atmosphere becomes warm and close (the air has 'warmed and thickened in the room', line 3). We may wonder whether, as well as the light, the generator has been powering a fan or an air-conditioner.

The speaker has an 'evidence bag' (line 3), a kind of small, resealable transparent plastic bag. He opens it.

He takes the object inside the bag and puts it on, 'finger by finger' (lines 3 to 4), a delicacy of action that suggests the speaker is treating the glove as something precious.

The speaker explains that the woman who formerly owned the glove had 'large hands' (line 4). This is why he can slip it on easily. The fact that her hands had been bigger than the speaker's had been a joke between them, something he remembers from when they held hands as they walked 'through the market' (line 5).

In the darkness the speaker puts his gloved hand to his face, breathes in the scent of the woman, and feels that she is still with him (lines 5 to 6).

Composition

'The Glove' is a prose poem. Prose poetry is a relatively infrequently encountered form. It is poetry written as prose, without the line breaks and verse form associated with poetry writing. It manifests other characteristics of poetry, among which may be heightened imagery, metaphor, repetition, figures of speech, rhyme, poetic metre and emotional effects. Whilst not looking at first sight like a poem, prose poetry preserves the both the original Greek root of the word 'poem' (*poiēma* [ποίημα], meaning 'what is made or created, workmanship') and the Oxford English Dictionary definition of the term as 'a piece of writing in which the expression of feelings and ideas is given intensity by particular attention to diction (sometimes involving rhyme), rhythm, and imagery'.

'The Glove' is set out in a tight block of text, which suggests the enclosed intimacy — dark, warm and private — of the setting in which the poem's events unfold.

The poem opens with a sentence written in trochees, giving it a strongly rhythmic character. The rest of the piece does not use regular metre, nor does the poet employ rhyme.

The poem's punctuation is, as we might expect, conventional for a passage written in prose.

The work is richly descriptive of atmosphere. The poet describes the creation of a closed, private, warm, dark personal space: this will, as we see, enhance the senses of touch and smell in which to enter into what is almost a form of communion with the glove — a close personal, emotional, almost spiritual contact. However, this atmospheric effect is achieved with a light use of language: metaphor is limited to 'thickened' (descriptive of the air becoming warm and dense-feeling, line 3), and 'she was still there' in the final line which suggests how the woman's smell on the glove evokes the sense of her presence.

The poignancy of the speaker's sense of loss and longing in this secret sensory encounter is touchingly apparent.

Message

Sadly, loss is a part of life. Often there is nothing we can do to prevent it. We may lose people from our lives for many reasons.

It is usual to feel bad about our loss, which may range in intensity from a sense of missing the person, through sadness in varying degrees, to an almost unbearable level of emotional pain.

Sometimes we may find that an object, perhaps something that belonged to the person we have lost or that they gave to us or that we experienced with them, may remind us of them. Interacting with this object can be a very intense sensation, and for a little while it can almost feel as though the person is back with us. Something as simple as a particular smell or the taste of a certain food can be enough to evoke a very powerful emotional response within us.

We may often find that it is helpful to us to identify our own quiet space, away from others, in which to think about our loss.

Lesson plan: 'The Glove' by Peter Kalu

Resources

Copies of the poem — ideally one per pupil, pens and pencils, plain or lined paper, rulers for SEND pupils to follow a line when reading.

Copies of pupils' safety plans to which they can refer throughout the session/lesson.

The lesson will cover oracy and reading skills.

The session can be done in the round, or as a circle time activity, or at tables, or in an unstructured group. It is suitable for Upper Key Stage 2, 3 and 4.

Links with the PSHE Association PSHE Education Programme of Study

The learning opportunities below are not covered by the DfE statutory guidance: Health Education and Relationships Education/RSE but they form part of a broader programme for schools when they are covering work on bereavement.

Links have been made to the PSHE Association PSHE Education Programme of Study at Key Stage 2, 3 and 4 as follows:

KS2

- *H23. about change and loss, including death, and how these can affect feelings; ways of expressing and managing grief and bereavement*

KS3

- *R22. the effects of change, including loss, separation, divorce and bereavement; strategies for managing these and accessing support*

KS4

- *R13. ways to manage grief about changing relationships including the impact of separation, divorce and bereavement; sources of support and how to access them*

Links with the National Curriculum

Links have been made to the National Curriculum for English at Key Stage 2, 3 and 4 as follows:

KS2 (Years 5 and 6) English programme of study

- *maintain attention and participate actively in collaborative conversations, staying on topic and initiating and responding to comments*
- *discuss and evaluate how authors use language, including figurative language, considering the impact on the reader*
- *provide reasoned justifications for their views*

KS3 English programme of study

- *participating in formal debates and structured discussions, summarising and/or building on what has been said*
- *knowing how language, including figurative language, vocabulary choice, grammar, text structure and organisational features, presents meaning*

KS4 English programme of study

- *listening to and building on the contributions of others, asking questions to clarify and inform, and challenging courteously when necessary*
- *analysing a writer's choice of vocabulary, form, grammatical and structural features, and evaluating their effectiveness and impact*

Teaching and learning activities

This is an intriguing and thought-provoking poem for discussion about remembrance and loss. We are not sure what has happened to the owner of the glove. We are left wondering whether the person has died or left the speaker's life. It is up to the reader to decide.

- Introduction — share aims of lesson.
- Refer pupils to their safety plans. Remind them of what a safety plan is for. Ask them to read through their own safety plan before they go further and answer any questions they may have.
- Read the poem (teacher/leader to read it aloud). Ask the following key questions with the whole class:
  - What is the poem about?
  - What kind of poem is it?
  - What is the significance of the title?
  - Why is the glove important to the speaker?
  - Why did the speaker wait until night before taking out the glove?
  - What is the effect of using personal pronouns 'I' and 'she' in the poem?
- Think about a time when you were given an emotionally significant or memorable item. Who gave it to you? Why was it given to you? What positive/happy things can you draw from that memory? Give pupils the option to write about their memory or to draw and write using key words and phrases to encapsulate their memory.
- Review what has been achieved in the lesson.
- Refer pupils to their safety plans as a place to look if they need help after leaving the lesson.

Extension activities

- Pupils to write responses to the questions in the teaching and learning section.
- Produce a story board of the poem with images that catch the essence of the poem. Key words and phrases may be taken from the poem and included in the pictures.
- How does the poem make you feel? How does it do this? Give reasons for your opinions.
- Pupils to write their own narrative poems based on 'The Glove'.
- Pupils to turn 'The Glove' into a piece of descriptive writing.
- Do you like the poem? Why? Give reasons and justify your answer by reference to the poem.
- What is the meaning of the poem? What message do you think it gives? Why do you think this?

- Write a story based on the poem. You may want to use a flashback technique to recount events that took place between the speaker and the woman in the poem. What happened between them? Why are they no longer together?

Cross-curricular/topic links

Cross-curricular and topic links may be explored for use in follow-up and for extension work in
- English
- PSHE
- Art and Design

Differentiation

Opportunities for discussion in mixed ability pairs.

Differentiation by outcome e.g. quantity or complexity of issues identified, sophistication of response, level of inclusion/contribution, empathy.

Writing quantity outcomes will be differentiated/assessed/moderated according to teacher's expectations of quantity and depth; otherwise by outcome.

Differentiation may also be through key words rather than written sentences, or through artwork as a means of expression.

the view from here
by Paul Morris

Commentary

The blinds are drawn with this ending day,
and nothing will be the same.

Walls have been stripped, the boards laid bare,
to wait for other columns of colour, other sticky labels to appear.
The floor is prickled with staples, and bits of paper
no longer relevant
taken down, given back —
this a keepsake, that a memory —
my time in this place sketched in sun-faded pictures, biroed words.

One more look out of windows that have lit the landscape of my mind,
the view from here
where lost thoughts and flashbulb moments filled
my time, this space.

My chair still there but already a bit too small.

I linger to check my named drawer one last time,
knowing it's empty but for the sadness crumbed into the corners.

I am moving on,
like it or not:
growing into a wide world still too big for my shoulders,
where opportunities and new horizons are promised.

And this is my last day here and I'm
a little
lost,
a little
empty.

To open my new chapter I
must close this book, I
must leave the friendships and happy times, I
must leave people who cared and looked after me, I
must leave the familiar smells
of hot school dinners and disinfectant,
of library books and sugar paper,
of poster paint and rubber glue,
of wet coats and muddy shoes
clagged with the smell of school field.

My bag brims with personal effects,
with letters and gifts from friends to say
'Have a great holiday' and
'Be in touch' and
'See you soon' and
in a world that's shifting and new, scribbled
goodbyes on torn-off scraps.

A final smile from my teacher and a gift to say goodbye.
A wave as we traipse
> under the banner that signs *OUR* farewell,

then

one deep breath more, one
back-cast glance, one
heart-heavy sigh more, one
to say

goodbye

old place, old room,
old school, old friends.

Context

The 2021 poem 'the view from here' was commissioned and written especially for the anthology *Face in the Mirror*. It was intended to address specifically the emotional challenges that young people face when moving schools, though its treatment of that very particular circumstance might also be applied to other instances in life that involve relocation accompanied by the dislocation of separation.

The events the poem describes were based upon the poet's personal memories, combined with those of his wife and her close observations over many years of children leaving her Year 6 class and feeling all the mingled hope and distress that change so often entails, the sense of the unfamiliar among the familiar.

The disturbance of leaving primary school and starting afresh at secondary school is a rite of passage that almost all young people undergo, yet it is all too easy to underestimate the impact it can have upon a young person. Similarly, leaving a school when moving house, or later leaving secondary school for higher education or work, are times of significant change. This poem examines the rich mixture of emotions that a young person might experience in the final moments before leaving the school they have known for many years.

Content

The poem opens with the speaker describing how, at the end of the day, the blinds are being closed (line 1). With that simple action comes the realisation that something in the speaker's life has changed (line 2).

The speaker describes the room in which they stand. It is a school classroom that has been stripped of decoration and displays (lines 3 and 4), and the floor is strewn with staples and scraps of paper (line 5). Among the pieces of paper are items that are 'no longer relevant' either because the lessons to which they refer are long past or because the child who created the piece of work is now leaving the school (lines 5 to 7): some pieces are being given to children as 'a keepsake' (lines 7 and 8). Though they have been faded by the sun these papers remind the speaker in words and pictures of their time in the class (line 9).

Perhaps to remind themselves of the view that they find special, the speaker looks out of the classroom windows (line 10). This view has formed part of their mindscape, the view from a place that they know has given rise to new thoughts and realisations ('flashbulb moments') that have filled both their time and the room they have spent it in (lines 10 to 13). In many respects the line 'the view from here' (line 11), which is also the title of the poem, captures the theme of the entire work — the broader viewpoint of a young person who, in the place they are in on that day, is now seeing a long-familiar scene almost as though for the first time, though in fact it may be for the last time. Interestingly, the poet — who is known to consider a poem's title to be a significant element of its content — has stated that the title of this piece is all in lower case letters in order to avoid emphasis on place, because it is not one particular physical view or location that is depicted but rather the fluid, indefinite and shifting viewpoint of a young person in a state of change.

The speaker notes the presence of their chair in the room, a familiar object though it already seems 'a bit too small' (line 14) — a sign, perhaps, of their awareness of outgrowing these surroundings.

Though they stop to look at their classroom work tray ('my named drawer', line 15), the speaker already knows that it is empty. They seem to see their own sadness in that emptiness (line 16).

The speaker is 'moving on' (line 17) — leaving, whether they 'like it or not' (line 18). They are aware that they are changing, moving out into a world that seems too big to fit them comfortably (line 19), though they are told that there are good things and good progress to be had there (line 20).

Having looked around and taken new note of the familiar surroundings that they are about to leave, the speaker declares both where they stand and how they feel. This is their last day (line 21), and they feel lost and empty (lines 23 and 25). It is significant that both of these adjectives are preceded by 'a little' (lines 22 and 24), the repetition of which suggests a deeper connotation to the phrase: that the speaker is also sensing their youth and feeling somewhat 'little' in the face of this big change — insignificant, inexperienced, and perhaps unprepared.

Realising now what the change may entail, the speaker sees how they must move forward by leaving this phase of life behind (lines 26 and 27). They must leave behind the friendship and happiness of this familiar school (line 28), and the caring they associate with it (line 29): these are all associations that young people often have with the nurturing ethos of primary schools. The speaker must also leave the specific sensations they associate with the place (line 30): the smells of food and cleaning (line 31), books and stationery (line 32), art materials (line 33), the smells of wet clothes and shoes and mud, and the scent — easier to recognise than to describe — that they identify particularly with the school playing field (lines 34 and 35). These are the markers of the ebb and flow of daily life in a school, usually barely noticed but now cast into vivid clarity. The speaker will leave all this familiar sensory and emotional landscape behind, and the intensely personal nature of the experience is emphasised by the repetition of 'I' at the end of lines 26 to 29.

In contrast to the sense of emptiness and loss the speaker has been describing, their school bag is full of personal items (line 36), things given by friends (line 37) to wish them well over the school holiday (lines 38 to 40). However, the speaker seems aware that this is not a holiday like previous ones: in their new and changing world (line 41), these are really makeshift ways of friends saying goodbye (line 42).

The speaker describes how the teacher smiles and a gift is given 'to say goodbye' (line 43), though it is not clear whether the smile is for the speaker alone or for everyone there, nor do we know whether the gift is given to the speaker or by them. These things are only mentioned in passing. The children finally take their leave, waving as they walk reluctantly (line 44) under a banner (presumably put up by the teacher) that displays its 'farewell' especially for these leavers (line 45). As this is happening the speaker breathes deeply, perhaps to catch those classroom scents for the final time (line 47), looking back (line 48) with a heavy sigh (line 49). This is a sigh that says goodbye (line 51), just as clearly as the banner, to the school and the classroom (lines 52 to 53), We are left to wonder whether the 'friends' (line 53) the speaker is leaving are in fact just their classmates, or perhaps include the familiar places in school that the speaker now thinks of as friends in themselves.

Composition

The poem is a narrative piece, telling the story of the speaker's last day at primary school, and is written in free verse, unrhymed and without regular metre.

The work consists of fourteen stanzas which serve the progression of the poem's narrative: the closure of the blinds and of the day; the clearing of the classroom, the removal of the familiar, previously inconsequential items that now have the sense of being valued relics; the familiar view from the window, a scene the speaker is now leaving; the realisation of already outgrowing the place; going through familiar motions but finding only sadness; the realisation of moving on, willingly or not; the realisation of finality and admitting a sense of being out of one's depth in this change; the necessity of change and a list of the familiar things that will be missed; the little personal rituals of leave-taking; leaving as a communal experience; realisation; the emotionality of goodbyes; the goodbye itself; the familiarity and closeness that remains. Each of these forms a distinct yet linked part of the speaker's emotional experience.

The language of the poem is conversational and accessible, the emotion of the young speaker suggested by a certain hesitancy and reservation of expression.

There are a few words of which the young reader might appreciate clarification: 'keepsake' (= 'souvenir', line 8), 'biroed' (= 'written with a ballpoint pen', line 9), 'clagged' (= 'clogged or stuck, as with mud', line 35), 'brims' (= 'is full', line 36).

Punctuation is conventional, and such as might be used had the piece been presented as prose. Elsewhere, the use of enjambment throughout the poem follows the natural flow of the language. In lines 48 and 49, hyphenated compound adjectives are used to slow the delivery, creating forms that are as difficult to articulate as the speaker's emotion is to feel.

The layout of the work is organised so as to support and enhance the language. Distinct ideas, briefly conveyed, are often given their own line, as in the case of lines 6 (the ending of relevance), 11 (the view from the window and from the young person's general viewpoint), 14 (outgrowing one's surroundings), 17 (transition), 18 (volition), 23 (loss), 25 (emptiness) and 51 (valediction). Elsewhere, the organisation of the text on the page helps suggest and support other effects of the piece. The separation of lines 21 to 25 emphasises the speaker's hesitancy, whilst the grouping of lines 26 to 35 suggests the rush of successive impressions or ideas occurring to the speaker. The separation and indentation of line 45 suggests the unwelcome awkwardness of walking beneath the 'farewell' banner.

Meanwhile, textual organisation within individual lines allows the poet to create an unusual 'special effect' of metre, which is more apparent for the poem not having a regular metrical structure. In lines 11, 13, 17, 18, 22, 24, 52 and 53 (and less obviously in lines 6, 7, 27, 47, 49) the poet constructs a line of two iambs (in fact these are single iambs in lines 22 and 24), which within the confines of the short line creates a tight two-beat 'da-DUM-da-DUM' suggestive of the heartbeat of the emotional speaker. It is upon such a repeated heartbeat that the poem closes.

In stanzas 8 and 12 the poet uses caesuras late in the line to create an effect of timing. The repetition of the hanging personal 'I' and the singular 'one' create a pause followed by a monosyllabic sob, emphasising the isolation and intensity of the speaker's emotional state and suggesting the tears that seem inevitable on days such as this.

Figurative language in the poem consists entirely of metaphor, suggesting the immediacy of the situation rather than its being 'like' anything the speaker has previously experienced. The strewn staples pulled out of dismantled wall displays result in a floor that is 'prickled' (line 5). Past moments of learning and realisation are 'flashbulb moments' (line 12). The speaker's sadness, like the bits of detritus left in a drawer, is 'crumbed into the corners' (line 16), suggesting both the physical object and the scrappiness of the speaker's emotions.

Message

The message of the poem is that transition is inevitable, and that we may expect the experience to be filled with emotion. Sooner or later we have to leave places that we have loved, or at least that have been familiar to us, and this is especially the case with our schools. We may feel that we are ready to move on, only to be surprised by the vividness of our feelings of attachment when we try to do so.

Transition is a rite of passage, and whilst this may make it no less difficult to experience it can be helpful for us to realise that everyone has passed, or will pass, through similar experiences in life.

It may only be when we are faced with leaving a place that we realise how much it has become a part of us — or how much we have become a part of it.

We may be surprised by the sensations we feel when we are moving on. We may experience apparently familiar sights, sounds and other sensations with a new vividness. This can be disconcerting, but is quite usual — a result of our taking particular notice, whilst we are emotional, of things that have previously blended into the background.

We may only realise the true importance of a place or person to us as we are moving on and leaving them behind. However, no place or person that we love ever truly leaves us, but always remains part of us. What we have gained from them never goes away.

Lesson plan: 'the view from here' by Paul Morris

Resources

Copies of the poem — ideally one per pupil, pens or pencils, plain or lined paper, rulers for SEND pupils to follow a line when reading.

Copies of pupils' safety plans to which they can refer throughout the session/lesson. The lesson will cover oracy and reading skills.

The session can be done in the round. or as a circle time activity, or at tables, or in an unstructured group. It is suitable to use with pupils at Upper Key Stage 2, 3 and 4.

Links with the PSHE Association PSHE Education Programme of Study

Links have been made to the PSHE Association PSHE Education Programme of Study at Key Stage 2, 3 and 4 as follows:

KS2

- *H19. a varied vocabulary to use when talking about feelings; about how to express feelings in different ways;*
- *H20. strategies to respond to feelings, including intense or conflicting feelings; how to manage and respond to feelings appropriately and proportionately in different situations*
- *H23. about change and loss, including death, and how these can affect feelings; ways of expressing and managing grief and bereavement*
- *H24. problem-solving strategies for dealing with emotions, challenges and change, including the transition to new schools*

KS3

- *H6. how to identify and articulate a range of emotions accurately and sensitively, using appropriate vocabulary*
- *R22. the effects of change, including loss, separation, divorce and bereavement; strategies for managing these and accessing support*

KS4

- *H6. about change and its impact on mental health and wellbeing and to recognise the need for emotional support during life changes and/or difficult experiences*

Links with the National Curriculum

Links have been made to the National Curriculum for English at Key Stage 2, 3 and 4 as follows:

KS2 (Years 5 and 6) English programme of study
- *listen and respond appropriately to adults and their peers*
- *maintain attention and participate actively in collaborative conversations, staying on topic and initiating and responding to comments*
- *identifying how language, structure and presentation contribute to meaning*
- *provide reasoned justifications for their views*

KS3 English programme of study
- *participating in formal debates and structured discussions, summarising and/or building on what has been said*
- *knowing how language, including figurative language, vocabulary choice, grammar, text structure and organisational features, presents meaning*
- *recognising a range of poetic conventions and understanding how these have been used*

KS4 English programme of study

- *listening to and building on the contributions of others, asking questions to clarify and inform, and challenging courteously when necessary*
- *analysing a writer's choice of vocabulary, form, grammatical and structural features, and evaluating their effectiveness and impact*

Teaching and learning activities

This poem is about transition. It encapsulates the thoughts and feelings of the speaker who is sad about leaving behind all that is familiar and comfortable about his/her school. Transition to high school, or between high school and further education, can be very daunting for young people, and this poem can be used to explore their worries and concerns and to prepare them for the changes that lie ahead in life, whether in education or elsewhere. It can be used at KS3 to continue work on transition, to help young people access new opportunities at high school. It may also be helpful at KS4 when young people are preparing to leave their secondary school, or at any time that a school move is necessary.

- Introduction — share aims of lesson.
- Refer pupils to their safety plans. Remind them of what a safety plan is for. Ask them to read through their own safety plan before they go further and answer any questions they may have.
- Read the poem (or teacher/leader to read it aloud) and ask the following key questions:
  - What do you think this poem is about?
  - How does the person in the poem feel about leaving school? What evidence can you find to justify your views?
  - The poem is called 'the view from here'. What do you think the title refers to? Where is 'here', and how is it a 'view'? Do you think the title means more than one thing? If the title's meaning can be read as a metaphor, what does the metaphor mean? Why does the classroom look different to the speaker today, and what difference does that make? (Note: the speaker's 'view from here' refers not only to the literal view from the classroom window but also the speaker's new awareness of what is going on around and within them — a new view of an old familiar scene.)
- In pairs or in small groups discuss how this poem made you feel. How did it do this? If you have left primary school what memories does the poem bring to your mind?
- Think about a time you felt anxious or worried. If you feel able to discuss it, what were the circumstances? Pupils may want to reflect on how they felt during the Covid-19 lockdown and their subsequent return to school. How did you deal with these feelings?
- Ask for feedback.
- What opportunities lie ahead when leaving primary school/secondary school? Discuss in pairs or small groups. What opportunities do you/did you want to find there? Think of some good ways to make the best of the opportunities secondary school has to offer.
- Ask for feedback.
- Share sources of available help that pupils can access if they need to talk to someone about worries and concerns they have about going to high school, finding their way in high school life, or leaving to go to sixth form college.
- Review what has been achieved in the lesson.
- Refer pupils to their safety plans as a place to look if they need help after leaving the lesson.

Extension activities
- Pupils to write their answers to the key questions.

- In circle time activities or in a one-to-one situation ask pupils to reflect on issues that make them feel anxious about going to high school. For example, making new friends, adapting to new routines, worries about getting lost at high school, concerns about homework, being late for lessons, etc. Discuss ways of dealing with these issues.

- Invite speakers to come into school to talk about transition, including former pupils and secondary teachers.

- What will you/did you miss most about primary school? What sights and sounds and smells will you/did you miss? What experiences will you/did you miss? What will you miss about high school if you are moving to sixth form college?

- Write a description of your view of a familiar space (e.g. your classroom) without using your sense of sight. Describe only what you can smell, hear, touch or taste.

- Pupils to produce their own self-help guides and pamphlets on the theme of transition.

- Discuss the use of language in the poem — think of things such as alliteration, the use of the personal pronoun 'I', the use of the imperative verb 'must'.

- Write about what you will miss about your primary school/secondary school and why. Write about what you are looking forward to at your new school.

- What questions do you have about your high school/sixth form college? Make a list. These may be addressed when high school teachers visit or by the class teacher.

- Did you like or dislike the poem? Why do you think this? Give reasons for your opinion.

- Write your own poem about leaving primary school/secondary school and what you will miss.

- Write a short list of advice for someone who is moving from primary to secondary school or from secondary school to sixth form college. What things do you think it is important for them to know? Think of things you wish you had known or would still like to know.

- Design a public advice poster including your most important advice to people who are moving from primary to secondary school.

Cross-curricular/topic links

Cross-curricular and topic links may be explored for use in follow-up and for extension work in
- English
- PSHE
- Art and Design

Differentiation

Opportunities for discussion in mixed ability pairs/groups.

Differentiation by outcome e.g. quantity or complexity of issues identified, sophistication of response, level of inclusion/contribution, empathy.

Writing quantity outcomes will be differentiated/assessed/moderated according to teacher's expectations of quantity and depth; otherwise by outcome.

Differentiation may also be through key words rather than written sentences, or through artwork as a means of expression.

Facing My Trauma

This section is about trauma, anxiety and post-traumatic stress...

Beyond the Morning Sun

by Paul Morris

Commentary

My daddy was a soldier,
The best you've ever seen,
With great big boots of shiny black
And a uniform of green.

My daddy was a sergeant,
His shout was very loud;
He wore a shiny cap-badge
Of which he was so proud.

And all the men looked up to him
And they would all agree
He was a *proper* soldier
As smart as smart could be.

He told new soldiers what to do
As they marched around the square,
And he shouted things like, 'Left, right, left!'
And he made them cut their hair.

We all lived on the army base,
My dad, my mum and me,
With lots of other soldier folk —
An army family!

I'd ride on daddy's shoulders
As high as high could be,
And I'd wear his hat and shiny badge
For all the world to see.

He loved to laugh and dance about
And bounce me all around
And he'd tell me jokes and sing daft songs
Till my ears hurt with the sound!

Then late one summer evening
When I had gone to bed
I heard dad talk to mum downstairs
And this is what he said:

'We're shipping out tomorrow:
The big plane goes at one.
Don't worry — it's only Helmand
And at least I'll get some sun.'

Then I heard my mother crying,
I'm almost sure I did,
And dad say, 'Be strong, lovey,
For me and for the kid.

I won't be gone forever
And six months goes so fast —
And when I'm back here with you
It'll all be in the past.'

Next day we went out early
And we drove out of the base,
Dad with his great big army bag
And his smiling army face.

We drove down to the airfield
With lots of other folks,
And all the soldiers stood around
Laughing and cracking jokes.

Then someone shouted orders
And everyone fell dumb,
And dad reached down and scruffed my hair,
Said, 'Look after your mum.'

Dad hugged mum, whispered in her ear —
I don't know what or why —
But what he whispered made her laugh
And also made her cry.

Then dad and all the soldiers
Got on the big green plane;
We waved till it flew out of sight
Then just went home again.

I didn't go to school that day.
Granny came round instead.
She sat with mum, drank tea and talked
Till it was time for bed.

And though I tried to ask them
Neither of them would say
Where the big green army plane had gone
That took my daddy away.

Next day, as day was dawning,
I lay wide awake in bed
With oh-so-many questions
Running through my head.

I heard a noise downstairs and I
Came down the stairs to find
My mother sitting by the window
Staring through the blind

As the distant dawning sun lit up
The sky with streaks of red;
And I asked her about daddy,
And this is what she said:

She pointed through the window
At the early morning sun
And she said, 'That's east: and east is where
Your soldier daddy's gone.

To a land they call Afghanistan —
There's a job there to be done.
That's where your daddy is right now:
Beyond the morning sun.'

Mum said he'd gone to fight for peace,
To make their people free
To live a safe and happy life —
To live like you and me.

And she said he was a hero,
But I have never known
Just why he had to go away
And leave us on our own.

For the Afghans may need heroes
To fight to make then free,
But I wanted daddy home with mum —
And I wanted him with *me*.

But days turn into weeks, and weeks
Turn into months, and so
The days and weeks and months passed
Since I saw my daddy go.

Until, one cold day in the spring
When the tarmac shone with rain,
The big green army aircraft
Brought my daddy home again.

And it brought *some* of the soldiers
Who'd gone away with him —
But nobody was cheerful,
And everyone was grim.

No, it didn't bring as many back
As it had taken away,
And no-one laughed and no-one joked
As they'd done on that day.

And when I asked where they all were
Dad said that every one
Had come home through Wootton Bassett
From beyond the morning sun.

And my daddy's great loud sergeant's shout
And his smiling soldier's face:
He must have left them out there
In that oh-so-far-off place.

Now, I don't like Afghanistan
And I will tell you why:
Whatever it is they did out there,
It makes my daddy cry.

He says it's not the Afghans' fault
And while that may be true,
I know the daddy they sent home
Is not the man I knew.

Oh, he doesn't talk about it much,
Says it was 'just a tour',
But the medals that they gave him
Lie forgotten in his drawer.

Yes the shiny silver medals
Lie forgotten in the drawer,
For he says it's no parade-ground
When the guns begin to roar;

And he says it doesn't matter
How loud a man can shout,
You'd just better keep your head down
When the bullets fly about;

And he won't play soldiers with me
And he will not tell me why,
But he says that it's no playground
When the rockets start to fly.

And he won't laugh or sing or smile
And he never will have fun,
But he just sits and stares for hours
Beyond the morning sun.

He goes all silent when he thinks
Of all his friends who fell
Beneath the bombs and bullets that
Turned Helmand into Hell...

One day *I'll* be a soldier too;
One day *I'll* have a gun,
And join the ranks of those who've gone
Beyond the morning sun.

Context

'Beyond the Morning Sun' was written in the summer of 2011 and first published in 2014, since when it has been used extensively in school sessions with pupils from Year 3 upwards, secondary and tertiary education settings, and adult poetry workshops.

The poet describes how the poem was written whilst he was working on a novel. He had stopped writing to make some tea, and as he was doing so he switched on the lunchtime BBC television news. On screen was a live news report, and the picture was split in two. On one side of the screen, British soldiers returning from Afghanistan to a UK RAF base were being reunited with their loved ones, and everyone was joyful. But on the other side, flag-draped caskets containing fallen service personnel were being taken from a military aircraft at RAF Lyneham and laid into hearses to be driven away through the town of Wootton Bassett, where people lined the streets to pay their respects. As the long line of caskets was carried from the aircraft, watched by grieving families, the BBC reporters spoke to many people: senior military officers, MPs, religious and community leaders, local dignitaries, political commentators, bereaved partners bravely carrying on with tearful children clinging silently to their coats. But nobody spoke to the children. They had no voice. The poet decided to give them a voice, and the poem was composed in one sitting that same afternoon.

The work, published as a single volume illustrated with photographs supplied by the UK Ministry of Defence, was published in late 2014 just before the major drawdown of British troops from Afghanistan. It has since been used to raise much-needed funds for Combat Stress, a leading UK charity that supports service veterans with mental health difficulties.

For four and a half years RAF Lyneham in Wiltshire served as the principal reception point for the repatriation of fallen service personnel to the UK. During that time the local community of Wootton Bassett stood in quiet reverence to pay its respect to the three hundred and fifty-five service personnel whose final journey of return took them through its heart. This respectful devotion led Queen Elizabeth II to confer upon the town the permanent title of Royal Wootton Bassett as an enduring symbol of the nation's admiration and gratitude.

On 28th December 2014, NATO formally ended combat operations of its International Security Assistance Force in Afghanistan, transferring full security responsibility to the Afghan government. Following the election of a new US president in November 2020, the alliance of Western military forces began to withdraw NATO troops from the country, a step that led to the launch of a Taliban offensive against the Afghan government. Order collapsed quickly, the Afghan president fleeing the country. A restored, Taliban-led Islamic Emirate of Afghanistan was swiftly declared amid social, political and military chaos.

The conflict in Afghanistan continues.

Content

The poem opens with the voice of a child, who narrates the story that the poem tells.

We are not told any personal details about the child except that 'My daddy was a soldier' (stanza 1, line 1), which places the child into a military family. As to the child's other personal characteristics — age, sex, colour, religion and so on — the reader is left to imagine the character in any way they choose. It is for this reason that the gender-neutral pronoun 'they/their' is used in this commentary.

The child introduces the father and we learn that he was a sergeant in the British Army (stanza 2, line 2) who was a model soldier (stanzas 2 and 3) and trained new recruits (stanza 4). The family lived on an army base and the child speaks of their being 'An army family!', which could mean that their own family was one with a history of military service or perhaps that they felt they were part of the wider 'family' of the army (stanza 5).

The child describes a happy home life with a father who was jovial, playful and a friend to the child (stanzas 6 and 7). However, this is all described in the past tense, and we may be left with an uneasy feeling that this is because the father is no longer alive.

We learn that the child remembers overhearing a conversation between father and mother in which he tells her that he is leaving the following day for a sunny place called 'Helmand' (stanza 9, line 3). This is the Helmand province of Afghanistan, located in the south of the country and one of the main focuses for fighting. The child hears their mother crying, and the compassionate father reassure her that the six months of his tour of duty will pass quickly (stanzas 10 and 11).

The following day the family drives to the airfield and in an atmosphere of jocularity — almost of celebration — the soldiers board 'the big green plane' (stanzas 12 and 13). Before they do, the child's father tells them to 'Look after your mum', giving them a responsibility to fulfil whilst he is away (stanza 14). The father takes his leave of the child's mother, whispering to her privately and making her both laugh and cry, the conflicted emotions of such a parting and a hope for safe return (stanza 15). The aircraft takes off with all the soldiers aboard, and the child and mother can only wave until they lose sight of it, then go home together (stanza 16).

The child stays home from school as their grandmother comes to visit, presumably to keep the mother company and to reassure her (stanza 17). The child tries to ask where the father has gone, but neither of the adults will answer (stanza 18).

The child awakes at dawn the next day with a head full of questions (stanza 19), and comes downstairs when they hear the sound of the mother. She is sitting and looking out of the window (stanza 20) as the sun rises. It is clear that she has been unable to sleep and has come down to watch the sunrise. The child asks her again 'about daddy', and this time receives a reply (stanza 21). The mother points to the rising sun and says that its direction is east: this is the direction towards which the child's father has travelled to 'a land they call Afghanistan', and he has gone there for a purpose (stanzas 22 and 23). She explains that he has gone to help restore peace to the people of that country, to allow them to 'live a safe and happy life', and she says he is a hero (stanzas 24 and 25). Yet the child cannot grasp why he has gone away and left both of them (stanza 25): the child holds in the balance the Afghan people's need for help from people like the father in his role as a soldier, and the compelling personal wants of the mother and themselves to have the father as 'daddy' at home for them (stanza 26).

Time passes. Months have elapsed since the father left (stanza 27).

The 'big green army aircraft' returns to the base (stanza 28). There is no laughing or jocularity as there had been when the troops departed, and now there is a sense of foreboding gloom that makes us afraid that the child's father might not be among the depleted count of soldiers who are returning alive from the war zone (stanzas 29 and 30).

Our concern is quickly dispelled in a bittersweet stanza (stanza 31) in which the child asks the father, who we are relieved to learn has in fact returned alive, where all the other soldiers are. He replies that they have returned from the east 'through Wootton Bassett', the small Wiltshire town which, as we know, remains famous for its respectful reception of fallen service personnel repatriated through RAF Lyneham (see **Context** above). This is the father's way of saying gently that the missing soldiers are all dead.

Our hopes are raised that the soldier-father is not only alive but well. But these hopes are dashed as quickly as they were raised. The child says that he has left his smile and his loud shout in Afghanistan, and that whatever has happened to him there makes him weep (stanzas 32 and 33). The child tells us plainly 'Now, I don't like Afghanistan', a disfavour acquired because of the changes the father has undergone: he is no longer the man the child knew (stanza 34), and he blames whatever unknown events happened in that distant place.

In a section of increasingly emphatic and insistent rhythm (stanzas 35 to 39) the child tells us how the once proud soldier now dismisses his time in Afghanistan as 'just a tour' (stanza 35). He is not concerned with the medals he has been awarded, suggesting that they are the trivial stuff of the parade-ground rather than the hard reality of war signified by the roar of artillery fire (stanza 36). He is no longer loud and outgoing, and he no longer sees these things as the mark of a man, but thinks only of the need to take cover when under the fire of the battlefield (stanza 37). He will not 'play soldiers' anymore, and though he will not explain his experiences to the child it is clear that he no longer sees conflict, the business of the soldier, as a matter for play (stanza 38). Unlike the version of himself who went away, the father shows no signs of happiness but 'just sits and stares for hours' towards the east — the direction of Afghanistan and the origin of whatever dreadful experiences have affected him so profoundly (stanza 39).

We may remember that the poem opened with 'My daddy was a soldier' (stanza 1, line 1) and ask ourselves whether the past tense is used there because the father has now left the army, or perhaps because he no longer behaves in a way that the child associates with his being a soldier. Either way, the result is similar.

We are told that the father, whom we know to have been an ebullient and carefree soldier, becomes silent when he thinks about the comrades who died in Helmand which became, for the troops there, 'Hell' (stanza 40).

The final stanza is enigmatic. The child says that one day they too will be a soldier with a gun, and will become one of those who have gone east 'Beyond the morning sun' (stanza 41). It is a statement that sounds almost oracular. Is the child saying that they know that one day they will follow the father's footsteps and join the army, that they too will fight in this place? Certainly the British Army relies upon 'army families', in which succeeding generations follow each other into the services. It may be that the child wants to do the same, regardless of what has happened in the family. Perhaps the child wishes to go to Afghanistan to avenge the father: this seems harsh but it is not impossible, especially if the child does not yet know what this would entail. Perhaps the child sees the father's military service as a source of pride and wishes to share it. But a compelling possibility is that the child wishes to join the army, so much associated with the carefree family life they remember, and to go to Afghanistan in their turn and learn the secret of what happened to the once proud soldier-father. We may be forgiven for hoping that their wish is never fulfilled.

Composition

'Beyond the Morning Sun' is a narrative poem written in forty-one stanzas of quatrains. It is composed in ballad metre with the rhyme scheme ABCB.

The language of the poem is direct, its vocabulary straightforward as befits a poem composed in the voice of a child. The only word for which one might expect younger readers to appreciate assistance is the compound noun 'cap-badge' (= 'a badge worn on military headgear to indicate the wearer's nationality or branch of the armed services', stanza 2, line 3). It may be noted that the speech of the central child character becomes more adult in tone as the poem goes on, and particularly after the return of the changed father, indicating the extent to which the child's experience causes them to grow up or to try to see the matter through more adult eyes.

The poem's punctuation is sparing and conventional.

Throughout the work the poet has left the noun 'daddy' uncapitalised, even when its usage as a proper noun would make capitalisation usual. This also applies to the less frequently used 'dad' and 'mum' where they occur. This not only suggests the youthfulness of the speaker, but makes it clear that the child makes no distinction between 'daddy' as a role and 'Daddy' as an individual (and likewise for the mother). To the loving and innocent child, person, role and relationship are all one.

There is extensive use of enjambment throughout the piece, which promotes the flow of line and is, to some extent, necessitated by the short line structure the poet has chosen to use. The final stanza is indented to approximately three quarters of an average line length, and this sets apart and emphasises the brief internal drama of its enigmatic significance.

The poem contains a number of voltas, both major and minor. These occur at: stanza 8, line 1, where the child's happy life is interrupted by the father's departure; stanza 28, lines 3 and 4, where the father returns but we suspect he may be dead; stanza 31, lines 2 to 4, where we learn that the father has survived; stanza 33 where we learn that the father is unwell; and stanza 41, where we find that the child now wants to join the army rather than being put off it. The effect of these multiple voltas is to send the reader in a quick succession of changing emotional directions.

The poet uses direct speech extensively — it appears in stanzas 4, 9, 10, 11, 14, 22, 23 and 35. This enhances the dramatic effect and immediacy of the action in the narrative at those points. However, elsewhere the poet uses reported speech with similar effect, notably in the child's tense account in stanzas 36 to 38 of things that the changed and unfamiliar father says about the relationship between the innocent (or trivial) 'play' of military matters and the stark reality of the combat zone.

There is an unusual and striking use of rhythm in stanzas 35 to 39. This is a point of high tension in the narrative, conveying the extent to which the soldier-father has been changed by his experience of war and revealing the child's growing and shocked realisation of the extent of that change. From the middle of stanza 35 the rhythm becomes increasingly emphatic, picking up in stanza 36 to a marching pace (or indeed a military drumbeat) that is achieved through the syllabic and tonal values of the line. As this proceeds through stanzas 37 and 38 this takes on a tense, hard (indeed almost frantic) quality, suggestive of the father's stressed and agitated state of mind. This breaks as we get into stanza 39 as we are introduced to the father sitting passively, thinking about his fallen comrades; this is achieved through the use of sibilance in the first and third lines, giving them a sigh-like sense of release. It has been noted that the rhythmic effect across stanzas 35 to 39 resembles that used by Rudyard Kipling in the refrains of his poem 'Tommy', which also deals with the plight of the ordinary British soldier, and the poet has stated that this is a deliberate homage to Kipling's work.

The use of simile and metaphor in the poem appear to be restrained. However, it should be noted that the phrase 'beyond the morning sun', a phrase that occurs four times in the poem in addition to being its title, may be understood to be meant metaphorically as well as literally. The soldier-father has gone to a place in the east, the direction of the rising sun, but he, like others, has also gone to an otherworldly place that is beyond the light of understanding for those who have never seen it, where things happen that take away life for some and change it forever for others. Beyond the light of morning the soldier-father has found a kind of darkness. Perhaps this, after all, is why the child wishes to go there: to learn for him- or herself just what kind of trauma it is that can change life for someone so profoundly, and perhaps with that understanding to help bring back the lost light.

Message

Life presents us with changes. These may be caused by trauma, sometimes to ourselves and sometimes to others: injury, separation, physical or mental illness, and many other causes of traumas may happen to anybody. We may not feel ready to face these things when they occur, we may not want things to change, and they may make us grow up far more quickly than we might have liked, but we can learn to adjust to them and the changes they bring. Life may not be the same, but it goes on and we can still learn to be happy and to achieve.

When we experience trauma we may sometimes feel a sense of loss or helplessness, and wish that life had not changed for us. With the help of others — family, friends or professionals — we may be able to find new ways in life that help us to cope with our trauma and its effects, and to reduce our negative feelings about how life has changed.

We may sometimes find ourselves dwelling upon changes that have occurred, either to us or to those who are close to us. It is to be expected that we may sometimes wish to return to the memory of these things, perhaps to analyse them and see if we can make sense of them. However, we should seek help if we find ourselves doing this as the experience, especially if repeated, can sometimes prevent us from moving on with our lives as we might otherwise do.

Life can leave us with questions. Why did a particular thing happen to us? Is there a reason why it 'chose' us to happen to, rather than happening to someone else? Can we get back to being the way we were before? We may need help, and careful thought too, to get these questions into perspective and begin to find answers. Often things do not 'choose' us, but just happen randomly — accidents, for example. With guidance we can identify the most helpful questions to ask, and find our way towards answers.

Even when very traumatic events have happened, we may remember that we are still here and that we are capable of improving life. Others may not really understand what we have gone through, because some things are so far beyond many people's lived experience. We may find it helpful to try to find ways to explain, at least to ourselves, what we feel and how we will try to make positive changes to our lives.

Even when things seem dark, we know that there is always light to be found.

Lesson plan: 'Beyond the Morning Sun' by Paul Morris

Resources

Copies of the poem — ideally one per pupil, pens and pencils, marker pens, flip chart paper, rulers for SEND pupils to follow a line when reading.

Copies of pupils' safety plans to which they can refer throughout the session/lesson.

The lesson will cover oracy and reading skills.

The session can be done in the round, or as a circle time activity, or at tables, or in an unstructured group. It is suitable for Upper Key Stage 2, 3 and 4.

Links with the PSHE Association PSHE Education Programme of Study

Links have been made to the PSHE Association PSHE Education Programme of Study at Key Stage 2, 3 and 4 as follows:

KS2

- *H17. to recognise that feelings can change over time and range in intensity*
- *H21. to recognise warning signs about mental health and wellbeing and how to seek support for themselves and others*
- *H22. to recognise that anyone can experience mental ill health; that most difficulties can be resolved with help and support; and that it is important to discuss feelings with a trusted adult*

KS3

- *H7. the characteristics of mental and emotional health and strategies for managing these*
- *H11. the causes and triggers for unhealthy coping strategies, such as self-harm and eating disorders, and the need to seek help for themselves or others as soon as possible [NB It is important to avoid teaching methods and resources that provide instruction on ways of self-harming, restricting food/inducing vomiting, hiding behaviour from others etc., or that might provide inspiration for pupils who are more vulnerable (e.g. personal accounts of weight change).]*
- *H12. how to recognise when they or others need help with their mental health and wellbeing; sources of help and support and strategies for accessing what they need*

KS4

- *H6. about change and its impact on mental health and wellbeing and to recognise the need for emotional support during life changes and/or difficult experiences*
- *H8. to recognise warning signs of common mental and emotional health concerns (including stress, anxiety and depression), what might trigger them and what help or treatment is available*

Links with the National Curriculum

Links have been made to the National Curriculum for English at Key Stage 2, 3 and 4 as follows:

KS2 (Years 5 and 6) English programme of study

- *maintain attention and participate actively in collaborative conversations, staying on topic and initiating and responding to comments*
- *drawing inferences such as inferring characters' feelings, thoughts and motives from their actions, and justifying inferences with evidence*
- *discuss and evaluate how authors use language, including figurative language, considering the impact on the reader*
- *provide reasoned justifications for their views*

KS3 English programme of study

- *participating in formal debates and structured discussions, summarising and/or building on what has been said*
- *making inferences and referring to evidence in the text*
- *knowing how language, including figurative language, vocabulary choice, grammar, text structure and organisational features, presents meaning*

KS4 English programme of study

- *listening to and building on the contributions of others, asking questions to clarify and inform, and challenging courteously when necessary*
- *analysing a writer's choice of vocabulary, form, grammatical and structural features, and evaluating their effectiveness and impact*
- *seeking evidence in the text to support a point of view, including justifying inferences with evidence*

Teaching and learning activities

This poem is about stress and trauma caused by change. Change may be due to a divorce, a death, the sudden loss of a family member or beloved pet, the loss of a job, losing a friend, a change of school, etc., all of which can have a profound effect on a young person's life.

The poem is very accessible to all key stages. There are few words that might require explanation. However, two place names which are likely to require clarification are Helmand and Wootton Bassett: the former is a province in Afghanistan notorious for its reputation as the most dangerous in the country; the latter is the Wiltshire market town famous for its respectful reception of fallen service personnel from the Afghan conflict. Pupils may also need to know the term 'cap badge' (stanza 2 line 3) and the importance of insignia in relation to military uniform and service.

- Introduction — share aims of lesson.
- Refer pupils to their safety plans. Remind them of what a safety plan is for. Ask them to read through their own safety plan before they go further and answer any questions they may have.
- Read the poem (teacher/leader to read it aloud) and discuss its content. Ask the following key questions:
  - What is the poem about?
  - Who is the speaker in the poem? How do you know?
  - How did the poem make you feel? Why? How does it do this?

- What is the poem's message?

- Analyse the phases of the child's life as delineated by the poem. There are four phases: the innocent time before the father goes away; his absence and the child missing him; his return, changed; and the time of the child coming to terms with change that follows.. Ask the pupils to work with a partner or in a small group to identify and describe the phases. Record on flip chart paper.

- Take feedback.

- Introduce the key term 'volta' to the pupils. A volta is a place in a poem where the direction of thought or story or feeling changes. Pupils can usually find three clear voltas in this poem and possibly a fourth. Pupils to work with a partner or in small groups to identify the changes. Text mark where the changes occur.

- Take feedback.

- Discuss the rhyme scheme, which is an ABCB scheme. The vocabulary starts off quite simple. As the child gains experience in the poem the vocabulary becomes more adult and so does the structure. The child has become involved with the adult world. There is a particular part of the poem from 'yes the shiny silver medals' when the poem then becomes heavily rhythmical. The poem takes on a rhythm which is like the refrains in Rudyard Kipling's 'Tommy'.

- Ask pupils to reflect on what has happened to the child's father. The father is suffering from post-traumatic stress disorder (PTSD). If pupils are not familiar with this term it will need to be explained to them. What changes occur in the father's behaviour and personality? What impact does it have on the child and the mother? Why does it have this effect? Discuss with a partner or in a small group.

- Ask for feedback.

- Explain to pupils that PTSD is a mental illness that can be caused by a variety of unresolved stress. Give some examples such as a family breakup, sudden death or departure of a loved one, accident, injury or sickness. Events such as these can have a deep impact on the wellbeing of an individual. Discuss how this illness might have a negative effect on a person's behaviour and on their daily life. Record ideas on a flip chart.

- Ask for feedback.

- Discuss the help that is available to deal with post-traumatic stress. Discuss coping responses that can help to alleviate stress such as seeking help, practising deep breathing and relaxation, exercising or going out for a walk, etc.

- Review what has been achieved in the lesson.

- Refer pupils to their safety plans as a place to look if they need help after leaving the lesson.

Extension activities

- Pupils to write responses to the key questions.

- Write about the form, structure and rhyme scheme of the poem.

- Comment on the poem. Did you like or dislike the poem? Why? Give reasons for your opinion.

- Think of alternative titles for the poem and give reasons why you have chosen them.

- Why does dad not talk about the experiences that have obviously affected him so much? Ask pupils to reflect on this.

- Why do you think that no one speaks to the child about the change in their father's behaviour?

- Ask pupils to review the poem. What did they like and dislike about it? Why did they feel this way about the poem?
- Look at situations in pupils' own lives that could have been made better if they had been explained and understood e.g. why we must keep moving houses/schools.
- Research the effects war had on soldiers in WWI. At the time PTSD was often dismissed as shell shock, cowardice, or was otherwise not understood. What do we know about PTSD today? What sort of help is available nowadays?
- Imagine you are the child in the poem. Write a letter to your father explaining why you are worried about him.
- Imagine you are the child in the poem. Write diary entries tracking the changes in your father's behaviour.
- Imagine you are the child's father in the poem. Write about your experiences, thoughts and feelings during your last tour of duty with the army in Afghanistan.

Cross-curricular/topic links

Cross-curricular and topic links may be explored for use in follow-up and for extension work in

- English
- PSHE
- History

Differentiation

Opportunities for discussion in mixed ability pairs.

Differentiation by outcome e.g. quantity or complexity of issues identified, sophistication of response, level of inclusion/contribution, empathy.

Writing quantity outcomes will be differentiated/assessed/moderated according to teacher's expectations of quantity and depth, otherwise by outcome.

Dulce et Decorum est

by Wilfred Owen

Commentary

Bent double, like old beggars under sacks,
Knock-kneed, coughing like hags, we cursed through sludge,
Till on the haunting flares we turned our backs
And towards our distant rest began to trudge.
Men marched asleep. Many had lost their boots
But limped on, blood-shod. All went lame; all blind;
Drunk with fatigue; deaf even to the hoots
Of tired, outstripped Five-Nines that dropped behind.

Gas! GAS! Quick, boys! — An ecstasy of fumbling,
Fitting the clumsy helmets just in time;
But someone still was yelling out and stumbling
And flound'ring like a man in fire or lime…
Dim, through the misty panes and thick green light,
As under a green sea, I saw him drowning.

In all my dreams, before my helpless sight,
He plunges at me, guttering, choking, drowning.

If in some smothering dreams you too could pace
Behind the wagon that we flung him in,
And watch the white eyes writhing in his face,
His hanging face, like a devil's sick of sin;
If you could hear, at every jolt, the blood
Come gargling from the froth-corrupted lungs,
Obscene as cancer, bitter as the cud
Of vile, incurable sores on innocent tongues, —
My friend, you would not tell with such high zest
To children ardent for some desperate glory,
The old Lie: *Dulce et decorum est*
Pro patria mori.

Context

'Dulce et Decorum est' was first drafted by Wilfred Owen during a stay at the Craiglockhart War Hospital near Edinburgh in 1917, at the height of the First World War. Owen had been admitted for treatment for shell shock, a condition he had developed following his involvement in the heavy fighting of the Battle of the Somme in 1916.

The poem's title is taken from the Latin tag *'dulce et decorum est pro patria mori'* ('sweet and fitting it is to die for one's country') which appears in the *Odes* (III.2.13) of Horace (Quintus Horatius Flaccus), the Roman first century BCE lyric poet. In Owen's own poem, however, through vivid evocations of trench warfare he exposes the stark and brutal truth behind this long-propagated, sanitised notion of the glorious patriotic death — what he calls 'the old Lie'.

During Owen's stay at Craiglockhart he met fellow officer and poet Siegfried Sassoon whose sentiments against the conduct of the war were expressed through his refusal to return to the battlefield (a resolution he was later to withdraw) contained in a letter that was to find its way to being read to the House of Commons, and in his own poem 'Sick Leave'. The encounter with Sassoon was to have far-reaching effects upon Owen's life. Owen appears to have seen it as his duty to add his voice to that of Sassoon, telling of the true horror of war.

Owen's simple description of this work as 'a gas poem', made when he sent an early draft of it to his mother, seems inadequate to represent the depth and intensity of experience that lies at its heart. The deathly exhaustion of the marching column of soldiers, the mud, the barely-noticed howls of the 'Five-Nines' (German 5.9-inch artillery shells loaded with poison gas), the speaker who sees from behind the 'misty panes' of his gas mask the plight of the comrade who has not got his own mask on in time, the shattering descriptions of the effects of that gas, a candid and appalled gaze at the hideous reality of war, set the poem apart. Surely nobody could find anything 'sweet' or 'fitting' about this horrid, mundane, squalid business of death.

Owen addressed an early version of the poem 'to a certain poetess'. This is thought to have been Jessie Pope, a poet and journalist who had expressed 'patriotic' enthusiasm for the war, and she may be the 'friend' to whom line 25 refers so bitterly. The poem left no moral space in which to claim glory for such an undertaking.

Although he might have remained on home-duty indefinitely, far from the fighting, Owen was impatient to return to active service in France. His decision to do so was probably a consequence of Sassoon's return to England after he had suffered a head wound that same month. Sassoon himself was profoundly opposed to Owen's return to the trenches, even going to the alarming extreme of threatening to 'stab [him] in the leg' if he tried to do so, presumably in the knowledge that a further wound would prevent Owen from carrying out his plan. Owen's response was to return to France in July 1918, but only to tell Sassoon once he was there.

On 1st October 1918, Owen led his men in storming enemy positions near the village of Joncourt, an action in which he earned the award of the Military Cross and promotion to the rank of lieutenant. He lived to see neither. On 4th November 1918, Second Lieutenant Wilfred Edward Salter Owen MC was killed in action during the crossing of the Sambre-Oise Canal, exactly one week — almost to the very hour — before the signing of the Armistice that would end the war.

Content

The poem opens upon a column of soldiers, of whom the speaker is one, marching — or rather trudging — through the mud. They are bent, coughing and swearing ('cursed', line 2), moving away from the battlefield with its 'haunting flares' (burning lights fired into the air to illuminate the ground, line 3) towards their 'distant rest' (line 4). They are so worn out that some of them seem to be asleep even as they are marching (line 5). Many have lost their boots in the battlefield's sticky mud, and their feet are torn and bloody (line 6). All of them are having difficulty walking ('lame', line 6) and seeing. They are so tired that they seem to be drunk, and not to hear the howling of the German 5.9 inch artillery shells that are falling behind them (lines 7 and 8), shells that are carrying poison gas.

A warning is shouted to the men: 'Gas! GAS! Quick, boys!' (line 9). In a frenzy ('ecstasy', line 9) the men fumble to put on their gas masks ('the clumsy helmets' of line 10) 'just in time' before the poison gas reaches them. One of the soldiers is still shouting and struggling like somebody who is on fire or who is caught in a caustic, corrosive substance ('like a man in fire or lime', line 12). The speaker watches him through the foggy lenses of his gas mask ('misty panes', line 13), in the dim light that is coloured green by the poison gas. It is as though the speaker is 'under a green sea' (line 14), and the stricken soldier looks as though he is 'drowning' (line 14) as he struggles to breathe.

The speaker describes how in all his dreams he watches helplessly as he sees that soldier who 'plunges' at him, 'choking, drowning', on the poison gas (lines 15 and 16).

We may infer that the speaker's dreams are 'smothering' (line 17): this may describe the way they stifle and overwhelm the speaker, or perhaps a more literal reference to the gassed soldier's smothering and asphyxiation by the choking gas. It is in such smothering dreams, of which the speaker clearly has knowledge, that he suggests the reader might walk behind the wagon into which his comrade was 'flung' (lines 17 and 18), a remarkably unfeeling verb to describe the treatment of a dying man. We are told of seeing the stricken soldier's contorted face (lines 19 and 20), and hearing the sound of him choking on blood and froth which has been produced by the corrosive gas (lines 21 to 23), and of the horror of the sores it causes 'on innocent tongues' (line 24). These are the terrible truths the reader may see in such dreams of the reality the speaker has endured.

The speaker asserts that were they to experience such things, even in dreams, then the reader would no longer delight in repeating ('to tell with such high zest', line 25) to young people who are keen to win 'glory' in war (line 26) the 'old Lie' that 'it is sweet and fitting to die for one's country' (lines 27 and 28). The apparent beauty and dignity of the Latin tag are an illusion, and to see the hideous reality of war would dispel such old myth-making in a moment.

Composition

'Dulce et Decorum est' is written as four stanzas of iambic pentameter with a rhyme scheme of ABAB, the end rhymes changing as the poem progresses through its seven quatrains (of which, it should be noted, two are spread across the second and third stanzas).

The poem's language is formalised, with a use of syntax that demands close attention, such that the poet does not allow us to slip lightly over the awful truths he depicts.

There are several words for which the younger reader may appreciate clarification: 'hags' (= 'old women', line 2), 'outstripped' (= 'gone beyond the range of, expired', line 8 — the idea here is that the men are beyond the range of the exploding shells, but not the poison gas they release), 'ecstasy' (= 'an emotional frenzy or concentrated experience', line 9), 'lime' (= 'quicklime, a caustic alkaline substance consisting of calcium oxide', line 12), 'flound'ring' (= 'floundering, struggling or staggering clumsily', line 12, 'guttering' (= 'flickering and burning unsteadily, usually of a candle flame', line 16), 'cud' (= 'partly digested food chewed by a ruminant animal such as a cow', line 23), 'zest' (= 'great enthusiasm', line 25), 'ardent' (= 'very enthusiastic, passionate', line 26), 'desperate' (= 'having a great need or desire for something', line 26).

The poem's punctuation, though relatively complex in places, avoids elaborateness and is precisely as required to convey meaning as if the poem were a passage written in prose.

The poet deploys a number of literary devices in the composition, particularly for the effect of emphasis and focus. The amplification of 'Gas! GAS!' at the opening of line 9 conveys the frantic urgency of focus upon the impending deadly vapour: the emphatic capitalisation of the second word is often omitted in reproductions of the poem, but is clearly present in the poet's original. Owen uses an anadiplosis in the repeated emphasis of 'his face, / His hanging face' at the end of line 19 to the opening of line 20. It is easy to miss the epiphora the poet uses in his repetition of 'drowning' at the ends of lines 14 and 16, although once noticed the effect is not merely emphatic but feels almost like the rising to the surface of someone who is actually in the process of drowning — the 'drowning' man is seen, disappears, then rises again to our now focused attention.

The use of simile and metaphor in the poem carries particular force. The similes include 'like old beggars under sacks' (line 1), 'coughing like hags' (line 2), 'flound'ring like a man in fire or lime' (line 12), 'As under a green sea' (line 14), 'like a devil's sick of sin' (line 20), and the searing 'Obscene as cancer, bitter as the cud' (line 23). The metaphors are numerous: 'we cursed through sludge' (line 2), 'Men marched asleep' (line 5), 'blood-shod' (line 6), 'Drunk with fatigue' (line 7), 'tired, outstripped Five-Nines' (line 8), 'An ecstasy of fumbling' (line 9), 'drowning' (which is not literal, lines 14 and 16), 'guttering' (usually used of a flickering candle flame, line 16). It may be noted that the greater part of the simile and metaphor in the poem occurs in the middle section of the work, particularly in the treatment of the column of soldiers, the gas attack and its awful effects. We may speculate that this is because in seeking to show the non-combatant reader a scene which is so far beyond their experience, the soldier poet chooses to appeal to the non-literal and the representative, daring our imaginations to approach something we must hope never to have to live through.

The 'old Lie' that it is sweet and fitting to die for one's country — *'Dulce et decorum est / Pro patria mori'* (lines 27 and 28), is conveyed in Classical Latin. This was the traditional academic language of the English public schools of the nineteenth and early twentieth centuries, the fertile ground in which the British Empire cultivated the sense of patriotism among the burgeoning officer class that was necessary for its own support. When, a decade after the Battle of Waterloo, the Duke of Wellington had suggested that 'the battle of Waterloo was won on the playing fields of Eton' he did not intend it literally, but meant that the sports and games ethos of the British public school developed the qualities that made men good soldiers and particularly good officers. The Classical Roman belief in the 'glorious death' in battle was part of that mythology, as outmoded as the dead language of Latin. A century after Wellington the notion of glorious war, the illusion of glorious death in the cause of one's country, was to be one more fatality of the Great War.

Message

When we are facing our trauma it can be difficult to describe to others just what we have experienced and the effect it has had upon us. People's imaginations may be limited by the extent of their own experiences in life, and they may find it difficult to understand precisely what we have gone through. We should try to persist, to find other ways of helping them to understand. If we are asked to share the thoughts of others who have experienced their own trauma, we may find it helpful to try to find experiences in our own lives that those traumas might resemble. Often we can find within ourselves a key to understanding others' pain, or to help others to understand ours.

Sometimes when we experience trauma it can feel as though we are merely spectators, watching things happen to us — or perhaps to other people. We should try to remember that often we cannot do anything about the trauma we experience, and we should try not to blame ourselves for being unable to prevent it.

Trauma may lead to us developing problems that require professional help. In some circumstances we may develop problems such as post-traumatic stress disorder that have been brought on by our trauma. If this happens we should try to accept all the help we can from professionals who are qualified to help us, including doctors, counsellors, therapists, teachers and others.

Traumatic experiences may sometimes remain with us. We may dream about them, or we may experience flashbacks or waking visions in which we seem to be visited again by our trauma. We should remember that this is part of having experienced trauma, an example of the overwhelm we felt and the intolerable nature of it. We should try to remember that with professional and specialist help it is possible to overcome this.

If we have experienced trauma it may be distressing, or even annoying, if we hear someone speaking lightly of the thing that has caused us pain. It may help us to remember that it is easy for people to dismiss experiences they do not understand. As we face our trauma, we gain understanding and strength to go forward.

Lesson plan: 'Dulce et Decorum est' by Wilfred Owen

Resources

Copies of the poem — ideally one per pupil, pens and pencils, marker pens, A4 or A5 plain paper, rulers for SEND pupils to follow a line when reading, thesaurus or access to iPads/computers.

Copies of pupils' safety plans to which they can refer throughout the session/lesson.

The lesson will cover oracy, reading and writing skills.

The session can be done in the round, or as a circle time activity, or at tables, or in an unstructured group. It is suitable for Upper Key Stage 2, 3 and 4.

Links with the PSHE Association PSHE Education Programme of Study

Links have been made to the PSHE Association PSHE Education Programme of Study at Key Stage 2, 3 and 4 as follows:

KS2

- *H17. to recognise that feelings can change over time and range in intensity*
- *H21. to recognise warning signs about mental health and wellbeing and how to seek support for themselves and others*

KS3

- *H7. the characteristics of mental and emotional health and strategies for managing these*
- *H12. how to recognise when they or others need help with their mental health and wellbeing; sources of help and support and strategies for accessing what they need*

KS4

- *H6. about change and its impact on mental health and wellbeing and to recognise the need for emotional support during life changes and/or difficult experiences*
- *H8. to recognise warning signs of common mental and emotional health concerns (including stress, anxiety and depression), what might trigger them and what help or treatment is available*

Links with the National Curriculum

Links have been made to the National Curriculum for English at Key Stage 2, 3 and 4 as follows:

KS2 (Years 5 and 6) English programme of study

- *maintain attention and participate actively in collaborative conversations, staying on topic and initiating and responding to comments*
- *drawing inferences such as inferring characters' feelings, thoughts and motives from their actions, and justifying inferences with evidence*
- *discuss and evaluate how authors use language, including figurative language, considering the impact on the reader*
- *provide reasoned justifications for their views*
- *writing — noting and developing initial ideas, drawing on reading and research where necessary*

KS3 English programme of study

- *participating in formal debates and structured discussions, summarising and/or building on what has been said*
- *making inferences and referring to evidence in the text*
- *knowing how language, including figurative language, vocabulary choice, grammar, text structure and organisational features, presents meaning*
- *plan, draft, edit and proof-read through:*
  considering how their writing reflects the audiences and purposes for which it was intended

KS4 English programme of study

- *listening to and building on the contributions of others, asking questions to clarify and inform, and challenging courteously when necessary*
- *analysing a writer's choice of vocabulary, form, grammatical and structural features, and evaluating their effectiveness and impact*
- *seeking evidence in the text to support a point of view, including justifying inferences with evidence*
- *make notes, draft and write, including using information provided by others*

Teaching and learning activities

This poem was written during the First World War. Wilfred Owen wrote it following his experiences fighting in the trenches in northern France. It will be necessary to give pupils some background information about the First World War and the effects it had on soldiers. This will include talking about post-traumatic stress disorder (shell shock) and trauma linked to the horrific scenes that soldiers witnessed. Some of the words in the poem may need explaining to younger pupils to aid understanding.

- Introduction — share aims of lesson.
- Refer pupils to their safety plans. Remind them of what a safety plan is for. Ask them to read through their own safety plan before they go further and answer any questions they may have.
- Read the poem (teacher/leader to read it aloud) and discuss its content. Ask the following key questions:
  - What does the title of the poem mean? (Note: it means 'It is sweet and fitting to die for one's country'.) Why might such a death ever have been thought of as 'sweet'? Why might it ever have been thought of as 'fitting'?

- What is the poem about?
- How did the poem make you feel? Why? Give reasons for your opinions.
- What is the poem's message?

- The poet uses the words 'Dulce et decorum est pro patria mori' in the poem. Does Wilfred Owen agree or disagree with this saying that 'it is sweet and fitting to die for one's country'? Why do you think this? What is Owen's view of war, and why do you think this? Discuss with a partner or in a small group.

- Take feedback.

- Try to identify some of the themes that run through the poem. These might include such themes as war, propaganda, politics, hero worship and patriotism. Briefly discuss some of these themes with the pupils.

- What is the image of war that Wilfred Owen presents? Ask pupils to discuss in pairs or small groups and to find and highlight key words and phrases in the poem that help to create this image.

- Ask for feedback.

- Wilfred Owen saw some terrifying, traumatic things in the trenches. Imagine you are Wilfred Owen and describe some of the things you saw (using evidence from the poem) and how the experience made you feel. Is it just fear, or are there other things? What are they? For pupils who may find this task difficult, they could find alternative synonyms for the words 'fear' or 'trauma' in a thesaurus and record them around a picture of Wilfred Owen with reasons why he felt these things. Alternatively, write a short account of a traumatic experience that has happened to you. Describe what happened and how it made you feel: you may have felt many things all at once. The account could be recorded for those pupils who may struggle with the writing task.

- Review what has been achieved in the lesson.

- Refer pupils to their safety plans as a place to look if they need help after leaving the lesson.

Extension activities

- Pupils to write responses to the key questions.
- Write about the form, structure and rhyme scheme of the poem.
- Read other poems by war poets that recount the horrors and trauma of war. In what ways are they similar to, or different from, Owen's poem?
- Research Wilfred Owen's life. Write a short biography about him.
- Comment on the poem. Did you like or dislike the poem? Why?
- Write your own poem about war or about a frightening or traumatic incident that may (or may not — you can write a fictional piece) have happened to you.
- Is war ever justified? Write a balanced argument.
- Find examples of similes and metaphors in the poem. Can you explain their meaning? Why does the poet use them?
- A symbol that pervades the poem is the idea of a nightmare. Produce a piece of artwork that depicts a nightmare. What colours will you use? Will you incorporate some of the things Wilfred Owen describes in his poem?
- What do we mean by trauma? What traumatic events can impact on people's lives? What help is available? Discuss in PSHE lessons.

Cross-curricular/topic links

Cross-curricular and topic links may be explored for use in follow-up and for extension work in

- English
- PSHE
- History
- Art and Design

Differentiation

Opportunities for discussion in mixed ability pairs.

Differentiation by outcome e.g. quantity or complexity of issues identified, sophistication of response, level of inclusion/contribution, empathy.

Writing quantity outcomes will be differentiated/assessed/moderated according to teacher's expectations of quantity and depth; otherwise by outcome.

Alternative tasks to meet the needs of pupils have been provided in the main part of the lesson.

Differentiation may also be through key words rather than written sentences, or through artwork as a means of expression.

Your Poem Here

by Hannah Kate

Commentary

So I try to put it on paper, like they say,
creating a set of rhythmic lines to unwind
the knot that built up inside the night before
when I formed my words with a different pen,
scribbled marks and underscores
that tasted of copper and heat.
I take a sheet of empty paper,
as white and clean as an exposed arm
and recreate eloquence I found before.
Replace one form with another
to answer other people's questions.
This therapy they sell me
is only an act of translation.

Context

'Your Poem Here' was written by Hannah Kate, a Manchester-based poet, short story writer, editor, publisher and broadcaster.

The poem takes as its theme the difficult topic of self-harm. It explores how self-harm can, for some, be a means of release and self-expression, and what it means to try to find an alternative and less self-destructive way of expressing oneself.

Self-harm is the name given to the practice of deliberately injuring or harming oneself. It is typically done as a manifestation of emotional distress and is one way of coping with or expressing overwhelming emotional pain. People who harm themselves may have one or more of a number of purposes in mind: to punish themselves; to express distress; to relieve or dissipate unbearable tension; as a cry for help; as an act of particular autonomy; or many other personal reasons, depending upon the individual.

The UK's National Health Service suggests that more than half of the people in the country who die by suicide have a history of self-harm.

'Your Poem Here' has its basis in the poet's own life experience, a circumstance that she has particularly asked to be mentioned here. The poem is a reflection of her own experiences of mental health difficulties and self-harm, and her striving to articulate these.

In 'Your Poem Here', the poet explores a moment in which the energy of self-harm is being rechannelled into the positive self-expressive creativity of writing poetry.

Content

The speaker says that she is trying to put down on paper 'a set of rhythmic lines' (line 2) — that is, a poem — to undo the emotional knot that grew inside her 'the night before' (line 3).

On that previous night the speaker 'formed [her] words' (line 4) — that is, expressed herself — with a different instrument whose marks 'tasted of copper and heat' (line 6). The speaker is describing the taste of blood: the marks she has made with the instrument she has described as 'a different pen' (line 4) are cuts to her own skin.

The speaker takes a sheet of white paper, 'clean as an exposed arm' (line 8), and tries to write in a way that is expressive: either as expressive as her writing has been before, or as expressive as she has found self-harm to be (lines 9 to 11) — her precise meaning is ambiguous, and she might very well mean both.

The speaker is trying to replace one form of expression, self-harm, with another one, writing poetry, which can 'answer other people's questions' (lines 10 to 11). The speaker may be referring to the fact that by expressing her inner emotion though poetry, rather than by self-harm, she will be doing so in a way through which is easier for others (therapists, one might perhaps speculate) to find meaning and understanding of her mental and emotional landscape.

The speaker says she has been told that the therapy of writing poetry is 'only an act of translation' (line 13) — that is, of converting one form of expression into another, possibly more readily intelligible, form. Both self-harm and writing poetry consist of using an instrument (a blade and a pen respectively, in this case) to make marks that express emotion and offer release. Though the cuts she makes are not words but 'scribbled marks and underscores' (line 5), to this extent the speaker's act of self-harm is like scribing a poem of sorts into her own skin.

Composition

'Your Poem Here' is written in free verse, without rhyme or regular metre.

The language is quite conversational, and as such feels approachable and accessible to the reader. The poem's punctuation is conventional, being just as it would be had the text of the poem been written as a piece of prose. There is a sense of the poem being an account or report of a real event, but the poet's choice of vocabulary and expression is unmistakably poetic.

The pace of the piece is slow, almost languid, with the poet's language constructed so as to slow down its delivery — it is a poem that is difficult to read quickly — and this serves to sharpen focus on the actions of the speaker.

As in other works by this poet, the poem's capitalisation reinforces its conversational tone, with capital letters being used only to begin a sentence or for proper nouns rather than following the poetic convention of capitalising the initial word of each line.

The poet's use of simile is restricted to the single powerful image of line 8, in which her sheet of paper is 'as white and clean as an exposed arm' — the medium on which the speaker has previously made her marks.

Metaphor is similarly restrained. The 'scribbled marks and underscores' of line 5 are the cuts the speaker makes in her skin.

Message

For some people, what may appear to be a destructive, or indeed self-destructive, act can be a search for catharsis. This does not mean that their actions are a healthy or positive form of release, even if they are all that seem to be available.

There are many ways of dissipating anger, frustration, anguish, desperation, or any of the many other forms of emotional pain we may feel. We should try hard to be open to ways that do not harm or hurt ourselves or others.

We may find that acts of conscious creation allow us to manage our feelings and to express them in ways which help others who are also struggling. These may offer just as much release and relief as our destructive behaviour, or perhaps even more. They might involve an activity such as writing poetry, keeping a diary, painting, music, dance or something else that helps us to express ourselves.

There are many ways to communicate and to express the pain we feel. We should try, perhaps with the help of teachers or therapists or others who are willing to help us, to find those ways which allow us to build and grow a sense of happiness, wellbeing, achievement and healthy self-expression.

Lesson plan: 'Your Poem Here' by Hannah Kate

Resources

Copies of the poem — ideally one per pupil, pencils or pens, flip chart paper, rulers for SEND pupils to follow a line when reading.

Copies of pupils' safety plans to which they can refer throughout the session/lesson. The lesson will cover oracy and reading.

The session can be done in the round, or as a circle time activity, or at tables, or in an unstructured group. It is suitable to use with pupils at Key Stage 3 and 4.

Links with the PSHE Association PSHE Education Programme of Study

Links have been made to the PSHE Association PSHE Education Programme of Study at Key Stage 3 and 4 as follows:

KS3

- *H11. the causes and triggers for unhealthy coping strategies, such as self-harm and eating disorders, and the need to seek help for themselves or others as soon as possible [NB It is important to avoid teaching methods and resources that provide instruction on ways of self-harming, restricting food/inducing vomiting, hiding behaviour from others etc., or that might provide inspiration for pupils who are more vulnerable (e.g. personal accounts of weight change).]*
- *H12. how to recognise when they or others need help with their mental health and wellbeing; sources of help and support and strategies for accessing what they need*

KS4

- *H8. to recognise warning signs of common mental and emotional health concerns (including stress, anxiety and depression), what might trigger them and what help or treatment is available*

- *H9. the importance of and ways to pre-empt common triggers and respond to warning signs of unhealthy coping strategies, such as self-harm and eating disorders in themselves and others [NB It is important to avoid teaching methods and resources that provide instruction on ways of self-harming, restricting food/ inducing vomiting, hiding behaviour from others etc., or that might provide inspiration for pupils who are more vulnerable (e.g. personal accounts of weight change).]*

- *H10. how to recognise when they or others need help with their mental health and wellbeing; to explore and analyse ethical issues when peers need help; strategies and skills to provide basic support and identify and access the most appropriate sources of help*

Links with the National Curriculum

Links have been made to the National Curriculum for English at Key Stage 3 and 4 as follows:

KS3 English programme of study

- *participating in formal debates and structured discussions, summarising and/or building on what has been said*

- *making inferences and referring to evidence in the text*

- *knowing how language, including figurative language, vocabulary choice, grammar, text structure and organisational features, presents meaning*

KS4 English programme of study

- *listening to and building on the contributions of others, asking questions to clarify and inform, and challenging courteously when necessary*

- *seeking evidence in the text to support a point of view, including justifying inferences with evidence*

- *analysing a writer's choice of vocabulary, form, grammatical and structural features, and evaluating their effectiveness and impact*

Teaching and learning activities

This poem lends itself to a lot of discussion — individual, paired, group and class discussion — around the theme of self-harm.

- Introduction — share aims of lesson.

- Refer pupils to their safety plans. Remind them of what a safety plan is for. Ask them to read through their own safety plan before they go further and answer any questions they may have.

- Read the poem (or teacher/leader to read it aloud) and ask the following questions:
  - What is this poem about?
  - What can you infer from the title?
  - What did the person in the poem do to herself? Why do you think she did this?

- What is self-harm? Can you come up with a definition? Pupils to work in pairs or small groups.

- Record answers on flip chart paper.
- Ask for feedback.
- Share and discuss the definition of self-harm from the NHS website https://www.nhs.uk/conditions/self-harm/
- What do you know about self-harming? Why do you think people hurt themselves? What life events could lead to self-harm? Prompt with examples such as divorce or separation, someone close to them dying, anxiety, a relationship breaking up or bullying. Discuss in pairs or in small groups.
- Refer to the overview page about self-harm on the NHS website (see above) which provides reasons why some people self-harm.
- How do people self-harm? Why would they do this rather than choose to express themselves in some other way? Is it really a matter of choice? Begin by referring to the person in the poem and how she self-harms. Discuss with the whole class.
- Ask pupils to identify 'feelings that are hard to deal with' and 'feelings that are easier to deal with' and to place them down in the appropriate column on a flip chart. Ask pupils to explain why they have placed them in each column. What makes feelings easy or hard to deal with?
- Each group to feed back.
- What therapy is offered in the poem? Discuss with the whole class or group.
- What help is available to those who self-harm? Share with the class the different organisations that can help
- Review what has been achieved in the lesson.
- Refer pupils to their safety plans as a place to look if they need help after leaving the lesson.

Extension activities

- Pupils to write answers to the key questions.
- Invite speakers to come into school to raise awareness around mental health e.g. Kooth, Mind, Childline, Samaritans, Mental Health Foundation, a GP, an educational psychologist.
- Produce and display posters around school/setting so pupils know where to go to access help and support.
- Produce a poster or an information booklet that raises the profile of self-harm. What is self-harm? Why do people self-harm? What help is available?
- What should you do if you see cuts/marks on a friend's arms or legs, or if you suspect that a friend may be self-harming? Discuss in PSHE lessons.
- Find an example of a simile in the poem. Can you explain what it is being compared to?
- Find an example of a metaphor in the poem and explain its meaning.
- What does the phrase 'recreate eloquence' (line 9) mean in the poem?
- Who is being referred to in the line 'to answer other people's questions' (line 11)? Why must these questions be answered?
- Write about the importance of strong, supportive friendships.
- Write about the form, structure and rhyme scheme of the poem.
- Produce a piece of creative artwork on the theme of 'a cry for help'.

Cross-curricular/topic links

Cross-curricular and topic links may be explored for use in follow-up and for extension work in

- English
- PSHE
- Art and Design

Differentiation

Opportunities for discussion in mixed ability pairs/groups.

Differentiation by outcome e.g. quantity or complexity of issues identified, sophistication of response, level of inclusion/contribution, empathy.

Writing quantity outcomes will be differentiated/assessed/moderated according to teacher's expectations of quantity and depth; otherwise by outcome.

Differentiation may also be through key words rather than written sentences, or through artwork as a means of expression.

On Pudding Lane

by Elaine Bousfield

Commentary

I hear your voice through the wall
But Miss, I can't face facts today
And words stick like tar in rain.
I am someplace else, lost and small,
Frozen in time as you turn the page
To the Fire of London.
Pictures of children, barefoot, and running
Flames dancing, market stalls scorching,
And you, teacher, talking
About Pudding Lane.

I hear your voice through the wall
But Miss, it's Dad I hear today
His words glued to my brain
Back there in his kitchen.
I am one with words spat in rage
But you're talking about the Fire of London.
My brother's crying, my mum's hiding
Fists are flailing, my father's baying
And you, teacher, talking, talking
About Pudding Lane.

I hear your voice through the wall
But Miss, I cannot learn today.
I'm with my mum at A&E again
You see the doctor's checking my brother and me
And mum's saying we'll manage
But you're talking about the Fire of London.
Dad is steaming, mum's denying
Social worker's spying, I am lying
And you, teacher, talking, talking
About Pudding Lane.

I hear your voice through the wall
And Miss, I need to learn today:
Like how to feel whole again,
Not history stuff but warmer stuff,
To be like them and turn the page —
Not like the Fire of London.
Like how to push the scare away,
To face the day and face my pain
But I fear my words will stick like tar in rain
If I try to explain.

I see you see me through the wall.
I felt your look slip in astray —
Shiny wet, a glance of shame.
Nothing can ever be the same.
I hear your voice, its clearer now. I'm centre-stage.
No fire now. No London.
You're standing here, beside me somehow.
You smile. You see me now.
The flames subside,
I feel calmer, calmer, still: inside
Hope is shining, my dad was lying
And I'm not nothing. And I will tell you something
'Cos you, teacher, you'll understand my pain.

Context

'On Pudding Lane' was written in 2019. The poet, Elaine Bousfield, worked for many years as a therapist with young people. Her poem draws upon her direct and personal experience of children and young people who have experienced the internal conflict caused by having to deal with a home life that is difficult — or, as in the case of the child in this poem, conflict-riven or violent — whilst still having to maintain their everyday world of education and social interaction.

Content

The poem examines the internal dialogue of a school pupil who is taking part in a history lesson.

The teacher is talking about the events of the Great Fire of London which took place in 1666, and particularly about Pudding Lane which was reputedly the location at which the conflagration began. However, the child is unable to concentrate on the lesson because his or her mind is filled with the memory of conflict, threat and violence that comes from living in a household with a violent father. The child's mind returns constantly to the recent, stark and all too real matters that occupy it, matters to which he or she might very well be returning after school. It is a domestic world of anger and pain, of well-meaning professionals whose solicitousness seems to make the situation worse for a mother who is trying to move on with life without her violent partner being moved to commit further excesses. In many ways, by the teacher referring to events of long ago that are not of direct daily relevance, she is similarly not helping the child's situation. The child wants help and advice on practical matters, not stories from history.

The child's memories are so vividly intrusive that they drown out the details of the lesson; but the teacher's voice similarly intrudes repeatedly into the child's contemplation. It is clear that the child is compelled towards the memories and thoughts that occupy his or her mind, whilst at the same time being aware of feeling that they should be taking part in the lesson. It becomes apparent that the child wants to learn, but cannot do so because of the stress and sheer internal volume of his or her inner conflict and preoccupation with their violent home life. We see that the child just wants someone to talk to.

The late volta of the poem occurs when a simple glance from the teacher makes a connection with the child. We are led to speculate whether he or she has seen some element of recognition or understanding in the teacher's look. Whatever it might be, the child grasps keenly at the moment of perceived acceptance, seeing in the teacher someone to whom he or she can talk, and resolves to approach the teacher as someone who will 'understand my pain'. Perhaps this is the first step towards the child getting further support, and even towards healing.

Composition

The poem consists of five stanzas, the first four of ten lines and the last of thirteen lines to accommodate the denouement of the poem's narrative.

The structure of the work is complex and internally intricate.

Every stanza begins with a similar line — 'I hear your voice through the wall' — except for the final stanza which substitutes 'I see you see me through the wall'. The 'wall' referred to in each of these initial lines may be considered metaphorically as the sense of separation from reality that the speaker feels, the sense that they are somehow removed from contact with their surroundings, excluded by the sheer pressure of their thoughts and feelings. Yet even across that distance, and through the teacher's distracting drone, there is a degree of contact to which the speaker clings.

The second line of each stanza addresses the teacher as 'Miss', except for the final stanza in which the speaker uses the more direct 'you', reflecting the directness of contact that he or she now senses.

There is a rhyming, or at least phonemic, regularity between each of the first, second and third lines ('-all', '-ay' and '-ain' or '-ame') and the seventh, eighth and ninth lines ('-ing' or '-ay'/'-ain'). The final lines of the first three stanzas locate the teacher's monologue in 'Pudding Lane', a mundane-sounding setting that is at odds with the dynamic internal life of the speaker's mind. This builds the feeling of familiarity to the point of monotony very effectively from stanza to stanza. For the young speaker, this experience is going on and on; but his or her response becomes ever more emphatic — hearing the teacher, asserting their need, then recalling what prevents their full involvement in the life of their classroom. This is almost mantric or incantatory, with a sense of the near-hypnotic state of an outsider looking in. One may imagine the tension between the speaker's internal landscape and the external manifestation of his or her apparent inattentiveness: a young person who appears to be distracted, absent-minded, but who is actually absorbed wholly in the intensity of their internal world.

The sixth lines of each stanza refer to the Fire of London. This is the point at which each stanza turns. Each is a point at which the speaker pulls focus on what is being discussed in class, and reiterates its immediate irrelevance to him or her. It might be seen as an indication that the speaker is still, at a deeper level, engaged with the teacher's lesson — a point to which they return repeatedly.

The seventh, eighth and ninth lines of each stanza are a desperate expression of the speaker's pain, except for the final stanza in which the emotional loading is reversed to a redemptive realisation of finally being understood.

Beyond its sixth line the final stanza departs from the repetitive structure of the earlier poem, building and elaborating upon the speaker's sense of being understood, of finding a forum in which to speak, of the final possibility of relief and catharsis.

Message

This is a poem of redemption, of realisation that however alone we might feel there is someone out there who understands our pain and is willing to listen. This realisation is essential to the process of healing and validation: that we are worthy of being heard, understood, supported.

The young speaker in the poem is admirable because he or she finds their way through their internal noise, not succumbing to the darkness of their daily home life but remaining determined to be connected with the broader world around them and recognising an opportunity to seek help when it presents itself. Theirs is a quietly patient and determined bravery, to be admired and celebrated.

Lesson plan: 'On Pudding Lane' by Elaine Bousfield

Resources

Copies of the poem — ideally one per pupil, pens and pencils, marker pens, flip chart paper, rulers for SEND pupils to follow a line when reading.

Copies of pupils' safety plans to which they can refer throughout the session/lesson.

The lesson will cover oracy and reading skills.

The session can be done in the round, or as a circle time activity, or at tables, or in an unstructured group. It is suitable for Upper Key Stage 2, 3 and 4.

Links with the PSHE Association PSHE Education Programme of Study

Links have been made to the PSHE Association PSHE Education Programme of Study at Key Stage 2, 3 and 4 as follows:

KS2

- *R9. how to recognise if family relationships are making them feel unhappy or unsafe, and how to seek help or advice*

KS3

- *R37. the characteristics of abusive behaviours, such as grooming, sexual harassment, sexual and emotional abuse, violence and exploitation; to recognise warning signs, including online; how to report abusive behaviours or access support for themselves or other*

KS4

- *R30. to recognise when a relationship is abusive and strategies to manage this*

Links with the National Curriculum

Links have been made to the National Curriculum for English at Key Stage 2, 3 and 4 as follows:

KS2 (Years 5 and 6) English programme of study

- *maintain attention and participate actively in collaborative conversations, staying on topic and initiating and responding to comments*
- *drawing inferences such as inferring characters' feelings, thoughts and motives from their actions, and justifying inferences with evidence*
- *discuss and evaluate how authors use language, including figurative language, considering the impact on the reader*
- *provide reasoned justifications for their views*

KS3 English programme of study

- *participating in formal debates and structured discussions, summarising and/or building on what has been said*
- *making inferences and referring to evidence in the text*
- *knowing how language, including figurative language, vocabulary choice, grammar, text structure and organisational features, presents meaning*

KS4 English programme of study

- *listening to and building on the contributions of others, asking questions to clarify and inform, and challenging courteously when necessary*
- *analysing a writer's choice of vocabulary, form, grammatical and structural features, and evaluating their effectiveness and impact*
- *seeking evidence in the text to support a point of view, including justifying inferences with evidence*

Teaching and learning activities

- Introduction — share aims of lesson.
- Refer pupils to their safety plans. Remind them of what a safety plan is for. Ask them to read through their own safety plan before they go further and answer any questions they may have.
- Read the poem (teacher/leader to read it aloud) and discuss its content. Ask the following key questions:
  - What is the poem about?
  - Why do you think the young person in the poem is unable to concentrate or learn in class? Look for evidence in the poem to support your views.
  - How does the young person in the poem manage to get through the lesson? Who is there for him/her?
  - How did the poem make you feel? Why do you think this?
  - What is the poem's message?
- In pairs or in small groups discuss the reasons that people argue. Ask pupils to record ideas on flip chart paper.
- Ask for feedback.
- The young person in the poem is clearly very distressed by events that have happened at home. What do you think has taken place and what have been the effects on family members?
- Ask for feedback.
- What are the signs that an argument is getting out of hand? Discuss in pairs or small groups. Pupils to record their ideas on flip chart paper.
- Ask for feedback.
- Domestic violence should never be tolerated. What is domestic violence? Discuss. Explain to pupils that there are agencies that can help if an argument/conflict gets out of hand. Discuss other sources of help such as extended family members, friends and friends' families, teachers, other members of the school community.
- What stops people asking for help? What might encourage them to get help? Discuss with the whole class or group.
- Review what has been achieved in the lesson.
- Refer pupils to their safety plans as a place to look if they need help after leaving the lesson.

Extension activities

- Pupils to write responses to the key questions.
- Write about the form, structure and rhyme scheme of the poem.
- Pupils to produce information posters about where to go for help if an argument or conflict gets out of hand. Display posters in class and around school.
- What do you think the young person in the poem should do next? Devise a plan to help him/ her to move forward.
- Imagine you are the young person in the poem. Write a letter to a friend, teacher or extended family member about how you feel.
- How does the young person in the poem show bravery?
- What are the warning signs that someone might be in an abusive relationship? Discuss in PSHE lessons.

Cross-curricular/topic links

Cross-curricular and topic links may be explored for use in follow-up and for extension work in

- English
- PSHE
- Art and Design

Differentiation

Opportunities for discussion in mixed ability pairs.

Differentiation by outcome e.g. quantity or complexity of issues identified, sophistication of response, level of inclusion/contribution, empathy.

Writing quantity outcomes will be differentiated/assessed/moderated according to teacher's expectations of quantity and depth; otherwise by outcome.

Differentiation may also be through key words rather than written sentences, or through artwork as a means of expression.

I'm Standing Strong

This section is about building firm foundations,
being resilient and having a positive outlook on life...

Recovery will come

by Emily Jane

Commentary

There is a young girl too afraid to breathe.
She is soft with a range of rough edges she wishes she could smooth out.
The world has instilled an idea of perfection into her mind.
Chiselled an acidic thought into her alkali mind.
She is stunning, breath taking.
Every time someone dares mention her beauty she blurts out utterances of flaws. Hundreds of poisonous lies spew from her mouth.
Have you ever watched a rose shudder at the mere thought that it could be beautiful?
I have.
Each time she traces a delicate hand over her figure while her mistaken eyes burn into the mirror, she wishes it would set alight.
There was a time, it felt like an age, when she refused to allow any trace of food to pass her lips.
She locked herself away with merely a lighter and the suffocating abyss of black.
I watched as she decayed, my voice drowned out in the ocean of wicked words that overwhelmed her.
She was destroying herself. Did she know?

Every day felt like a year.
One day I remember looking up.
I saw her.
She seemed different.
She was smiling, genuinely smiling.
I gazed after her as she hugged her friends tight and allowed a smile to light her features.
She was recovering.
Though I will never understand how she picked herself up whilst completely alone,
I am proud of the person that I never knew but always understood.

She finally chose to live.
She knows she is worth this life.

Context

Emily Jane has written often about the effects that mental health issues can have upon people, and began doing so in her teens. She has focused particularly on the effects upon wellbeing of stress, low confidence, feelings of being different, and issues of body image. The reacquisition of a sense of self-worth is a recurrent theme in her poetry.

Content

'Recovery will come' is a poem in which we may speculate that the subject, a young girl, might be the speaker herself, or an earlier version of her.

The speaker tells us that the girl of whom she is speaking is afraid, though at first she does not state what it is that she fears. She seems to be driven to focus solely upon her imperfections, or at least her own perception of these, when compared with a notion of perfection that has come to her from 'the world' — presumably from society or her peers. She may have body dysmorphia: she is highly self-critical and appears to be unhappy with her appearance to the point of revulsion.

The speaker says that she has seen somebody experience these things. We are left to infer that she may have seen them in herself, in her own experience and in her own behaviour.

We are told that the girl has mistreated herself. She has deprived herself of food and shown signs of an eating disorder, locked herself away, and possibly self-harmed (the reference to a lighter may relate to this). The speaker has watched the girl do this, but has been unable to make herself heard among the negative noise — presumably internal — that the girl has been experiencing. The speaker wonders, perhaps rhetorically (and certainly so if the girl and the speaker are the same person), whether the girl really knows that she is 'destroying herself'.

The speaker tells us that the situation seemed to go on for a long time, but that one day she saw the girl smiling and realised that she seemed happier — the first signs of the girl's recovery. She does not know how the girl achieved this alone: we infer that she entered this state of recovery without any outside assistance or intervention. However, the recovery seems real and the speaker expresses her pride at the girl's achievement; her reference to 'the person that I never knew but always understood' again inclines us to infer that she is speaking of herself.

In closing the poem, the speaker reveals what it is that has made a difference to the girl: she has chosen to live, and accepted that 'she is worth this life'.

Composition

The poem is written in free verse, without a rhyme scheme or regular metrical structure.

It is organised in three stanzas. These progress thematically. The first stanza, which is by far the longest with seventeen lines, deals with the girl's situation as the speaker sees it. The second, of middle length with nine lines, addresses the girl's recovery. The third stanza, the shortest with a mere two brief lines, offers what might be understood as a reason for her recovery, but might also be a summary of the recovery's consequences. The effect of this is to suggest a process of emergence, from the press of words and impressions with which the poem opens to the sparse clarity of the final couplet.

Punctuation and spelling are conventional. It should be noted that no fewer than twenty-two of the poem's twenty-eight lines end with a full stop, which gives the poem the feeling of being a series of statements, together with a sense of authority and frank openness befitting what is, after all, a work that deals with the revelation of painful experience.

The poet employs enjambment in three locations: lines 10 to 11, 12 to 13 and 15 to 16, all the foregoing being in the first stanza. The effect of this is to place the emphasis in the first stanza upon the telling of the girl's story, rather than permitting the confinement of the storyteller's expression within the strictures of limited poetic line. As the poem continues towards its resolution the need for this intensity of delivery diminishes, and lines are allowed to become simpler and more succinct.

The poem is particularly notable for its extensive and effective use of figurative language.

The work includes a liberal, diverse and highly imaginative use of metaphor. The instances of this include 'too afraid to breathe' (line 1), 'soft with a range of rough edges' (line 2), the almost forensic contrast of 'chiselled an acidic thought into her alkali mind' (line 4), 'poisonous lies' (line 7), the extended metaphor of lines 8 to 9 by which the girl is likened to a rose, 'mistaken eyes burn / into the mirror' (line 11 to 12), 'suffocating abyss of black' (line 14), 'she decayed, my voice drowned out in the ocean of wicked words' (line 15), 'She was destroying herself' (line 17). All of this is contained within the first stanza, in which it serves to build and enhance the complex image of the girl's internal emotional landscape; yet metaphor is almost absent in the second and third stanzas, in which there is a shift from the internal, solitary and imaginative towards the external, social and literal. It could be argued that the poem's last two lines use metaphor, but this is applied with a lighter hand. One might also consider that the poet/speaker might very well be using throughout the poem the extended metaphor of her observation of the girl who, as we have already considered, may be the speaker/poet herself considered from the perspective of her own internal but detached viewpoint.

Interestingly for a poem constructed with such a wealth of metaphor, simile appears to be absent from the composition. However, the discipline that the poet displays in choosing to concentrate on metaphor to construct her imagery serves to keep the work from straying into figurative ostentation.

Message

The message of the poem is salutary: we may be aware of negative aspects of our own wellbeing, almost observing our own behaviour as a detached bystander, without necessarily being able to control that negativity.

We may not understand the reasons for our actions, thoughts and feelings, and may emerge from negativity without ever really gaining full understanding about what we have been going through.

Ultimately, however, the poet offers us an outlook that is hopeful, redemptive and positive. We can move on from our pain, perhaps even without help from others, and in doing so we can gain strength and insight. We can move from solitude to the warmth of happiness and friendship. And we may gain comfort from the poet's assurance that, however dark matters may seem, when we are at our lowest still we may expect that, as the poem's title tells us, recovery will come.

Lesson plan: 'Recovery will come' by Emily Jane

Resources

Copies of the poem — ideally one per pupil, pens or pencils, flip chart paper, marker pens, plain paper, rulers for SEND pupils to follow a line when reading.

Copies of pupils' safety plans to which they can refer throughout the session/lesson. The lesson will cover oracy and reading skills.

The session can be done in the round, or as a circle time activity, or at tables, or in an unstructured group. It is suitable to use with pupils at Key Stage 2, 3 and 4.

Links with the PSHE Association PSHE Education Programme of Study

Links have been made to the PSHE Association PSHE Education Programme of Study at Key Stage 2, 3 and 4 as follows:

KS2

- *H15. that mental health, just like physical health, is part of daily life; the importance of taking care of mental health*
- *H21. to recognise warning signs about mental health and wellbeing and how to seek support for themselves and others*

KS3

- *H11. the causes and triggers for unhealthy coping strategies, such as self-harm and eating disorders, and the need to seek help for themselves or others as soon as possible [NB It is important to avoid teaching methods and resources that provide instruction on ways of self-harming, restricting food/inducing vomiting, hiding behaviour from others etc., or that might provide inspiration for pupils who are more vulnerable (e.g. personal accounts of weight change).]*
- *H12. how to recognise when they or others need help with their mental health and wellbeing; sources of help and support and strategies for accessing what they need*

KS4

- *H9. the importance of and ways to pre-empt common triggers and respond to warning signs of unhealthy coping strategies, such as self-harm and eating disorders in themselves and others [NB It is important to avoid teaching methods and resources that provide instruction on ways of self-harming, restricting food/ inducing vomiting, hiding behaviour from others etc., or that might provide inspiration for pupils who are more vulnerable (e.g. personal accounts of weight change).]*
- *H10. how to recognise when they or others need help with their mental health and wellbeing; to explore and analyse ethical issues when peers need help; strategies and skills to provide basic support and identify and access the most appropriate sources of help*

Links with the National Curriculum

Links have been made to the National Curriculum for English at Key Stage 2, 3 and 4 as follows:

KS2 (Years 5 and 6) English programme of study
- *maintain attention and participate actively in collaborative conversations, staying on topic and initiating and responding to comments*
- *discuss and evaluate how authors use language, including figurative language, considering the impact on the reader*
- *provide reasoned justifications for their views*

KS3 English programme of study
- *participating in formal debates and structured discussions, summarising and/or building on what has been said*
- *knowing how language, including figurative language, vocabulary choice, grammar, text structure and organisational features, presents meaning*

KS4 English programme of study

- *listening to and building on the contributions of others, asking questions to clarify and inform, and challenging courteously when necessary*
- *analysing a writer's choice of vocabulary, form, grammatical and structural features, and evaluating their effectiveness and impact*

Teaching and learning activities

The poem 'Recovery will come' is about a young female with a dysmorphia condition who struggles to come to terms with her body shape and appearance. She also has an eating disorder and may self-harm.

- Introduction — share aims of lesson.
- Refer pupils to their safety plans. Remind them of what a safety plan is for. Ask them to read through their own safety plan before they go further and answer any questions they may have.
- Read the poem (or teacher/leader to read it aloud) and ask the following key questions:
  - What do you think this poem is about?
  - Why do you think the poem is called 'Recovery will come'?
  - What are the stages involved in the girl's condition and her recovery?
  - How did the poem make you feel? How did it do this? Give reasons for your opinions.
- In pairs or in small groups discuss what you know about the young girl in the poem. Record ideas on flip chart paper.
- Ask for feedback from each group. One of the group members could act as a spokesperson.
- In pairs or in small groups discuss the stages of the girl's condition and her recovery. What can we say about each of the stages? How could she have broken the cycle of her unhappiness at each stage, and accelerated her recovery? Is there anything we think she did well? Is there anything we think she might have done better? Record ideas on flip chart paper.
- Ask for feedback from each group. Again, one of the group members could act as a spokesperson.
- What does the line 'The world has instilled an idea of perfection into her mind' (stanza 1 line 3) mean? Where do you think this idea has come from? How important is pressure from society or our peers in affecting how we think and what we do? List some of the things to which this pressure and ideas of perfection might relate — the things about which young people can be made to feel 'imperfect'.
- Look up the term 'body dysmorphia'. What does this mean?
- Discuss reasons why people develop eating disorders. Ask pupils to come up with ideas. List ideas on the whiteboard.
- How do people with eating disorders feel about their bodies? Discuss with the whole class or group.
- If someone feels unhappy about themselves, when do you think is the right time for them to seek help? Why do you think this? Where could they go to look for help? If someone came to you for help, how could you respond?
- Share and signpost sources of available help.
- Review what has been achieved in the lesson.
- Refer pupils to their safety plans as a place to look if they need help after leaving the lesson.

Extension activities

- Pupils to write their answers to the key questions.

- Pupils to write about the form, structure and rhyme scheme of the poem.
- Invite speakers to come into school to raise awareness around mental health e.g. Mind, Kooth, Childline, Samaritans, Mental Health Foundation, a GP, an educational psychologist.
- Display posters around school/setting so pupils know where to go to access help and support.
- KS3/4 pupils might like to read Samuel Pollen's book *The Year I Didn't Eat*. The novel chronicles a year in the life of a fourteen-year-old boy called Max who struggles with anorexia. This reading may be done as a class/group activity.
- In PSHE lessons discuss ways of reducing the stress and anxiety around body image that social media might cause.
- How might an eating disorder affect a person's family and social life? How could it affect school? Discuss in PSHE lessons.

Cross-curricular/topic links

Cross-curricular and topic links may be explored for use in follow-up and for extension work in

- English
- PSHE

Differentiation

Opportunities for discussion in mixed ability pairs/groups.

Differentiation by outcome e.g. quantity or complexity of issues identified, sophistication of response, level of inclusion/contribution, empathy.

Writing quantity outcomes will be differentiated/assessed/moderated according to teacher's expectations of quantity and depth; otherwise by outcome.

The Rainy Day

by Henry Wadsworth Longfellow

Commentary

The day is cold, and dark, and dreary;
It rains, and the wind is never weary;
The vine still clings to the mouldering wall,
But at every gust the dead leaves fall,
And the day is dark and dreary.

My life is cold, and dark, and dreary;
It rains, and the wind is never weary;
My thoughts still cling to the mouldering past,
But the hopes of youth fall thick in the blast,
And the days are dark and dreary.

Be still, sad heart, and cease repining;
Behind the clouds is the sun still shining;
Thy fate is the common fate of all,
Into each life some rain must fall,
Some days must be dark and dreary.

Context

Henry Wadsworth Longfellow was born in Portland in the US state of Maine (then part of Massachusetts) in 1807. He was descended from English colonists who had arrived in New England in the early 1600s, including some of the original Mayflower Pilgrims.

Starting at a private elementary school at the age of just three, Longfellow progressed under his mother's enthusiasm for learning, particularly for reading. His first poem, a short patriotic piece entitled 'The Battle of Lovell's Pond' was published in *The Portland Gazette* newspaper on 17th November 1820, when Longfellow was only thirteen years old.

Two years later Longfellow became a student at the college founded by his grandfather, Bowdoin College in Brunswick, Maine. There he formed a lifelong friendship with Nathaniel Hawthorne, who would also go on to become a luminary of American literature. Longfellow's own literary aspirations flourished and he submitted poetry and prose to newspapers and magazines, including nearly forty poems during his final college year (over half of them were published in *The United States Literary Gazette*). His graduation was followed promptly by the offer of a job as professor of modern languages at his college which, after three years travelling in Europe, he initially declined — though he eventually accepted it, aged only twenty-two, when the salary offer was increased and he was offered the additional post of college librarian.

Two years later Longfellow married, but the union was ill-fated. His wife Mary, a childhood friend, died after just four years as the result of a miscarriage she suffered whilst the couple were travelling in Europe, a trip that had been a condition of an offer of a professorship for Longfellow at Harvard

University. Mary's death in 1835 was to be a tragic theme to which the poet returned repeatedly for many years afterwards.

Longfellow began publishing his poetry in 1839 and his work achieved swift popularity. He had begun to court Frances Appleton, the daughter of a wealthy industrialist, but at first she refused his offers of marriage. She finally accepted in 1843 after several years of dedicated and determined courtship by the poet. The couple had six children. Longfellow's literary attainments were flourishing, enabling him to retire from his post at Harvard 1854 to concentrate on his writing career. However, the couple's happiness was brought to an abrupt end in 1861 when Frances died after her clothing caught fire, possibly caused by a lit candle or burning sealing wax. Longfellow tried in vain to save her, suffering such serious burns in the attempt that he was unable to attend her funeral.

Longfellow never recovered fully from the death of Frances. He lived for a further twenty-one years, during which he continued to write and was a noted supporter of the abolition of slavery.

'The Rainy Day' dates from 1842, some seven years after the death of Longfellow's first wife Mary and during the period when Frances was still refusing marriage. Though he was a successful and popular Harvard professor and his writing career was thriving, 'The Rainy Day' provides us with what might be considered to be a deeply personal glimpse into the poet's state of mind, the storms and dark clouds within his psyche.

Content

The speaker tells us that the day is cold and dark, with rain and constant wind (lines 1 and 2). Outside, a vine is still clinging to an old wall but leaves blow off it with every gust of wind (lines 3 and 4).

We are told that, like the day, the speaker's life is also 'cold, dark, and dreary' (line 6). In it, too, the rain falls and the wind blows constantly (line 7). His thoughts cling to the past, like the vine did to the old wall (line 8); the hopes of his younger days have blown away like the leaves did from the vine (line 9). The days of his life are dark and tedious (line 10).

The speaker tells his sad heart to be still, to stop being despondent ('repining', line 11). Behind the clouds the sun still shines (line 12): we may understand the speaker to mean this both literally and in terms of the world still having the capacity for happiness behind the apparent misery of his life. What has happened to his heart, his emotions, is what happens to everyone (line 13), as some unhappiness must occur in everyone's life (line 14) and some days must feel dark and cheerless. Though unhappiness is inevitable, and perhaps universal from time to time, there is always the hope of happiness beyond it.

Composition

'The Rainy Day' is written in three stanzas of quintains (verses of five lines). The first two stanzas have a rhyme scheme of AABBA, with the end rhymes changing from stanza to stanza, whereas that of the final stanza is AABBC for reasons that are suggested below. The metrical scheme for each stanza consists broadly of iambic tetrameter, changing to trochaic tetrameter in the fifth line (iambs going da-DUM and trochees reversing to go DUM-da).

The punctuation of the poem is conventional, following expression naturally. Its layout divides the work thematically, with the first stanza addressing the day's inhospitable weather, the second stanza the similarly dismal 'weather' of the poet's internal life, and the third his cathartic effort to suppress his dolorous feelings and put his unhappy outlook into perspective.

The poem's vocabulary is largely straightforward and consists mostly of monosyllabic words. Few words are likely to present a challenge to the young reader: 'dreary' (= 'unhappy' or 'tedious', lines 1, 5, 6, 10 and 15), 'mouldering' (= 'decaying', lines 3 and 8), and 'repining' (= 'being unhappy or despondent', line 11).

The poet makes generous use of repetition in the piece, and indeed much of its dramatic effect is derived from his skilful use of the device. Through it the poem's dark focus is rendered cyclical, stressed, its recurrent and monotonous nature thrown into stark relief. Anaphora is used to strong effect in the first and second lines of the first and second stanzas; symploce is used in the repetition of the phrase 'dark and dreary' in the first and final lines of the first two stanzas and the final line of the third. The effect is to emphasise the dull hopelessness of both the day and the poet's internal mindscape, and the relationship between them, a relationship assisted by the internal repetition of 'still cling[s] to the mouldering' in the third lines of both the first and second stanzas.

The repetitive rhyming construction conveys adroitly the cyclical nature of suffering expressed in the poem. Just as the weather becomes worse and then better (first stanza), so life brings its unhappinesses and reliefs (second stanza). The cyclical pattern of suffering and turmoil described in the first two stanzas is supported by their common rhyme scheme AABBA, a structure that brings the stanza back cyclically to where it began, each time with the recurrent and monotonous rhyme 'dreary'. But this pattern is broken in the first two lines of the third stanza, in which the recurring 'dreary/weary' rhymes of the preceding stanzas are overturned as unhappiness is banished and the sun is glimpsed. The stanza shifts to a rhyme scheme of AABBC, in which the unhappiness of the final line, whilst acknowledged as inevitable by the poet's philosophy and still present, no longer sits easily but feels as out of place to us as unhappiness should.

The entire work may be seen as an extended metaphor in which the darkness and misery of the weather is mirrored in the psyche of the poet. Just as the day is 'cold, dark, and dreary', so is the poet's internal life; his memory clings to the past as the vine clings to the decaying wall; the hopes of his youth are blown away just as the vine's leaves are carried away by the gale. Yet the inner light may still shine for him as the sun does behind the storm clouds.

With the realisation that it is a common, if not universal, fate for people to be unhappy sometimes comes the strength of the poet's insight that unhappiness is a 'common fate' of all people, the common lot of humanity, expressed in Longfellow's proverbial aphorism that 'into each life some rain must fall'. Some days must be dull, tedious and joyless; but behind them, if we stand strong, is the reassuring promise of an ever-present bright sun to shine on us when the clouds disperse.

Message

Just as the weather is sometimes dark and miserable, and affects us all whoever we may be, so sometimes unhappiness visits each of us. It is part of the human condition, part of being alive. We should not forget, though, that behind the darkness is the light of something better, always there and waiting to break through.

Sometimes it may seem that our lives are cold and dark. We may fret about the past, perhaps longing for things that have gone. There may be things — the weather perhaps, or other associations and memories — that trigger these feelings. But we may stand strong in the knowledge that unhappiness is not reserved for us alone. We are experiencing what everyone experiences, and whilst this may not be enough to take away our pain it may provide us with some comfort, consolation and hope.

It may be better not to cling to negative memories of the past. The present and the future may have better things to offer us.

Each of us may look within ourselves for the power to stand strong before our unhappiness, the ability to speak internally to our sadness and say 'no, enough'. It may not make our unhappiness go away completely, but our inner realisation, wisdom and strength can be enough to help us make it through to a clearer day.

Lesson plan: 'The Rainy Day' by Henry Wadsworth Longfellow

Resources

Copies of the poem — ideally one per pupil, pens or pencils, A4 or A3 plain paper, rulers for SEND pupils to follow a line when reading.

YouTube 'The Rainy Day' by Henry Wadsworth Longfellow set to music by Erik Quisling: https://www.youtube.com/watch?v=BkC8cSuRKzU

Copies of pupils' safety plans to which they can refer throughout the session/lesson. The lesson will cover oracy and reading skills.

The session can be done in the round, or as a circle time activity, or at tables, or in an unstructured group. It is suitable to use with pupils at Key Stage 2, 3 and 4.

Links with the PSHE Association PSHE Education Programme of Study

Links have been made to the PSHE Association PSHE Education Programme of Study at Key Stage 2, 3 and 4 as follows:

KS2

- *H15. that mental health, just like physical health, is part of daily life; the importance of taking care of mental health*
- *H21. to recognise warning signs about mental health and wellbeing and how to seek support for themselves and others*

KS3

- *H7. the characteristics of mental and emotional health and strategies for managing these*
- *H9. strategies to understand and build resilience, as well as how to respond to disappointments and setbacks*
- *H12. how to recognise when they or others need help with their mental health and wellbeing; sources of help and support and strategies for accessing what they need*

KS4

- *H5. the characteristics of mental and emotional health; to develop empathy and understanding about how daily actions can affect people's mental health*
- *H8. to recognise warning signs of common mental and emotional health concerns (including stress, anxiety and depression), what might trigger them and what help or treatment is available*

Links with the National Curriculum

Links have been made to the National Curriculum for English at Key Stage 2, 3 and 4 as follows:

KS2 (Years 5 and 6) English programme of study

- *maintain attention and participate actively in collaborative conversations, staying on topic and initiating and responding to comments*
- *discuss and evaluate how authors use language, including figurative language, considering the impact on the reader*
- *provide reasoned justifications for their views*

KS3 English programme of study

- *participating in formal debates and structured discussions, summarising and/or building on what has been said*
- *knowing how language, including figurative language, vocabulary choice, grammar, text structure and organisational features, presents meaning*

KS4 English programme of study

- *listening to and building on the contributions of others, asking questions to clarify and inform, and challenging courteously when necessary*
- *analysing a writer's choice of vocabulary, form, grammatical and structural features, and evaluating their effectiveness and impact*

Teaching and learning activities

In the poem 'The Rainy Day' themes of lost and renewed hope, youth and grief are explored to show how past experiences and the presence of sadness affect our lives and how we can overcome multiple struggles in life.

It may be necessary to go through some of the vocabulary to aid understanding of the poem particularly with younger pupils. Words such as 'vine', 'dreary', 'weary', 'mouldering', 'youth' and 'repining' may need to be explained.

- Introduction — share aims of lesson.
- Refer pupils to their safety plans. Remind them of what a safety plan is for. Ask them to read through their own safety plan before they go further and answer any questions they may have.
- Read the poem (or teacher/leader to read it aloud) or listen to Erik Quisling perform it to music on YouTube (see link above) and ask the following key questions:
  - What do you think this poem is about?
  - What does the title 'The Rainy Day' make you think of? What thoughts, feelings and emotions resonate with you?
- Introduce the art/visualisation activity. Ask each pupil to draw a picture based on the details of each stanza. Pupils who find it difficult to work on their own can work with a partner. Allow ten minutes drawing time for each stanza. Pupils can accompany their drawings with words and phrases if they wish. After thirty minutes or so, go around the class and assign each pupil the number of a stanza. Ask all the pupils who have been given a number one, a number two or a number three to sit together in their groups. If you feel there are too many pupils in each group then have two groups for each stanza. Ask each person in the group to show their sketch to the rest of the group and to talk about what it shows. Ask pupils to

reflect on each other's work. Which drawing contains the most information about the contents of the stanza?

- Ask for feedback from each group and reflections on the activity.
- Explain to pupils that if a person is clinically depressed, they often find it difficult to get out of their low mood. It affects the person's ability to carry on with daily life. When the feelings of sadness, hopelessness or despair last longer than a few weeks and interfere with school life and activities, professional help may be needed. Professionals can give counselling and medication to help them get back to feeling normal again. It is important to talk about the help available so that pupils know where to go for support.
- Share and signpost sources of available help.
- Review what has been achieved in the lesson.
- Refer pupils to their safety plans as a place to look if they need help after leaving the lesson.

Extension activities

- Pupils to write their answers to the key questions.
- Pupils to write about the form, structure and rhyme scheme of the poem.
- Pupils to write about the poet's use of metaphorical language in the poem.
- In circle time activities or in a one-to-one situation, ask pupils to reflect on issues that worry them, make them feel down, or make them sad. For example, exam stress, COVID-19, starting a new school, the loss of a family pet or family member. Discuss ways of coping with these issues.
- Invite speakers to come into school to raise awareness around mental health e.g. Mind, Kooth, Childline, Samaritans, Mental Health Foundation, a GP, an educational psychologist.
- Display posters around school/setting so pupils know where to go to access help and support.
- Listen to Erik Quisling's song on YouTube. How did the song make you feel? How and why did it do this?
- Pupils to sing along to Erik Quisling's rendition of 'The Rainy Day'.
- Working in pairs or small groups, pupils to produce and perform their own music to accompany the words of the poem, or choreograph expressive actions to go with the Erik Quisling song.

Cross-curricular/topic links

Cross-curricular and topic links may be explored for use in follow-up and for extension work in

- English
- PSHE
- Music
- Art and Design

Differentiation

Opportunities for discussion in mixed ability pairs/groups.

Differentiation by outcome e.g. quantity or complexity of issues identified, sophistication of response, level of inclusion/contribution, empathy.

Writing quantity outcomes will be differentiated/assessed/moderated according to teacher's expectations of quantity and depth; otherwise by outcome.

Differentiation may also be through key words rather than written sentences, or through artwork as a means of expression.

Differentiation through musical participation as a means of expression.

Promise Yourself
by Christian D. Larson

Commentary

To be so strong that nothing
can disturb your peace of mind.
To talk health, happiness, and prosperity
to every person you meet.

To make all your friends feel
that there is something in them.
To look at the sunny side of everything
and make your optimism come true.

To think only the best, to work only for the best,
and to expect only the best.
To be just as enthusiastic about the success of others
as you are about your own.

To forget the mistakes of the past
and press on to the greater achievements of the future.
To wear a cheerful countenance at all times
and give every living creature you meet a smile.

To give so much time to the improvement of yourself
that you have no time to criticize others.
To be too large for worry, too noble for anger, too strong for fear,
and too happy to permit the presence of trouble.

To think well of yourself and to proclaim this fact to the world,
not in loud words but great deeds.
To live in faith that the whole world is on your side
so long as you are true to the best that is in you.

Context

Christian Daa Larson was born in Iowa in 1874, just a few years after end of the devastating American Civil War, and was of Norwegian descent.

Larson attended Iowa State College and Pennsylvania's Meadville Theological School, and it is believed that he intended to enter a Lutheran seminary to train for Christian ministry. However, in his early twenties he began to follow the teaching of Mental Science, one of the schools of thought that flourished in the later nineteenth century interested in the power and potential of the human mind and spirit.

Larson went on to become a founder of the New Thought movement, which was (and in a revised form still remains) concerned with beliefs in metaphysics, life force, personal power, spirituality, positive thinking and creative visualisation. Broadly, New Thought held that God (or, as they had it, the 'Infinite Intelligence') is everywhere, that spirit is everything, that true human selfhood is divine, divine thought a force for good, and that so-called 'right thinking' was capable of healing. In 1898, aged just twenty-four, Larson organised the New Thought Temple at his home in Cincinnati, Ohio, and three years later began to publish a leading New Thought periodical entitled *Eternal Progress* which grew to enjoy a circulation of over a quarter of a million. Meanwhile, he began his book writing career and became the prolific author of metaphysical and New Thought works.

'Promise Yourself' was written in 1912, and was adopted by then-new Optimist Club such that it became known by the alternative title of 'The Optimist Creed'. The organisation grew to become the modern Optimist International, a volunteer organisation working in more than twenty countries, who explain their mission as 'By providing hope and positive vision, [to] bring out the best in youth, our communities and ourselves', their purpose 'To develop optimism as a philosophy of life utilizing the tenets of the Optimist Creed… in the belief that the giving of one's self in service to others will advance the well-being of humankind, community life and the world'. 'The Optimist Creed' consists of the ten precepts that form the first five stanzas of the poem. As such, 'Promise Yourself' is the only poem in this book around which an entire shared life philosophy has been consciously built.

Content

The poem addresses the reader directly and contains two affirmations in each stanza, each of which should be read as being preceded by the title phrase 'promise yourself'; so that for example the first becomes 'Promise yourself to be so strong that nothing can disturb your peace of mind'.

The first stanza talks of promising to be so strong that our peace of mind cannot be disturbed, and of talking of success — 'health, happiness, and prosperity' (lines 3 and 4) — to everyone we meet.

The second stanza refers to making our friends feel that there is 'something' (line 6), by which we may infer 'something special', in them. We are advised to see the 'sunny side of everything' (line 7) and to make our optimism come true — an essential step beyond simply wishing for the best.

We are encouraged in the third stanza to be guided by 'the best' and to pursue it (lines 9 and 10), being as keen to see others succeed as we are for our own success (lines 11 and 12).

The errors of past times are to be set aside as we progress to the greater attainments of the future (lines 13 and 14). We must always put on a cheerful look and smile at every living thing we encounter (lines 15 and 16).

We should, we are told, devote so much of our time to making ourselves better that we have no time to be critical of other people (lines 17 and 18). We should be spiritually too great to worry, we should be above anger, we should be too strong within ourselves to feel afraid, and our internal happiness should not allow us to feel troubled (lines 19 and 20).

Our good opinion of ourselves should be announced to the world in what we do, rather than what we say about ourselves (lines 21 and 22). We should live in the belief that as long as we are faithful to the best that is within us, the world will be on our side (lines 23 and 24).

Composition

'Promise Yourself' is a didactic epistolary poem. It is written in the form of a direct address to the reader that seeks to teach, particularly in terms of knowledge or morals.

The poem is written in free verse, in six stanzas of quatrains, without rhyme scheme or regular metre.

The poem's language is direct, though not especially informal. The effect of this is to retain a certain degree of dignified authority, as befits an extended piece of instruction. The vocabulary is accessible, with few instances of words that are likely to be unfamiliar to the young reader: 'prosperity' (= 'wealth', line 3), 'countenance' (= 'face', line 15), 'large' (= 'great of character', line 19), 'proclaim' (= 'announce, make known', line 21).

Each stanza, consisting of a quatrain, contains two instructions each of couplets (that is, two lines' length). The poet uses enjambment freely to provide easy continuation across the two lines of the majority of these couplets, the device being used in nine out of twelve cases.

Every couplet ends in a full stop, demarcating the self-contained nature of the instruction it contains.

Anaphora is used throughout the poem in the 'To' opening of every couplet. This adds a declamatory feel to the poem, especially when it is read aloud. The poet also makes effective use of epistrophe (the repetition of a word or phrase at the end of successive lines or clauses) with the triple occurrence in lines 9 and 10 of 'only [for] the best', a device that both creates a rhythm in the line and emphasises the repeated phrase, here amplifying a key concept in the poem.

For such an idealistically committed poem, 'Promise Yourself' is remarkably pragmatic and does not concern itself with flights of fancy. Figurative language is kept to the minimum. The only clearly discernible metaphor in the work, 'the sunny side of everything' (line 7), is unobtrusive and barely metaphorical at all.

In many ways the poem reads like a manifesto — or, as it has become known, a creed. It might certainly have been rendered as a prose poem, and perhaps purely as prose. Poetry, however, achieved through the work's lineation and its quality of expression, is perhaps the most suitably elevated medium for a work that conveys such a concentrated focus of worthy thought.

Message

It can be helpful to have a set of principles or guidance in life by which to help regulate and inform our daily behaviour, a set of principles or guidelines that we may set out for ourselves as a kind of roadmap to guide our way. This may give us a sense of strength and security. Some people may find this in religion, in philosophy, in one of the many secular life guidance pathways, or it may be something we create for ourselves.

We should aim to develop and improve our inner strength and resilience, which can help us to deal with many of the difficulties that life can present.

Positivity and a resolve to be as cheerful as we can be may help us through dark times, and they may also communicate themselves to others who are in need of the light we can show. Our own strength may be infectious.

Making others feel that they are appreciated, valued and wanted is good not only for the world around us but also for ourselves, as we will be seen in a better light by others who may be happy to have us around. Positivity has a way of coming back to us.

If we always try to do our best, try hard and aim for the best outcome we can achieve, we can always assure ourselves that we have sought what is good for us and for the world around us. We should not try to do things that cause harm to others, but rather things that help the general good.

Teaching ourselves to feel joyful about the good fortune of others helps us to avoid envy and jealousy which can be corrosive to our mental health. We should try to be as happy for others' success as we would hope that they would be for ours.

Sometimes it is easy to feel that we are held back or pulled down by the past, by the memory of bad or negative things. It may be that these are very significant events with which we need help, and we should try to get that help where we need it. However, so far as we can we should try hard to set aside smaller causes of negativity: just because things have not gone well in the past is no reason why they will not go well for us in the future. We may very well do better if we go forward with positivity, optimism and the resolve that both we and the things around us will become better.

We should allow ourselves to succeed, and not stand in our own way.

Strength often comes in the form of gentleness, and if we are gentle and helpful to others whilst we are trying to go forward, we help both ourselves and the world. It is not necessary for us to be self-centred, brash or hard. Gentleness and persistence may achieve what mere brute strength cannot: rock is hard, water is soft, yet water's gentle power will wear away the hardest stone.

Lesson plan: 'Promise Yourself' by Christian D. Larson

Resources

Copies of the poem — ideally one per pupil, pens, pencils or marker pens, flip chart paper, rulers for SEND pupils to follow a line when reading. Extra paper should be made available for use if required.

The lesson plan is suitable to use with pupils at Upper Key Stage 2, 3 and 4.

The lesson will cover oracy and reading skills.

The session can be done in the round, or as a circle time activity, or at tables, or in an unstructured group, for all age groups.

Links with the PSHE Association PSHE Education Programme of Study

Links have been made to the PSHE Association PSHE Education Programme of Study at Key Stage 2, 3 and 4 as follows:

KS2

- *H15. that mental health, just like physical health, is part of daily life; the importance of taking care of mental health*
- *H16. about strategies and behaviours that support mental health — including how good quality sleep, physical exercise/time outdoors, being involved in community groups, doing things for others, clubs, and activities, hobbies and spending time with family and friends can support mental health and wellbeing*

- *H28. to identify personal strengths, skills, achievements and interests and how these contribute to a sense of self-worth*

KS3

- *H1. how we are all unique; that recognising and demonstrating personal strengths build self-confidence, self-esteem and good health and wellbeing*
- *H7. the characteristics of mental and emotional health and strategies for managing these*
- *H10. a range of healthy coping strategies and ways to promote wellbeing and boost mood, including physical activity, participation and the value of positive relationships in providing support*

KS4

- *H5. the characteristics of mental and emotional health; to develop empathy and understanding about how daily actions can affect people's mental health*
- *H7. a broad range of strategies — cognitive and practical — for promoting their own emotional wellbeing, for avoiding negative thinking and for ways of managing mental health concerns*

Links with the National Curriculum

Links have been made to the National Curriculum for English at Key Stage 2, 3 and 4 as follows:

KS2 (Years 5 and 6) English programme of study

- *maintain attention and participate actively in collaborative conversations, staying on topic and initiating and responding to comments*
- *discuss and evaluate how authors use language, including figurative language, considering the impact on the reader*
- *provide reasoned justifications for their views*

KS3 English programme of study

- *participating in formal debates and structured discussions, summarising and/or building on what has been said*
- *knowing how language, including figurative language, vocabulary choice, grammar, text structure and organisational features, presents meaning*

KS4 English programme of study

- *analysing a writer's choice of vocabulary, form, grammatical and structural features, and evaluating their effectiveness and impact*
- *make an informed personal response, recognising that other responses to a text are possible and evaluating these*

Teaching and learning activities

This poet speaks about the reasons to be positive and optimistic in life.

- Introduction — share aims of lesson.
- Refer pupils to their safety plans. Remind them of what a safety plan is for. Ask them to read through their own safety plan before they go further and answer any questions they may have.
- Read the poem (or teacher/leader to read it aloud) and discuss its content. Ask key questions:
  - What is this poem about?

- How does this poem make you feel? Why do you feel that way? How does the poem do this?

- The poet uses the lines 'To look at the sunny side of everything / and make my optimism come true' (lines 7 and 8). What does this line mean to you?

- Divide the class into small groups of three or four. Give each group a line from the poem to discuss. What does the line mean to you? How would you put this promise into practice? How would it help to make you stronger? How might it help others or the world around you? Record ideas on a flip chart.

- Take feedback from the groups.

- Ask pupils to write their own promise to themselves. Ask them to reflect on how they will keep their promise. What strategies will they employ? For example, they may want to track their progress by recording it in a journal. What obstacles might stand in the way and how can these be overcome? The promise can be revisited on a frequent basis.

- Review what has been achieved in the lesson.

- Refer pupils to their safety plans as a place to look if they need help after leaving the lesson.

Extension activities

- Pupils to write their answers to the key questions.

- Pupils to decorate the poem using positive, affirming images.

- Ask each pupil to write their own 'I Promise Myself' poem. Each line should begin with the phrase 'I promise myself'.

- Think of alternative titles for the poem 'Promise Yourself'.

- Prepare the poem to read aloud and to perform, showing understanding through intonation, tone and volume so that the meaning is clear to an audience. It could be read as a class or group poem, or with individuals being chosen to recite a line.

- Pupils to write their own class or school promise poems. These could be displayed in the classroom or around school. This is a good activity when pupils are moving class or school and can help to establish a positive culture at the start of an academic year.

- Ask pupils to reflect on the phrase 'how to stay optimistic'. What does this mean to you? Think of ways to stay optimistic in your outlook.

- Ask pupils to find famous quotes on the theme of optimism. Display the quotes in the classroom and around school.

- The following quote is taken from AA Milne's famous book *Winnie the Pooh*. Read the quote out loud.

    'What day is it?' asked Pooh.

    'It's today', squealed Piglet.

    'My favourite day', said Pooh.

Discuss with a partner your favourite school day. Why is it your favourite school day? Which day do you like the least? Why is that day your least favourite? How can you make your least favourite day feel better for yourself?

- Write a class poem called 'I Promise Myself'. Each pupil is to write a line.

Cross-curricular/topic links

Cross-curricular and topic links may be explored for use in follow-up and for extension work in

- English

- Drama
- PSHE
- Art and Design

Differentiation

Opportunities for discussion in mixed ability pairs.

Differentiation by outcome e.g. quantity or complexity of issues identified, sophistication of response, level of inclusion/contribution, empathy.

Writing quantity outcomes will be differentiated/assessed/moderated according to teacher's expectations of quantity and depth; otherwise by outcome.

Differentiation may also be through artwork as a means of expression.

Old Tree

by Judy Morris

Commentary

Snap!
A knotty-gnarled finger breaks.
A creaking sigh
As you inhale,

                Exhale...

Drinking in life's ever-changing seasons,
Weathering all storms,
A monolithic frame of towering strength
You stand: proud —

Grounded.

Tracing and retracing
The footsteps of time;
Of cherished afternoons spent smiling with you.

Context

'Old Tree' was written when the poet had been thinking about the oldest tree in her garden, which had recently been pollarded and had had all its branches removed. She was looking at a sawn log that had been saved. The tree was over a hundred and fifty years old and had withstood time's tide, and this inspired the poet to think about her relationship with the tree.

Content

The poem talks about how we stand strong, sometimes blending into the scenery but withstanding whatever life throws at us. The tree is a living, breathing organism, just like humans, and it has its own rhythms of life that vary through the seasons. Like the tree, we all have our roots and we all have our memories. The poem is metaphorical and comparisons are drawn between humans and the natural world.

Composition

The opening line is a single sharp, sudden sound — the breaking of a twig, perhaps. But 'snap!' is also a common exclamation. It is something we shout when we realise that something is broken. We may also shout 'snap!' when we realise that something is very similar to something else, like when we are wearing similar clothes to another person.

The poet suddenly realises the similarity between herself and the old tree. We break too, and bits of our lives 'fall off' or are trimmed away. But we keep growing, and we can get stronger. The poem is optimistic: though the tree has been through a lot in its long life, it is still standing strong and it will heal and recover. The final line, 'Of cherished afternoons spent smiling with you', could refer to the poet's thoughts about having known the tree for a long time; or perhaps she is thinking about someone she has known and with whom she has enjoyed the tree's company.

'Old Tree' is written in free verse, with no regular metre or rhyme scheme. The lines are organised in groups of 4, 1, 4, 1 and 3. The spacing of the lines is arranged so as to emphasise certain words — 'exhale' and 'grounded' (lines 5 and 10) — and to slow down the poem's pace by making the reader pause and breathe.

Message

The message of the poem is that sometimes we need to search our innermost selves for those happy memories of favourite moments. These memories can keep us rooted, grounded, strong.

It can be too easy to lose sight of what we value, especially when there have been big changes in our lives, or when we are going through those changes. Sometimes we need to remember something simple and happy — like being with an old friend, smiling.

Lesson plan: 'Old Tree' by Judy Morris

Resources

Copies of the poem — ideally one per pupil, rulers for SEND pupils to follow a line when reading, Post-it notes, pens and pencils or marker pens. Extra paper should be made available for use if required.

The lesson plan is suitable to use with pupils at Upper Key Stage 2, 3 and 4.

The lesson will cover oracy and reading skills.

The session can be done in the round, or as a circle time activity, or at tables, or in an unstructured group, for all age groups.

Links with the PSHE Association PSHE Education Programme of Study

Links have been made to the PSHE Association PSHE Education Programme of Study at Key Stage 2, 3 and 4 as follows:

KS2

- *H16. about strategies and behaviours that support mental health — including how good quality sleep, physical exercise/time outdoors, being involved in community groups, doing things for others, clubs, and activities, hobbies and spending time with family and friends can support mental health and wellbeing*
- *H27. to recognise their individuality and personal qualities*

KS3

- *H1. how we are all unique; that recognising and demonstrating personal strengths build self-confidence, self-esteem and good health and wellbeing*
- *H10. a range of healthy coping strategies and ways to promote wellbeing and boost mood, including physical activity, participation and the value of positive relationships in providing support*

KS4

- *H1. to accurately assess their areas of strength and development, and where appropriate, act upon feedback*
- *H7. a broad range of strategies — cognitive and practical — for promoting their own emotional wellbeing, for avoiding negative thinking and for ways of managing mental health concerns*

Links with the National Curriculum

Links have been made to the National Curriculum for English at Key Stage 2, 3 and 4 as follows:

KS2 (Years 5 and 6) English programme of study

- *maintain attention and participate actively in collaborative conversations, staying on topic and initiating and responding to comments*
- *discuss and evaluate how authors use language, including figurative language, considering the impact on the reader*
- *provide reasoned justifications for their views*

KS3 English programme of study

- *participating in formal debates and structured discussions, summarising and/or building on what has been said*
- *knowing how language, including figurative language, vocabulary choice, grammar, text structure and organisational features, presents meaning*

KS4 English programme of study

- *analysing a writer's choice of vocabulary, form, grammatical and structural features, and evaluating their effectiveness and impact*
- *make an informed personal response, recognising that other responses to a text are possible and evaluating these*

Teaching and learning activities

This poem is about searching our innermost selves for those happy memories of favourite moments. The tree is a symbol of strength and endurance, resilience and the familiar.

- Introduction — share aims of lesson.
- Refer pupils to their safety plans. Remind them of what a safety plan is for. Ask them to read through their own safety plan before they go further and answer any questions they may have.
- Read the poem (or teacher/leader to read it aloud) and discuss its content. Use of questions 'what-who-where-when-how-why':
  - What is this poem about?
  - Who is speaking in the poem?
  - Where/when is the poem set?
  - How does it make you feel? How does it do this?
  - Why do you think the poet has chosen a tree as a metaphor to talk about human feelings?
- Discuss the following with a talk partner. Think of a time when you have felt low. What was your experience and how did you deal with that feeling? Did it help you to think about happy times, friends or family, or something else? For those pupils who do not wish to share emotional experience openly, responses can be written down and posted into a worry box for

the teacher/leader to read out, respecting anonymity. It is important to keep asking 'Why do you think that?' to encourage pupils to reflect.

- Take feedback and comments from pupils.
- Pupils to be given time to reflect upon their personal strengths. Using Post-it notes, pupils to write down key words or phrases that help them to get through difficult situations. Pupils to read out their key words or phrases to share with the group.
- Explore together common experience and responses to the above activity. Where can you go for help and support? Who can you talk to? What might get in the way of you talking about your situation? How might you get over these barriers?
- Finish by asking pupils to say one positive thing about themselves and one positive thing about the session. Go around the group as many times as you can.
- Review what has been achieved in the lesson.
- Refer pupils to their safety plans as a place to look if they need help after leaving the lesson.

Extension activities

- Pupils to write their answers to the 'what-who-where-when-how-why' questions.
- Pupils to write about a personal experience of a time in their life when they felt low, how they reacted to that feeling, what they did to try to remedy it and how this worked.
- Words and phrases written on Post-it notes can be displayed on a working wall for pupils to see and refer back to.
- Agony aunt/uncle situation, working with a partner. Write a letter to an agony aunt or agony uncle about a personal experience. Exchange letters with your partner. Write advice to your partner based on their letter.
- Write a letter to the tree in the poem, or to a long-lasting object that is familiar to you in your life (it might be a building, a statue, a wall, a local landmark, etc.) talking about how the object has remained strong. Think about how you could use some of those characteristics of strength in your own life.
- Write your own 'tower of strength' poems, based on the tree or on a long-lasting object that is familiar to you in your life.
- Think of alternative titles for the poem 'Old Tree'.
- Put together collages or mixed media work (images, cuttings, painting and drawing) using images of strength and endurance. What do we think of as 'strong'? Are there some unusual ways of being strong that we often miss?
- Prepare the poem to read aloud and to perform, showing understanding through intonation, tone and volume so that the meaning is clear to an audience.

Cross-curricular/topic links

Cross-curricular and topic links may be explored for use in follow-up and for extension work in

- English
- Drama
- PSHE
- Art and Design

Differentiation

Opportunities for discussion in mixed ability pairs.

Differentiation by outcome e.g. quantity or complexity of issues identified, sophistication of response, level of inclusion/contribution, empathy.

Writing quantity outcomes will be differentiated/assessed/moderated according to teacher's expectations of quantity and depth; otherwise by outcome.

Differentiation may also be through artwork as a means of expression.

Past, Present, Future

by Emily Brontë

Commentary

Tell me, tell me, smiling child,
What the past is like to thee?
'An Autumn evening soft and mild
With a wind that sighs mournfully.'

Tell me, what is the present hour?
'A green and flowery spray
Where a young bird sits gathering its power
To mount and fly away.'

And what is the future, happy one?
'A sea beneath a cloudless sun;
A mighty, glorious, dazzling sea
Stretching into infinity.'

Context

For detail regarding Emily Brontë's life, see the **Context** section to her poem 'Love and Friendship' in the **My Love, My Friendships** section of this guide.

'Past, Present, Future' is usually dated to 1836, but did not appear in the 1846 volume of collected poetry of Emily and her two sisters Charlotte and Anne, *Poems by Currer, Ellis, and Acton Bell*. It remained unpublished during the poet's lifetime, being first printed privately by Dodd, Mead and Company of New York in 1902 and later appearing in *The Complete Poems of Emily Brontë* in 1908.

The poem was written when the poet was just seventeen years old and preparing to become a teacher at Roe Head School near Mirfield in West Yorkshire, having attended the school briefly as a pupil the previous year. It is tempting to speculate whether the poem's preoccupation with the thoughts of children is a product of Emily's inclination towards her teaching vocation.

Content

The speaker addresses a child directly.

The speaker invites the happy child to tell her what the past is like to him or her (lines 1 and 2). The child replies that it is like a 'soft and mild' autumn evening (line 3) in which the wind 'sighs mournfully' (line 4).

The speaker asks the child to tell her about what the present time is like (line 5). The child answers that it is like green, flowery foliage (line 6) where a young bird sits to gather its strength (line 7) before it takes off and flies away (line 8).

Lastly the speaker asks the child to describe the future (line 9). The child says that it is like the sea beneath a clear sunny sky (line 10); it is mighty, glorious and dazzling (line 11) and stretches away endlessly (line 12).

The child finds the past gentle, but slightly sad. The present is a time of hope and expectation, of gathering new strength to do greater things. The future is dazzlingly brilliant and beautiful, an infinite vista of possibility.

Composition

'Past, Present, Future' is an epistolary poem and is written in three stanzas, each of which is a quatrain. The rhyme scheme ABAB is used for the first two stanzas, the end rhymes changing between them, whilst the final stanza uses the scheme AABB.

The metre varies with each stanza: the syllabic pattern in the first is 7, 7, 8, 8; in the second it is 8, 6, 9, 6 (assuming that 'gathering' is read as an elided two syllables); and in the final stanza 9, 8, 9, 8. Whilst not strictly regular, this variation imparts to the work a lilting and almost hymn-like pace that is easy to read aloud.

The poem's three-stanza structure lends itself to the thematic treatment of past, present and future, one stanza being focused upon each of these in order.

The poem's language is somewhat archaic even for its time, an effect that adds a sense of importance to the words of both the main speaker and the child. This is achieved chiefly through phrasing, with some assistance from the poet's choice of vocabulary such as 'thee' (line 2). There is little vocabulary with which the young reader is likely to be unfamiliar: 'thee' (= 'you', line 2), 'spray' (= 'branch, foliage, greenery', line 6), 'mount' (= 'take off', line 8).

Although the language of the poem is generally direct, as one might expect for a conversation between an adult and a young child, there is an element of formality that adds weight to the exchange. This occurs in formulations such as 'Tell me, tell me, smiling child' (line 1) and 'happy one' (line 9), which one might suggest would have been as unlikely in daily conversation in the poet's own time as they are in our own. Likewise the child's answers have a precocious sophistication that adds gravitas among the supposed simplicity — one must suspend disbelief to accept that even in the early nineteenth century a young child would refer to 'a wind that sighs mournfully' (line 4), 'A green and flowery spray' (line 6), or 'A mighty, glorious, dazzling sea' (line 11). This linguistic sophistication, whilst indicating wisdom, is slightly unsettling. Perhaps this is less a happily innocent child, more a wise Spirit of Childhood or perhaps Youth personified, with a deeper insight into the truth of the values he or she depicts of optimism, innocence, hope and strength. We might extend this concept further: this is not a lesson in which the adult teaches the child, but an encounter in which the natural order of things is suspended and Experience as personified by the main speaker learns from Innocence — albeit a rather oxymoronically knowing kind of innocence — in the person of the child.

The poet makes extensive use of figurative language, particularly extended metaphor and simile. In each stanza the child says what the past, present or future is like (or is) in metaphorical terms that show them as seen through the unjaundiced and hopeful eyes of youth. There is no place here to admit the usual poetical tropes of the lost happy past, the fearful present, the dreaded future. Here the past is a time of gentle sadness, the present a point of gathering strength to take wing, and the future a shining place of boundless horizons. In the child's innocence there is a strength to look forward, facing the future unafraid and grasping what life has to give.

Message

The past, present and future are not seen in the same way by everyone.

It is easy to think that the past should always be viewed nostalgically as a place to be longed for, but it is alright to think of it with less happy recollections. The present may take on a different complexion if one sees it as a time to gather strength to move forward and to grow. The future does not have to be something we must fear, but can be an unblemished prospect of fresh possibility and opportunity. So much depends on how we see things.

Sometimes we may feel that it is somehow expected of us that we should be hesitant, anxious or even afraid of something, especially if others seem to be. These may be learned behaviours. We may be able to change how we see things, to look on them in a way that does not provoke fear but expectation, hope, optimism and the determination to stand strong.

The way we see life can make a difference to how we experience it. If we are inclined to see the negative, then that may be what we will tend to experience. To try to see things positively, to take a strong stance, may help us to have more positive life experiences.

Even if we think we know how life works, we may still learn positive lessons from how others approach it. We can learn good things from anyone: it is the lesson that matters, whoever the teacher may be.

Lesson plan: 'Past, Present, Future' by Emily Brontë

Resources

Copies of the poem — ideally one per pupil, pens and pencils or marker pens, flip chart paper, rulers for SEND pupils to follow a line when reading, PSHE files, journals or exercise books. Extra paper should be made available for use if required.

The lesson plan is suitable to use with pupils at Upper Key Stage 2, 3 and 4.

The lesson will cover oracy and reading skills.

The session can be done in the round, or as a circle time activity, or at tables, or in an unstructured group, for all age groups.

Links with the PSHE Association PSHE Education Programme of Study

Links have been made to the PSHE Association PSHE Education Programme of Study at Key Stage 2, 3 and 4 as follows:

KS2

- *H16. about strategies and behaviours that support mental health — including how good quality sleep, physical exercise/time outdoors, being involved in community groups, doing things for others, clubs, and activities, hobbies and spending time with family and friends can support mental health and wellbeing*

KS3

- *H10. a range of healthy coping strategies and ways to promote wellbeing and boost mood, including physical activity, participation and the value of positive relationships in providing support*

KS4

- *H7. a broad range of strategies — cognitive and practical — for promoting their own emotional wellbeing, for avoiding negative thinking and for ways of managing mental health concerns*

Links with the National Curriculum

Links have been made to the National Curriculum for English at Key Stage 2, 3 and 4 as follows:

KS2 (Years 5 and 6) English programme of study

- *maintain attention and participate actively in collaborative conversations, staying on topic and initiating and responding to comments*
- *discuss and evaluate how authors use language, including figurative language, considering the impact on the reader*
- *provide reasoned justifications for their views*

KS3 English programme of study

- *participating in formal debates and structured discussions, summarising and/or building on what has been said*
- *knowing how language, including figurative language, vocabulary choice, grammar, text structure and organisational features, presents meaning*

KS4 English programme of study

- *analysing a writer's choice of vocabulary, form, grammatical and structural features, and evaluating their effectiveness and impact*
- *make an informed personal response, recognising that other responses to a text are possible and evaluating these*

Teaching and learning activities

'Past, Present, Future' is a classic poem. The speaker asks a child about the meaning of the past, present, and future. The child says that the past is a place of gentle sadness, the present a place to gather strength to grow and to take wing, and the future a bright place of infinite prospects.

- Introduction — share aims of lesson.
- Refer pupils to their safety plans. Remind them of what a safety plan is for. Ask them to read through their own safety plan before they go further and answer any questions they may have.
- Read the poem (or teacher/leader to read it aloud) and discuss its content. Ask the following key questions:
  - What is this poem about?
  - Who is asking the questions?
  - Who is giving the answers?
  - What is the past like for the child?
  - What is the present like for the child?

- Is the child optimistic about the future? Give reasons for your opinions.
- Divide the class into small groups of three or four. What is the poet trying to say through the poem? Do you agree with the child's views? Give reasons for your thinking. Record comments on flip chart paper.
- Take feedback from the groups.
- Think about a happy experience or memory in your past. Share it with a partner or in a group. How does it make you feel talking about it? Why do you feel this way? Reminiscing about happy events may increase positive feelings and dampen the release of stress hormones.
- Ask pupils to reflect on their own futures. Where do you see yourself in ten years' time? What possibilities do you think are waiting for you? What things might be holding you back? Who/ what can help you to stay positive about the future? Ask pupils to discuss with a partner or in a small group.
- Each pupil to write their own short-term, medium-term and long-term personal goals in their PSHE folders, books or journals. What do they really want to achieve? It is important to think **SMART** when considering your goals: break them down into steps that are **S**pecific, **M**easurable, **A**ttainable, **R**ealistic and **T**imely. Pupils to revisit their goals on a regular basis and to rewrite/update them as necessary. Achieving personal goals can seem like a big thing. How do you eat an elephant? One small bite at a time!
- Review what has been achieved in the lesson.
- Refer pupils to their safety plans as a place to look if they need help after leaving the lesson.

Extension activities

- Pupils to write their answers to the key questions.
- Pupils to illustrate the poem using positive, affirming images.
- Ask each pupil to write about their own future. This is a follow-up activity to the discussion in the main part of the lesson.
- Think of alternative titles for the poem 'Past, Present, Future'.
- Prepare the poem to read aloud and to perform, showing understanding through intonation, tone and volume so that the meaning is clear to an audience. It could be read as a class or group poem, or with individuals being chosen to be the speaker asking questions or the child giving answers.
- Write a short biography of Emily Brontë.
- 'Past, Present, Future' is a classic poem and was written a long time ago. How is its message still relevant to people today? Discuss.
- Ask pupils to reflect on ways to stay positive in life. What does this mean to you? Ask pupils to think about their own learning, friendships, family. Pupils to write their own personal notes and reflections.
- Write your own poem using a question and answer technique on a subject of your own choice.
- Does the poem have a regular rhyme scheme? Write about it. How does it make the poem more (or less, if you think this) effective?
- Draw or paint three pictures to encapsulate the message/meaning in each of the three stanzas.
- Describe how the poet uses metaphors to convey the past, present and future.
- Did you like or dislike the poem? Give reasons for your opinions.

Cross-curricular/topic links

Cross-curricular and topic links may be explored for use in follow-up and for extension work in

- English
- PSHE
- History
- Art and Design

Differentiation

Opportunities for discussion in mixed ability pairs.

Differentiation by outcome e.g. quantity or complexity of issues identified, sophistication of response, level of inclusion/contribution, empathy.

Writing quantity outcomes will be differentiated/assessed/moderated according to teacher's expectations of quantity and depth; otherwise by outcome.

Differentiation may also be through artwork as a means of expression.

See It Through

by Edgar Albert Guest

Commentary

When you're up against a trouble,
Meet it squarely, face to face;
Lift your chin and set your shoulders,
Plant your feet and take a brace.
When it's vain to try to dodge it,
Do the best that you can do;
You may fail, but you may conquer,
See it through!

Black may be the clouds about you
And your future may seem grim,
But don't let your nerve desert you;
Keep yourself in fighting trim.
If the worst is bound to happen,
Spite of all that you can do,
Running from it will not save you,
See it through!

Even hope may seem but futile,
When with troubles you're beset,
But remember you are facing
Just what other men have met.
You may fail, but fall still fighting;
Don't give up, whate'er you do;
Eyes front, head high to the finish.
See it through!

Context

For detail regarding Edgar Guest's life, see the **Context** section to his poem 'Be A Friend' in the **My Love, My Friendships** section of this guide.

'See It Through' is believed to date from the later part of Edgar Guest's long writing career. It is a considerable distinction for the poem that among Guest's prolific production — more than twenty volumes taken from over eleven thousand poems written during his lifetime — 'See It Through' remains one of his most celebrated and popular works.

Like so much of the poetry of this 'poet of the people' (though Guest saw himself more as 'a newspaper man who wrote verses'), 'See It Through' is an inspirational, optimistic and unashamedly sentimental piece that celebrates the simple and old-fashioned virtues of an idealised America, reflecting life in an empathetic, moral and rather rose-tinted glow.

Content

The speaker addresses the reader directly, offering advice person-to-person. The tone is not didactic but affable, avuncular and robust.

We are advised that when we encounter trouble we should face it head on (lines 1 and 2), bracing ourselves against it (lines 3 and 4). When it is not possible to avoid trouble we should just do the best we can (lines 5 and 6): we might not succeed, but then again we might get the better of the situation and win (line 7). We must 'See it through' (line 8) — that is, persist and continue to be engaged with the situation until it is finished.

The situation may seem dark and the future uninviting (lines 9 and 10), but we should not lose our courage (line 11). We should try to keep ourselves ready to fight back against what assails us (line 12). If, in spite of all we can do, the worst is going to happen and we cannot stop it and running away will not help (lines 14 and 15), then we must 'See it through'.

When we are overwhelmed by problems it may seem useless even to hope for things to be better (lines 17 and 18). But we should remember that what we are facing, others have faced in the past (lines 19 and 20). The speaker tells us that even if we do not succeed in opposing the troubles we have, we should keep on trying throughout and never give up (lines 21 and 22). Looking ahead, head held high, we should carry on to the finish and 'See it through' (lines 23 and 24).

The poem is an exhortation to the reader never to give up, however hard things might seem and however many troubles they may seem to have. The speaker considers it best to face a difficult situation with determination and persistence, and follow the problem through to the finish.

Composition

'See It Through' is written in three stanzas of octaves (verses of eight lines) composed in trochaic tetrameter with a rhyme scheme of ABCBDEFE.

The poem's language, like much of Guest's poetry, is a mixture of informal, conversational, 'folksy' American English embellished with some aesthetic or poetic word-forms that would be unusual in everyday speech (e.g. 'vain' , line 5; 'beset', line 18; 'whate'er', line 22), and syntactic inversions that would usually be absent from everyday speech forms (e.g. 'Black may be the clouds about you', line 9; 'When with troubles you're beset', line 18). These somewhat self-conscious features seem intended to give the piece a 'poetic' feel, likely for the casual reader who may not be a regular consumer of poetry. We should remember that Guest was a writer of popular verse for mass publication, usually in newspapers, and that his adroit use of characteristics such as accessible language, a straightforward and jaunty metre, a clear rhyme scheme and the use of just enough 'artistic' words to mark the piece as 'poetic' was key to his significant popularity and the success of his work.

The poem's punctuation is conventional. It is perhaps more characteristic of an epistolary form — a letter of direct address to the reader — than the clear flow of speech that would be achieved, for example, through the use of enjambment. But the poem flows clearly as a source of valuable homespun advice, and one can imagine such contents in a letter from a worthy aunt, uncle or grandparent.

The poet's use of figurative language is restrained. An interesting example is the idiomatic advice 'Keep yourself in fighting trim' (line 12): the latter part of the phrase originally applied to sailing ships and indicated a vessel kept in a stable state so as to float evenly or, by extension, a state of preparedness to sail into battle. Indeed the poet makes use elsewhere of the language of combat, or at least of confrontation — though it is redolent of the language of the pugilist, of a hand-to-hand scrap rather than of warfare. Lines 2, 3 and 4 '(Meet it squarely' to 'take a brace') suggest a boxer taking up his stance; the reader is advised 'don't let your nerve desert you' (line 11); there is a suggestion that where running away will not help one should stand and fight (lines 13 to 16); 'You may fail, but fall still fighting' (line 21) is a clear and direct reference, with the tenacious fighter standing 'Eyes front, head high to the finish' (line 23) at the end.

Message

The emphatic message of the poem is to stand strong in the face of adversity.

It may not be easy — indeed it might be very hard — to face up to trouble. There are times when the poet's advice to 'see it through' would not be appropriate, and we should seek help rather than trying to endure a situation we should not have to tolerate. But so often we find that it can be helpful for us to try to develop an inner resilience that will help us to deal with the difficulties of life. This inner resilience is something we can grow and develop for ourselves, which we can practise, and which may grow stronger with time. It can be very fulfilling and affirming to feel that we have been able to cope better with a problem because of our strong inner resources.

Life's problems can teach us many lessons, not just about the world and other people but also about ourselves. In time we can learn when we should turn to others for help and when we can choose to draw on our inner reserves of strength, persistence and personal courage. Courage is not necessarily about fighting battles or dealing with extreme danger: it can be about having the determination to come back from difficulties, to take another step when we would rather give up, to remain committed to do the right thing and be true to ourselves.

Even if things do not go well for us, we may feel better about ourselves because of the way we have faced our problems.

It can sometimes feel as though we are being assailed by all sorts of troubles in life — or perhaps just one particularly troublesome problem might be more than enough for us. Deciding to stand our ground, to stand strong, to exercise the gentle strength of our own inner courage and determination, can help us to rise to meet life's challenges.

Lesson plan: 'See It Through' by Edgar Albert Guest

Resources

Copies of the poem — ideally one per pupil, rulers for SEND pupils to follow a line when reading, Post-it notes or strips of paper for the tags (displaying phrases) pens or pencils. Extra paper should be made available for use if required.

The lesson plan is suitable to use with pupils at Upper Key Stage 2, 3 and 4.

The lesson will cover oracy and reading skills.

The session can be done in the round, or as a circle time activity, or at tables, or in an unstructured group, for all age groups.

Links with the PSHE Association PSHE Education Programme of Study

Links have been made to the PSHE Association PSHE Education Programme of Study at Key Stage 2, 3 and 4 as follows:

KS2

- *H15. that mental health, just like physical health, is part of daily life; the importance of taking care of mental health*

KS3

- *H9. strategies to understand and build resilience, as well as how to respond to disappointments and setback*

KS4

- *H7. a broad range of strategies — cognitive and practical — for promoting their own emotional wellbeing, for avoiding negative thinking and for ways of managing mental health concerns*

Links with the National Curriculum

Links have been made to the National Curriculum for English at Key Stage 2, 3 and 4 as follows:

KS2 (Years 5 and 6) English programme of study

- *maintain attention and participate actively in collaborative conversations, staying on topic and initiating and responding to comments*
- *drawing inferences such as inferring characters' feelings, thoughts and motives from their actions, and justifying inferences with evidence*
- *discuss and evaluate how authors use language, including figurative language, considering the impact on the reader*
- *provide reasoned justifications for their views*

KS3 English programme of study

- *participating in formal debates and structured discussions, summarising and/or building on what has been said*
- *making inferences and referring to evidence in the text*
- *knowing how language, including figurative language, vocabulary choice, grammar, text structure and organisational features, presents meaning*

KS4 English programme of study

- *listening to and building on the contributions of others, asking questions to clarify and inform, and challenging courteously when necessary*
- *seeking evidence in the text to support a point of view, including justifying inferences with evidence*
- *analysing a writer's choice of vocabulary, form, grammatical and structural features, and evaluating their effectiveness and impact*

Teaching and learning activities

This poem explores how meeting one's problems 'face to face' (line 2) with confidence, determination and perseverance can help us feel to feel stronger and happier when we encounter challenging life experiences. This lesson plan brings the concept of resilience into pupils' consciousness and provides them with lots of opportunities to talk about ways of developing inner resilience and fortitude.

- Introduction — share aims of lesson.
- Refer pupils to their safety plans. Remind them of what a safety plan is for. Ask them to read through their own safety plan before they go further and answer any questions they may have.
- Read the poem (or teacher/leader to read it aloud) and discuss its content. Ask key questions:
  - What does the title of the poem mean to you? Why do you think the poet chose to call the poem 'See It Through'?
  - What is this poem about? It may be necessary to write key vocabulary and phrases on the whiteboard to help younger pupils to better understand the poem.
  - What is the message of the poem? Give reasons for your opinions.
- Explore with the pupils the meaning of resilience. Brainstorm a collective definition.
- Is resilience the same as 'just get on with it'? What is the difference? Discuss this in groups.
- How can developing resilience help to maintain good mental health? Discuss with all pupils and compare ideas.
- Ask pupils to think of ways in which they are resilient, or would like to be. Discuss in pairs or small groups.
- Prepare tags for the wall completing the phrase 'I am resilient because...' or 'I can be resilient by....' or 'I can be resilient when...'.
- Working in pairs or small groups, pupils to think about how they can help or support others who are trying to be resilient. This might include not undermining others' attempts to be resilient, and exercising empathy.
- Take feedback and comments from pupils.
- Review what has been achieved in the lesson.
- Refer pupils to their safety plans as a place to look if they need help after leaving the lesson.

Extension activities

- Pupils to write their answers to the key questions.
- Write about the form and structure of the poem.
- Write your own motivational/resilience poem drawing on the work covered in the lesson.
- Think of alternative titles for the poem 'See It Through'.
- What is the effect or repeating the line 'See it through!' in each of the stanzas?
- Plan and write a short story about a character who did not use resilience. What happened? How could the outcome have been different by exercising resilience? How could the character have achieved that? Think particularly about the decision the character had to make.
- Keep your own resilience journal. Add to the journal every time you do something that demonstrates resilience.
- Draw or paint an image to go with the title of the poem.
- Illustrate the poem with motivational images or words.

Cross-curricular/topic links

Cross-curricular and topic links may be explored for use in follow-up and for extension work in

- English
- PSHE
- Art and Design

Differentiation

Opportunities for discussion in mixed ability pairs.

Differentiation by outcome e.g. quantity or complexity of issues identified, sophistication of response, level of inclusion/contribution, empathy.

Writing quantity outcomes will be differentiated/assessed/moderated according to teacher's expectations of quantity and depth; otherwise by outcome.

Differentiation may also be through key words rather than written sentences, or through artwork as a means of expression.

Looking for Happiness

This section is about finding happiness in things that we do
and in the natural world...

Delaunay's Dye

by Hannah Kate

Commentary

We went halves on a 99p palette,
pocket money colours,
purples, blues and greys.
Giggling mirrorless to St. Peter's
where, with one sponge brush,
we painted each other's eyes
amongst brambles and gravestones,
graffiti and angels.
When our curfew was passed
and it was too dark to see
our newly grown-up faces,
we watched the stars switch on,
writing the dyeworks into the sky.
Wandered home slowly,
mauve eyes on Turkey Red streets
where, once, colours were made.

Note:
Angel Delaunay and his family introduced the Turkey Red dyeing process to North Manchester in 1788. The family owned land in Crumpsall and Blackley, and their dyeworks was one of the major businesses in the area.

Context

'Delaunay's Dye' is a modern work by Hannah Kate, a poet, short story writer, editor, publisher and broadcaster based in Manchester.

The poem is set in the North Manchester of Hannah's childhood and teenage years, an area which, as the poet's note explains, included land acquired in the late eighteenth century by the Delaunay family whose dyeworks grew to be a major local business.

'Delaunay's Dye' remembers a simple, happy episode of two young friends enjoying being together and experimenting with makeup. The poem is also an exercise in colour, blending several allusions to the theme with a reference to the dye of the title. These elements include the shades of makeup bought by the girls who populate the poem, the colours of their eyes, and the streets that were a home to the old dyeworks.

Content

The poem opens with the word 'We', locating it in the personal experience of the speaker, who we may assume to be the poet herself. As readers we are invited to assume that the work has an autobiographical basis or that it has its foundation in first-hand experience.

We encounter the speaker with a friend, each paying half of the price of a palette of inexpensive eyeshadow ('pocket money colours', line 2). Laughing between themselves, and without a mirror, the girls make their way to the grounds of St. Peter's, a local church. In the churchyard, amid the carved stonework and undergrowth, they use a single sponge brush to make up each other's eyes, which we can understand as a bonding experience between the two young friends as they experiment with a grown-up item.

When it is time for the girls to go home they make their way through the dark streets together. They are feeling 'grown-up' (line 11) because of the mauve (line 15) eyeshadow they are wearing. As they walk slowly, they see the stars becoming visible in the sky (lines 12 to 13). The speaker remembers that this is the place where Turkey Red, a bright red dye used to colour or print cotton textiles in the northern cotton trade, used to be made.

Composition

The poem is composed as a single stanza of free verse, with no regular metre or rhyme scheme.

The poem's language and vocabulary create a conversational tone, and this impression is supported by its punctuation which is just as it would be were the text presented as prose.

The poem's capitalisation reinforces its conversational tone further. Unusually for poetry, in which there is a convention that the initial word of each line should be capitalised, capital letters are used in 'Delaunay's Dye' precisely as they would have been in a piece of prose — that is, only to begin a sentence or for proper nouns. This contributes to a sense of the poem being an account or report of a real event, one which might equally have been delivered as prose but which has been given the touch of poetry by the poet's consciously creative act.

Although it certainly has prose-like features, the piece is clearly distinguished as poetry by three factors: the poet's particular attention to the use of language; the layout or arrangement of line, which informs how the verse is read; and the poet's intention that the piece should be recognised, and therefore encountered and read, as poetry.

Lines are arranged so as to present a series of steps, line by line, each with a small, incremental advance in scene or action. The poet controls the measured and languid pace of the work, redolent of the girls' reluctance to go home and to part from each other's company.

The poet has chosen to use little figurative language. There is no use of simile. Metaphor is limited: 'pocket money colours' (line 2), 'watched the stars switch on' (line 12), and 'writing the dyeworks into the sky' (line 13). However, the text is deliciously descriptive, especially of the girls' joyful relationship, the contrast of the tangled churchyard, and the splashes of light and colour in the eyeshadow, the stars, the girls' 'painted' eyes, and the placement of all in the 'streets / where, once, colours were made'. The sheer joy and colour of an innocent amusement, at once a rite of passage, shines from the page.

Message

Our friendships may be a source of joy, fun, companionship and shared experience.

Our friends may be not just the faces we see every day, but important features of our lives with whom we try new things and take steps towards adulthood. Even apparently insignificant experiences such as trying out eye makeup can feel like small but important progress on the way to being our grownup selves.

We may find that even something of little or no real monetary cost can be a source of shared delight when we are able to enjoy it with friends. Often the act of shared experience can make things even more special and give us memories to treasure.

The warmth of friendship may add colour and light to what would otherwise be dull and familiar, and help us to see the world differently.

Lesson plan: 'Delaunay's Dye' by Hannah Kate

Resources

Copies of the poem — ideally one per pupil, pens and pencils or marker pens, rulers for SEND pupils to follow a line when reading. Extra paper should be made available for use if required.

Copies of pupils' safety plans to which they can refer throughout the session/lesson.

The lesson will cover oracy, reading and writing skills.

The session can be done in the round, or as a circle time activity, or at tables, or in an unstructured group. The lesson plan is suitable to use with pupils at Upper Key Stage 2, 3 and 4.

Links with the PSHE Association PSHE Education Programme of Study

Links have been made to the PSHE Association PSHE Education Programme of Study at Key Stage 2, 3 and 4 as follows:

KS2

- *H18. about everyday things that affect feelings and the importance of expressing feeling*

KS3

- *H10. a range of healthy coping strategies and ways to promote wellbeing and boost mood, including physical activity, participation and the value of positive relationships in providing support*

KS4

- *H7. a broad range of strategies — cognitive and practical — for promoting their own emotional wellbeing, for avoiding negative thinking and for ways of managing mental health concerns*
- *H8. to recognise warning signs of common mental and emotional health concerns (including stress, anxiety and depression), what might trigger them and what help or treatment is available*

Links with the National Curriculum

Links have been made to the National Curriculum for English at Key Stage 2, 3 and 4 as follows:

KS2 (Years 5 and 6) English programme of study

- *maintain attention and participate actively in collaborative conversations, staying on topic and initiating and responding to comments*
- *identifying how language, structure and presentation contribute to meaning*
- *discuss and evaluate how authors use language, including figurative language, considering the impact on the reader*

KS3 English programme of study

- *participating in formal debates and structured discussions, summarising and/or building on what has been said*
- *knowing how language, including figurative language, vocabulary choice, grammar, text structure and organisational features, presents meaning*

KS4 English programme of study

- *listening to and building on the contributions of others, asking questions to clarify and inform, and challenging courteously when necessary*
- *analysing a writer's choice of vocabulary, form, grammatical and structural features, and evaluating their effectiveness and impact*

Teaching and learning activities

'Delaunay's Dye' is about a happy occasion when two friends decide to spend their pocket money on inexpensive eyeshadow colours and have fun putting on the makeup. As they walk home the colours of their make-up are a reminder of Delaunay's Dyeworks which used to manufacture dyes in the neighbourhood. The speaker recalls happy memories of the experience.

- Introduction — share aims of lesson.
- Refer pupils to their safety plans. Remind them of what a safety plan is for. Ask them to read through their own safety plan before they go further and answer any questions they may have.
- Read the poem (or teacher/leader to read it aloud) and discuss its content. Ask the following key questions:
  - What is the poem about? Does the title give you any clues?
  - Do you like the poem? Justify your answer with reference to the poem.
  - How does the poem make you feel? Why? How does it do this?
- Spend a few minutes reflecting on how the experience made the two friends feel. What sort of relationship do they have — serious, fun, or something else? Ask pupils to highlight words in the poem that reflect their feelings.
- Take feedback.
- Ask pupils to work with a partner or in a small group. Can you recount a happy occasion or time in your life that you shared with a friend or group of friends? Why was it special? Can you remember how you felt at the time? How do you feel now when you think about the event?
- Spend a few minutes inviting pupils to share their personal memories of friendship with the whole class.
- Why is it important to reflect on happy times in your life? Discuss with the whole class. Research shows that high levels of serotonin in the brain are linked to elevated mood and feeling happy. Feeling happy and positive can help young people build resilience to stress and reduce vulnerability to depression. 'Mood induction' can help to increase the levels of

serotonin in our brains — visualising a happy moment from your memory, thinking about a positive experience, looking at photos of things that make you happy (friends, places, pets, etc.). You may want to share this with the pupils: thinking about happy things really can help you to feel happier.

- Review what has been achieved in the lesson.
- Refer pupils to their safety plans as a place to look if they need help after leaving the lesson.

Extension activities

- Pupils to write their answers to the key questions in the first part of the lesson.
- Do you like the poem? Pupils to write their own responses, giving reasons.
- What is the theme of the poem? Is there more than one theme and if so, what are they?
- Describe the mood of the poem.
- Write a short play based on the poem. Make up fictitious names for the two friends. Think particularly about the dialogue that they might use.
- Turn the poem into a piece of descriptive prose writing, recreating the events of that evening and capturing thoughts and feelings.
- Create a painting or drawing based on the poem. You might want to think about abstracts, which capture mood rather than representational imagery.
- What do you think are the ingredients for a happy life?
- Is happiness the same as pleasure? Discuss.
- Keep a journal or a 'happy scrapbook'. Collect thoughts, song lyrics, poems, photos and images of things that make you feel happy or positive. You can go to it to 'top up' when you feel low.

Cross-curricular/topic links

Cross-curricular and topic links may be explored for use in follow-up and for extension work in

- English
- PSHE
- Art and Design

Differentiation

Opportunities for discussion in mixed ability pairs.

Differentiation by outcome e.g. quantity or complexity of issues identified, sophistication of response, level of inclusion/contribution, empathy.

Writing quantity outcomes will be differentiated/assessed/moderated according to teacher's expectations of quantity and depth; otherwise by outcome.

Differentiation may also be through key words rather than written sentences, or through artwork as a means of expression.

How Still, How Happy

by Emily Brontë

Commentary

How still, how happy! Those are words
That once would scarce agree together;
I loved the plashing of the surge —
The changing heaven the breezy weather,

More than smooth seas and cloudless skies
And solemn, soothing, softened airs
That in the forest woke no sighs
And from the green spray shook no tears.

How still, how happy! now I feel
Where silence dwells is sweeter far
Than laughing mirth's most joyous swell
However pure its raptures are.

Come, sit down on this sunny stone:
'Tis wintry light o'er flowerless moors —
But sit — for we are all alone
And clear expand heaven's breathless shores.

I could think in the withered grass
Spring's budding wreaths we might discern;
The violet's eye might shyly flash
And young leaves shoot among the fern.

It is but thought — full many a night
The snow shall clothe those hills afar
And storms shall add a drearier blight
And winds shall wage a wilder war,

Before the lark may herald in
Fresh foliage twined with blossoms fair
And summer days again begin
Their glory-haloed crown to wear.

Yet my heart loves December's smile
As much as July's golden beam;
Then let us sit and watch the while
The blue ice curdling on the stream —

Context

For detail regarding Emily Brontë's life, see the **Context** section to her poem 'Love and Friendship' in the **My Love, My Friendships** section of this guide.

'How Still, How Happy' may be dated to 1838, in the September of which Emily became a teacher at Law Hill School near Halifax. The school was actually situated in the village of Southowram, to the south-east of the town, with a view (as contemporary engravings confirm) of the smoky factory chimneys of a thriving nineteenth century industrial town whose wealth came from the cotton, wool and carpet industries. Emily's biographers generally agree on the distressing homesickness she suffered on the few occasions — only four as far as we know — that she lived away from her home village of Haworth. We may speculate that the prospect of the industrial town, a mere a mile and a half distant, may have turned the poet's mind towards the open, natural spaces of the moors around Haworth.

The poem did not appear in the 1846 volume of collected poetry of Emily and her two sisters Charlotte and Anne, *Poems by Currer, Ellis, and Acton Bell.* Perhaps it was too acute and private a reminder of her homesickness for Emily to wish it to be included. The work remained unpublished during the poet's lifetime, being first printed privately by Dodd, Mead and Company of New York in 1902 and later appearing in *The Complete Poems of Emily Brontë* in 1908.

Content

The poem opens with the speaker asserting that once she felt that the words 'still' and 'happy' did not go together: rather than immobility and immutability, she enjoyed movement and change such as the splash of the tide ('plashing of the surge', line 3), the changing sky and the wind (line 4) more than 'smooth seas and cloudless skies' (line 5) or the calm atmosphere that makes no sound in the forest (lines 6 and 7) and does not shake water drops from the leaves (line 8).

Now the speaker feels that silence is 'sweeter' (line 10) than happy laughter (line 11), even at its most joyous and pure (lines 11 and 12).

The speaker invites the reader to sit with her on a 'sunny stone' (line 13) in her evocation of the wintery moors (line 14). She and the reader will be alone (line 15) under a clear sky (line 16). She thinks that she might be able to recognise the buds of spring, new leaves and violet flowers in the faded winter grass (lines 17 to 20).

This, however, is merely her imagination (line 21). There will be many nights of storms, snow and winds before spring returns (lines 25 and 26) and then the glory of summer (lines 27 and 28).

The speaker loves the 'smile' of December (line 29) as much as the golden sun of July (line 30). She invites the reader to sit with her and watch 'the blue ice' forming and thickening on the surface of the stream (lines 31 and 32).

Composition

The poem is composed in quatrains of iambic tetrameter with a rhyme scheme of ABAB.

The language of the poems feels somewhat archaic, which may be due partly to its age and partly to the poet's use of syntactical inversions including 'That in the forest woke no sighs / And from the green spray shook no tears' (lines 7 and 8), 'Where silence dwells is sweeter far' (line 10), 'And clear expand heaven's breathless shores' (line 16), 'Spring's budding wreaths we might discern' (line 18), 'blossoms fair' (line 26), and 'glory-haloed crown to wear' (line 28). However, its tone is light and joyful as befits a speaker who has discovered her enthusiasm not just for the beauty of summer but also for the pale, stark beauty of the wild, frozen winter. This is a poem of joy, and the winter's cold is just as joyous as summer's heat, stillness just as joyous as lively motion. There is as much to be found in stillness as in movement, perhaps more.

The poem's vocabulary is generally accessible, though there are a few words for which younger readers might appreciate guidance: 'plashing' (= 'splashing', line 3), 'spray' (= 'leafy or flowery branch', line 8), 'raptures' (= 'intense pleasures', line 12), 'o'er' (= 'over', line 14), 'shoot' (= 'grow', line 20), 'blight' (= 'nuisance, trouble, affliction', line 23), 'curdling' (= 'freezing, thickening', line 32).

Overall the effect of the poet's language is joyful, effusive, conveying an infectious sense of enthusiasm about the beauties of her surroundings in all their seasons. It is a beauty that we may suspect comes from within as much as being observed externally. The work is also highly sensual, with focus on sound, light, colour, movement, warmth, cold, calm, rage, movement and stillness — a broad spectrum of sensory experience that finds reflection in the poet's feelings.

The poet uses sibilance in the second stanza, particularly its second line. The recurrent 's' sounds across the stanza evoke the susurration of the breeze, the water and windblown foliage. The 's' is encountered repeatedly in the fourth, fifth and sixth stanzas, again in vivid descriptions of wild nature, and the sixth stanza is also ended, unusually, by a repeated 'w' sound that could be intended to suggest the 'waah' sound of storm winds.

The poem is remarkably light in its use of figurative language. There is some use of metaphor: the 'tears' of line 8 are rain or dew rather than actual tears; the 'eye' of the violet in line 19 is a metaphorical description of the personified flower (or perhaps its centre, which is streaked like the coloured iris of an eye). Personification and metaphor are used especially in the seventh and eighth stanzas: summer days 'wear' a 'glory-haloed crown' in line 28, whilst December has a 'smile' in line 29.

It is with punctuation, unusually, that the poet leaves her final impression on the reader. Throughout the poem punctuation has been quite minimal, serving conventionally to point up its language but largely giving way to the poet's extensive use of enjambment, which adds particular flow to stanzas 2, 3, 6 and 7. But at the end of the poem's final line the poet chooses to close not with a full stop but with a dash — a mark that indicates that there is more left to be said, and that this is not really the end of the scene. The world goes on, always presenting us with new scenes, new opportunities for appreciation and new causes for happiness, if we open our eyes and hearts to experience.

Message

Our experience of the world changes. But what we take from our experiences changes too. We may find that we begin to take happiness from things we have never noticed before, or that we thought we did not like. Sometimes, all it needs for us to find a new source of happiness is for us to open our minds and hearts to something new.

It has been said that there are no uninteresting things, only uninterested people. If we learn not to close our minds we may find that not only does the world seem a wider and more fascinating place, but that we can see how we fit into it more easily. There is more to the world than our narrow experience may lead us to believe, and somewhere there are people who think like us, who like what we like and value what we value.

It is good for us to be able to take pleasure from all sorts of things, from all sorts of environments and weather and people and ways of life. Why should we not be able to take as much pleasure in a bright, chilly day as a bright, warm one, when both are beautiful? Variety of experience can add depth to who we are and how we see ourselves, and how we understand the world and the people around us too.

Even when things are not good for us, we may see that they will get better again. In our winter, we can look forward to spring. Meanwhile we can take pleasure in simple things. We can not only look for happiness, but learn to find it wherever we look.

Lesson plan: 'How Still, How Happy' by Emily Brontë

Resources

Copies of the poem — ideally one per pupil, pens and pencils or marker pens, rulers for SEND pupils to follow a line when reading. Extra paper should be made available for use if required.

Copies of pupils' safety plans to which they can refer throughout the session/lesson.

The lesson will cover oracy, reading and writing skills.

The session can be done in the round, or as a circle time activity, or at tables, or in an unstructured group. The lesson plan is suitable to use with pupils at Upper Key Stage 2, 3 and 4.

Links with the PSHE Association PSHE Education Programme of Study

Links have been made to the PSHE Association PSHE Education Programme of Study at Key Stage 2, 3 and 4 as follows:

KS2

- *H15. at mental health, just like physical health, is part of daily life; the importance of taking care of mental health*
- *H16. about strategies and behaviours that support mental health — including how good quality sleep, physical exercise/time outdoors, being involved in community groups, doing things for others, clubs, and activities, hobbies and spending time with family and friends can support mental health and wellbeing*

KS3

- *H10. a range of healthy coping strategies and ways to promote wellbeing and boost mood, including physical activity, participation and the value of positive relationships in providing support*

KS4

- *H7. a broad range of strategies — cognitive and practical — for promoting their own emotional wellbeing, for avoiding negative thinking and for ways of managing mental health concerns*

Links with the National Curriculum

Links have been made to the National Curriculum for English at Key Stage 2, 3 and 4 as follows:

KS2 (Years 5 and 6) English programme of study

- *maintain attention and participate actively in collaborative conversations, staying on topic and initiating and responding to comments*
- *identifying how language, structure and presentation contribute to meaning*
- *discuss and evaluate how authors use language, including figurative language, considering the impact on the reader*

KS3 English programme of study

- *participating in formal debates and structured discussions, summarising and/or building on what has been said*
- *knowing how language, including figurative language, vocabulary choice, grammar, text structure and organisational features, presents meaning*

KS4 English programme of study

- *listening to and building on the contributions of others, asking questions to clarify and inform, and challenging courteously when necessary*
- *analysing a writer's choice of vocabulary, form, grammatical and structural features, and evaluating their effectiveness and impact*

Teaching and learning activities

'How Still, How Happy' is about finding happiness and fulfilment that depends on being and perceiving rather than doing. It is about taking pleasure from calm and continuity rather than activity and change. It is also about how our preferences change as we grow.

It may be necessary to go through each stanza with younger pupils so that they have a clear understanding of what the poem is about. Encourage pupils to annotate their copies of the poem. The commentary provides background information which will help pupils understand more about the environment the poet lived in.

- Introduction — share aims of lesson.
- Refer pupils to their safety plans. Remind them of what a safety plan is for. Ask them to read through their own safety plan before they go further and answer any questions they may have.
- Read the poem (or teacher/leader to read it aloud) and discuss its content. Explain that some of the words in the poem are archaic and have fallen out of usage. Ask pupils to see if they can work out the meaning of the words 'tis' and 'o'er' Ask the following key questions:
  - What is the poem about? Does the title give you any clues?
  - What are the speaker's reasons for liking winter?
  - How does the speaker interact with her environment? What does the speaker like doing? Why do you think this?
- Can you recount a time where you enjoyed the peace and quiet of the countryside or of some other place where you felt relaxed? Share thoughts with a partner or in a small group.
- Spend a few minutes inviting pupils to share their personal memories with the whole class.

- Is there anything that you now enjoy that you used to dislike? It could be anything: a place, a food, a sport, or a school subject. Why do you think you have changed? What does this tell you about how you grow as a person?
- Does the ability to be still and be contemplative contribute to happiness? Do you ever think about your inner life? What do you think? Discuss with the whole class.
- Ask pupils to reflect on their favourite season and why they like it. Ask pupils to make notes and to share their thoughts with the class.
- Review what has been achieved in the lesson.
- Refer pupils to their safety plans as a place to look if they need help after leaving the lesson.

Extension activities

- Pupils to write their answers to the key questions in the first part of the lesson.
- Do you like the poem? Pupils to write their own responses giving reasons.
- What is the theme of the poem?
- How did the poem make you feel? How and why did it make you feel this way?
- Can you find examples of metaphors and personification? Are there any instances where both are combined?
- What is the mood of the poem? Can you find evidence to support your views?
- Imagery is used in the line 'blue ice curdling on the stream'. Can you explain what this image means?
- The poem is full of symbolism. Find examples and explain how they are used.
- Write out the poem decoratively with illustrated borders. Hang it in a prominent place.
- Write your own poem in the style of 'How Still, How Happy'.
- Write about your favourite season. Why do you prefer this season to others?
- Paint or draw a picture of your own peaceful, idyllic scene.
- Select part of the poem that appeals to you. Create a painting or drawing that reflects the poet's words.
- In PSHE lessons explore ways of relaxing, the importance of making time for oneself and the effect this can have in helping to calm the mind.
- Pupils to produce a piece of stimulus writing using images suggested in the poem. Pupils/ teachers to find images of moorland heaths showing how they change over the seasons in the UK. The aim is to write about the content of a picture and the thoughts and feelings it inspires, rather than simply describing the image. What would it be like to be there? How would you feel? What sounds, smells, tastes or other sensations would you experience? What might you be doing there? Would you be with someone, and if so whom? What would you be doing and why? Try to think of positive associations.
- Is there any single thing that will always make us happy? Think about the reasons for your answer.

Cross-curricular/topic links

Cross-curricular and topic links may be explored for use in follow-up and for extension work in

- English
- PSHE
- Art and Design

Differentiation

Opportunities for discussion in mixed ability pairs.

Differentiation by outcome e.g. quantity or complexity of issues identified, sophistication of response, level of inclusion/contribution, empathy.

Writing quantity outcomes will be differentiated/assessed/moderated according to teacher's expectations of quantity and depth; otherwise by outcome.

Differentiation may also be through artwork as a means of expression.

When You Grow Up

by Rosie Garland

Commentary

At night, she leaps and does not land. Spreads her arms and soars
above the fenced and neatly weeded garden. Her dreams
are practice sessions where she lifts cars, sees through walls, fights

dragons. She is a pirate captain, a queen, a horse. She is neither girl
nor boy: the distinctions are irrelevant when her small body encompasses
male and female; human, beast. A turbulent child figure-heading

the prow of her beaked ship, she buckles on armour, rescues
princesses from charming princes and spinning wheels.
She is fearless of the shapes beneath the bed. Too soon

she hears the summons: Breakfast! Now!
Blinks this world into focus. Hushes battle cries,
sheathes her sword between the pages of her book.

Every bedtime her mother tucks in
the sheet of marriage, husband, children: tucks it in tight.

Context

Award-winning poet, novelist, cabaret artist and post-punk band singer Rosie Garland has often written about the experiences of childhood.

The memories she writes about are often bittersweet. Rosie describes herself as having been 'born in London to a runaway teenager', whilst also recalling that one of her earliest and happiest memories is of being read to by her grandmother, an experience that gave her a lifelong love of reading.

'When You Grow Up' is a delicately poignant poem examining the contrast between the unfettered, unlimited imagination of a child and the latent forces of restriction that come from adult influence.

Content

The poem describes, from the point of view of an unidentified observer, the fantastical, unrestrained dream life that a young girl lives every night.

She dreams of being able to fly, soaring high above the ordinary world (lines 1 and 2).

The girl's dreams are rehearsals of having superpowers and being able to fight monsters (lines 2 to 4).

There is no limit to the girl's identity: she can be male, female or even an animal (lines 4 to 6) — the 'distinctions are irrelevant' (line 5).

The dreaming girl is an adventurer and a warrior and a leader, not just the crew but the very emblem of the ship of imagination she sails ('figure-heading / the prow of her beaked ship', lines 6 and 7), inhabiting the reality of fairy tales and unafraid (lines 6 to 9).

The world of dreams is interrupted by reality as the girl is woken by a call to breakfast (lines 9 and 10). Waking, she calms the action in her mind, putting her sleeping fantasies to rest within the book from which her rich landscape of imagination may take its inspiration (lines 11 and 12).

The speaker tells us that every night the child's mother puts her to bed, figuratively wrapping her tightly with her own hopes and expectations that her daughter will marry into a life that will consist of having a husband and children. Perhaps this is something that the mother says to her child; or it may be a hope that as she is tucking in her own child, so the girl will one day be a mother herself and do the same for her own children; or it may represent the wishes that the mother imposes on the child in many ways, both spoken and unspoken. There is a powerful contrast between the notional shackles of expectation that the mother tries to place, however lovingly, on her daughter and the girl's wild, unlimited, free imagination — her still-pristine belief that she can do and be anything she wishes.

Composition

'When You Grow Up' is written as free verse, in five stanzas without rhyme scheme or regular metre.

Though the poem is punctuated as though it was written as prose, it is not classified as a prose poem. Prose poems are not usually divided into poetic line and stanza, though they manifest other characteristics of poetry such as symbolism, metaphor and other figures of speech.

The poem's capitalisation dispenses with the poetic convention that the initial word of each line should be capitalised, and capital letters are used just as they would have been in a piece of prose — to begin sentences or for proper nouns. This is congruent with the feeling of the poem being a story as well as verse, an account of the girl's experiences in her boundless world of dreams.

Though the poet's adroit storytelling magnifies its prosaically narrative qualities, 'When You Grow Up' is clearly distinguished as poetry rather than prose by three factors: the poet's careful attention to the use of language; the arrangement of line, which helps to govern and pace how the verse is read; and the poet's intention that the piece should be read as poetry. The word 'poem' originates from an ancient Greek root word, *poiēma* [ποίημα], which means 'what is made or created', and hence the poet's intention is crucial to the identity of the text.

The Oxford English Dictionary definition of 'poem' notes that '…the expression of feelings and ideas is given intensity by particular attention to diction (sometimes involving rhyme), rhythm, and imagery'. In 'When You Grow Up', the rich language and vocabulary, selected with notable care and sensitivity to nuanced meaning, create a highly descriptive linguistic landscape and a deliberately rich, poetic tone which heighten the poet's evocative and opulently imaginative treatment of fantastical matter.

The poem is a fertile garden of imagery, forgoing the relative plainness of simile for a closely-woven fabric of figurative expression that abounds in metaphor, and through which boundaries are blurred ('neither girl / nor boy', line 4; 'male and female; human, beast', line 6). Images are packed densely, a mosaic of identification and cross-identification and personification that evoke a vivid maelstrom of successive dreamlike impressions.

The first four stanzas consist of three lines each, over which the poet builds and delivers a succession of waves of description of the child's dream world. It is sobering that the final stanza, consisting of only two lines, creates so readily the sense of the wild and whirling world of possibility being brought down by the simple, well-intentioned yet stifling mundaneness of the mother's imposed expectation, clipping the wings of her daughter's flights of fancy and freedom. There is a significant irony in the apprehension that in order to fulfil the mother's ideas of happiness, the girl may have to give up her own.

Message

Our imagination is a powerful thing. It can help us to shape our ambitions, our plans and expectations, and to see ourselves and others differently.

Freedom of imagination is something that many people are born with, but which is often stifled by adults, the media, friends or others. We may be told to 'get real', to 'grow up', or that we are 'living in a dream'. This may make us feel that imagination is a negative thing, and that we will be more acceptable to others if we live a plain, nondescript life.

We may feel pressured to give up our ideas of happiness in order to fulfil what others think we should do or be. Sometimes we may be made to feel that they know best, even when perhaps they do not. But we should be careful not to allow others to make us feel that their happiness is more important than our own. We should be considerate of others and take their feelings into account when we do things, but we must not forget that our own happiness matters too.

We are capable of achieving much if we dare to dream. Many people feel happy and fulfilled by following a dream — to have a particular career, to go to a particular place, to be a particular kind of person. Sometimes we do not even have to achieve the dream in order to be happy — it is enough just to be able to pursue it.

We may not be able to live exactly as we do in our dreams, but we should try to retain, or even develop, our powers of imagination and visualisation. They can help us to follow new and interesting paths, to meet life's challenges, and to accept that each of us is and should always be uniquely ourselves.

Lesson plan: 'When You Grow Up' by Rosie Garland

Resources

Copies of the poem — ideally one per pupil, pens and pencils or marker pens, Post-it notes, rulers for SEND pupils to follow a line when reading. Extra paper should be made available for use if required.

Copies of pupils' safety plans to which they can refer throughout the session/lesson.

The lesson will cover oracy, reading and writing skills.

The session can be done in the round, or as a circle time activity, or at tables, or in an unstructured group. The lesson plan is suitable to use with pupils at Upper Key Stage 2, 3 and 4.

Links with the PSHE Association PSHE Education Programme of Study

Links have been made to the PSHE Association PSHE Education Programme of Study at Key Stage 2, 3 and 4 as follows:

KS2

- *H18. about everyday things that affect feelings and the importance of expressing feelings*
- *H27. to recognise their individuality and personal qualities*

KS3

- *H1. how we are all unique; that recognising and demonstrating personal strengths build self-confidence, self-esteem and good health and wellbeing*
- *H5. to recognise and manage internal and external influences on decisions which affect health and wellbeing*

KS4

- *H2. how self-confidence, self-esteem, and mental health are affected positively and negatively by internal and external influences and ways of managing this*
- *H4. strategies to develop assertiveness and build resilience to peer and other influences that affect both how they think about themselves and their health and wellbeing*

Links with the National Curriculum

Links have been made to the National Curriculum for English at Key Stage 2, 3 and 4 as follows:

KS2 (Years 5 and 6) English programme of study

- *listen and respond appropriately to adults and their peers*
- *maintain attention and participate actively in collaborative conversations, staying on topic and initiating and responding to comments*
- *discuss and evaluate how authors use language, including figurative language, considering the impact on the reader*

KS3 English programme of study

- *participating in formal debates and structured discussions, summarising and/or building on what has been said*
- *knowing how language, including figurative language, vocabulary choice, grammar, text structure and organisational features, presents meaning*

KS4 English programme of study

- *listening to and building on the contributions of others, asking questions to clarify and inform, and challenging courteously when necessary*
- *analysing a writer's choice of vocabulary, form, grammatical and structural features, and evaluating their effectiveness and impact*

Teaching and learning activities

This poem shows a dichotomy between a mother and her child. The child's imagination is unfettered and free, unconstrained by convention or expectation. The mother's plans for her daughter's future are limited to the social norms of marriage and motherhood, an expectation in which she figuratively wraps the child.

- Introduction — share aims of lesson.
- Refer pupils to their safety plans. Remind them of what a safety plan is for. Ask them to read through their own safety plan before they go further and answer any questions they may have.
- Read the poem (or teacher/leader to read it aloud) and discuss its content. Ask the following key questions:
  - What is the poem about?
  - Did you like the poem? Give reasons for your opinions.
  - What is the poem's message?
  - Which words in the poem reveal the child's strength when she is dreaming?
- What future expectations does the mother have of her daughter? How do these differ from her daughter's hopes and dreams? Discuss with the whole class or group.
- What are your hopes and dreams for the future? Discuss in pairs or in small groups. Are there any barriers that prevent you from realising your dreams? What can you do to overcome them?
- Each pair or group to feed back.
- On a Post-it note, write three words or phrases to help you to feel empowered and strong. Keep the Post-it note in the front of your journal or file and refer to it regularly.
- Review what has been achieved in the lesson.
- Refer pupils to their safety plans as a place to look if they need help after leaving the lesson.

Extension activities

- Pupils to write their answers to the key questions in the first part of the lesson.
- What are your future ambitions? What job would you like to do one day? Why do you want these things? How do you think they will make you happy?
- Think of a book that you have read where you admired the central character. What made that person stand out for you? What actions or characteristics made them special?
- Create your own superhero. What special powers do they have?
- Draw, paint or produce a collage of your superhero.
- Would you like to be the child in the poem 'When You Grow Up'? Why do you think this?
- Have you ever found yourself daydreaming? What kinds of things do you daydream about?
- Produce a comic strip of the poem with captions taken from the poem's text.
- Write about the form and structure of the poem.
- Write your own short story (up to five hundred words) about a dream you have which turns you into an exciting, strong, powerful character.
- Write your own poem in the style of Rosie Garland.
- Think of alternative titles for Rosie's poem.
- List some of the powerful verbs used in the poem. Can you find alternative words for these in a thesaurus?

Cross-curricular/topic links

Cross-curricular and topic links may be explored for use in follow-up and for extension work in

- English

- PSHE
- Art and Design

Differentiation

Opportunities for discussion in mixed ability pairs.

Differentiation by outcome e.g. quantity or complexity of issues identified, sophistication of response, level of inclusion/contribution, empathy.

Writing quantity outcomes will be differentiated/assessed/moderated according to teacher's expectations of quantity and depth; otherwise by outcome.

Differentiation may also be through key words rather than written sentences, or through artwork as a means of expression.

Happy Thought

by Robert Louis Stevenson

Commentary

The world is so full of a number of things,
I'm sure we should be as happy as kings.

Context

'Happy Thought' is taken from Stevenson's book *The Child's Garden of Verses*, a collection of poetry for children first published in 1885 that covers themes of childhood, play, solitude and illness.

Stevenson suffered from ill health all his life, making him extremely thin, and he had a particular tendency to develop fevers, coughs and other bronchial problems.

Content

The poem is a simple and joyful rhyming couplet that reminds us how big and varied is the world in which we live.

The poet asserts that among all the plenty that the world has to offer we should be able to find a source for happiness. We are encouraged to reflect on the unspecified but boundless aspects of the world from which we may derive a sense of personal richness.

Composition

The two lines of the poem have a regular, though relatively unusual, metre of eleven syllables, none of which is especially stressed.

The language consists mostly of simple monosyllables, except for the antepenultimate word of each line, which is disyllabic. The overall effect is mantra-like, or like a playground rhyme with a bounding, skipping sense of happiness.

Message

The message of the poem is simple: that in such a broad and varied world as ours we should be able to find things that help to make us happy. The poet does not suggest what might do this — wealth, status or anything else — but gently encourages us to seek for ourselves.

Lesson plan: 'Happy Thought' by Robert Louis Stevenson

Resources

Copies of the poem — ideally one per pupil, pens and pencils or marker pens, rulers for SEND pupils to follow a line when reading. Extra paper should be made available for use if required.

Copies of pupils' safety plans to which they can refer throughout the session/lesson.

The lesson will cover oracy, reading and writing skills.

The session can be done in the round, or as a circle time activity, or at tables, or in an unstructured group. The lesson plan is suitable to use with pupils at Upper Key Stage 2, 3 and 4.

Links with the PSHE Association PSHE Education Programme of Study

Links have been made to the PSHE Association PSHE Education Programme of Study at Key Stage 2, 3 and 4 as follows:

KS2

- *H15. that mental health, just like physical health, is part of daily life; the importance of taking care of mental health*
- *H18. about everyday things that affect feelings and the importance of expressing feelings*

KS3

- *H10. a range of healthy coping strategies and ways to promote wellbeing and boost mood, including physical activity, participation and the value of positive relationships in providing support*

KS4

- *H7. a broad range of strategies — cognitive and practical — for promoting their own emotional wellbeing, for avoiding negative thinking and for ways of managing mental health concerns*

Links with the National Curriculum

Links have been made to the National Curriculum for English at Key Stage 2, 3 and 4 as follows:

KS2 (Years 5 and 6) English programme of study
- *explain and discuss their understanding of what they have read, including through formal presentations and debates, maintaining a focus on the topic and using notes where necessary*
- *provide reasoned justifications for their views*
- *draft and write by:*
  selecting appropriate grammar and vocabulary, understanding how such choices can change and enhance meaning

KS3 English programme of study
- *participating in formal debates and structured discussions, summarising and/or building on what has been said*
- *knowing how language, including figurative language, vocabulary choice, grammar, text structure and organisational features, presents meaning*
- *recognising a range of poetic conventions and understanding how these have been used*
- *write accurately, fluently, effectively and at length for pleasure and information through poetry*

KS4 English programme of study
- *analysing a writer's choice of vocabulary, form, grammatical and structural features, and evaluating their effectiveness and impact*

307

- *make an informed personal response, recognising that other responses to a text are possible and evaluating these*
- *make notes, draft and write including using information provided by others*

Teaching and learning activities

This is a really good poem for deep philosophical debate and for analysing our own attitudes towards happiness. It is a simple rhyming poem as it is a single couplet, but despite its simplicity it has great depth and meaning.

- Introduction — share aims of lesson.
- Refer pupils to their safety plans. Remind them of what a safety plan is for. Ask them to read through their own safety plan before they go further and answer any questions they may have.
- Read the poem (or teacher/leader to read it aloud) and discuss its content. Ask the following key questions:
  - What do we mean by 'the world'?
  - Do we have access to the world or just a small part of it?
  - How can we increase our 'reach' into the world?
  - The world is full of things, as the poet suggests, but how can we find out about them and decide what is right for us?
  - Is there such a thing as a right choice?
  - What sort of things make us happy? Is it just objects, and if not then what other things can give us happiness?
  - Is happiness internal or external?
  - Is it realistic to expect to be happy all the time? Is anyone always happy all the time?
  - How can we pursue happiness?
  - Think about the poet's phrase 'as happy as kings'. What does this mean? Are kings really happy? What makes them happy — or stops them from being truly happy?
- This lesson can be approached by defining what we do and do not mean by happiness. Provide each pupil with a piece of A4 paper. Divide the paper in landscape into two halves vertically. On the centre line write HAPPINESS, in the top left hand corner write IS NOT, and in the top right hand corner write IS, so you have one end of the page for the negatives and the other end for the positives. Start to populate the paper with things that are associated with happiness — things that, to you, happiness is or is not. Think whether there are some things that can appear on both sides, things that make you both happy and unhappy. For example, your favourite football team might do both, as might your family or friends. Explore why something can have the power to make you both happy and unhappy. How does this apply to something like wealth and popularity? Pupils can work on their own, in a small group, or with a partner on this activity.
- Hone ideas that have been written down, so as to create a personal philosophy of happiness (e.g. I want good friends who support me and who I support; I want to be good at something and recognised for it; I want to have enough money for my needs). This could be turned into either a personal statement (e.g. John's Law of Happiness, Jiang's Advice for a Happy Life), or it could be turned into a two line couplet. For example:

> *Happiness is not about having a lot:*
> *It's having enough, and liking what you've got.*

If it cannot be confined to one couplet it might be extended to two or three couplets, but brevity is the ideal as it encourages critical thinking.

- Review what has been achieved in the lesson.
- Refer pupils to their safety plans as a place to look if they need help after leaving the lesson.

Extension activities

- Pupils to write their answers to the key questions in the first part of the lesson.
- Pupils to write their own couplet poems on the topic of happiness and what makes them truly happy. These can be displayed in the setting for other pupils to read.
- Do you like the poem? Pupils to write their own responses giving reasons.
- Learn the poem 'Happy Thought' by heart.
- Prepare your own poem to read aloud and to perform, so that the meaning is clear to an audience.

Cross-curricular/topic links

Cross-curricular and topic links may be explored for use in follow-up and for extension work in

- English
- PSHE

Differentiation

Opportunities for discussion in mixed ability pairs.

Differentiation by outcome e.g. quantity or complexity of issues identified, sophistication of response, level of inclusion/contribution, empathy.

Writing quantity outcomes will be differentiated/assessed/moderated according to teacher's expectations of quantity and depth; otherwise by outcome.

Trying to Find Answers

This section is about resilience, determination and positivity
in the face of the challenges life brings...

Heartbeat Number 2

by Paul Morris

Commentary

This is heartbeat number two:
Number one is inside you —

> *Question:*
> *If half of you was early lost*
> *And half was never found,*
> *Is there Anyone for taking*
> *When the Reaper comes around?*

Every fall of the hammer, the hurtle and spin
Each twist of the drama, the trouble we're in
The smack of your heartbeat, the rattle and hum
In the heights that you've dared and the distance you've come
In the distance you've fought and the height that you fell
And the climb and the grind as you fought back as well
In each breath that you grasp and each heartbeat you feel
Through the slip of the clay and the kick of the wheel
Every cause that you fight, every question you ask
And your right to the might as you strike to your task
It's the scream as each dream finds the courage you lack
And you bleed but you need it and find your way back
It's the heat of the love and the chill of the rage
And the jolt of the ink as you bleed on the page
It's when hate won't be sated, its cuts bleed you hollow
Till love cuts across all the dross that you follow
It's the bite of the knife and the twist of the blade
And the light in your life of the Good that you've made
It's your push through the crush as you're rocking your style
Through the last centimetre and metre and mile
Till you drop you don't stop and you go it alone
Through the crack of the smile and the snap of the bone
Through the dash and the din
And the thrash and the spin
And the thick and the thin
But you bear it and grin
And you never —
                    you never —
                              you ***never*** give in.

Context

'Heartbeat Number 2' was written in the spring of 2018.

311

The poet describes how the poem was written during one sleepless night. Having worked long into the night (a usual habit of his), he went to bed at about 3.00am but could not sleep. After lying awake for some time he became aware of a single line of verse that was forming and reforming itself in his mind, apparently independently of his conscious thought. This was followed by another, then another, until he could no longer disregard them. He got out of bed, found pen and paper and wrote the poem in one continuous flow that was, as he has said, 'as though I was taking dictation'. When he had finished, he threw down the writing materials, returned to bed and instantly fell into a deep sleep. In the morning he went to inspect the night's work and found the poem written at odd angles all over the paper, with lines crossing lines and some lines written around the edge of the page. He copied it down precisely as he had written it, only tidying the layout but with no revisions or redrafting because, as he said, 'It was a poem that seemed to come *to* me rather than *from* me, and it was not up to me to change a word of it'.

Asked about the poem's cryptic title, the poet has explained it as referring to 'the second heartbeat that is within and outside us all — whether it is the silent beat of freedom, courage, determination or something else, it is the impetus and the internal energy that drives each of us through life'.

Content

The poem opens by introducing itself, defining itself as distinct from what we may think of as 'heartbeat number one', the first heartbeat (that is, the physical pulse) that lies within the reader. It is clear that 'heartbeat number two' is not describing a physical phenomenon but something more.

The reader is then confronted with a question, displaced from the flow of the poem — literally an aside. He or she is invited to consider what it means to be oneself: whether, if we have 'lost' some of what it means to be ourselves early in life (perhaps as a result of parental, social or educational influence, although this is not stated explicitly), then we fail to find ourselves (i.e. to encounter our true identity) as we go through life, we can really consider ourselves to have been 'Anyone' as life comes to an end. This is a stark challenge, and one which requires self-reflection; the reader may take a moment for thought before entering the main body of the work.

The poem then moves into a rapid, impressionistic and seemingly disparate series of scenes, a jagged mix of descriptions both literal and metaphorical of snapshotted experiences from life. These include: the blows that life deals us, in its speed and confusion (line 8); the rapid change of life's direction, with the problems it brings (line 9); the sense of energetic striving and fall that are implicit in life's achievements and setbacks, with the constant determination to fight back against the reversals we experience (lines 10 to 13); the investment of life in the act of creating something (lines 14 and 15); the right to believe, to question and be devoted to a cause (lines 16 and 17); the pain of finding that we fall short of our ambitions, but persisting nevertheless (lines 18 and 19); the need to express ourselves, however hard or painful it may be to do so (lines 20 and 21); the power of hate to leave us feeling drained and weakened, and its powerlessness in the face of love (lines 22 and 23); the seeming cruelty of life, through which our good deeds shine like a light (lines 24 and 25). These are all common experiences that, whilst difficult, we may expect to encounter in life and to have to find our way through.

We are told that throughout all of these challenges we must push onwards, resolutely being true to ourselves ('rocking your style', line 26) every centimetre along life's path, even though we may be alone, whatever the pain and confusion we may face, however it may seem that life's difficulties are somehow intended to hurt or deceive us ('the thrash and the spin' of line 31).

We must find our way, try to remain resolute and keep our good humour, and never yield or concede that life has defeated us.

Composition

'Heartbeat Number 2' is written in three stanzas. These are: the first two lines, identifying the 'heartbeat' of the title; the question or challenge to the reader of lines 3 to 7; and the main body of the poem that follows (lines 8 to 36).

The poem is written in anapaestic tetrameter, a poetic metre that has four anapestic metrical feet per line, each foot having two unstressed syllables followed by a stressed syllable (in effect, 'da-da-DUM', though the initial unstressed beat of a line may be omitted). This form has found use in a wide variety of poetry, from Dr Seuss to the epic of Lord Byron. The poet's use of the metre in this work gives it a sense of energy and momentum that suits the poem's theme, and particularly the notion that life's insistent pace may present us with a rapid succession of 'one thing after another'. It should be noted that the strict metre shifts from line 30, where the four metrical feet are at first halved, or rather shared, across pairs of lines (lines 30–31, 32–33), and then across the three lines that end the poem (lines 34–36). This metre produces a rapid, driving pace with a regularity that has been likened to the pace and rhythm of a cantering horse's hoofbeats; the shift from line 30 gives the impression of that horse being pulled up, ready for the dramatic conclusion of the final line.

The rhyme scheme is three-fold, varied across the three stanzas. There is an introductory rhyming couplet; followed by a quatrain with the rhyme scheme ABCB (this has an appended, irregular line that fronts it — the single word 'Question' of line 3 which steps out of rhyme to perform its function); then reverting to rhyming couplets in the main body of the poem.

The language and vocabulary are direct and dramatic, and selected so as to create numerous internal rhymes. Although the vocabulary seems everyday, there are three usages which may be relatively unfamiliar: 'Reaper' (= 'death', as in 'Grim Reaper', line 7), 'sated' (= 'satisfied', line 22), and 'dross' (= 'rubbish', line 23).

Punctuation is scant, consisting solely of marks within the line, rather than at line ends. This helps to create the impression of flow, pace and drive.

Capitalisation is used conventionally for the beginning of each line. Three further words are capitalised, namely 'Anyone' (line 6), 'Reaper' (line 7), and 'Good' (line 25): in the second case this may be understood as a proper noun, but for the first and third the capitalisation seems to be intended to add status and universality to the words.

Anaphora is used for emphasis throughout the poem, including the line openings 'In' (lines 11, 12 and 14), 'It's' (lines 18, 20, 22, 24 and 26), 'Till' (lines 23 and 28), and 'Through' (lines 27, 29 and 30). There is also the highly insistent repetition of 'you never' (the third 'never' in heavy type for particular emphasis) in lines 34, 35 and 36, which act like hammer blows to drive home the poet's final point.

Figurative language is used throughout the poem. No intrusive similes are used, the poet confining himself to short, impactful metaphors which often depend for their effect upon the connotations of a single word.

Message

The message of the poem is forceful both in expression and intent.

We should be aware that our lives are not merely a physical process, but depend upon something further within us, our minds and hearts, that carries us forward — 'the silent beat of freedom, courage, determination or something else… the impetus and the internal energy that drives each of us through life' of which the poet has spoken. We may each find our own spur, our own drive.

We are to understand that life is full of challenges, triumphs and setbacks, but that we should try to meet each occurrence and development with determination and persistence. There are many things that we will find we need, and that are worth fighting and hanging on for, even though it is an effort, or perhaps causes us pain, to do so.

We should try to maintain a strong sense of self, and the resolve and fortitude to pursue what we feel to be our purpose in life.

Life is not easy — in fact it is often very hard indeed — but we should never give up trying.

Lesson plan: 'Heartbeat Number 2' by Paul Morris

Resources

Copies of the poem — ideally one per pupil, rulers for SEND pupils to follow a line when reading, pens or pencils, thesauruses, flip chart paper. Extra paper should be made available for use if required.

The lesson plan is suitable to use with pupils at Upper Key Stage 2, 3 and 4.

The lesson will cover oracy and reading skills.

The session can be done in the round, or as a circle time activity, or at tables, or in an unstructured group, for all age groups.

Links with the PSHE Association PSHE Education Programme of Study

Links have been made to the PSHE Association PSHE Education Programme of Study at Key Stage 2, 3 and 4 as follows:

KS2

- *H29. about how to manage setbacks/perceived failures, including how to re-frame unhelpful thinking*

KS3

- *H2. to understand what can affect wellbeing and resilience (e.g. life changes, relationships, achievements and employment)*
- *H4. simple strategies to help build resilience to negative opinions, judgments and comments*

KS4

- *H7. a broad range of strategies — cognitive and practical — for promoting their own emotional wellbeing, for avoiding negative thinking and for ways of managing mental health concerns*
- *H4. strategies to develop assertiveness and build resilience to peer and other influences that affect both how they think about themselves and their health and wellbeing*

Links with the National Curriculum

Links have been made to the National Curriculum for English at Key Stage 2, 3 and 4 as follows:

KS2 (Years 5 and 6) English programme of study

- *maintain attention and participate actively in collaborative conversations, staying on topic and initiating and responding to comments*
- *discuss and evaluate how authors use language, including figurative language, considering the impact on the reader*
- *provide reasoned justifications for their views*

KS3 English programme of study

- *participating in formal debates and structured discussions, summarising and/or building on what has been said*
- *knowing how language, including figurative language, vocabulary choice, grammar, text structure and organisational features, presents meaning*

KS4 English programme of study

- *listening to and building on the contributions of others, asking questions to clarify and inform, and challenging courteously when necessary*
- *analysing a writer's choice of vocabulary, form, grammatical and structural features, and evaluating their effectiveness and impact*

Teaching and learning activities

We all have days when life is not easy. We experience challenges, triumphs, and setbacks. What is important is how we deal with the ups and downs of life, showing an inner resolve to push through challenges with determination and persistence.

- Introduction — share aims of lesson.
- Refer pupils to their safety plans. Remind them of what a safety plan is for. Ask them to read through their own safety plan before they go further and answer any questions they may have.
- Read the poem (or teacher/leader to read it aloud) and discuss its content. It may be necessary to explain the meaning of some of the words in the poem. The meaning can be found in the **Commentary**.
- Ask key questions:
  - What does the title of the poem 'Heartbeat Number 2' mean to you?
  - What is this poem about? Why do you think this?
  - What is the poem's message?
  - Did you like the poem? Give reasons for your opinion.
- In pairs or in small groups talk about a setback or a challenge that you have had in your life. Describe what happened and how you came through it.
- Ask for feedback.
- Working with a partner or on your own, highlight some of the words the poet has used to describe how to get through life's challenges and setbacks. What positive behavioural traits do you think are necessary to deal with life's challenges and setbacks? Pupils to come up with a list of words and phrases. Write an example on the whiteboard e.g. 'resilience' so that pupils understand what they are being asked to think about. Pupils to be encouraged to use a

thesaurus to find additional synonyms for the words they come up with. Words and phrases to be recorded on a flip chart.

- Ask for feedback. Write the words and phrases on the whiteboard.
- Ask each pupil to select a word or phrase from the whiteboard and to design a calligram of the word/phrase. A calligram is a word or piece of text in which the design and layout of the letters creates a visual image related to the meaning of the words themselves, for example the word 'strong' in the shape of a fist. Show pupils examples of calligrams taken from the web (there are many) to provide inspiration and ideas for their own designs.
- Review what has been achieved in the lesson.
- Refer pupils to their safety plans as a place to look if they need help after leaving the lesson.

Extension activities

- Pupils to write their answers to the key questions.
- Write about the form, structure and rhyme scheme of the poem.
- Pupils to produce calligrams of words for behavioural traits discussed in the main lesson. Pupils can use a range of media including paints and felt pens to produce a piece of word art. Display the calligrams in the classroom so that pupils can see them regularly.
- Work on performing 'Heartbeat Number 2' to an audience. This might be for an assembly or for parents, the whole school, etc. This can also be done on a one-to-one basis with student and teacher/session leader.
- Ask pupils to find examples of short impactful metaphors in the poem and to write about them.
- Why is it important to develop inner resilience in life? Ask pupils to carry out their own research and to produce a booklet or poster about the importance of resilience.
- Pupils to write their own poems about inner resilience based on 'Heartbeat Number 2'.
- What are the barriers to developing inner resilience? Discuss in PSHE lessons. Discuss ways of overcoming some of these barriers.
- Pupils to write letters to themselves, either advising how to deal with one or more of the negative things that has happened in their lives, or putting them into perspective. Try to incorporate things like empathy, forgiveness, tolerance, strength and being kind to themselves and others.
- Keep a journal to record your emotions and feelings. Try to write about good things in your life and reflect on events that have made you feel bad about yourself. In each case describe what happened and how it made you feel. How might things have been done better? What lessons did you learn from this? It is important to remember that nobody is perfect. By reflecting on the negative things as well as the positive it can help you to keep things in perspective.

Cross-curricular/topic links

Cross-curricular and topic links may be explored for use in follow-up and for extension work in

- English
- PSHE
- Art and Design

Differentiation

Opportunities for discussion in mixed ability pairs.

Differentiation by outcome e.g. quantity or complexity of issues identified, sophistication of response, level of inclusion/contribution, empathy.

Writing quantity outcomes will be differentiated/assessed/moderated according to teacher's expectations of quantity and depth; otherwise by outcome.

Differentiation may also be through key words rather than written sentences, or through artwork as a means of expression.

On the Stork Tower
(登鸛雀樓)

by Wang Zhihuan

Commentary

The sight of the moving bright sun is blocked by the shape of the end of the mountain,
The ever-running flow of the Yellow River ends in the infinite wild sea.
To exhaust your thousand-mile sight
You must ascend the tower, go one level further: rise.

Translation by Kelvin Pak
from the Tang Dynasty original (8th century CE)

Context

'On the Stork Tower' (in Mandarin Chinese '登鸛雀樓' or '*Dēng guàn què lóu*') was written in the early 8th century, during the Kaiyuan era of China's Tang Dynasty. The poet, Wang Zhihuang, was born in Jin Yang, near Taiyuan, capital of Shanxi province. He mastered the classics before his thirties and became a famous poet during the high point of the Tang Dynasty. Many of his poems were made into songs by musicians, which brought him fame and influence. Only six of his poems have survived to modern times.

The Stork Tower (sometimes referred to in anthologies and histories as Heron Lodge) is a 73.9 metre (242 feet) high watchtower first constructed in the 5th century CE. It is said that after the tower was built storks often perched upon it, and so it acquired its name.

Religion appears to have played a lesser role in the daily life of the ancient Chinese people than it did in many other cultures. There are very few religious ideas that originated in China, and China's tradition of religious thinking is largely imported. It is significant that the Chinese people, historically a largely agrarian society in daily contact with the powers of Nature, have often sought personal, spiritual and artistic inspiration from that natural source rather than from religion. This is largely reflected in the great body of ancient Chinese literature that survives today. 'On the Stork Tower' draws on this distinctive tradition.

Content

The poem describes the view from the Stork Tower, reflecting the inspiration that ancient Chinese poetry often draws characteristically from the natural world.

While the poem is brief, it is intended to be a focus for personal meditation, a reminder that in a world where natural forces shape life our own efforts can make a significant difference. The piece draws together elements of Taoist, Buddhist and Confucian thought and popular tradition: the stork of the title is an emblem of long life, and in the Chinese imperial hierarchy is a 'bird of first rank' whose flight symbolises the hope for higher position.

The piece integrates natural scenery with the human spirit beautifully, taking as its underlying motif an aspiration for constant self-improvement and personal elevation. The view we are invited to meditate upon is grand: the vivid description of the moving sun and running river, stretching away as far as one's eye can see, presents an uplifting epigram in its conclusion, a message of encouragement to seek out new and better prospects through our efforts. Like Nature, we progress by not standing still.

The poem uplifts the reader's spirit through the display of Nature's majestic powers, suffused by an atmosphere of quiet and restraint, whilst exhorting us to seek personal growth to improve our own lives.

Composition

The poem in the original Chinese follows the conventions of the *jueju* or Chinese quatrain, a type of *jintishi* ('modern form poetry') popular among Chinese poets of the Tang Dynasty (618 to 907CE) though originating before that period.

Jueju poems consist of two couplets, each line of which has five or seven syllables. In the original Chinese this is expressed as a strict composition of four strictly rhythmical lines, each of five characters. It is not possible to reproduce this precisely in translation due to the inherent differences between the Chinese and English languages, although the meaning and beauty of language of the original are preserved in our version above.

The piece presents us with a magnificent vista of nature in movement. It leads the observer's eye, with the steady motion of the setting sun and the river beneath, along the stony ridge of mountains to where we encounter the vast flow of the sea. We are invited to be aware of our place in the vastness of the natural world, part of its daily rhythms yet distinctly human.

The poem's final word in translation, 'rise', reflects the sense of the original Chinese with its definite implication of motion.

Message

The message is inspiring: one should not be idle, but instead be prepared at all times to take a step further to attain a higher goal.

Nature may appear peaceful, but its beauty is the result of dynamism, of unceasing motion. So we too may become better and more positive versions of ourselves through what we choose to do.

Just as we climb the tower, so in life we must be prepared to go onwards and upwards. To see further, to go further, we must both aspire and take action.

Lesson plan: 'On the Stork Tower' by Wang Zhihuan

Resources

Copies of the poem — ideally one per pupil. Pens and pencils. Plain paper should be made available for use if required. Rulers for SEND pupils to follow a line when reading.

Copies of pupils' safety plans to which they can refer throughout the session/lesson.

The lesson will cover oracy, reading and writing skills.

The lesson plan is suitable to use with pupils at Upper Key Stage 2, 3 and 4.

The session can be done at tables or in an unstructured group, for all age groups.

Links with the PSHE Association PSHE Education Programme of Study

Links have been made to the PSHE Association PSHE Education Programme of Study at Key Stage 2, 3 and 4 as follows:

KS2

- *H28. to identify personal strengths, skills, achievements and interests and how these contribute to a sense of self-worth*
- *H16. about strategies and behaviours that support mental health — including how good quality sleep, physical exercise/time outdoors, being involved in community groups, doing things for others, clubs, and activities, hobbies and spending time with family and friends can support mental health and wellbeing*

KS3

- *H1. how we are all unique; that recognising and demonstrating personal strengths build self-confidence, self-esteem and good health and wellbeing*
- *H7. the characteristics of mental and emotional health and strategies for managing these*
- *H10. a range of healthy coping strategies and ways to promote wellbeing and boost mood, including physical activity, participation and the value of positive relationships in providing support*

KS4

- *H1. to accurately assess their areas of strength and development, and where appropriate, act upon feedback*
- *H2. how self-confidence self-esteem, and mental health are affected positively and negatively by internal and external influences and ways of managing this*
- *H7. a broad range of strategies — cognitive and practical — for promoting their own emotional wellbeing, for avoiding negative thinking and for ways of managing mental health concerns*

Links with the National Curriculum

Links have been made to the National Curriculum for English at Key Stage 2, 3 and 4 as follows:

KS2 (Years 5 and 6) English programme of study
- *articulate and justify answers, arguments and opinions*
- *provide reasoned justifications for their views*
- *plan their writing by:*
  identifying the audience for and purpose of the writing, selecting the appropriate form and using other similar writing as models for their own
- *noting and developing initial ideas, drawing on reading and research where necessary*

KS3 English programme of study

- *participating in formal debates and structured discussions, summarising and/or building on what has been said*
- *knowing the purpose, audience for and context of the writing and drawing on this knowledge to support comprehension*
- *making inferences and referring to evidence in the text*
- *knowing how language, including figurative language, vocabulary choice, grammar, text structure and organisational features, presents meaning*

KS4 English programme of study

- *listening to and building on the contributions of others, asking questions to clarify and inform, and challenging courteously when necessary*
- *seeking evidence in the text to support a point of view, including justifying inferences with evidence*
- *analysing a writer's choice of vocabulary, form, grammatical and structural features, and evaluating their effectiveness and impact*
- *drawing on knowledge of the purpose, audience for and context of the writing, including its social, historical and cultural context and the literary tradition to which it belongs, to inform evaluation*

Teaching and learning activities

The poem is an extended call for a positive life. The message is inspiring: just as Nature is never entirely still, so one should always be prepared to move onwards, to take a step further to reach better things.

- Introduction — share aims of lesson.
- Refer pupils to their safety plans. Remind them of what a safety plan is for. Ask them to read through their own safety plan before they go further and answer any questions they may have.
- Provide background information about the poem and explain that it was written in the Tang Dynasty, a Chinese imperial dynasty (that is, a sequence of rulers from the same family or clan) that ruled from 618 to 907CE.
- Read the poem (or teacher/leader to read it aloud) and discuss its content.
- Ask key questions:
  - What is the Stork Tower? Discuss and show images of watchtowers. This is about developing positive visualisation.
  - What can you see in the poem?
  - What is the message of the poem? How is it different from other poems you have read? Refer to other poems you have read, or that the pupils might have encountered.
- Take feedback and comments from pupils.
- It may help pupils to sketch/draw what they see in the poem.
- Pupils to write inspirational mottos or a positive message for their own personal journeys and to sketch a scene or an image to accompany it.
- Pupils to share their own personal mottos.
- Plan a journey from a problem you have to its solution e.g. a journey from being angry with your friend to being on good terms with him or her. What are the steps on your journey? What are the important stages you will pass through? How will you know that you have got there?

- Review what has been achieved in the lesson.
- Refer pupils to their safety plans as a place to look if they need help after leaving the lesson.

Extension activities

- Pupils to write their answers to the key questions.
- Pupils to write their own written journeys building on the planning session and to make changes to their work through editing.
- Paint or use multi-media to work up sketches and mottos so they can be displayed in the classroom/setting. Pupils can also research images of Chinese watchtowers to find out more about the Tang Dynasty and the importance of the natural world and humankind's place in it.
- Describe a beautiful place that you have visited, either real or imaginary. How did it make you feel? What was special about it? Share your experience with a friend or write about it.
- Read other examples of Tang Dynasty poetry.
- Research the Tang Dynasty period in Chinese history.

Cross-curricular/topic links

Cross-curricular and topic links may be explored for use in follow-up and for extension work in

- English
- Drama
- PSHE
- Art and Design
- History (Chinese)

Differentiation

Opportunities for discussion in mixed ability pairs.

Differentiation by outcome e.g. quantity or complexity of issues identified, sophistication of response, level of inclusion/contribution, empathy.

Writing quantity outcomes will be differentiated/assessed/moderated according to teacher's expectations of quantity and depth; otherwise by outcome.

Differentiation may also be through key words rather than written sentences, or through artwork as a means of expression.

If

by Rudyard Kipling

Commentary

If you can keep your head when all about you
    Are losing theirs and blaming it on you,
If you can trust yourself when all men doubt you,
    But make allowance for their doubting too;
If you can wait and not be tired by waiting,
    Or being lied about, don't deal in lies,
Or being hated, don't give way to hating,
    And yet don't look too good, nor talk too wise:

If you can dream — and not make dreams your master;
    If you can think — and not make thoughts your aim;
If you can meet with Triumph and Disaster
    And treat those two impostors just the same;
If you can bear to hear the truth you've spoken
    Twisted by knaves to make a trap for fools,
Or watch the things you gave your life to, broken,
    And stoop and build 'em up with worn-out tools:

If you can make one heap of all your winnings
    And risk it on one turn of pitch-and-toss,
And lose, and start again at your beginnings
    And never breathe a word about your loss;
If you can force your heart and nerve and sinew
    To serve your turn long after they are gone,
And so hold on when there is nothing in you
    Except the Will which says to them: 'Hold on!'

If you can talk with crowds and keep your virtue,
    Or walk with Kings — nor lose the common touch,
If neither foes nor loving friends can hurt you,
    If all men count with you, but none too much;
If you can fill the unforgiving minute
    With sixty seconds' worth of distance run,
Yours is the Earth and everything that's in it,
    And — which is more — you'll be a Man, my son!

Context

'If' was written by Rudyard Kipling, who was born in 1865 in Bombay, then one of the most important cities in British India, the name given to the territories of the Indian subcontinent that came under Imperial British colonial rule between 1612 and 1947.

The British Raj (the latter word meaning 'rule' in Sanskrit and Hindustani) was the system of rule by the British Crown in India between 1858 and 1947. It, and indeed the British Empire as a whole, is now generally viewed as a phase of British imperialist colonialism that was inherently racist and that caused considerable damage and pain among the people into whose lands the Empire sought to expand. It is against this reprehensible history that Kipling's work must be set, as he was a product of that world no less than we are of our own. The Raj depended largely upon the British expatriates who set up home in India. Kipling's parents were such and considered themselves to be Anglo-Indians, the term used to describe people of British origin who were living in India. Their son Rudyard, who was named after the Staffordshire lake where his parents had carried out much of their courting before marrying and moving to India, spent a good deal of his childhood speaking Hindi with his nurse and, as he recalled, spoke English to his parents 'haltingly translated out of the vernacular idiom that one thought and dreamed in'.

Kipling wrote 'If' in or about 1895 and recorded in his posthumously published autobiography, *Something of Myself* (1937), that he had done so as a tribute to the Scottish colonial politician Leander Starr Jameson. Jameson had assembled a private army outside the Transvaal in the then South African Republic, preparing to overthrow the Boer government in the hope of invading and annexing the territory for Britain. The failed incident, motivated by the patriotism that was seen as laudable at the time, became known as the Jameson Raid. Though the British Colonial Secretary was implicated in its events much of the blame for the raid rested upon Jameson himself. The failure of the mercenary armed coup d'état intensified political tensions between Great Britain and the Boers, and was one of the factors that led to the Second Boer War.

Though the colonialist motivations we may ascribe to Jameson would now be thoroughly and rightly condemned, according to the now unacceptable standards of the time Kipling saw his actions as patriotic. His handling of the personal trouble that the Jameson Raid caused him, and indeed his personal qualities and stoicism in general, appear to have inspired a devotion from many of his contemporaries that would be inexcusable in our own more enlightened times given the imperialist, expansionist actions that Jameson had committed. Though we might now see being 'a Man', as Kipling describes it, as having connotations of empire and stiff upper lip that we recognise as symptoms of toxic masculinity, according to his own standards Kipling saw Jameson's outlook as a model of Victorian-era stoicism, and worthy of celebration in verse. It is important that Kipling's verse should be seen in its historical context.

It is often observed that the poem, though still extremely popular, is not without its problems for the modern reader. It is frequently identified as a poem that includes elements of 'toxic masculinity', the set of attitudes and behaviours stereotypically associated with or expected of men that are regarded as having a negative impact on individuals and on society as a whole. This may be found, for example, in the poem's encouragement to suppress emotion (e.g. 'start again at your beginnings / And never breathe a word about your loss', lines 19 and 20), or to keep going when it might be healthier to stop ('force your heart and nerve and sinew / To serve your turn long after they are gone', lines 21 to 24). The poem is also particularly male-centred, as is clear from the final line 'you'll be a Man, my son'. However, these points of difficulty give considerable scope for debate and discussion, helping us to reach a view on how this and other such poems can be understood according to modern social standards and be relevant to all sexes and genders.

The poem is written in the form of paternal advice to Kipling's son John. It was first published in *Rewards and Fairies* (1910), a collection of Kipling's poetry and short stories.

Content

The poem is written in the form of advice from the speaker to his son (see line 32).

The speaker presents to the person he is addressing, and hence to the reader, a series of 'ifs': *if* you can do certain things and not do others, *if* you can behave in certain ways (most of them evincing Victorian stoicism and a certain 'stiff upper lip'), *if* you can maintain a certain approach to life, then you will have become a better person and more equipped to get on in life. These 'ifs' may therefore be read as ideal advice about what one should do and how one should conduct oneself in order to become what Kipling considered to be a better person.

We are advised to stay clear-minded when everyone around us is not only losing their self-control but also blaming their panic on us (lines 1 and 2).

We should trust ourselves even when other people doubt us, but we should also take into account the reasons why they might not believe in us or our ability (lines 3 and 4).

The speaker tells us that we should be able to wait without becoming tired of waiting (line 5). If we are lied about, we should not indulge in lying about others (line 6), and if we are hated we should not then allow ourselves to hate (line 7). While we are doing these things we should not try to make ourselves 'look too good', nor should we try to sound clever about our own virtue (line 8).

We should have dreams but not be governed by them (line 9), and we should think but not just for its own sake — that is, we should remember to be practical too (line 10).

The speaker advisers us to meet with success and failure whilst treating both of them the same way (lines 11 and 12). He refers to them as 'those two impostors', and we may speculate that this is because both success and failure are similarly fleeting and insubstantial.

We should be prepared to bear seeing unscrupulous people twist the things we have said, and using this in order to deceive others (lines 13 and 14). We may have to see everything we have given our lives to build up being broken down, and we may have to put our lives back together with poor resources (lines 15 and 16).

We are to ask whether we could take all we have won in life and stake it all on a single chance; then, having lost everything, whether we could carry on without complaining (lines 17 to 20). We may ask ourselves whether what is being suggested by the speaker is an unhealthy suppression of our emotions, or whether there really may be times in life when our emotions cannot take first place.

The speaker challenges us with having the will to force ourselves — mentally and physically — to keep going even after our bodies and minds have exhausted their strength (lines 21 and 22), so that we can remain firm even when we are only doing so by the power of our determination (lines 23 and 24). Again, we may ask whether the speaker is urging us to push on even when it seems unhealthy for us to do so, or whether he is suggesting that there are extraordinary and rare times in life when such extreme singlemindedness is the only way to get through.

We should be able to interact with many people without our sense of right and wrong being affected by a mob mentality (line 25). Yet we should also be able to mix with wealthy and powerful people without forgetting our ordinariness (line 26): people are just people.

It is advised that we should be sufficiently strong in ourselves that neither friends nor enemies can harm our feelings (line 27): here the poet is clearly aware of the ability of even our closest friends to hurt us emotionally, albeit that they perhaps do so unintentionally. Everybody should matter to us, but nobody should become disproportionately important in our lives (line 28).

Time is 'unforgiving' because it carries on running in spite of us, so we should fill every minute with valuable activity and not let time go to waste (lines 29 and 30). Life is like running a race, and we should keep on running for the full sixty seconds of every minute.

If we can do all of these things then the world, figuratively speaking, will belong to us — we might say 'the world is our oyster' (line 31). More than this, and more valuably than this, we will also be what the poet calls (using social conventions and social norms of his time where desirable traits were expressed in masculine terms), 'a Man' (line 32); that is to say, a person of fine character who, from the traits the speaker has described in the poem, will be his ideal of a fully-rounded, capable, decent, stoical human being.

Composition

'If' is written in four stanzas, each an octave of iambic pentameter with the rhyme scheme ABABABAB. The odd-numbered lines in fact have an eleventh syllable (remembering that iambic pentameter consists of disyllabic feet with a short and long syllable, making ten to a line). This is achieved by using a so-called 'feminine ending' to those odd-numbered lines, using an amphibrach in the fifth foot.

The poem is broadly epistolary, in the form of a letter or address from the speaker to his son giving moral and practical advice for life.

The language is everyday, using a light vernacular within the context of the poet's social class and the linguistic conventions of the day. This is shown through forms such as the abbreviations of 'don't' (lines 6, 7 and 8) and 'you've' (line 13), and the colloquially casual 'talk too wise' (instead of 'too wisely', line 8) and "em' (for 'them', line 16).

There are two items of vocabulary in particular for which the younger reader may appreciate clarification: 'knaves' (= 'dishonest or unscrupulous people, line 14), 'pitch-and-toss' (= 'a game in which players take turns to throw a coin at a wall and the player with the coin that lands closest to the wall wins all the other coins', line 18).

The poem's punctuation is more open than might be the case had the piece been composed in prose. The entire thirty-two-line poem consists of only two sentences. The first of these is twenty-four lines long and makes generous use of colons and semicolons to help govern its progress; whilst the second, only eight lines long, relies on commas with a single semicolon and one pair of dashes. The poet makes use of enjambment at a number of points in the poem (lines 1 to 2, 11 to 12, 13 to 14, 17 to 18, 19 to 20, 21 to 22, 23 to 24 and 29 to 30) to enhance its flow.

Kipling uses anaphora extensively in the poem, with the recurring 'if' that opens lines 1, 3, 5, 9, 10, 11, 13, 17, 21, 25, 27, 28 and 29: of these, all are 'if you can', with the exception of 27 and 28 which refer not to 'you' but to others ('foes', 'loving friends' and 'all men') . The effect of this is to keep returning the focus of the advice to its intended subject, and therefore to 'you' the reader. The repetition accumulates to have the feeling of a challenge: the traits the speaker requires of us are numerous and varied, reaching into many aspects of our daily lives.

Kipling uses symploce in dealing with the traits of which we must be wary. This occurs in lines 3 and 4 ('doubt' / 'doubting'), line 4 ('wait' / 'waiting'), line 5 ('lied' / 'lies'), line 7 ('hated' / 'hating'), line 9 ('dream' / 'dreams') and line 10 ('think' / 'thoughts'). Again the effect is one of emphasis, reiterating the trait of which the speaker (and hence the poet) wishes us to be mindful and reinforcing our awareness of it.

There is some personification in the second stanza where, in line 11, the poet introduces 'Triumph and Disaster', which are personified by his capitalising the words as though they were proper nouns. They are presented as 'two impostors', deceivers who are not to be trusted.

Kipling appears to prefer the use of metaphor to that of simile for the purposes of this poem, the latter being essentially absent. There are numerous uses of metaphor: 'keep your head' (line 1) has a familiar usage in the sense of 'remain composed'; the breaking of 'the things you gave your life to' (line 15) also appears metaphorical, as do the 'worn-out tools' — the reduced or enfeebled resources that may be the only things we have left with which to respond when, despite our efforts, what we have worked hard for has been destroyed. The 'one turn of pitch-and-toss' (line 18) is no less likely intended metaphorically, as an image of the simple all-or-nothing chance that can sometimes attach to even the simplest or most apparently innocent occurrence — or one upon which we consciously risk losing everything. Our 'heart and nerve and sinew' (line 21) may be physical or may be emblematic of our inner and corporeal resources, but the will we are urged to exert when these resources are exhausted is no less real in either case. The association with crowds and kings in lines 25 and 26 are again metaphorical, as few of us ever consort with either of these as such; but the poet's point — that we should beware the influence on our sensibilities of either the mob or of privilege — is eminently clear. We will not gain 'the Earth' (line 31), nor will many of us become (or ever wish to become) 'a Man' as Kipling seems to intend the word, but we may very well want the integrity, self-reliance, steadfastness and stoicism that his advice promises, and find some answers to our needs in the positive effects these may have upon our lives.

Message

The message of the poem is that we can set out to develop personal values and behaviours that may help us to find some answers in our lives. These may not be the same as Kipling's suggestions, but we may find good in them.

Kipling advises us to be calm, clear-headed, even-tempered, self-reliant, slow to judge people negatively, patient, not to return hate for hate or lies for lies, to be modest, have realistic goals and dreams, to be thoughtful, to accept success and failure with equanimity, to be resilient, to have humility, to try to keep going even when we think we can do no more, not to be influenced too much by others so that we forget our true selves, to use our time wisely and well. This is a long list, and a difficult one to follow in every detail. But we may see how any of these traits might be of value to us in finding answers to some of our needs in life.

Nothing can provide us with all the answers, but a good place to start is within ourselves. When we may be unable to influence the world around us, within us is where we may still be able to make positive changes.

Whether it is remaining calm, avoiding conflict, increasing our self-reliance and resilience, not giving up, or perhaps something else, we can identify and try to develop practices and personal values that will help us to find answers to some of our needs.

Lesson plan: 'If' by Rudyard Kipling

Resources

Copies of the poem — ideally one per pupil, rulers for SEND pupils to follow a line when reading, pens or pencils, flip chart paper. Extra paper should be made available for use if required.

The lesson plan is suitable to use with pupils at Upper Key Stage 2, 3 and 4.

The lesson will cover oracy and reading skills.

The session can be done in the round, or as a circle time activity, or at tables, or in an unstructured group, for all age groups.

Links with the PSHE Association PSHE Education Programme of Study

Links have been made to the PSHE Association PSHE Education Programme of Study at Key Stage 2, 3 and 4 as follows:

KS2

- *H15. that mental health, just like physical health, is part of daily life; the importance of taking care of mental health*
- *H16. about strategies and behaviours that support mental health — including how good quality sleep, physical exercise/time outdoors, being involved in community groups, doing things for others, clubs, and activities, hobbies and spending time with family and friends can support mental health and wellbeing*
- *H28. to identify personal strengths, skills, achievements and interests and how these contribute to a sense of self-worth*

KS3

- *H10. a range of healthy coping strategies and ways to promote wellbeing and boost mood, including physical activity, participation and the value of positive relationships in providing support*
- *H5. to recognise and manage internal and external influences on decisions which affect health and wellbeing*

KS4

- *H7. a broad range of strategies — cognitive and practical — for promoting their own emotional wellbeing, for avoiding negative thinking and for ways of managing mental health concerns*
- *H2. how self-confidence self-esteem, and mental health are affected positively and negatively by internal and external influences and ways of managing this*

Links with the National Curriculum

Links have been made to the National Curriculum for English at Key Stage 2, 3 and 4 as follows:

KS2 (Years 5 and 6) English programme of study

- *maintain attention and participate actively in collaborative conversations, staying on topic and initiating and responding to comments*
- *discuss and evaluate how authors use language, including figurative language, considering the impact on the reader*
- *provide reasoned justifications for their views*

KS3 English programme of study

- *participating in formal debates and structured discussions, summarising and/or building on what has been said*
- *knowing how language, including figurative language, vocabulary choice, grammar, text structure and organisational features, presents meaning*

KS4 English programme of study

- *listening to and building on the contributions of others, asking questions to clarify and inform, and challenging courteously when necessary*
- *analysing a writer's choice of vocabulary, form, grammatical and structural features, and evaluating their effectiveness and impact*

Teaching and learning activities

This poem is addressed to the speaker's son. He is telling him how, in his view and according to the standards of the day, a good man should be. The poem is written as a list of things he should do and believe. The speaker lists a number of conditionals, saying that 'if' his son does these things, he will live a fulfilling existence and be 'a Man', a person of fine character who, from the traits the speaker describes, will be a fully-rounded, capable, decent, stoical human being.

- Introduction — share aims of lesson.
- Refer pupils to their safety plans. Remind them of what a safety plan is for. Ask them to read through their own safety plan before they go further and answer any questions they may have.
- Read the poem (or teacher/leader to read it aloud) and discuss its content. Ask key questions:
  - What is this poem about?
  - Who might be speaking in the poem? Why might they be giving this advice?
  - Why do you think Rudyard Kipling wrote 'If' in second person? (The poet is giving advice.)
- Write a list of personal values you think are necessary for a happy, meaningful life. What would you include? Why? How might these values impact on your mental health and emotional wellbeing? What are the barriers/influences that might keep you from attaining or developing these values? How might you overcome them? Discuss with a partner or in a small group. Record ideas on a flip chart.
- Pupils to feed back their thoughts and ideas.
- Is it ever really a good idea to suppress your feelings, as the speaker seems to suggest in lines 19 and 20? Can you think of any circumstances in which strong emotions might actually get in the way? (Suggestion: think of emergencies.) Discuss this as a group or class. How can you deal with powerful emotion when there is no time to take stock? What can you do afterwards to help come to terms with your feelings and ensure that you stay healthy?
- The poem is written as an address from a male speaker to his son. To what extent do you think it is applicable to girls and women? What about people of all genders? Discuss in groups or as a class.

- Review what has been achieved in the lesson.
- Refer pupils to their safety plans as a place to look if they need help after leaving the lesson

Extension activities

- Pupils to write their answers to the key questions.
- Write about the form, structure and rhyme scheme of the poem.
- Find an example of a metaphor in the poem. Explain its meaning.
- Find an example of personification in the poem. What has the poet personified and why do you think he has done this?
- Think of alternative titles for the poem.
- Choose **one** of these lines from the poem, 'If you can trust yourself when all men doubt you', 'Or being lied about, don't deal in lies', 'Or being hated, don't give way to hating'. Write a short story (which may be fiction or based on real-life experience) which involves one of these situations. Who was involved? How did the situation arise? What happened? How was it handled?
- Did you like the poem? Give reasons for your opinion.
- Find three examples in the poem where if something bad is done to you, you do not do the same bad thing in return.
- What is the moral lesson of the poem?
- What are the most important lessons you have learned so far in your life?
- Write your own recipe for a happy life.
- Poetry can teach us life lessons. Discuss this statement with reference to other poems you may have read.

Cross-curricular/topic links

Cross-curricular and topic links may be explored for use in follow-up and for extension work in

- English
- PSHE

Differentiation

Opportunities for discussion in mixed ability pairs.

Differentiation by outcome e.g. quantity or complexity of issues identified, sophistication of response, level of inclusion/contribution, empathy.

Writing quantity outcomes will be differentiated/assessed/moderated according to teacher's expectations of quantity and depth; otherwise by outcome.

Differentiation may also be through key words rather than written sentences.

you will heal

by Emily Jane

Commentary

sometimes,

you have to allow yourself to exist amongst your sadness.

cradle the rejected emotions, allow yourself to endure everything you wickedly locked away.

feel. every. emotion.

the anger you shunned, forcing it into a corner only ever causing it to prosper.

exhale the self destruction living in your veins.

you. are. human.

an entity overflowing with tenderness. the purity of joy is yet to come.

the dark storm will evaporate.

although, for now you must allow yourself to inhale what you are afraid to know.

it will hurt. ache unlike any other.

sadness will suffocate you, allowing you to breathe enough to die and live all at once.

then it will release its grasp. you will be free.

but until you are able to calm storms with your whispers,

you must allow yourself to exist amongst your sadness.

Context

Emily Jane has often focused her writing upon the effects of mental health issues, and began to do so in her teens. She has examined particularly the effects of stress, low confidence, the sense of being different, and issues of body image on the individual's wellbeing. Healing and the reacquisition of a sense of self-worth are recurrent themes in her poetry.

Content

The poem's speaker addresses the reader directly. She speaks as though giving the reader a gentle permission to experience their sadness and suppressed emotion, in an uncritical act of acceptance and validation.

She begins by observing that sometimes we have to allow ourselves 'to exist amongst your sadness' (line 2). This appears to be an encouragement to live unhappily, to merely 'exist' rather than live, and to do so sorrowfully; but this is not actually so, as will be seen at the poem's conclusion.

The reader is encouraged supportively to allow him- or herself to feel the emotions they have within, even the painful ones. The speaker refers to the suppression of such emotions as their being 'wickedly locked away' (line 3 to 4). The word 'wickedly' seems strange, at odds with the common notion of people finding relief in repressing negative feelings, and we may wonder whether she is encouraging us to feel bad; but it becomes clear that the speaker considers that by confining and imprisoning such emotions we are allowing them to prosper.

By giving audience to negative or painful emotions, acknowledging their presence, we can cause them to pass from us and we are told to 'exhale the self destruction living in your veins' (line 7). It should be noted that the poet does not merely refer to self-destruction in the usual hyphenated construction. We may be considering self-destruction or the presence of self-destructive forces, means through which we turn against ourselves, but this is more than just that. This is 'self destruction', two words with their own individual nuances. It is the force of destruction *of* self, whether it has come from the self or from others. It is also the selfhood of destruction, the self or thing that is destruction in itself. This allows for a nuanced concept of destructive forces that are turned against us, and that come from both within and outside us.

With careful emphasis we are reminded of our humanity. Our emotional overload and the darkness it may bring does not deprive us of that humanity and all its complexity. As human beings we are 'overflowing with tenderness' and may expect to feel 'the purity of joy' (line 9).

The speaker reassures us: 'the dark storm will evaporate' (line 10), and we may expect the tempest of negative emotion to leave us at some time 'yet to come' (line 10).

We are advised 'to inhale what you are afraid to know' (line 11), that is to take in and assimilate the things that cause us problems, though we are warned that 'it will hurt. ache unlike any other' (line 12). The sadness we experience will, the speaker says, be suffocating, enough so to make us feel that we 'die and live all at / once' (lines 13 to 14). This is a process of taking ownership of the things that hurt us. Once we have embraced something that has caused our pain, it will help us to be free from 'its grasp' and we 'will be free' (line 15).

The speaker tells us that until we are able to free ourselves of the things that cause our pain by the application of our gentle will — 'to calm storms' with our 'whispers' (line 16) — we must allow ourselves 'to exist among your sadness' (line 17). It is at this point, after we have been counselled throughout the poem to be patient and to be open to our emotions and to accept ownership of our pain, that the speaker's message from the opening of the poem becomes clear. The poet's emphasis is not upon the sadness, but upon *allowing ourselves to exist*. We are not being told to commit ourselves to living in unhappiness, but rather to still allow the inner essence of our *self* to exist, even though we are surrounded by that unhappiness. We may not be able to escape that unhappiness just yet, but among it our inner self must survive and be allowed to continue.

In time, as the poet promises in the poem's title, you will heal.

Composition

'you will heal' is written as free verse, without rhyme scheme or regular metre. It is conceived as a single stanza with a blank line space between each of the lines, the only exceptions being the two locations (lines 3–4 and 13–14) where textual length requires it to run on to the line below: the effect of this is to focus the reader closely upon the content of each line, giving emphasis to that content.

The poem is a didactic epistolary work of catharsis, exploring the process of releasing, and thereby providing relief from, strong or repressed emotions. The poet, through the speaker, addresses the reader directly to pass on her insight about dealing with, and eventually emerging from, negative and painful emotion. As such, the vocabulary and language of the piece are personal and direct, accessible and measured. The poet avoids the use of capital letters, which adds a sense of gentle flow to the advice rather than it having the appearance of a stark series of instructions.

Punctuation is minimal, limited to that necessary to clarify meaning. The poet avoids complex constructions, preferring to address the reader in simple phrases and sentences. In lines 5 and 8, full stops are used between each word as a device to add particular emphasis to them in a short but fundamentally important point of address. The overall effect is to render the poet's advice into a series of short, easily grasped and digested bites, each of which is delivered with a quiet emphasis and insistence.

The poet makes highly effective use of sibilance, in which the recurring 's' consonant suggests the release of exhalation. This may be seen in lines 1–2, 7, 14, 15, 16 and 17, in the first and last of which it is particularly noticeable in the repeated phrase 'allow yourself to exist amongst your sadness'. It is the breath of release.

Use is made of personification at lines 3–4 and 6, in which emotion and anger are described in terms of entities that can be cradled, locked away, shunned or forced into a corner. Sadness is personified in lines 13 and 15 as something that can suffocate you and in whose grasp you can be held, again as though it were a person. This emotion is inside you, but may have a sort of personality of its own. The description of negative emotion in such terms helps to lend it a sense of identity that is separate from the individual who feels it, perhaps suggesting that one might manage a relationship with it as one would with another person.

One might think of the 'separate personhood' of negative emotion as being a kind of extended metaphor throughout the poem. It is something, someone, with whom we may negotiate, bide our time and await our moment of release and freedom.

Message

Everyone becomes unhappy sometimes. When we do, it is important to remember that although we may feel swamped by our sadness or negative feelings, we are still ourselves.

We should try whenever possible not to hide from the negative emotions we feel, but to acknowledge them. Locking away negativity and unhappiness can make it grow.

We should remember that we are people, capable of all sorts of good feelings and happiness. We may not feel those positive things at the moment, but they will come.

Often it is not necessary to fight against negative emotions as such, but to simply relax and try to let them go. To do this, it can be very helpful for us to know what is causing our unhappiness and negative feelings.

If we are particularly unhappy, especially if it makes us feel unwell (as may occur, for example, if we are experiencing depression), it can help us if we realise that it is a natural process that has led us to feel that way. But the pain will not last. It will go away, especially if we seek help from others.

As time goes by we may become more skilled at dealing with unhappiness and negative emotions when we feel them, and more able to realise that we are not to be overwhelmed by our sadness. There is still room to be ourselves.

Lesson plan: 'you will heal' by Emily Jane

Resources

Copies of the poem — ideally one per pupil, pens or pencils, flip chart paper, marker pens, plain paper, rulers for SEND pupils to follow a line when reading.

Copies of pupils' safety plans to which they can refer throughout the session/lesson. The lesson will cover oracy and reading skills.

The session can be done in the round, or as a circle time activity, or at tables, or in an unstructured group. It is suitable to use with pupils at Upper Key Stage 2 (Year 6), 3 and 4.

Links with the PSHE Association PSHE Education Programme of Study

Links have been made to the PSHE Association PSHE Education Programme of Study at Key Stage 2, 3 and 4 as follows:

KS2

- *H15. that mental health, just like physical health, is part of daily life; the importance of taking care of mental health*
- *H21. to recognise warning signs about mental health and wellbeing and how to seek support for themselves and others*
- *H22. to recognise that anyone can experience mental ill health; that most difficulties can be resolved with help and support; and that it is important to discuss feelings with a trusted adult*

KS3

- *H7. the characteristics of mental and emotional health and strategies for managing these*
- *H10. a range of healthy coping strategies and ways to promote wellbeing and boost mood, including physical activity, participation and the value of positive relationships in providing support*

KS4

- *H5. the characteristics of mental and emotional health; to develop empathy and understanding about how daily actions can affect people's mental health*
- *H7. a broad range of strategies — cognitive and practical — for promoting their own emotional wellbeing, for avoiding negative thinking and for ways of managing mental health concerns*
- *H8. to recognise warning signs of common mental and emotional health concerns (including stress, anxiety and depression), what might trigger them and what help or treatment is available*

Links with the National Curriculum

Links have been made to the National Curriculum for English at Key Stage 2, 3 and 4 as follows:

KS2 (Years 5 and 6) English programme of study

- *maintain attention and participate actively in collaborative conversations, staying on topic and initiating and responding to comments*
- *drawing inferences such as inferring characters' feelings, thoughts and motives from their actions, and justifying inferences with evidence*
- *discuss and evaluate how authors use language, including figurative language, considering the impact on the reader*
- *provide reasoned justifications for their views*

KS3 English programme of study

- *participating in formal debates and structured discussions, summarising and/or building on what has been said*
- *making inferences and referring to evidence in the text*
- *knowing how language, including figurative language, vocabulary choice, grammar, text structure and organisational features, presents meaning*

KS4 English programme of study

- *listening to and building on the contributions of others, asking questions to clarify and inform, and challenging courteously when necessary*
- *seeking evidence in the text to support a point of view, including justifying inferences with evidence*
- *analysing a writer's choice of vocabulary, form, grammatical and structural features, and evaluating their effectiveness and impact*

Teaching and learning activities

The poem 'you will heal' is about recovery from unhappiness and negative emotions. In an extreme form this might include feelings of depression. For healing to take place the poet says that one should first acknowledge one's pain and sadness, as this is part of being human. It is important not to lose one's sense of self among the negative feelings.

- Introduction — share aims of lesson.
- Refer pupils to their safety plans. Remind them of what a safety plan is for. Ask them to read through their own safety plan before they go further and answer any questions they may have.
- Read the poem (or teacher/leader to read it aloud) and ask the following key questions:
  - What can you infer about the poem from the title 'you will heal'?
  - What is this poem about?
  - What is the poet's message?
- Class discussion about sadness and negative emotions. What are they and where do they come from? How can they be encouraged to go away? What is it like to live with these feelings?
- (KS3/4) What is depression? Why do people feel depressed? What are the signs of depression and do they differ from person to person? How is depression different from feeling sad? It is worth mentioning to pupils that while depression is a serious illness, it is also a treatable one.

- In pairs or in small groups discuss the feelings associated with sadness, negative emotion or depression in the poem and record them on flip chart paper. Why is it important not to suppress these feelings? What should we do with them?
- Ask for feedback from each group. Perhaps one of the group members could act as a spokesperson.
- Why do you think the poet uses the line 'you. are. human.'? As a person you are capable of feeling happiness as well as sadness, love as well as loneliness. Your emotional darkness does not take away your humanity. Is it helpful to be reminded of this? Why (or why not)?
- What sort of things can you do to avoid feelings of sadness and negative emotion? Discuss with the whole class.
- (KS3/4) What sort of things can you do to avoid triggering or exacerbating instances of depression? Discuss with the whole class.
- If someone feels sad or depressed, when do you think is the right time for them to seek help? Where could they go to look for help? If someone came to you for help, how could you respond?
- Share and signpost sources of available help.
- Review what has been achieved in the lesson.
- Refer pupils to their safety plans as a place to look if they need help after leaving the lesson.

Extension activities

- Pupils to write their answers to the key questions.
- Pupils to write about the form, structure and language of the poem.
- Can you find an example where personification is used in the poem? Can you explain its meaning?
- Invite speakers to come into school to raise awareness around mental health e.g. Mind, Kooth, Childline, Samaritans, Mental Health Foundation, a GP, an educational psychologist.
- Display posters around school/setting so pupils know where to go to access help and support.
- In PSHE lessons discuss further some of the factors that can lead a young person to feel sad or depressed. Discuss what can be done to prevent these feelings from building up.
- Roleplay a discussion between someone who is feeling sad, negative or depressed and someone to whom they have gone for help (it might be a friend). Think carefully about how you listen, how you speak, what questions you ask and how you deal with the answers you receive.
- Did you like the poem? Give reasons for your opinions. Justify your answers by reference to the text.

Cross-curricular/topic links

Cross-curricular and topic links may be explored for use in follow-up and for extension work in

- English
- Drama
- PSHE

Differentiation

Opportunities for discussion in mixed ability pairs/groups.

Differentiation by outcome e.g. quantity or complexity of issues identified, sophistication of response, level of inclusion/contribution, empathy.

Writing quantity outcomes will be differentiated/assessed/moderated according to teacher's expectations of quantity and depth; otherwise by outcome.

Facing the Future Without Fear

This section is about feelings of optimism, personal happiness and building a way forward to face the future...

The Hourglass

by Paul Morris

Commentary

A hundred hungry voices
A million things to say
And every word must be loved and heard
In my ordinary day

> And all our lives are an hourglass
> And all our days are sand
> But I know we hold forever
> When we hold each other's hand

So truant time goes hiding
As faces look to me
To teach them so their hearts can grow
To live their yet-to-be

> And all our lives are an hourglass
> And all our days are sand
> But I know we hold forever
> When we hold each other's hand

Seems every moment's hungry
To take my each and all
And my turncoat clock has no time to stop
Turns her cold face to the wall

> And all our lives are an hourglass
> And all our days are sand
> But I know we hold forever
> When we hold each other's hand

But life is no rehearsal
And as time slips by unseen
She won't steal away my chance today
To live my might-have-been

> And all our lives are an hourglass
> And all our days are sand
> But I know we hold forever
> When we hold each other's hand.

Context

'The Hourglass' was written in 2004, when the poet's wife was a primary school teacher, as a response to her description of the challenge of being 'all things to all people' whilst still leaving time for her family and herself. As the school year was nearing its end, the poem was couched in terms that would be accessible to Year 6 children and could equally apply to the challenges that they would face in their everyday lives, fitting in all that was asked of them.

The poem's song-like form, as exemplified by its recurrent chorus, was chosen because the poet's wife wanted to have original words to put to music in a songwriting and musical composition course she was undertaking at the time.

Content

The poem describes how external needs and pressures intrude into the subject's everyday world — the pressure to listen to others and respond to their needs, to help others and to be empathetic. Time does not seem to be on our side, and often seems to be against us. Yet we realise that we only have once chance to live our lives, and so we remain determined to live to the full and to fulfil our potential.

The repeated chorus is an affirmation of our understanding that time may seem to pass quickly, like sand slipping through an hourglass, but that we may find a point of security in a loved one or a friend.

Composition

The form of the poem resembles that of a song, and in fact it was set to music shortly after it was written. The work consists of eight four-line stanzas, in the arrangement of alternating verse and chorus, each with a regular rhyme scheme of ABCB. Metre is not strict but proceeds with a 'tick-tock' rhythm.

The absence of punctuation adds to the sense of the language, and by extension time itself, moving along swiftly without any barrier to slow or regulate it save for its own internal rhythm. The emphatic effect of the alternating chorus stanzas is mantra-like, a repeated declaration of belief that whilst time runs quickly we can be anchored by the love and care of someone else.

Message

The poem's message is to recognise the pressures to which we may all feel subject from time to time — or perhaps all the time. We have to fulfil what we expect of ourselves, but often we have to meet the needs (or demands) of others too. Whilst this may make us feel that we do not have enough time to do all that is required, or that time itself is against us, we should do our best with the one chance we have at life. And we can often be helped in this through the love and care of others for whom we in turn care.

Lesson plan: 'The Hourglass' by Paul Morris

Resources

Copies of the poem — ideally one per pupil, pens and pencils or marker pens, rulers for SEND pupils to follow a line when reading, Post-it notes, a copy of the musical score (including a suggested melodic line) or sound file for singing.

Copies of pupils' safety plans to which they can refer throughout the session/lesson.

The lesson will cover oracy and reading skills.

The session can be done in the round, or as a circle time activity, or at tables, or in an unstructured group. The lesson plan is suitable to use with pupils at Upper Key Stage 2 and Key Stage 3.

Links with the PSHE Association PSHE Education Programme of Study

Links have been made to the PSHE Association PSHE Education Programme of Study at Key Stages 2 and 3 as follows:

KS2

- *H15. that mental health, just like physical health, is part of daily life; the importance of taking care of mental health*
- *H2. about the elements of a balanced, healthy lifestyle*

KS3

- *H7. the characteristics of mental and emotional health and strategies for managing these*
- *H13. the importance of, and strategies for, maintaining a balance between school, work, leisure, exercise, and online activities*

Links with the National Curriculum

Links have been made to the National Curriculum for English at Key Stages 2 and 3 as follows:

KS2 (Years 5 and 6) English programme of study
- *maintain attention and participate actively in collaborative conversations, staying on topic and initiating and responding to comments*
- *discuss and evaluate how authors use language, including figurative language, considering the impact on the reader*
- *provide reasoned justifications for their views*

KS3 English programme of study
- *participating in formal debates and structured discussions, summarising and/or building on what has been said*
- *knowing how language, including figurative language, vocabulary choice, grammar, text structure and organisational features, presents meaning*

Links with KS2 and KS3 Music Programme of Study

Links have been made to the National Curriculum for Music at Key Stages 2 and 3 and link to the music extension exercise as follows:

KS2 Music programme of study

- *play and perform in solo and ensemble contexts, using their voices and playing musical instruments with increasing accuracy, fluency, control and expression*

KS3 Music programme of study

- *play and perform confidently in a range of solo and ensemble contexts using their voice, playing instruments musically, fluently and with accuracy and expression*
- *identify and use the interrelated dimensions of music expressively and with increasing sophistication, including use of tonalities, different types of scales and other musical devices*

Teaching and learning activities

- Introduction — share aims of lesson.
- Refer pupils to their safety plans. Remind them of what a safety plan is for. Ask them to read through their own safety plan before they go further and answer any questions they may have.
- Read the poem (or teacher/leader to read it aloud) and discuss its content. Use of questions 'what-who-where-when-how-why':
  - What is this poem about?
  - Who might be speaking in the poem? Are there any clues?
  - Where can you find examples of metaphors within the poem? Revise understanding of metaphors as necessary.
  - When might somebody say the sorts of things the speaker says in this poem?
  - How did the poem make you feel? Why? How did it do this? Give reasons for your opinions.
  - Why do you think the poet chose an hourglass (metaphor) to talk about the passing of time? Can you suggest any alternative metaphors that might work?
- Discuss the following with a talk partner or in a small group. Have you ever felt like there is not enough time in your life for everything you want to do? When have you felt like this? How did it make you feel? Did you tell anyone? What are the important things you would like more time for in your life?
- Take feedback and comments from pupils.
- How can we make more time for the things that are important to us? Think of three changes that you can make to your life to include things that are important to you. Write them on Post-it notes or card that can go in your pocket, purse, wallet or homework diary as a daily reminder.
- Take feedback and comments from pupils.
- Play the music that accompanies the words (see the musical score that follows this lesson plan) and concentrate on singing the chorus collectively (KS2 and KS3 only).
- Review what has been achieved in the lesson.
- Refer pupils to their safety plans as a place to look if they need help after leaving the lesson.

Extension music activities

Upper Key Stage 2

- The music can first be played on a piano or keyboard to familiarise pupils with the tune, and the verses and chorus can be sung collectively.
- As pupils become more familiar with the melody instruments can be brought in to provide an introduction such as a drum, a tambourine and a recorder.
- A soloist or a group can be selected to sing each of the verses.
- The class can be divided into two groups. The first group to sing the first line of the chorus. The second group to sing the second line of the chorus. The whole class can then sing the last two lines.

Key Stage 3

- Divide the class into two groups for a staggered start to sing the piece as a round. Group 1 to sing the first verse. Group 2 to start singing verse one when Group 1 begins the chorus. Both groups continue singing all of the remaining verses and chorus. The song could also be performed by two soloists rather than two groups.
- A variation may be that soloists can be selected to sing each of the verses with the rest of the class singing the chorus. In the last line of the chorus the last word 'hand' can have multiple harmonies.
- Improvise more parts of musical accompaniment with older pupils — percussion, wind, string, etc.

Further extension activities

- Pupils to write their answers to the key questions.
- Pupils to try writing some new verses for the song.
- Divide the class into groups of two or three. Each group to perform a verse of the poem with everyone joining in with the chorus. Explain that they are going to perform the poem to another class or in assembly. Talk about how the poem will be delivered and where there needs to be emphasis.
- PSHE circle time activity — explore ways in which pupils can maximise their learning opportunities in school. What are you doing well with? What do you need to focus on? What support do you need? What do you need to avoid doing? Spend time talking about each of the questions. Encourage pupils to reflect on the positive.

Cross-curricular/topic links

Cross-curricular and topic links may be explored for use in follow-up and for extension work in

- English
- PSHE
- Music

Differentiation

Opportunities for discussion in mixed ability pairs.

Differentiation by outcome e.g. quantity or complexity of issues identified, sophistication of response, level of inclusion/contribution, empathy.

Differentiation may also be through musical participation as a means of expression and the level of difficulty with regards to harmonies and use of tuned instruments to accompany the melody.

The Hourglass

Words by Paul Morris

Music by Judy Morris

A hun – dred hun gry voi – ces A mill – ion things to say And

ev – ry word must be loved and heard In my ord – in – ar – y day And all our lives are an

hour – glass And all our days a – re sand But I know we hold for – ev – er When we

hold each oth – er's hand

Note: *This score shows the first verse and chorus.*
Subsequent verses are sung to bars 1 to 9, with the chorus 'And all...' sung to bars 9 to 17.

Life

by Charlotte Brontë

Commentary

Life, believe, is not a dream
So dark as sages say;
Oft a little morning rain
Foretells a pleasant day.
Sometimes there are clouds of gloom,
But these are transient all;
If the shower will make the roses bloom,
O why lament its fall?

Rapidly, merrily,
Life's sunny hours flit by,
Gratefully, cheerily,
Enjoy them as they fly!

What though Death at times steps in
And calls our Best away?
What though sorrow seems to win,
O'er hope, a heavy sway?
Yet hope again elastic springs,
Unconquered, though she fell;
Still buoyant are her golden wings,
Still strong to bear us well.
Manfully, fearlessly,
The day of trial bear,
For gloriously, victoriously,
Can courage quell despair!

Context

Charlotte Brontë was an English poet and novelist, the eldest of the three talented Brontë sisters whose novels became classics of English literature.

Charlotte was in fact the third child born to her parents, her elder sisters Maria and Elizabeth being respectively two years and one year her senior. However, both girls died in 1825 when Charlotte was just nine years old. Charlotte's birth was followed by that of brother Branwell and sisters Emily and Anne: she was to outlive them all. Tuberculosis, which had killed both Maria and Elizabeth in 1825, eventually carried off the rest of Charlotte's siblings.

The family moved to the parsonage in Haworth, in the West Riding of Yorkshire, in 1820, shortly after Anne was born. Here Charlotte wrote her first known poem at the age of thirteen. Many of her poems were about her fictional Glass Town Confederacy and first appeared in *Branwell's Blackwood's Magazine*, a homemade magazine produced by her brother. Charlotte and her siblings created their own fictional worlds, and Charlotte and Branwell wrote Byronic stories about their own imagined

345

country of Angria. This almost obsessive interest during childhood and early adolescence is likely to have given Charlotte a good preparation for her literary vocation in adulthood.

In 1831, Charlotte was enrolled at Miss Wooler's school in Roe Head, Mirfield. It had a good reputation, and Margaret Wooler was fond of Charlotte — so much so that she accompanied her to the altar at her marriage in 1854. Charlotte was happy at Roe Head, making many lifelong friends, though she remained at the school as a pupil for only a year.

Back home in Haworth, Charlotte wrote a novella entitled *The Green Dwarf: A Tale of the Perfect Tense*, under the elaborate pen-name of Lord Charles Albert Florian Wellesley.

Charlotte was to return to the school at Roe Head in 1835 after she was offered a position as Miss Wooler's assistant. She was accompanied by her sister Emily, whose school fees were partly paid by Charlotte's salary. Charlotte taught, rather unhappily, and was to remain at the school until 1838.

Leaving Roe Head, Charlotte took a number of positions as governess to Yorkshire families between 1839 and 1841. She did not enjoy the work and considered that her employers humiliated her, treating her almost as a slave.

After a period studying and teaching at a school in Brussels, Charlotte returned to Haworth. It is believed that her experiences at the school were the basis for some of the events later described in her novels *The Professor* and *Villette*. She and her sisters worked to establish their own boarding school in the parsonage — The Misses Brontë's Establishment for the Board and Education of a Limited Number of Young Ladies — and advertised it in 1844, but no pupils were forthcoming.

The year of 1845 was a key one for the public literary life of Charlotte and her sisters. Charlotte found poems written by her sister Emily, and urged their publication. The sisters now discussed their poetry, some of which had been written in secret, and they decided to publish a collection of their work at their own expense. The following year of 1846 saw the publication of their poetry under the title *Poems by Currer, Ellis, and Acton Bell* — male pseudonyms adopted by the three sisters (Charlotte was Currer, Emily was Ellis, and Anne was Acton) to preserve their anonymity and, Charlotte admitted, because they 'had a vague impression that authoresses are liable to be looked on with prejudice'. Charlotte contributed nineteen of the book's sixty-one poems, Emily and Anne twenty-one each. The book was not a commercial success — only two copies were sold — but it was a start, and all three sisters continued to write for publication and began to write their first novels.

Charlotte's first manuscript, *The Professor*, did not secure a publisher, but her second was taken up readily and in October 1847 *Jane Eyre* was published under Charlotte's nom de plume of Currer Bell. It is perhaps her best-known work. She published three novels in her lifetime, *The Professor* being published posthumously and *Emma* being part finished at the time of her death in 1855.

The immense success of *Jane Eyre* has perhaps rather overshadowed both her accomplishments as a poet and the brilliance of the more than two hundred poems that Charlotte produced in her lifetime.

Content

The speaker tells us that life is not a dark dream as wise people say (lines 1 and 2). It may often rain a little in the morning but the day can be pleasant — that is, that an unpleasant episode can be followed by good things (lines 3 and 4). There are clouds of unhappiness but they all pass by (lines 5 and 6). We are asked why we should be sorry that it rains if the rain will make roses bloom — that is, why we should be sorry if passing unpleasantness gives way to a beautiful outcome (lines 7 and 8).

The bright times in life pass by quickly and happily (lines 9 and 10). We should enjoy these good times with thanks and cheerfulness as they rush by (lines 11 and 12).

We are asked rhetorically why we should be too concerned if death sometimes takes away the best people around us (lines 13 and 14), or if unhappiness seems to triumph over hope (lines 15 and 16). We are told that hope will bounce back (line 17) and will be undefeated, although it was knocked down (line 18). The 'golden wings' of hope still have their lift and are still strong enough to carry us (lines 19 and 20). We are advised to put up 'manfully, fearlessly' with the times when life challenges us (lines 21 and 22). Courage can 'gloriously, victoriously' subdue unhappiness (lines 23 and 24).

The speaker advises us overall to remember that bad times are often followed by good ones, to enjoy the good times in life when they happen, not to be too downcast when things seem to be at their worst, but to remember that hope will return and carry us through.

Composition

'Life' is composed in three stanzas of eight, four and twelve lines. It has a rhyme scheme of ABAB.

The poem has a complex rhythmic structure. The first stanza alternates three lines of catalectic trochaic tetrameter (i.e. four metrical feet of trochees with a DUM-da beat, but missing a syllable to leave the final foot incomplete) with three lines of iambic trimeter (three metrical feet of da-DUM), finishing with a line of iambic tetrameter followed by one of iambic trimeter. The second stanza alternates two lines of cretic dimeter (two feet of DUM-da-DUM) with two lines of iambic trimeter. The long third stanza is actually composed as a combination of the rhythmic structures of the first two stanzas, its first to eighth lines mirroring the first stanza (save that its fifth line is in iambic tetrameter) and its ninth to twelfth mirroring the second stanza (save that the penultimate line is in iambic tetrameter). Metrically, therefore, the poet could have organised the work as four stanzas — long, short, long, short — rather than three.

The effect of introducing simple, metrically brief stanzas after longer ones is to give a verse/chorus feel to the piece. It reads with a rather hymn-like quality, which is perhaps not surprising given the poet's ecclesiastical home life.

The punctuation of the poem is conventional, the language straightforward as befits the poem's didactic nature. Its vocabulary contains some words with which the younger reader may be unfamiliar: 'sages' (= 'wise people', line 2), 'oft' (= 'often', line 3), 'foretells' (= 'predicts, anticipates', line 4), 'transient' (= 'passing, temporary', line 6), 'lament' (= 'grieve, be sorrowful for', line 8), 'flit' (= 'dash, dart', line 10), 'fly' (= 'rush by', line 12), 'sway' (= 'rule, domination', line 16), 'elastic' (= 'bouncy, able to bounce back', line 17), 'buoyant' (= 'able to rise', line 19), 'quell' (= 'subdue', line 24).

The wisdom of lines 3 and 4, 'Oft a little morning rain / Foretells a pleasant day' is proverbial, and versions of this sentiment appear in various sources of the poet's time and earlier including popular songs, ballads and sea shanties.

The poet makes extensive use of metaphor. Whilst assuring us that life is 'not a dream / So dark as sages say' (lines 1 and 2), there is still the suggestion that it might yet be a dream. The 'clouds of gloom' (line 5) are a readily accessible, if not conventional, metaphor, as is the idea that follows it of not regretting bad weather that brings rain but helps beautiful flowers to bloom (lines 7 and 8). In lines 13 to 16 the poet uses rhetorical questioning metaphorically: to both questions we seem to be invited to reply that neither death nor sorrow matter as long as we have hope. The third stanza moves towards its end with an elaborate personification of hope, who is imagined as a resilient presence, golden-winged, unconquered and strong, able to bear us up (lines 14 to 20). Our courage, strength and fortitude can help us to win a glorious victory over anguish, hopelessness and unhappiness (lines 21 to 24).

Message

Despite what some seemingly wise people may tell us, life is not necessarily bad, dark or sad.

Sometimes a little unhappiness can come before a time of great joy, and when it does the contrast can make our happiness seem all the better.

The gloom of unhappiness passes: unhappiness does not last forever. Even seemingly unpleasant or negative things can have positive results and produce what is good and beautiful.

We should enjoy life's happiness whenever we have the chance, being joyful and thankful for the good times we are enjoying.

Even though bad things may happen and we may experience sorrow, we still have hope. If our hope is resilient, we can bounce back from those times when life knocks us down.

If we try to be strong and fearless, we can beat many of the challenges that life puts in our way. Our courage can help us to stand and face the world, unafraid and proud.

Lesson plan: 'Life' by Charlotte Brontë

Resources

Copies of the poem — ideally one per pupil, pens and pencils or marker pens, dictionaries, flip chart paper, rulers for SEND pupils to follow a line when reading. Extra paper should be made available for use if required.

Copies of pupils' safety plans to which they can refer throughout the session/lesson.

The lesson will cover oracy and reading skills.

The session can be done in the round, or as a circle time activity, or at tables, or in an unstructured group. The lesson plan is suitable to use with pupils at Upper Key Stage 2, 3 and 4.

Links with the PSHE Association PSHE Education Programme of Study

Links have been made to the PSHE Association PSHE Education Programme of Study at Key Stage 2, 3 and 4 as follows:

KS2

- *H15. that mental health, just like physical health, is part of daily life; the importance of taking care of mental health*
- *H16. about strategies and behaviours that support mental health — including how good quality sleep, physical exercise/time outdoors, being involved in community groups, doing things for others, clubs, and activities, hobbies and spending time with family and friends can support mental health and wellbeing*

KS3

- *H10. a range of healthy coping strategies and ways to promote wellbeing and boost mood, including physical activity, participation and the value of positive relationships in providing support*

KS4

- *H7. a broad range of strategies — cognitive and practical — for promoting their own emotional wellbeing, for avoiding negative thinking and for ways of managing mental health concerns*

Links with the National Curriculum

Links have been made to the National Curriculum for English at Key Stage 2, 3 and 4 as follows:

KS2 (Years 5 and 6) English programme of study

- *maintain attention and participate actively in collaborative conversations, staying on topic and initiating and responding to comments*
- *discuss and evaluate how authors use language, including figurative language, considering the impact on the reader*
- *provide reasoned justifications for their views*

KS3 English programme of study

- *participating in formal debates and discussions, summarising and/or building on what has been said*
- *knowing how language, including figurative language, vocabulary choice, grammar, text structure and organisational features, presents meaning*

KS4 English programme of study

- *listening to and building on the contributions of others, asking questions to clarify and inform, and challenging courteously when necessary*
- *analysing a writer's choice of vocabulary, form, grammatical and structural features, and evaluating their effectiveness and impact*

Teaching and learning activities

The poem 'Life' was written by Charlotte Brontë. Life comes with bad times followed by good times, sorrowful times and happy times, meetings and partings. In this poem the poet encourages people to be hopeful and optimistic and to see the sunny things in life.

- Introduction — share aims of lesson.
- Refer pupils to their safety plans. Remind them of what a safety plan is for. Ask them to read through their own safety plan before they go further and answer any questions they may have.
- Read the poem (or teacher/leader to read it aloud) and discuss its content. Ask the following key questions:
  - What is the poem about? It may be necessary to write key vocabulary and phrases on the whiteboard to help younger pupils better understand the poem, e.g. o'er = over, sages = people who are wise or exhibit signs of wisdom or intelligence, foretells = predicts, transient = temporary, lament = grief.
  - Why do you think the poem is called 'Life'?
  - What is the poem's message?

- What is the tone of the poem? Discuss with a partner or in a small group. The tone of the poem is hopeful and optimistic. Life is more joyful than people often believe.
- Take feedback.
- Discuss the rhyme scheme of the poem which is a simple ABAB. Why is it appropriate (or, if you think so, inappropriate) for a poem like this?
- Life has its ups and downs. It is easy to focus on the negative things in life and lose sight of the many positive things. Ask pupils to reflect on an event that made them feel low or sad. Describe what happened. How did you come through that experience? Did you talk to anybody? Has it made you stronger as a person? Ask pupils to work in pairs or small groups.
- How can we surround ourselves with more positivity in our lives? What should we avoid, and how can we do that? Ask pupils to work in small groups. Record ideas on a flip chart.
- Ask for feedback.
- Review what has been achieved in the lesson.
- Refer pupils to their safety plans as a place to look if they need help after leaving the lesson.

Extension activities

- Pupils to write their answers to the key questions.
- Do you like the poem? Pupils to write their own responses giving reasons.
- Write a short biographical piece about Charlotte Brontë.
- Illustrate the poem with images/words of positivity.
- Life is full of sorrowful times as well as times of happiness. Describe a happy event or time in your life and how it impacted on your sense of wellbeing.
- Make a list of things that have a positive effect on your mood. It might be listening to a favourite piece of music, going out on a favourite walk, reading a favourite book, taking part in a favourite sport, etc. How do they make you feel better?
- Reflect on an activity which you struggled with in school. Describe how you felt. Did you seek help with the activity? Did it have a positive outcome? What could you have done differently if the outcome was not very positive?
- Keep a diary and write notes about how you feel each day. Try to concentrate on the positives even if you have had a difficult day. Remember the lines in the poem 'Sometimes there are clouds of gloom, / But these are transient all'.
- Paint, draw or produce collages which depict positivity, happiness and hope.

Cross-curricular/topic links

Cross-curricular and topic links may be explored for use in follow-up and for extension work in
- English
- PSHE
- Art and Design

Differentiation

Opportunities for discussion in mixed ability pairs.

Differentiation by outcome e.g. quantity or complexity of issues identified, sophistication of response, level of inclusion/contribution, empathy.

Writing quantity outcomes will be differentiated/assessed/moderated according to teacher's expectations of quantity and depth; otherwise by outcome.

Differentiation may also be through key words rather than written sentences, or through artwork as a means of expression.

The Road Not Taken

by Robert Frost

Commentary

Two roads diverged in a yellow wood,
And sorry I could not travel both
And be one traveler, long I stood
And looked down one as far as I could
To where it bent in the undergrowth;

Then took the other, as just as fair,
And having perhaps the better claim,
Because it was grassy and wanted wear;
Though as for that the passing there
Had worn them really about the same,

And both that morning equally lay
In leaves no step had trodden black.
Oh, I kept the first for another day!
Yet knowing how way leads on to way,
I doubted if I should ever come back.

I shall be telling this with a sigh
Somewhere ages and ages hence:
Two roads diverged in a wood, and I —
I took the one less traveled by,
And that has made all the difference.

Context

'The Road Not Taken' was written in 1915. Frost used to go walking with his friend, the poet Edward Thomas, who, finding a choice of ways, was frequently indecisive about which road they should take and then often regretted the choice they had made. Frost wrote the poem as a joke for his friend, but soon complained to Thomas that an audience of college students to whom he had read it had taken the work seriously, despite his efforts to make it clear that it was not to be taken as such. It is interesting to consider, though, Frost's remark that 'I'm never more serious than when joking'.

Born in San Francisco, California, in 1874, Frost was to lose his father just after his eleventh birthday. He attended the prestigious Dartmouth College for only two months before returning home to teach and to work at a variety of jobs, including assisting his mother in teaching her class, delivering newspapers, and working in a factory. He was later to attend Harvard University for two years, leaving because of illness. Yet throughout these ups and downs Frost held to the belief that his real vocation lay in writing poetry.

Frost sold his first poem in 1894 to *The Independent*, a weekly magazine published in New York, and received the sum of $15. This relatively modest achievement seems to have been enough to encourage him to propose marriage to his sweetheart, whom he married the following year.

Moving to the UK in 1912, Frost continued to build a reputation as a poet. His first two volumes of collected poetry, *A Boy's Will* (1913) and *North of Boston* (1914), were published in London. He returned to America in 1915 following the outbreak of the Great War, pursuing a career of teaching, lecturing and writing.

Frost developed a colloquial approach to language that he called 'the sound of sense'. He went on to win several Pulitzer Prizes and numerous academic distinctions including — although he never formally graduated from university — more than forty honorary degrees from universities including Oxford, Cambridge and Princeton.

In January 1961, at the age of eighty-six, Frost read at the inauguration of President John F. Kennedy. Though he was to read his poem 'Dedication', written specially for the occasion, he was dazzled by the bright sunlight and was unable to read it, so recited his 'The Gift Outright' from memory.

Frost died a few months later. The epitaph on his tomb, taken from one of his own poems, records somewhat wryly that 'I had a lover's quarrel with the world'.

Content

'The Road Not Taken' describes how choice is inevitable, and meditates on the emotional consequences of the choices we make.

The speaker describes how he was walking in a 'yellow' autumnal wood and came to a fork in the path. He regretted that, being only one person and unable to be in two places at once, he could not take both roads at the same time. He stood for a long time and looked down one road as far as he could, to where it curved out of sight into the woodland.

The speaker then chose to take the other path, which looked just as good. It seemed a more appealing choice because it was covered with grass that had not been trodden down by walkers, though really both of the paths themselves seemed to have been worn by a similar amount. Both paths were covered in fallen leaves that nobody had yet walked on.

The speaker chose the second path, the one with the less worn grass, leaving the other path to be walked some other day — though he realised that because one footpaths leads on to another, it was doubtful that he would ever return to that same place.

He knows that he will be telling this story long into the future, with a sigh that is unexplained but may be of regret (perhaps he wonders what would have happened had he taken the other path), longing, relief or gratitude. He came to two paths, chose to walk along the one that was used less often, and the decision to take that path has been of great significance to him. Although the speaker does not tell us why or how it has been so, it seems that he feels strongly positive about having taken the less frequently used path — perhaps something we may understand as a metaphor for his having taken a direction in life that most people do not choose.

Composition

'The Road Not Taken' is composed as four stanzas of quintains written in iambic octameter. The rhyme scheme is ABAAB.

The poem's language is conversational, with traces of 'poetic' formality (e.g. 'long I stood', line 3). Spellings respect the American form (e.g. 'traveler' rather than 'traveller', 'traveled' rather than 'travelled').

The punctuation and spacing of the poem are conventional. The stanza layout follows the poet's chosen verse form, rather than stanzas each dealing with an episode or unit of progression of the poem's narrative.

The poem is resolutely narrative and appears quite literal, with no notable use of figurative language, simile or metaphor. The poet does not use obvious or obtrusive poetic devices, except perhaps for the modest anaphora by which lines 2 to 4 begin with the same 'And'. This compositional simplicity gives an impression of reportage and verisimilitude, as though the poet is giving a straightforward account of an actual occurrence. There is no particular weighting of any part of the poem's narrative, giving the tale a steady flow rather than emphasising or dwelling upon any part of it or allowing any aspect of meaning to dominate obviously. The messages of the poem do not seem to be deliberately created out of the narrative, but rather to arise out of it in a natural and uncontrived manner.

Message

Life presents us with choices all the time. The decisions we make in response to those choices are often unimportant: they do not make any real difference to our lives. But sometimes our choices have far-reaching consequences, and our lives may be better or worse according to the decisions we make. It is very important to be able to recognise those decisions which might be important in our lives, and to take care (and, if necessary advice) to make the right choices.

Once we have made a decision — especially an important one — it may not be possible to go back and change that choice, or its consequences for ourselves or others, afterwards.

When faced with an important decision we would do well to look as far ahead as we can, and to use all the information we can get, to make the right choices. If there are factors we do not understand or if we otherwise feel we need it, we should ask for help from someone whose advice we can trust. We should try to make decisions that are well informed, balanced and sensible, and we should take time to think carefully about the consequences of our choices for ourselves and others.

Often we will remember our important life decisions long into the future, and whether or not we made good choices. We owe it to ourselves to make the best decisions we can.

Sometimes it can be tempting to choose the same things that others seem to be choosing. It can be an easy choice for us to dress similarly, behave similarly and act similarly to others, even when those people's choices and behaviour are not necessarily what is best for us. But we should not be afraid to think independently and to choose what is best for us and those we care for. Sometimes the road through life that seems less popular is actually the best one for us, and we should choose our own path without fear.

Lesson plan: 'The Road Not Taken' by Robert Frost

Resources

Copies of the poem — ideally one per pupil, pens and pencils, flip chart paper, copies of the table in the teaching and learning section of this lesson plan, rulers for SEND pupils to follow a line when reading.

Copies of pupils' safety plans to which they can refer throughout the session/lesson.

The lesson will cover oracy and reading skills.

The session can be done in the round, or as a circle time activity, or at tables, or in an unstructured group. The lesson plan is suitable to use with pupils at Upper Key Stage 2, 3 and 4.

Links with the PSHE Association PSHE Education Programme of Study

Links have been made to the PSHE Association PSHE Education Programme of Study at Key Stage 2, 3 and 4 as follows:

KS2

- *H20. strategies to respond to feelings, including intense or conflicting feelings; how to manage and respond to feelings appropriately and proportionately in different situations*

KS3

- *H5. to recognise and manage internal and external influences on decisions which affect health and wellbeing*

KS4

- *H2. how self-confidence self-esteem, and mental health are affected positively and negatively by internal and external influences and ways of managing this*

Links with the National Curriculum

Links have been made to the National Curriculum for English at Key Stage 2, 3 and 4 as follows:

KS2 (Years 5 and 6) English programme of study

- *maintain attention and participate actively in collaborative conversations, staying on topic and initiating and responding to comments*
- *drawing inferences such as inferring characters' feelings, thoughts and motives from their actions, and justifying inferences with evidence*
- *discuss and evaluate how authors use language, including figurative language, considering the impact on the reader*
- *provide reasoned justifications for their views*

KS3 English programme of study

- *participating in formal debates and structured discussions, summarising and/or building on what has been said*

- *making inferences and referring to evidence in the text*
- *knowing how language, including figurative language, vocabulary choice, grammar, text structure and organisational features, presents meaning*

KS4 English programme of study

- *working effectively in groups of different sizes and taking on required roles, including leading and managing discussions, involving others productively, reviewing and summarising, and contributing to meeting goals/deadlines*
- *seeking evidence in the text to support a point of view, including justifying inferences with evidence*
- *analysing a writer's choice of vocabulary, form, grammatical and structural features, and evaluating their effectiveness and impact*

Teaching and learning activities

In life we are often presented with choices. When making choices we are required to make decisions. This is explored through the poem 'The Road Not Taken', which considers the consequences of an apparently simple, casual choice.

Younger pupils, especially those who are unfamiliar with the countryside, may need support to understand the content of the poem. It may be necessary to go through each stanza in turn.

- Introduction — share aims of lesson.
- Refer pupils to their safety plans. Remind them of what a safety plan is for. Ask them to read through their own safety plan before they go further and answer any questions they may have.
- Read the poem (or teacher/leader to read it aloud) and discuss its content. Ask the following key questions:
  - What is this poem about?
  - What can you infer from the title? What is 'the road not taken' and why is it significant?
  - What is the poem's message?
- Do you like the poem? Ask pupils to give reasons and to refer to the poem to help justify their views.
- Discuss the following with a talk partner or in a small group. What are some of the decisions you must make as you grow up? How can they be important to your life? Brainstorm thoughts and ideas on flip chart paper.
- Ask for feedback.
- There are often consequences if wrong decisions are made in life. Ask pupils to work in pairs or small groups to complete the table below.

Decision	Short term consequences	Long term consequences
Bullying a pupil online.		
Truanting from school.		
Behaving disrespectfully to teachers and other adults in authority.		
Drinking and smoking in the park with peers.		
Not handing in homework on time.		

- Ask for feedback.
- What influences young people to make bad decisions? Discuss with a partner or in a small group.
- What influences them to make good decisions? Discuss with a partner or in a small group.
- Why would people sometimes choose to make poor decisions rather than good ones?
- Take feedback.
- Review what has been achieved in the lesson.
- Refer pupils to their safety plans as a place to look if they need help after leaving the lesson.

Extension activities

- Pupils to write their answers to the key questions.
- Write a short story about a young person who did the right thing when friends wanted him/her to do the opposite. What happened? What was the outcome?
- Write about a time when you were faced with a choice between doing the right thing and doing the wrong thing. Describe what happened and how you felt. Given the choice, would you do the same thing again and why?
- Design and produce a pack of cards with good and bad situations written on alternate cards. Deal the cards between four or five group members. Each person to turn over a card and to read out the situation. Is it a good or bad situation? Suggest ways to make the situation better.
- Peers in your class try to tempt you to make bad choices. How do you stand up to this peer pressure? This could be explored in circle time activities in PSHE, or in drama as a roleplay.

Cross-curricular/topic links

Cross-curricular and topic links may be explored for use in follow-up and for extension work in

- English
- Drama
- PSHE

Differentiation

Opportunities for discussion in mixed ability pairs.

Differentiation by outcome e.g. quantity or complexity of issues identified, sophistication of response, level of inclusion/contribution, empathy.

Writing quantity outcomes will be differentiated/assessed/moderated according to teacher's expectations of quantity and depth; otherwise by outcome.

Differentiation may also be through key words rather than written sentences.

Barter

by Sara Teasdale

Commentary

Life has loveliness to sell,
    All beautiful and splendid things,
Blue waves whitened on a cliff,
    Soaring fire that sways and sings,
And children's faces looking up
Holding wonder like a cup.

Life has loveliness to sell,
    Music like a curve of gold,
Scent of pine trees in the rain,
    Eyes that love you, arms that hold,
And for your spirit's still delight,
Holy thoughts that star the night.

Spend all you have for loveliness,
    Buy it and never count the cost;
For one white singing hour of peace
    Count many a year of strife well lost,
And for a breath of ecstasy
Give all you have been, or could be.

Context

'Barter' was first published in 1917 in Sara Teasdale's fourth volume of poetry, *Love Songs*, which won both the 1918 Pulitzer Prize and the Poetry Society of America Prize.

Sara Trevor Teasdale was born in St. Louis, Missouri, in 1884. Her life was not without its trials. Prolonged ill-health meant that she had to be home-schooled until she was nine. She married in 1914, having chosen a husband who could provide for her in preference to a poorer rival suitor (a poet) whom she loved, but she endured much loneliness as a result of her husband's constant business travel, a situation which led to the couple divorcing in 1929.

Sara began writing poetry at an early age, and her first poetry collection was published in 1904 when she was just twenty years old. The eight published volumes of her twenty-nine year publishing career show the development of her poetic sensitivity and subtlety, the lucidity of her work, and her preference for romantic themes.

'Barter' was written in the early stages of Sara's ultimately unsuccessful marriage, and may be seen as a reflection of the optimism of that time in her life.

Content

The poem describes the many wonderful experiences that life has to offer to someone who is willing to pursue and accept them. She describes this in terms of a transaction, as reflected by the poem's title: a sort of deal, in which life offers a wealth of experience and sensation in return for what we put into it.

The poem's speaker describes life's precious experiences in terms of the natural world, such as the sea and the scent of pine trees; in human terms such as the faces of children, the delights of music and the warmth of a loving relationship; and in terms of spiritual and emotional experience. None of these is made to appear superior to any other, each being given its due value in the bargain of life, and they are intermingled through the stanzas of the poem. The unifying factor among these things is that they are not trivial, nor are they material things such as possessions: it is the greater emotions, activities and experiences of life to which the poem's speaker assigns the greatest value.

The final stanza encourages the reader to pursue what the speaker terms 'loveliness' such as that which has been described in the poem. The exhortation to 'Spend all you have for loveliness, / Buy it and never count the cost' (lines 13 and 14) is not an encouragement to spend all our money on lovely things, but rather to spend our energy and imagination on lovely experience. We are told that the enjoyment of such truly delightful experience is worth the investment of much time, effort and trouble. For a brief moment of 'ecstasy', no cost is too high.

Composition

'Barter' consists of three stanzas, each of them sestets. Each verse follows the rhyming pattern of ABCBDD, with those rhyming elements varying from stanza to stanza.

The effect of the metre seems regular, though the actual metrical value varies between seven and eight syllables to the line.

The vocabulary the poet employs is quite straightforward, with no words that would not be familiar to the modern reader save, perhaps, for the slightly archaic 'strife' (meaning 'trouble') of line 16 and less frequently encountered words for younger pupils such as 'struggle', 'ecstasy' and 'delight'.

Punctuation is conventional.

The poet makes vibrant use of imagery, almost every line containing a brief but powerful description of some element of human experience. These elements are varied and seem to have been selected so as to be either universal, or at least broadly applicable, as things that people might reasonably be expected either to have experienced or to anticipate experiencing at some time in their lives. The poet names a range of experiences from which she would expect the reader to be able to find something that relates to their own life.

For a poem that is so rich in imagery, 'Barter' contains remarkably little developed figurative language. There are the similes of line 6 and line 8, and the brief metaphorical devices of lines 3, 4 (including personification), 12, 15 and 17, but none of these is used as anything more than a passing embellishment. Yet the overall effect is one of beauty in simplicity, an effect to which the poet's unostentatious use of figurative language contributes greatly.

Message

We are invited to see wonder in the natural world and in our interactions with those around us.

Life, we are told, is a process of exchange in which we give of ourselves and receive experience and 'loveliness' in return. The beauty of such experience is something we should value, and for which we should strive.

The more we invest in our lives and in the pursuit of positive, beautiful and worthwhile experiences, the greater the sense of personal fulfilment we might hope to receive from life in return.

Lesson plan: 'Barter' by Sara Teasdale

Resources

Copies of the poem — ideally one per pupil, pens and pencils or marker pens, dictionaries, rulers for SEND pupils to follow a line when reading. Extra paper should be made available for use if required.

Copies of pupils' safety plans to which they can refer throughout the session/lesson.

The lesson will cover oracy, reading and writing skills.

The session can be done in the round, or as a circle time activity, or at tables, or in an unstructured group. The lesson plan is suitable to use with pupils at Upper Key Stage 2, 3 and 4.

Links with the PSHE Association PSHE Education Programme of Study

Links have been made to the PSHE Association PSHE Education Programme of Study at Key Stage 2, 3 and 4 as follows:

KS2

- *H15. that mental health, just like physical health, is part of daily life; the importance of taking care of mental health*
- *H16. about strategies and behaviours that support mental health — including how good quality sleep, physical exercise/time outdoors, being involved in community groups, doing things for others, clubs, and activities, hobbies and spending time with family and friends can support mental health and wellbeing*

KS3

- *H10. a range of healthy coping strategies and ways to promote wellbeing and boost mood, including physical activity, participation and the value of positive relationships in providing support*

KS4

- *H7. a broad range of strategies — cognitive and practical — for promoting their own emotional wellbeing, for avoiding negative thinking and for ways of managing mental health concerns*

Links with the National Curriculum

Links have been made to the National Curriculum for English at Key Stage 2, 3 and 4 as follows:

KS2 (Years 5 and 6) English programme of study

- *maintain attention and participate actively in collaborative conversations, staying on topic and initiating and responding to comment*
- *discuss and evaluate how authors use language, including figurative language, considering the impact on the reader*
- *provide reasoned justifications for their views*
- *draft and write by selecting appropriate grammar and vocabulary, understanding how such choices can change and enhance meaning*

KS3 English programme of study

- *participating in formal debates and structured discussions, summarising and/or building on what has been said*
- *knowing how language, including figurative language, vocabulary choice, grammar, text structure and organisational features, presents meaning*
- *recognising a range of poetic conventions and understanding how these have been used*
- *writing for a wide range of purposes and audiences, including well-structured formal expository and narrative essays*

KS4 English programme of study

- *listening to and building on the contributions of others, asking questions to clarify and inform, and challenging courteously when necessary*
- *analysing a writer's choice of vocabulary, form, grammatical and structural features, and evaluating their effectiveness and impact*
- *make an informed personal response, recognising that other responses to a text are possible and evaluating these*
- *adapting their writing for a wide range of purposes and audiences, to describe, narrate, explain, instruct, give and respond to information, and argue*

Teaching and learning activities

This is a good poem for helping pupils reflect on the many wonderful things out there in the world to be seen and explored. The message is that there is more to life than what you are striving for. We have to make a deal with ourselves to appreciate beauty and goodness when and where we can.

- Introduction — share aims of lesson.
- Refer pupils to their safety plans. Remind them of what a safety plan is for. Ask them to read through their own safety plan before they go further and answer any questions they may have.
- Read the poem (or teacher/leader to read it aloud) and discuss its content. Ask the following key questions:
  - What is the poem about? It may be necessary to write key vocabulary and phrases on the whiteboard to help younger pupils better understand the poem e.g. strife, struggle, ecstasy, delight.
  - Why is the poem called 'Barter'? Pupils to look up the meaning of the word. What do you think is being bartered in the poem?

- Which senses are evoked in the poem?
- What is the poem's message? How relevant is it to today's young people?

- Discuss the form and structure of the poem. Ask pupils to highlight metaphors and similes in the poem, and to find instances of alliteration.

- In pairs or in small groups discuss how easy it is to lose sight of all the wonderful things that the world has to offer. How do negative images get in the way? Why does the media focus so much on the bad news?

- How can thinking about magical moments or experiencing 'loveliness' help to lift a person's mood if they are feeling low? Talk about this with a partner or in a small group.

- The world has lots of wonderful things to offer. Can you recall a happy, memorable experience in your life? Begin to write a short piece recalling where and when this took place and how it made you feel. This can be continued in the next lesson if there is not enough time for pupils to finish their writing.

- Review what has been achieved in the lesson.

- Refer pupils to their safety plans as a place to look if they need help after leaving the lesson.

Extension activities

- Pupils to write their answers to the key questions in the first part of the lesson.

- Do you like the poem? Pupils to write their own responses giving reasons.

- Write a short biographical piece about Sara Teasdale.

- Illustrate the poem with your own images of loveliness.

- What positive things are happening in the world? Pupils to write an extended piece of writing that reflects on changes that are having positive effects on people.

- Compile a list of positive news stories over a day or over a week. Share these stories in class. The stories may be school based or taken from media reports.

- Pupils to produce a piece of stimulus writing using images suggested in the poem. Pupils/ teachers to bring in pictures of waves crashing on the rocks/cliff, pictures of happy faces, musical instruments, pine forests and bonfires. The aim is to write about the content of a picture and the thoughts and feelings it inspires, rather than simply describing the image. What would it be like to be there? How would you feel? What sounds, smells, tastes or other sensations would you experience? What might you be doing there? Would you be with someone, and if so whom? What would you be doing and why? Try to think of positive associations. If you think of negative ones, how can you make those associations positive by thinking about things differently?

Cross-curricular/topic links

Cross-curricular and topic links may be explored for use in follow-up and for extension work in

- English
- PSHE
- Art and Design

Differentiation

Opportunities for discussion in mixed ability pairs.

Differentiation by outcome e.g. quantity or complexity of issues identified, sophistication of response, level of inclusion/contribution, empathy.

Writing quantity outcomes will be differentiated/assessed/moderated according to teacher's expectations of quantity and depth; otherwise by outcome.

Differentiation may also be through artwork as a means of expression.

Invictus
by William Ernest Henley

Commentary

Out of the night that covers me,
    Black as the pit from pole to pole,
I thank whatever gods may be
    For my unconquerable soul.

In the fell clutch of circumstance
    I have not winced nor cried aloud.
Under the bludgeonings of chance
    My head is bloody, but unbowed.

Beyond this place of wrath and tears
    Looms but the Horror of the shade,
And yet the menace of the years
    Finds and shall find me unafraid.

It matters not how strait the gate,
    How charged with punishments the scroll,
I am the master of my fate,
    I am the captain of my soul.

Context

'Invictus' was written by the English poet, editor and critic William Ernest Henley. Henley's work fell into near oblivion after his death in 1903, but his reputation has since been revived through the popularity of this poem, a work that continues to be used in popular motivational references.

From the age of twelve, Henley suffered from tuberculosis of the bone, a disease that led to the amputation of his left leg below the knee when he was nineteen or twenty. As a result of this illness, Henley's early life was interspersed with episodes of extreme pain.

Frequent illness often kept the young Henley from school, but he was able to pass the Oxford Local Schools Examination. He moved to London to attempt to establish himself as a journalist. However, his work was interrupted by long hospital stays over the following eight years, caused by his right foot having also become diseased. Henley resisted the proposal that a second amputation was the only way to save his life, entering the care of pioneering surgeon Joseph Lister at the Royal Infirmary of Edinburgh from 1873 to 1875. The stay was a long one, but Henley's leg was saved.

Henley married in 1878, but further misfortune followed. The couple's daughter Margaret died of cerebral meningitis at the age of five. It was Margaret who was famously responsible for inspiring the name of the character Wendy Darling in J.M. Barrie's play *Peter Pan*: Barrie, whom Margaret called 'Fwendy' (that is, 'Friendy') was a friend of her parents.

Henley himself was the inspiration for another famous literary character created by his friend Robert Louis Stevenson, who recorded in his letters how the character of Long John Silver was influenced by him: 'It was the sight of your maimed strength and masterfulness that begot Long John Silver... the idea of the maimed man, ruling and dreaded by the sound, was entirely taken from you'.

Henley published poems in several volumes and editions, but is chiefly remembered for his 'hospital poems', written during his isolation of 1873–1875. These works developed his artistic motif of the 'poet as a patient', and contained compositional features that anticipated modern poetry. 'Invictus' dates from this period, being written in 1875 and published in 1888 in Henley's first volume of poems, *Book of Verses*, in the section entitled 'Life and Death (Echoes)'.

When one examines the accounts of Henley written by those who knew the poet well, the autobiographical tenor of 'Invictus' becomes evident. Henley's younger brother Joseph recorded how, after painful procedures to treat tuberculosis abscesses, his elder brother would 'Hop about the room, laughing loudly and playing with zest to pretend he was beyond the reach of pain'. And following the poet's death in 1903 at the age of only fifty-three, an acquaintance wrote that 'Deep in his nature lay an inner well of cheerfulness, and a spontaneous joy of living, that nothing could drain dry'. Henley's steadfast inner resolve and the resolute positivity of his character not only made their impression on his friends and peers, but left their indelible imprint upon his poetry.

Content

'Invictus' is a Latin word meaning 'unconquered', 'undefeated', or even 'invincible'. It was a title applied to several Roman deities including Jupiter, Apollo, Mars, Silvanus (god of the woods), Hercules, and Sol (the divine personification of the Sun, who was worshipped as Sol Invictus). As such, it is an epithet that carries considerable potency.

The poem's speaker (who, for reasons outlined above, we may assume to be the poet himself) addresses the world in general, rather than the reader in particular, in what seems to be an assertion not only of his personal survival but of the strength and indomitability of his spirit.

The speaker declares that he is entirely covered by a kind of darkness (which we may take to be a metaphorical description of his circumstances, rather than a literal obscurity) that is proverbially 'Black as the pit' (lines 1–2). From this dark place, the speaker thanks the unspecified divine powers of the universe for giving him a soul that cannot be defeated by the trials of life (lines 3–4).

Even when he has been caught in the grip of dreadful circumstances, the speaker has neither flinched nor complained (lines 5–6). Misfortune has seemed to strike him repeatedly, and though he has been wounded by its blows he has not submitted to it (lines 7–8).

The speaker is aware that after the anger and unhappiness of this life, the death that follows it may be only the shadowy oblivion that people fear (lines 9–10); but as he advances through the years of life the growing nearness of death does not make him fearful (lines 11–12).

It does not matter to the speaker how narrow and tight life's path might be, or how much ill-treatment life has in store for him (lines 13–14). He is undauntedly in charge of himself, of his own destiny and the direction of his own spirit (lines 14–15).

Composition

'Invictus' is written as four stanzas, each of four lines of iambic tetrameter with the rhyme scheme ABAB, the rhyme endings changing from stanza to stanza.

The language and vocabulary of the poem have something of a monumental feel, in line with the poet's apparent intention of celebrating and memorialising the enduring indomitability of his own spirit. This appears in such rather grand and sometimes archaic usages as 'unconquerable' (line 4) and 'unbowed' (line 8), both synonyms for the poem's Latin title, 'bludgeonings' (= 'blows', line 7), 'wrath' (= 'anger', line 9), 'looms' (= 'appears threateningly', line 10), and the soaring stateliness of the final stanza.

The poem's punctuation is conventional and simple, being kept to the minimum necessary to direct and convey meaning.

The poet makes extensive use of figurative language, in line with the dignity of his poem's theme. The first stanza contains the only instance of simile, 'Black as the pit' (line 2), which is itself incorporated into the metaphor established in line 1 of the 'night' that covers the speaker: this is a metaphorical night, the darkness of which is likened by simile to the blackness of 'the pit'. The speaker goes on to thank 'whatever gods may be' (line 3) for his indomitable nature, which we may take to be his gratitude to the powers of good fortune rather than any literally-intended deities. The somewhat violent second stanza contains both 'the fell clutch of circumstance' (line 5) and 'the bludgeonings of chance' (line 7), in which both the grasp of fate and its blows are intended metaphorically — as is the bloodiness of the speaker's head in line 8. Unfortunately the description of the world as a 'place of wrath and tears' (line 9) is not metaphorical as we would doubtless prefer it to be, and the many misfortunes of Henley's life would certainly have qualified his world for this epithet. In the final stanza, the 'strait' (= 'narrow') gate of line 13 and the 'scroll' that is 'charged with punishments' (line 14), the painful narrowness of life's path and its seemingly endless list of apparently punitive adversity, form a powerful metaphor of predestined tribulation. Still the speaker remains both 'master' and 'captain' (lines 15 and 16) — both nautical images referring to those who command vessels — resolutely and fearlessly in charge of the course through life steered by his inner self.

Message

The chief message of the poem is one of steadfast positivity in the face of adversity.

However hard life has been, however hard it may seem that it will be in future, we can make up our minds to meet it with determination, purpose and courage.

We may find it helpful to be determined that life with all its vicissitudes has not beaten us, nor will it.

However dark things may appear, we should remember that we remain uniquely ourselves. We all have strengths and inner abilities that we can bring to bear against a difficult world.

Whenever we have dealt successfully with life's problems, whether on our own or with the help of others, we can take a certain pride in our success. We may remember that success when encountering problems in the future: the remembrance of having succeeded before may help us to do so again.

Sometimes the blows that life can deal are severe. They may be genuinely painful, wounding, and it may be hard to see how we will recover from them. But we have a far better chance of doing so if we try to remain positive, to be faithful to our own special inner self and what it can achieve. We are stronger than we know.

There are things that we can find ourselves worrying about that we can really do nothing to change. This does not mean that such things should not worry or bother us, but we should try to keep our fears within manageable limits and in perspective, perhaps with the help of others. Wherever we can we should keep our resolve fixed on those things that we can improve in life.

It may seem sometimes that life sets out to cause us problems, to send us in directions we do not want to go, or make us feel confined and under pressure. Sometimes it may feel as though life is out to get us. But we may remember that we have the power within ourselves to control and improve many things, to make wise and well-informed decisions, to take responsibility for ourselves and our actions, and not to be turned aside by avoidable things that could harm us.

We can face the world and our future knowing that we have it within us to make good choices, to steer our lives for the better, and to be in charge of ourselves. Within us all there is something unconquerable.

Lesson plan: 'Invictus' by William Ernest Henley

Resources

Copies of the poem — ideally one per pupil, pens and pencils or marker pens, dictionaries, thesauruses, plain or lined paper, rulers for SEND pupils to follow a line when reading. Extra paper should be made available for use if required.

Copies of pupils' safety plans to which they can refer throughout the session/lesson.

The lesson will cover oracy and reading skills.

The session can be done in the round, or as a circle time activity, or at tables, or in an unstructured group. The lesson plan is suitable to use with pupils at Upper Key Stage 2, 3 and 4.

Links with the PSHE Association PSHE Education Programme of Study

Links have been made to the PSHE Association PSHE Education Programme of Study at Key Stage 2, 3 and 4 as follows:

KS2

- *H15. that mental health, just like physical health, is part of daily life; the importance of taking care of mental health*
- *H29. about how to manage setbacks/perceived failures, including how to re-frame unhelpful thinking*

KS3

- *H2. to understand what can affect wellbeing and resilience (e.g. life changes, relationships, achievements and employment)*

- *H4. simple strategies to help build resilience to negative opinions, judgments and comments*

KS4

- *H4. strategies to develop assertiveness and build resilience to peer and other influences that affect both how they think about themselves and their health and wellbeing*

Links with the National Curriculum

Links have been made to the National Curriculum for English at Key Stage 2, 3 and 4 as follows:

KS2 (Years 5 and 6) English programme of study

- *maintain attention and participate actively in collaborative conversations, staying on topic and initiating and responding to comments*
- *discuss and evaluate how authors use language, including figurative language, considering the impact on the reader*
- *provide reasoned justifications for their views*
- *use a thesaurus*
- *evaluate and edit by:*

  assessing the effectiveness of their own and others' writing

  proposing changes to vocabulary, grammar and punctuation to enhance effects and clarify meaning

KS3 English programme of study

- *participating in formal debates and structured discussions, summarising and/or building on what has been said*
- *knowing how language, including figurative language, vocabulary choice, grammar, text structure and organisational features, presents meaning*
- *understand increasingly challenging texts through:*

  learning new vocabulary, relating it explicitly to known vocabulary and understanding it with the help of context and dictionaries
- *writing for a wide range of purposes and audiences, including:*

  stories, scripts, poetry and other imaginative writing

KS4 English programme of study

- *listening to and building on the contributions of others, asking questions to clarify and inform, and challenging courteously when necessary*
- *analysing a writer's choice of vocabulary, form, grammatical and structural features, and evaluating their effectiveness and impact*
- *revise, edit and proof-read through:*

  reflecting on whether their draft achieves the intended impact

Teaching and learning activities

'Invictus' is a poem that focuses on the human spirit in order to overcome adversity. In the poem, the speaker is faced with daunting, seemingly insurmountable challenges. However, he perseveres and succeeds. He faces each challenge courageously, and believes he can overcome any hardship.

- Introduction — share aims of lesson.

- Refer pupils to their safety plans. Remind them of what a safety plan is for. Ask them to read through their own safety plan before they go further and answer any questions they may have.
- Read the poem (or teacher/leader to read it aloud) and discuss its content. Ask the following key questions:
  - What is the poem about? It may be necessary to write key vocabulary and phrases on the whiteboard and look at them one by one, to help younger pupils understand the poem better e.g. 'unconquerable soul', 'In the fell clutch of circumstance', 'wince', 'wrath', 'bludgeoning', 'My head is bloody but unbowed', 'wrath', 'menace', 'strait', 'scroll', 'fate'.
  - What does the title 'Invictus' mean? The word 'invictus' is Latin for 'unconquered'.
  - What is the poem's message?
- How does the poem make you feel? How does it do this? Discuss with a partner or in a small group.
- Ask for feedback.
- Pupils to write their own synonym poems. The idea is to think about how synonyms can be used in a meaningful context. Ask pupils to write the title 'Unconquered' on a piece of lined paper. Next, ask pupils to look up synonyms for the word 'unconquered' in a thesaurus or on the web and choose their favourite one to be the first line. For the second line of the poem, list three more synonyms for the word 'unconquered'. Finally, for the third line ask pupils to write a descriptive phrase about the synonym they used in the first line. Below is an example of a poem that can be shared with pupils.

> *Unconquered*
>
> *Champion:*
>
> *Winning, successful, top —*
> *I will not allow the bad things to win!*

- Ask pupils to read out their poems.
- Peers to provide helpful comments on the quality of the descriptive phrases they have heard.
- Review what has been achieved in the lesson.
- Refer pupils to their safety plans as a place to look if they need help after leaving the lesson.

Extension activities

- Pupils to write their answers to the key questions in the first part of the lesson.
- Do you like the poem? Pupils to write their own responses giving reasons.
- Write a short biographical piece about William Ernest Henley.
- Write about how you might have responded if you had to deal with life challenges similar to those that William Ernest Henley faced.
- Illustrate the poem 'Invictus' with images/words of positivity.
- Younger pupils can write their own acrostic poems using one of the synonyms for the word 'unconquered'.
- Pupils to write about the form, structure and rhyme scheme of the poem.
- Design a motto or emblem that symbolises the message of the poem.
- Pupils to write their own adversity stories where the central character shows his/her strength to overcome a difficulty or problem.
- Find out about Nelson Mandela and why he regularly recited Henley's poem during his time in prison.

- Try to find examples of songs that have the same sort of message as 'Invictus' about staying strong, not giving up and not letting life's difficulties win. You might start with songs such as 'Tubthumping' (or 'I Get Knocked Down But I Get Up Again') by Chumbawamba, 'I'm Still Standing' by Elton John, or 'The Impossible Dream' by Andy Williams. How are their messages similar to 'Invictus'? How do the songs make you feel, and why?

Cross-curricular/topic links:

Cross-curricular and topic links may be explored for use in follow-up and for extension work in

- English
- PSHE
- Art and Design
- History

Differentiation

Opportunities for discussion in mixed ability pairs.

Differentiation by outcome e.g. quantity or complexity of issues identified, sophistication of response, level of inclusion/contribution, empathy.

Writing quantity outcomes will be differentiated/assessed/moderated according to teacher's expectations of quantity and depth; otherwise by outcome.

Differentiation may also be through artwork as a means of expression.

Face in the Mirror

by Judy Morris

Commentary

Who am I?
Me: with my love, my friendships.
It's okay to be different,
But when good times turn to dark times
And I'm alone,
Losing and remembering,
It's me: facing my trauma,
Standing strong,
Looking for happiness.
Trying to find answers.
Facing the future without fear.

Context

This poem was written as a response to the increasingly stressful world in which young people find themselves. Questions of identity, how we relate to others and to the world around us, seem to be more complex than ever before, and young people are challenged to make sense of it all. 'Face in the Mirror' was the poet's reflection on how, despite the apparent proliferation of support networks around young people, coming to terms with the difficulties of life still remains very much an internal process.

Content

'Face in the Mirror' is an assertion of personal identity. It begins with the question that people, and especially young people, have asked themselves in all periods of history and all societies around the world: *Who am I?* It is the question that almost everyone has asked at some time, encompassing the nature of identity in both internal and external terms, including how we fit into family, society and the world around us. The answer the poet gives is simple: *Me.* Yet this answer reflects the profound truth that everyone in the world, everyone who ever has been and ever will be born, is the only person ever to have been that one, unique individual that is him- or herself. Underlying this is the complexity of understanding what it is to be oneself.

The poem acknowledges that it is good to celebrate our human individuality, and to engage with the realisation that we must each respond in our own distinctive way to whatever happens to us in life and, at least for the poet, interact powerfully with it. At ease with being our true selves, each of us should seek to go through life with confidence, resilience and strength.

Composition

'Face in the Mirror' is written as a single eleven-line stanza. As a piece of free verse, there is no rhyme scheme or regular metre.

The language avoids complexity. Vocabulary is accessible, containing nothing with which most young people of KS2 and above are likely to be unfamiliar. The verse form serves the conversational nature and taut phrasing of the content, with punctuation being conventional and generally following line endings. There are three notable exceptions to this. The first is the caesura marked by the colon in the second line, which creates a momentary space in which to consider the meaning of the familiar but loaded 'Me'. The second instance is the enjambment from line 4 to line 5, at the poem's volta, which serves to avoid excessive line length whilst simultaneously sharpening the reader's focus onto the pivotal 'And I'm alone'. The third exception is the colon which marks the caesura in line 7 and, like that in line 2, invites us to focus on the emphatic 'me' that declares self and identity whilst reminding us of our individual uniqueness.

The poet eschews the use of figurative expression in favour of linguistic approachability. Imagery is kept to the minimum, there is no use of simile, and metaphor is confined to the conservative and proverbial 'dark times'.

The poem appears philosophical, and indeed is so, but it is written from an intensely personal perspective and approaches its philosophy from the viewpoint of personal experience. References to 'I', 'me' and 'my' are recurrent, appearing no fewer than seven times in eleven lines, and the boldness of the last four lines is enhanced by the strongly personal anchor of the 'me' and 'my' of line 7. The poem's title contains an element of punning: 'Face in the Mirror' is an address to oneself that could well be delivered when facing the mirror. It is at its heart a poem about self.

It should be noted that the lines of the poem reflect the section titles for the poetry anthology *Face in the Mirror*.

Message

'Face in the Mirror' tells us that we must all accept ourselves for who we are. We do not have to be like anyone else, and should celebrate our difference and uniqueness. At the heart of everything, we have access to reserves of resilience, self-reliance and inner strength that can help us to face the world, respond to the challenges of life, and seek a happy future.

Lesson plan: 'Face in the Mirror' by Judy Morris

Resources

Copies of the poem — ideally one per pupil, pens and pencils, copies of planning sheets, pupil's journals, PSHE files, notes, copies of the poetry anthology *Face in the Mirror*, rulers for SEND pupils to follow a line when reading.

Copies of pupils' safety plans to which they can refer throughout the session/lesson.

The lesson will cover oracy and reading skills.

The session can be done in the round (or as a circle time activity), or at tables, or in an unstructured group. The lesson plan is suitable to use with pupils at Upper Key Stage 2, 3 and 4.

Links with the PSHE Association PSHE Education Programme of Study

Links have been made to the PSHE Association PSHE Education Programme of Study at Key Stage 2, 3 and 4 as follows:

KS2

- *H15. that mental health, just like physical health, is part of daily life; the importance of taking care of mental health*
- *H16. about strategies and behaviours that support mental health — including how good quality sleep, physical exercise/time outdoors, being involved in community groups, doing things for others, clubs, and activities, hobbies and spending time with family and friends can support mental health and wellbeing*

KS3

- *H10. a range of healthy coping strategies and ways to promote wellbeing and boost mood, including physical activity, participation and the value of positive relationships in providing support*

KS4

- *H7. a broad range of strategies — cognitive and practical — for promoting their own emotional wellbeing, for avoiding negative thinking and for ways of managing mental health concerns*

Links with the National Curriculum

Links have been made to the National Curriculum for English at Key Stage 2, 3 and 4 as follows:

KS2 (Years 5 and 6) English programme of study

- *maintain attention and participate actively in collaborative conversations, staying on topic and initiating and responding to comments*

KS3 English programme of study

- *participating in formal debates and structured discussions, summarising and/or building on what has been said*

KS4 English programme of study

- *listening to and building on the contributions of others, asking questions to clarify and inform, and challenging courteously when necessary*

Teaching and learning activities

The last, eponymously-titled poem in the anthology *Face in the Mirror* seeks to draw together all the themes in that book and summarises the journey the young person has been on in reading the collection of poetry. The teaching activity seeks to encapsulate this journey visually in a self-identity collage that draws from photographs, images, quotes, Post-it notes, positive messages, self-reflection notes from the poems and the lesson activities that the pupils have encountered. The final teaching activity is the creation of an art picture which celebrates one's identity and uniqueness.

- Introduction — share aims of lesson.
- Refer pupils to their safety plans. Remind them of what a safety plan is for. Ask them to read through their own safety plan before they go further and answer any questions they may have.

- Read the poem (or teacher/leader to read it aloud) and discuss its content. Ask the following key questions:
  - What is the poem about?
  - Why is the poem called 'Face in the Mirror'?
  - What is the poem's message?
  - Why do you think the poet chose to include this poem at the end of the poetry anthology, rather than earlier in the book? This question should be asked if pupils have had access to the section headings in the anthology. It may be necessary to revisit the headings with pupils to refresh their memories.
- Introduce the task to the class or to the individual. Show examples of self-portrait artwork. There are lots of examples of mixed media art on the internet which can be brought up on the interactive whiteboard. Pupils can also view them for themselves if they have access to laptops or computers in the classroom.
- Discuss how design sheets are to be completed and answer any questions pupils may have regarding this task.
- Each pupil to begin work on creating a design planning board in preparation for artwork which may take three or four lessons to produce. The design planning board may reflect some or all of the eleven themes in the poetry anthology. Each sheet of the board can be blown up to A3 so that pupils can attach notes, photos etc. to it. Decisions will need to be made about how to produce the image of a face and how to incorporate mixed media into the picture. Ask the pupils to look back through their journals, notes, PSHE files, poetry anthology for ideas for their collage. The pupil's artwork should include the image of a pupil's face which may be drawn or painted. A pupil may prefer to include their own photograph if he/she wants to. The following design planning board sheets may be photocopied for pupils' use.

My Design Planning Board for 'Face in the Mirror'

How will I produce my face for my artwork?

Will I use a photograph of myself or will I paint or draw my face?

Will it be a side view or a front view of my face?

These are decisions you will need to make. You may want to produce sketches to help with your planning.

My Design Planning Board for 'Face in the Mirror'

What messages, quotes and information do I want to include in my artwork?

Look through your journal, poetry anthology, notes, etc., and compile a list of things that you want to be inserted into your artwork.

What messages, quotes and information do I want to include in my artwork?

How will you produce key words and phrases?

You may want to type up key words/phrases, paint or handwrite them. You may want to produce some of them in coloured bubble writing or in 3-D. The choice is yours!

Sketch your ideas.

How will you incorporate the words and phrases into your picture? You may want to sketch what your picture will look like and plan things like background colours, effects and designs.

- Review what has been achieved in the lesson.
- Refer pupils to their safety plans as a place to look if they need help after leaving the lesson.

Extension activities

- The planning activity may need another lesson to complete, followed by several lessons to produce the artwork.
- Create a display of artwork either in the classroom or across the school. Each picture should have the pupil's name written underneath.
- Parents and carers could be invited to see the exhibition as well as the rest of the school community.

Cross-curricular/topic links

Cross-curricular and topic links may be explored for use in follow-up and for extension work in

- Art and Design
- PSHE
- English

Differentiation

Opportunities for discussion in mixed ability pairs.

Differentiation by outcome e.g. quantity or complexity of issues identified, sophistication of response, level of inclusion/contribution, empathy.

Writing quantity outcomes will be differentiated/assessed/moderated according to teacher's expectations of quantity and depth; otherwise by outcome.

Differentiation may also be through key words rather than written sentences, or through artwork as a means of expression.

Poet biographies

Aya Ahmad

Aya Ahmad was born in Syria and is of Kurdish origin. Aya wrote the work in this collection whilst a student at Cedar Mount Academy, Manchester. She and her family came to the UK to escape from war and oppression. In 2017 and 2018 she won prizes for her writing in the Portico Sadie Massey Awards for Young Readers and Writers. She often writes about the effects of war on people and its futility.

Marian Allen

Eleanor Marian Dundas Allen (18 January 1892 – 12 September 1953) was born in Sydney, Australia, and came to live in Oxford before 1908. In 1913 or 1914 Marian met Arthur Tylston Greg, whom she was to have married. Arthur joined the army on the outbreak of the First World War in August 1914. His death on St George's Day 1917 inspired Marian to write some of her finest poetry. Marian is recognised as one of the few women war poets of the Great War.

William Blake

William Blake (28 November 1757 – 12 August 1827) was an English poet, painter and printmaker. His work was largely unrecognised during his lifetime, but Blake is now considered to be a central figure in the Romantic Age for his poetry and visual arts. Blake's work is notable for its spiritual and visionary qualities.

Elaine Bousfield

Elaine Bousfield worked for many years as a counsellor with young people in community mental health settings, focusing on working with complex trauma. In 2001 she founded and led an online counselling organisation called XenZone (now Kooth plc). In 2004, as the CEO of XenZone, she developed Kooth.com, the UK's largest digital mental health service for children and young people, and later Qwell, an online service for adults. She was with the company for twenty years until it went to IPO. She is the CEO of ZunTold, a publishing company which publishes fiction and poetry to support people with their mental health and delivers a Fiction as Therapy counselling service. She is a writer herself, an editor and also a practising counsellor.

Charlotte Brontë

Charlotte Brontë (21 April 1816 – 31 March 1855) was an English poet and novelist. She was the eldest of the three talented Brontë sisters, whose novels became classics of English literature. Charlotte outlived all of her siblings. Her best-known work is the novel *Jane Eyre*, which was published under her pen name 'Currer Bell' in October 1847.

Emily Brontë

Emily Brontë (30 July 1818 – 19 December 1848) was an English novelist and poet. Best known for her novel *Wuthering Heights*, Emily Brontë wrote over two hundred poems. She was especially close to her youngest sister, Anne, with whom she created the imaginary world of Gondal, the setting of many of her finest poems. She was a keen observer of the natural world, including the wild moors around her home in Haworth, Yorkshire.

Abbie Farwell Brown

Abbie Farwell Brown (21 August 1871 – 5 March 1927) was an American author. Her first children's book, *The Book of Saints and Friendly Beasts*, was published in 1900. In addition to stories, Brown also produced poetry for children and was an accomplished writer of song lyrics.

Emily Dickinson

Emily Dickinson (10 December 1830 –15 May 1886) was an American poet. She was reclusive and showed little interest in publishing her work, but was a prolific writer who regularly enclosed her poems in letters to friends. Her most active writing period was in her late twenties and early thirties. From the mid-1850s, Dickinson's mother was confined to her bed with various chronic illnesses, remaining so until her death in 1882. Dickinson chose to remain with their mother at all times. She seems to have found that the quiet, retired life at home with her books suited her. But with her mother's continued decline, domestic responsibilities weighed more heavily upon Dickinson and from the mid-1860s she produced fewer poems. Though she was not publicly recognised during her lifetime, she has grown in status to become a key figure of American literature.

George Eliot

Mary Anne Evans (alternatively Mary Ann or Marian Evans; 22 November 1819 – 22 December 1880) is best known by her pen name of George Eliot. She was an English poet, novelist, journalist and translator, the author of seven novels known for their realism and psychological insight. Eliot is celebrated as one of the leading writers of the Victorian era. Her 1871–1872 novel *Middlemarch* has been described as the greatest novel in the English language.

Robert Frost

Robert Lee Frost (26 March 1874 – 29 January 1963) was an American poet whose work was published in England before it was released in his own country. Frost's work is notable for his use of colloquial American language and for his realistic portrayals of rural life. A four-time winner of Pulitzer Prizes for Poetry, Frost was much celebrated in his own lifetime and came to be seen as a living institution of American literary art.

Mary Frye

Mary Elizabeth Frye (13 November 1905 – 15 September 2004) was an American poet and florist. Her poem 'Do Not Stand at my Grave and Weep', believed to have been inspired by the story of a young Jewish girl who had been staying in Frye's household, is said to have been composed on a brown paper shopping bag. Though she circulated copies privately, Frye never published or copyrighted the poem and its creator's identity was unknown until the late 1990s when Frye revealed her authorship.

Rosie Garland

Rosie Garland is an award-winning poet, novelist and singer with post-punk band The March Violets. With a passion for language nurtured by libraries (she was appointed inaugural writer-in-residence at Manchester's historic John Rylands Library in 2018), she has been called 'one of the country's finest performance poets' (Apples & Snakes). http://www.rosiegarland.com/

Edgar Albert Guest

Edgar Albert Guest (20 August 1881 in Birmingham, England – 5 August 1959 in Detroit, Michigan) was an English-born American poet who was popular in the first half of the 20th century and became known as the People's Poet. A prolific writer, his poems often conveyed a very optimistic and positive view of everyday life.

William Ernest Henley

William Ernest Henley (23 August 1849 – 11 July 1903) was an English poet, editor and critic. It is sometimes suggested that he had as central a role in his time as Samuel Johnson had in the 18th century, in terms of his significant influence on cultural and literary perspectives in the late Victorian period. Henley published many tens of poems in several volumes and editions. He is remembered most often for his 'hospital poems' that were composed during his isolation as a consequence of early, life-threatening battles with tuberculosis.

Emily Jane

Emily Jane was born in Bolton and wrote the poems in this book whilst studying English, Media and Sociology at college. She is a past winner in the prestigious Portico Sadie Massey Awards for Young Readers and Writers for her creative writing, and continues to both blog and write creatively.

Peter Kalu

Of Danish-Nigerian parentage, Peter Kalu is the author of three young adult novels, *Silent Striker*, *Being Me* and *Zombie XI*; he also writes short fiction and poetry. As a storyteller he has told tales in Nigeria, France, Lebanon and Pakistan. His current research interests include the colonial connections of English country houses, artificial intelligence and tightrope walking.

Hannah Kate

Hannah Kate is a poet, short story writer and editor based in North Manchester. Her work has appeared in a number of magazines and anthologies, and she is the editor of several short story collections (most recently *Nothing*, published in 2019 by Hic Dragones). Hannah is the writer-in-residence at Manchester's historic Clayton Hall, and she also presents Hannah's Bookshelf, a weekly literature show on North Manchester FM radio.

Rudyard Kipling

Joseph Rudyard Kipling (30 December 1865 – 18 January 1936) was an English poet, novelist, journalist and short-story writer. He was born in India, a country which inspired much of his work. Kipling was one of the most popular prose and verse writers in the United Kingdom in the late nineteenth and early twentieth centuries, and was awarded the Nobel Prize in Literature in 1907 at the age of forty-one, the first English-language writer to receive the prize and still its youngest recipient.

Christian D. Larson

Christian Daa Larson (1874 – 1954: some sources vary from these dates) was an American poet, the leader and teacher of the New Thought movement (an American religious movement that originated in the nineteenth century), as well as a prolific author of metaphysical and New Thought books. Many of Larson's books remain in print today, more than a century after they were first printed.

Henry Wadsworth Longfellow

Henry Wadsworth Longfellow (27 February 1807 – 24 March 1882) was an American poet and educator who was born in Portland, Maine. He studied at Bowdoin College, spent time in Europe, and became a professor at Bowdoin and later at Harvard College. Longfellow's lyric poems are known for their musicality, often presenting stories of mythology and legend. He became the most popular American poet of his day and also enjoyed success overseas.

Judy Morris

Judy trained as a teacher. She taught hundreds of pupils over a twenty-five-year classroom career before becoming a headteacher and then a writer. For many years Judy was a curriculum lead teacher for PSHE, SEND and Literacy, and worked on the development of PSHE resources for her education authority. Since the earliest days of her teaching career she has written plays, poems and stories to use with children in the classroom. Judy has always been passionate about teaching, wholly committed to delivering high-quality education and giving students a voice in their learning.

Paul Morris

Paul Morris was a successful lawyer before becoming an author known for his meticulous research and exciting stories. His published works include YA fiction and poetry, including his chart-topping single-poem volume *Beyond the Morning Sun*, released in support of services charity Combat Stress. He has served as a judge in the Portico Sadie Massey Awards for Young Readers and Writers, has edited books including fiction, poetry and academic works, and is an educational consultant for Bletchley Park.

Mojisola Oladiti

A keen and accomplished junior athlete representing her county as a middle-distance runner, Nigerian-born Mojisola Oladiti was among the talented student writers of Manchester's Cedar Mount Academy when she wrote her dynamic poem 'Hidden Tears'. As a proud young woman writer, Mojisola is excited by the possibilities of her work reaching and helping others.

Wilfred Owen

Wilfred Edward Salter Owen, MC (18 March 1893 – 4 November 1918) was an English poet and soldier who discovered his love of poetry around 1904. He became a private tutor, teaching English and French, and was working in France when the First World War broke out. He enlisted on 21

October 1915, and on 4 June 1916 was commissioned as a probationary second lieutenant in the Manchester Regiment. Wounded in action, Owen was diagnosed as suffering from shell shock and sent to Scotland for treatment. He returned to active service in July 1918 and was killed in action on 4 November, exactly one week before the signing of the Armistice which ended the war. Owen has come to be acknowledged as one of the leading poets of the Great War.

Kelvin Pak

Kelvin Pak was born in Hong Kong and educated at universities and colleges in Hong Kong and England, where he qualified and practised as a solicitor. A passionate believer in the power of literature both ancient and modern, his original translation of the classic Chinese poem 'On the Stork Tower' was written in 2018.

Tesni Penney

Tesni Penney is a young poet from the Peak District of Derbyshire. Many of her poems, which she uses to explore her own feelings and emotions, take mental health as their theme. Tesni considers that poetry is a great way to work through one's emotions, and recommends it as a therapy to everyone. Her poems have been published in various places, including the Chester Cathedral website and the Marple Young Writers' anthology.

William Shakespeare

William Shakespeare (baptised 26 April 1564 – 23 April 1616) was an English poet, playwright and actor. He is widely regarded as the greatest writer in the English language and the world's greatest dramatist. Shakespeare's work includes thirty-eight or thirty-nine plays (the number is a matter of scholarly debate), two narrative poems, one hundred and fifty-four sonnets, and a number of other poems.

Robert Louis Stevenson

Robert Louis Stevenson (13 November 1850 – 3 December 1894) was a Scottish novelist and travel writer. Born in Edinburgh, Stevenson suffered from ill health for much of his life, but still wrote prolifically and travelled extensively. Stevenson is most noted for his modern classics *Treasure Island*, *Kidnapped*, *The Strange Case of Dr Jekyll and Mr Hyde* and *A Child's Garden of Verses*. Celebrated during his lifetime, Stevenson's work attracted poor critical reaction for most of the twentieth century, though his reputation has since been revitalised.

Sara Teasdale

Sara Trevor Teasdale (8 August 1884 – 29 January 1933) was an American lyric poet born in St. Louis, Missouri. Teasdale was a member of The Potters, a group of young female artists who published, from 1904 to 1907, *The Potter's Wheel*, a monthly artistic and literary magazine. Her first poem was published in a local newspaper, *Reedy's Mirror*, in 1907. Her first collection of poems, *Sonnets to Duse and Other Poems*, was published the same year, followed by others in 1911 and 1915. She won a Pulitzer Prize in 1918 for her 1917 poetry collection *Love Songs*.

Ella Wheeler Wilcox

Ella Wheeler Wilcox (5 November 1850 – 30 October 1919) was an American poet and author. She began to write poetry around the age of eight, and her first poem was published when she was only thirteen years old. Her poem 'Solitude' was inspired by the experience of her meeting with a young widow when travelling to the Governor's inaugural ball in Madison, Wisconsin.

Peter Dale Wimbrow

Peter Dale Wimbrow Sr. (6 June 1895 – 26 January 1954) was an American writer, composer and radio artist. His early career was in music and radio and he became known for his records and radio performances with orchestras. Wimbrow established *The Indian River News* newspaper in June 1948, which was published until September 1966, having been carried on by his wife for twelve years after his death in 1954. The poem 'The Man In The Glass' reproduced in this book is an anonymously-written work inspired by Wimbrow's 1934 poem 'The Guy In The Glass'.

Wang Zhihuan

Wang Zhihuan (688 – 742) was a Chinese poet of the Tang Dynasty's Kaiyuan era. He was born in Jin Yang, near Taiyuan, capital of Shanxi province. He mastered the classics before his thirties and became a famous poet during the high point of the Tang Dynasty. Many of his poems were made into songs by musicians, which brought him fame and influence. Only six of his poems have survived to modern times.

Glossary of terms used in this book

adjective
A word that describes a noun or pronoun.

adverb
A part of speech that provides greater description to a verb, adjective, another adverb, a phrase, a clause, or a sentence. Describing how an action was done, adverbs often end in '-ly'.

allegory
A story, poem, play or picture that can be interpreted to reveal a hidden meaning that relates to morals, religion, or politics.

alliteration
The occurrence of the same letter or sound at the beginning of adjacent or closely connected words.

amphibrach
A metrical foot consisting of a stressed syllable between two unstressed syllables.

amphimacer
See **cretic**.

anadiplosis
A literary device in which a word or group of words located at the end of a clause, sentence or line is repeated at or near the beginning of the following one.

anapest
A metrical foot consisting of two unstressed syllables followed by a stressed syllable (as in da-da-DUM).

anapestic tetrameter
A poetic metre that has four anapestic metrical feet per line with each foot having two unstressed syllables followed by a stressed syllable.

anapestic trimeter
Three anapestic feet per line.

anaphora
A figure of speech in which words repeat at the beginning of successive clauses, phrases or sentences.

anaphoric
A word or phrase that takes its reference from another word or phrase, especially from a preceding one.

anthropomorphism
The attribution of human characteristics, emotions or behaviours to animals or other nonhuman entities.

antithesis
A figure of speech that juxtaposes two contrasting or opposing ideas usually within parallel grammatical structures.

apophasis
The rhetorical strategy of mentioning something to deny its relevance or importance (also known as **paralepsis**).

archaic
A word or style of language that is no longer in everyday use but is sometimes used to impart an old-fashioned flavour.

ballad metre
A poetic metre consisting of four lines that alternate between **iambic tetrameter** and **iambic trimeter**, with each iambic foot consisting of an unstressed syllable followed by a stressed syllable.

cadence
A modulation or inflection of the voice.

caesura
A pause near the middle of a poetic line.

calligram
A word or piece of text in which the design and the layout of the letters creates a visual image which is related to the meaning of the words themselves or the theme of the poem.

catalectic
A metrically incomplete line of verse ending with an incomplete foot or lacking a syllable at the end.

catharsis
The release of emotions such as fear, sadness, and pity.

chorus stanza
A repeated verse.

colloquialism
A word or phrase that is not formal or literary and is used in ordinary or familiar conversation.

controlling metaphor
A metaphor that controls or dominates a poem. Similar to an extended metaphor but with an especially central nature.

couplet
A pair of successive lines of verse, typically rhyming and of the same length.

cretic
A cretic (otherwise known as an **amphimacer**) is a metrical foot containing three syllables: long, short, long (as in DUM-da-DUM).

cretic dimeter
Describes the construction of a line of poetry consisting of two sets of cretics.

diacope
A repetition of a word or a phrase with one or more words in between.

diacritic
Diacritics, otherwise known as diacritical marks, are marks placed above, below or next to a letter in a word to indicate a particular pronunciation (i.e. accent, tone, or stress). They may also assist in identifying meaning, as when a homograph exists without the marked letter or letters.

disyllabic
A word or metrical foot consisting of two syllables.

elegiac stanza
A **quatrain** in **iambic pentameter** with alternate lines rhyming.

ellipsis
A series of three dots that indicates an omission of a word, sentence, or whole section from a text. An ellipsis omits the writing of a word or words that are superfluous or which are able to be understood from contextual clues. It may also indicate a pause or something that has been left unsaid.

encomium
A speech or piece of writing that praises someone or something highly.

enjambment
The continuation of a sentence beyond the end of a line, such that the line flows to the next without end punctuation in a couplet or stanza.

epiphora
Another name for **epistrophe**.

epistolary
A literary work in the form of letters or personal addresses.

epistrophe
The repetition of a word or phrase at the end of successive lines or clauses. Otherwise known as **epiphora**.

epithet
An adjective or phrase expressing a quality or attribute regarded as characteristic of the person or thing referred to.

feminine caesura
A **caesura** that follows a short or unstressed syllable.
See also **masculine caesura** below.

feminine ending
A line of verse having an unstressed and usually extrametrical (exceeding the usual or prescribed number of syllables in a given metre) end.

figurative language
Figurative language uses figures of speech to be more effective, persuasive, and impactful. Figures of speech such as metaphors, similes and allusions go beyond the literal meanings of the words to give readers new insights.

foot
A poetic metrical unit of stressed and unstressed syllables that determines the metre or rhythmic measure in the lines of a poem.

free verse
Poetry that is free from limitations of regular metre or rhythm, and does not rhyme.

half rhyme
A type of rhyme formed by words with similar but not identical sounds.

iamb
A type of metrical foot in poetry, consisting of an unstressed syllable followed by a stressed syllable (as in da-DUM).

iambic pentameter
A line of verse with five metrical feet of iambs, each consisting of one short (or unstressed) syllable followed by one long (or stressed) syllable.

iambic tetrameter
A line of verse with four metrical feet of iambs, each consisting of one short (or unstressed) syllable followed by one long (or stressed) syllable.

iambic trimeter
A line of verse with three metrical feet of iambs, each consisting of one short (or unstressed) syllable followed by one long (or stressed) syllable.

idiomatic
Characteristic of an expression, word or phrase that is natural to a native speaker.

imperative sentences
A type of sentence that gives instructions or advice, and expresses a command, an order, a direction, or a request.

jueju
A form of poem otherwise known as the Chinese quatrain, a type of *jintishi* ('modern form poetry') that was popular among Chinese poets of the Tang Dynasty (618 to 907CE), though originating before that period. *Jueju* poems consist of two couplets, each line of which has five or seven syllables. In the original Chinese this is expressed as a strict composition of four strictly rhythmical lines, each of five characters.

lyrical poetry
Poetry that expresses the writer's emotions in an imaginative and beautiful way.

masculine caesura
A **caesura** that follows a long or stressed syllable.
See also **feminine caesura** above.

metre
A stressed and unstressed syllabic pattern in a verse or within the lines of a poem. Metre gives poetry a rhythmical and melodious sound.

metaphor
A literary device used to express a variety of emotions, images and expressions by combining and comparing to different objects or situations.

metrical
Poetry that has metre.

monosyllabic
Having only one syllable. Also used to describe a person who uses short, abrupt words in conversation.

neologism
A newly coined word or expression.

noun
The name applied to any of a class of people, places, or things (common noun) or to name a particular one of these (proper noun).

onomatopoeia
The formation of a word based upon the sound of what it names or describes (e.g. oink, roar, meow).

orthography
A set of conventions for writing a language. It includes norms of spelling, hyphenation, capitalisation, word breaks, emphasis, and punctuation.

oxymoron
A figure of speech in which two opposite ideas are joined to create an effect.

paradox
Contrary to expectations, existing belief, or perceived opinion. A paradoxical statement is one that appears to be self-contradictory.

paralepsis
See **apophasis**.

parody
An imitation of a subject, artist, writer, or genre that makes fun of or comments on the original work.

personification
A literary device in which an animal, an idea or thing is given human characteristics.

phonemic
Relating to phonemes, units of sound that distinguish one word from another in a particular language. How people interpret sounds.

polysyllabic
A word having more than one syllable.

pronoun
A word that substitutes for a noun or noun phrase.

proper noun
The name of specific people, places, ideas, or things.

prose poem/prose poetry
A poem written as prose, without the line breaks and verse form associated with poetry writing. It manifests other characteristics of poetry among which may be heightened imagery, metaphor, repetition, figures of speech, rhyme, poetic metre and emotional effects. Whilst not looking at first sight like a poem, prose poetry preserves both the original Greek root of the word 'poem' (*poiēma* [ποίημα], meaning 'what is made or created, workmanship') and the Oxford English Dictionary definition of the term as 'A piece of writing in which the expression of feelings and ideas is given intensity by particular attention to diction (sometimes involving rhyme), rhythm, and imagery'.

quatrain
A stanza or poetic unit of four lines. It may also be a full poem with four lines.

rhyme
Repetition of the same or similar sounds occurring in two or more words, usually at the ends of lines in poetry.

ruba'i or **rubaiyat**
A verse form of Persian origin, the stanzas of which consist of quatrains. Sometimes known as *chāhārgāna*.

sestet
A six-line stanza of poetry.

sibilance
A poetic device in which repeated consonant sounds are used with a hissing or whistling effect, from the Latin '*sibilant*' meaning 'hissing, whistling'. These consonant sounds can be s, sh, z, d, g (as in 'judge'), the s in both 'test' and 'vision', and the 'ch' in 'teacher'.

simile
A figure of speech that uses 'as' or 'like' to make a comparison between two different things.

slant rhymes
Rhymes formed by words that have similar but not identical sounds.

SMART
The acronym for a well-known planning strategy where goals are broken down into steps that are Specific, Measurable, Attainable, Realistic and Timely.

staccato
A poetic device that uses short words or word repeats, often to create an impression of rapidity or to be read as rapid-fire speech.

stanza
A group of lines of poetry that form a unit or division within the work.

stressed syllables
Syllables which are emphasised in speech. These are often louder than non-stressed syllables. They may have a higher or lower pitch, or be longer in pronunciation.

susurration
A whispering, rustling sound such as might be produced by sibilance.

syllable
Part of a word that contains a single vowel sound.

symploce
A figure of speech in which a word or phrase is used successively at the beginning of two or more clauses or sentences and another word or a phrase with a similar wording is used successively at the end of them. It is the combination of **anaphora** and **epistrophe**.

syntactic
Relating to syntax, the grammatical arrangement of words in a sentence.

syntax
A form of grammar. The way in which words are put together in sentences.

trochaic tetrameter
A poetic metre consisting of four trochees to a line (see **trochee**).

trochee
A foot consisting of one long or stressed syllable followed by one short or unstressed syllable (as in DUM-da).

unstressed syllable
Syllables which are not emphasised in speech. These are often quieter than stressed syllables. They may be shorter in pronunciation.

volta
A turning point or point of change in a poem.

worry box
A slotted cardboard box resembling a ballot box. Pupils may post a note to the teacher, enabling them to have a say when they feel uncomfortable about speaking in a classroom setting. Alternatively the teacher can make a worry wallet, a pouch or envelope fixed to the wall for the same purpose.

zeugma
The use of one word to link two thoughts, often ones which are apparently unconnected, and often with comic effect.

Useful contact organisations for young people

- **Anna Freud National Centre for Children and Families**
  The Youth Wellbeing Directory provides a list of free local and national organisations for anyone up to the age of 25.
  Website: https://www.annafreud.org/on-my-mind/youth-wellbeing/

- **Anti-Bullying Alliance**
  Website: https://anti-bullyingalliance.org.uk/

- **CEOP (Child Exploitation and Online Protection command)**
  Website: https://www.ceop.police.uk/Safety-Centre/How-can-CEOP-help-me-YP/

- **Child Bereavement UK**
  Helpline: 0800 02 888 40
  Website: https://www.childbereavementuk.org/

- **Childline**
  Helpline: 0800 1111 (24 hours)
  Website: https://www.childline.org.uk/

- **The Hideout**
  Domestic violence and abuse support.
  Website: https://www.thehideout.org.uk

- **Kooth**
  An online counselling and community programme for young people aged 11 plus.
  Website: https://kooth.com/

- **Mental Health Foundation**
  Website: https://www.mentalhealth.org.uk/your-mental-health/getting-help

- **Mind**
  Helpline: 0300 123 3393 (9am to 6pm on weekdays)
  Email: info@mind.org.uk
  Website: https://www.mind.org.uk/

- **NHS Choices**
  Call 111 to access NHS mental health services.
  For NHS advice on self-harm go to https://www.nhs.uk/conditions/self-harm/